HAMMOND

Explorer World Atlas

Contents

ENTIRE CONTENTS
© COPYRIGHT 2000 BY
HAMMOND WORLD ATLAS
CORPORATION
All rights reserved. No part of this book may be reproduced or utilized in any form or by any means, electronic or mechanical, including photocopying, recording or by any information storage and retrieval system, without permission in writing from the Publisher. Printed in The United States of America.

LIBRARY OF CONGRESS
CATALOGING-IN-
PUBLICATION DATA

Hammond World Atlas Corporation.
　Hammond explorer world atlas.
　　　p. cm.
　Rev. ed. of: Explorer Atlas of the World/Hammond Incorporated.
　Includes index.
　ISBN 0-8437-1357-7
　1. Atlases.
I Hammond Incorporated. Explorer atlas of the world. II. Title. III. Title: Explorer world atlas.
G1021.H2457 1999　<G&M>
912--DC21　　99-28550
　　　　　CIP
　　　　　MAPS

Australia
Page/Lo
Area: 2,

68/B3 Flixecourt
69/D4 Flize, Fran
69/D4 Floing, Fra
69/H4 Flonheim,
69/F5 Florange,
69/D3 Floreffe, B

Map Projections

Simply stated, the map-maker's challenge is to project the earth's curved surface onto a flat plane. To achieve this elusive goal, cartographers have developed map projections — equations which govern this conversion of geographic data.

This section explores some of the most widely used projections. It also introduces a new projection, the Hammond Optimal Conformal.

GENERAL PRINCIPLES AND TERMS

The earth rotates around its axis once a day. Its end points are the North and South poles; the line circling the earth midway between the poles is the equator. The arc from the equator to either pole is divided into 90 degrees of latitude. The equator represents 0° latitude. Circles of equal latitude, called parallels, are traditionally shown at every fifth or tenth degree.

The equator is divided into 360 degrees. Lines circling the globe from pole to pole through the degree points on the equator are called meridians, or great circles. All meridians are equal in length, but by international agreement the meridian passing through the Greenwich Observatory near London has been chosen as the prime meridian or 0° longitude. The distance in degrees from the prime meridian to any point east or west is its longitude.

While meridians are all equal in length, parallels become shorter as they approach the poles. Whereas one degree of latitude represents approximately 69 miles (112 km.) anywhere on the globe, a degree of longitude varies from 69 miles (112 km.) at the equator to zero at the poles. Each degree of latitude and longitude is divided into 60 minutes. One minute of latitude equals one nautical mile (1.15 land miles or 1.85 km.).

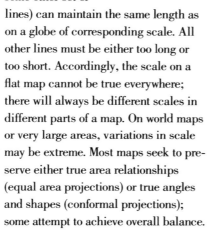

HOW TO FLATTEN A SPHERE: THE ART OF CONTROLLING DISTORTION

There is only one way to represent a sphere with absolute precision: on a globe. All attempts to project our planet's surface onto a plane unevenly stretch or tear the sphere as it flattens, inevitably distorting shapes, distances, area (sizes appear larger or smaller than actual size), angles or direction.

Since representing a sphere on a flat plane always creates distortion, only the parallels or the meridians (or some other set of lines) can maintain the same length as on a globe of corresponding scale. All other lines must be either too long or too short. Accordingly, the scale on a flat map cannot be true everywhere; there will always be different scales in different parts of a map. On world maps or very large areas, variations in scale may be extreme. Most maps seek to preserve either true area relationships (equal area projections) or true angles and shapes (conformal projections); some attempt to achieve overall balance.

PROJECTIONS: SELECTED EXAMPLES

Mercator (Fig. 1): This projection is especially useful because all compass directions appear as straight lines, making it a valuable navigational tool. Moreover, every small region conforms to its shape on a globe — hence the name conformal. But because its meridians are evenly-spaced vertical lines which never converge (unlike the globe), the horizontal parallels must be drawn farther and farther apart at higher latitudes to maintain a correct relationship.

FIGURE 1 Mercator Projection

FIGURE 2 Robinson Projection

Only the equator is true to scale, and the size of areas in the higher latitudes is dramatically distorted.

Robinson (Fig. 2): To create the thematic maps in Global Relationships and the two-page world map in the Maps of the World section, the Robinson projection was used. It combines elements of both conformal and equal area projections to show the whole earth with relatively true shapes and reasonably equal areas.

Conic (Fig. 3): This projection has been used frequently for air navigation charts and to create most of the national and regional maps in this atlas. (See text in margin at left).

HAMMOND OPTIMAL CONFORMAL

As its name implies, this new conformal projection (Fig. 4) presents the optimal view of an area by reducing shifts in scale over an entire region to the minimum degree possible. While conformal maps generally preserve all small shapes, large shapes can become very distorted because of varying scales, causing considerable inaccuracy in distance measurements. The concept underlying the Optimal Conformal is that for any region on the globe, there is an ideal projection for which scale variation can be made as small as possible. Consequently, unlike other projections, the Optimal Conformal does not use one standard formula to construct a map. Each map is a unique projection — the optimal projection for that particular area.

After a cartographer defines the subject area, a sophisticated computer program evaluates the size and shape of the region, projecting the most distortion-free map possible. All of the continent maps in this atlas, except Antarctica, have been drawn using the Optimal projection.

Using This Atlas

How to Locate Information Quickly
Our Maps of the World section is organized by continent. If you're looking for a major region of the world, consult the Contents on page two.

Australia
Page/Location: 70
Area: 2,966,136 sq
7,682,300 s
Population: 17,2
Capital: Canb

World Reference Guide
This concise guide lists the countries of the world alphabetically. If you're looking for the largest scale map of any country, you'll find a page and alpha-numeric reference at a glance, as well as information about each country, including its flag.

	Merlimont, Fran
/F4	**Mersch**, Luxembou
68/A3	**Mers-les-Bains**, France
69/F4	**Mertert**, Luxembourg
69/F4	**Mertesdorf**, Germany
69/G6	**Mertzwiller**, France
68/B5	**Méru**, France
68/B2	**Merville**, France
69/F2	**Merzenich**, Germany
69/F5	**Merzig**, Germany
'F4	**Messancy**, Belg

Master Index
When you're looking for a specific place or physical feature, your quickest route is the Master Index. This 6,000-entry alphabetical index lists both the page number and alpha-numeric reference for major places and features in Maps of the World.

This new atlas is created from a unique digital database, and its computer-generated maps represent a new phase in map-making technology.

HOW COMPUTER-GENERATED MAPS ARE MADE

To build a digital database capable of generating this world atlas, the latitude and longitude of every significant town, river, coastline, natural and political border, transportation network and peak elevation was researched and digitized. Hundreds of millions of data points describing every important geographic feature are organized into thousands of different map feature codes.

There are no maps in this unique system. Rather, it consists entirely of coded points, lines and polygons. To create a map, cartographers simply determine what specific information they wish to show, based upon considerations of scale, size, density and importance of different features.

New technology developed by mathematical physicist Mitchell Feigenbaum uses fractal geometry to describe and re-configure coastlines, borders and mountain ranges to fit a variety of map scales and projections. Dr. Feigenbaum has also created a computerized type placement program which allows thousands of map labels to be placed accurately in minutes. After these steps have been completed, the computer then draws the final map.

Each section of this atlas has been designed to be both easy and enjoyable to use. Familiarizing yourself with its organization will help you to benefit fully from its use.

WORLD FLAGS AND REFERENCE GUIDE

This colorful section portrays each nation of the world, its flag, important geographical data, such as size, population and capital, and its location in the Maps of the World section.

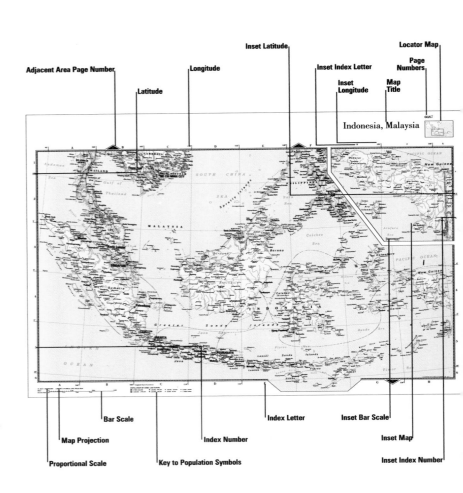

SYMBOLS USED ON MAPS OF THE WORLD

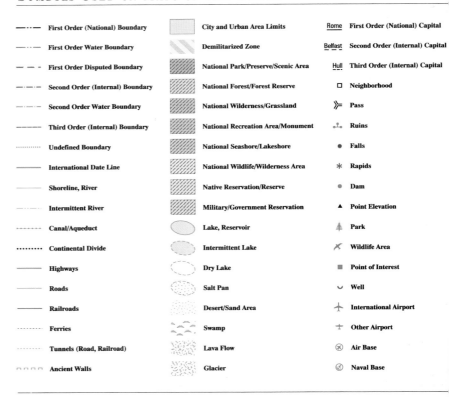

First Order (National) Boundary	City and Urban Area Limits	*Rome* First Order (National) Capital
First Order Water Boundary	Demilitarized Zone	*Belfast* Second Order (Internal) Capital
First Order Disputed Boundary	National Park/Preserve/Scenic Area	*Hull* Third Order (Internal) Capital
Second Order (Internal) Boundary	National Forest/Forest Reserve	Neighborhood
Second Order Water Boundary	National Wilderness/Grassland	Pass
Third Order (Internal) Boundary	National Recreation Area/Monument	Ruins
Undefined Boundary	National Seashore/Lakeshore	Falls
International Date Line	National Wildlife/Wilderness Area	Rapids
Shoreline, River	Native Reservation/Reserve	Dam
Intermittent River	Military/Government Reservation	Point Elevation
Canal/Aqueduct	Lake, Reservoir	Park
Continental Divide	Intermittent Lake	Wildlife Area
Highways	Dry Lake	Point of Interest
Roads	Salt Pan	Well
Railroads	Desert/Sand Area	International Airport
Ferries	Swamp	Other Airport
Tunnels (Road, Railroad)	Lava Flow	Air Base
Ancient Walls	Glacier	Naval Base

Point of Interest
National Park
Mountain Peak
Air Base
Desert / Sand Area
Dry Lake
Lake
National Recreation Area
Dam
River

Intermittent River
City / Urban Area
International Airport
Other Airport
1st Order (National) Boundary
2nd Order (Internal) Boundary
Principal Highway
Railroad

WORLD STATISTICS

World Statistics lists the dimensions of the earth's principal mountains, islands, rivers and lakes, along with other useful geographic information.

MAPS OF THE WORLD

These detailed regional maps are arranged by continent, and introduced by a political map of that continent. The continent maps, which utilize Hammond's new Optimal Conformal projection, are distinguished by individual colors for each country to highlight political divisions.

On the regional maps, different colors and textures highlight distinctive features such as parks, forests, deserts and urban areas. These maps also provide considerable information concerning geographic features and political divisions.

MASTER INDEX

This is an A-Z listing of names found on the political maps. It also has its own abbreviation list which, along with other Index keys, appears on page 110.

MAP SCALES

A map's scale is the relationship of any length on the map to an identical length on the earth's surface. A scale of 1:3,000,000 means that one inch on the map represents 3,000,000 inches (47 miles, 76 km.) on the earth's surface. Thus, a 1:1,000,000 scale is larger than 1:3,000,000, just as 1/1 is larger than 1/3.

The most densely populated areas are shown at a scale of 1:1,170,000, while selected metropolitan areas are covered at either 1:587,000 or 1:1,170,000. Other populous areas are presented at 1:3,500,000 and 1:7,000,000, allowing you to accurately compare areas and distances of similar regions. Remaining regions are scaled at 1:10,500,000. The continent maps, as well as the United States, Canada, Russia, Pacific and World have smaller scales.

PRINCIPAL MAP ABBREVIATIONS

ABOR. RSV.	ABORIGINAL RESERVE	IND. RES.	INDIAN RESERVATION	NWR	NATIONAL WILDLIFE RESERVE
ADMIN.	ADMINISTRATION	INT'L	INTERNATIONAL		
AFB	AIR FORCE BASE	IR	INDIAN RESERVATION	OBL.	OBLAST
AMM. DEP.	AMMUNITION DEPOT	ISTH.	ISTHMUS	OCC.	OCCUPIED
ARCH.	ARCHIPELAGO	JCT.	JUNCTION	OKR.	OKRUG
ARPT.	AIRPORT	L.	LAKE	PAR.	PARISH
AUT.	AUTONOMOUS	LAG.	LAGOON	PASSG.	PASSAGE
B.	BAY	LAKESH.	LAKESHORE	PEN.	PENINSULA
BFLD.	BATTLEFIELD	MEM.	MEMORIAL	PK.	PEAK
BK.	BROOK	MIL.	MILITARY	PLAT.	PLATEAU
BOR.	BOROUGH	MISS.	MISSILE	PN	PARK NATIONAL
BR.	BRANCH	MON.	MONUMENT	PREF.	PREFECTURE
C.	CAPE	MT.	MOUNT	PROM.	PROMONTORY
CAN.	CANAL	MTN.	MOUNTAIN	PROV.	PROVINCE
CAP.	CAPITAL	MTS.	MOUNTAINS	PRSV.	PRESERVE
C.G.	COAST GUARD	NAT.	NATURAL	PT.	POINT
CHAN.	CHANNEL	NAT'L	NATIONAL	R.	RIVER
CO.	COUNTY	NAV.	NAVAL	RA	RECREATION AREA
CR.	CREEK	NB	NATIONAL BATTLEFIELD	RA.	RANGE
CTR.	CENTER			REC.	RECREATION(AL)
DEP.	DEPOT	NBP	NATIONAL BATTLEFIELD PARK	REF.	REFUGE
DEPR.	DEPRESSION			REG.	REGION
DEPT.	DEPARTMENT	NBS	NATIONAL BATTLEFIELD SITE	REP.	REPUBLIC
DES.	DESERT			RES.	RESERVOIR, RESERVATION
DIST.	DISTRICT	NHP	NATIONAL HISTORICAL PARK		
DMZ	DEMILITARIZED ZONE			RVWY.	RIVERWAY
DPCY.	DEPENDENCY	NHPP	NATIONAL HISTORICAL PARK AND PRESERVE	SA.	SIERRA
ENG.	ENGINEERING			SD.	SOUND
EST.	ESTUARY	NHS	NATIONAL HISTORIC SITE	SEASH.	SEASHORE
FD.	FIORD, FJORD			SO.	SOUTHERN
FED.	FEDERAL	NL	NATIONAL LAKESHORE	SP	STATE PARK
FK.	FORK	NM	NATIONAL MONUMENT	SPR., SPRS.	SPRING, SPRINGS
FLD.	FIELD	NMEMP	NATIONAL MEMORIAL PARK	ST.	STATE
FOR.	FOREST			STA.	STATION
FT.	FORT	NMILP	NATIONAL MILITARY PARK	STM.	STREAM
G.	GULF			STR.	STRAIT
GOV.	GOVERNOR	NO.	NORTHERN	TERR.	TERRITORY
GOVT.	GOVERNMENT	NP	NATIONAL PARK	TUN.	TUNNEL
GD.	GRAND	NPP	NATIONAL PARK AND PRESERVE	TWP.	TOWNSHIP
GT.	GREAT			VAL.	VALLEY
HAR.	HARBOR	NPRSV	NATIONAL PRESERVE	VILL.	VILLAGE
HD.	HEAD	NRA	NATIONAL RECREATION AREA	VOL.	VOLCANO
HIST.	HISTORIC(AL)			WILD.	WILDLIFE,
HTS.	HEIGHTS	NRSV	NATIONAL RESERVE		WILDERNESS
I., IS.	ISLAND(S)	NS	NATIONAL SEASHORE	WTR.	WATER

World Flags and Reference Guide

Afghanistan
Page/Location: 53/H2
Area: 250,775 sq. mi.
649,507 sq. km.
Population: 23,738,085
Capital: Kabul
Largest City: Kabul
Highest Point: Noshaq
Monetary Unit: afghani

Albania
Page/Location: 39/F2
Area: 11,100 sq. mi.
28,749 sq. km.
Population: 3,293,252
Capital: Tiranë
Largest City: Tiranë
Highest Point: Korab
Monetary Unit: lek

Algeria
Page/Location: 76/F2
Area: 919,591 sq. mi.
2,381,740 sq. km.
Population: 29,830,370
Capital: Algiers
Largest City: Algiers
Highest Point: Tahat
Monetary Unit: Algerian dinar

Andorra
Page/Location: 35/F1
Area: 174 sq. mi.
450 sq. km.
Population: 74,839
Capital: Andorra la Vella
Largest City: Andorra la Vella
Highest Point: Coma Pedrosa
Monetary Unit: Fr. franc, Sp. peseta

Angola
Page/Location: 82/C3
Area: 481,351 sq. mi.
1,246,700 sq. km.
Population: 10,623,994
Capital: Luanda
Largest City: Luanda
Highest Point: Morro de Môco
Monetary Unit: new kwanza

Antigua and Barbuda
Page/Location: 104/F3
Area: 171 sq. mi.
443 sq. km.
Population: 66,175
Capital: St. John's
Largest City: St. John's
Highest Point: Boggy Peak
Monetary Unit: East Caribbean dollar

Argentina
Page/Location: 109/C4
Area: 1,068,296 sq. mi.
2,766,890 sq. km.
Population: 35,797,536
Capital: Buenos Aires
Largest City: Buenos Aires
Highest Point: Cerro Aconcagua
Monetary Unit: nuevo peso argentino

Armenia
Page/Location: 45/H5
Area: 11,506 sq. mi.
29,800 sq. km.
Population: 3,465,611
Capital: Yerevan
Largest City: Yerevan
Highest Point: Alagez
Monetary Unit: dram

Australia
Page/Location: 70
Area: 2,966,136 sq. mi.
7,682,300 sq. km.
Population: 18,438,824
Capital: Canberra
Largest City: Sydney
Highest Point: Mt. Kosciusko
Monetary Unit: Australian dollar

Austria
Page/Location: 33/L3
Area: 32,375 sq. mi.
83,851 sq. km.
Population: 8,054,078
Capital: Vienna
Largest City: Vienna
Highest Point: Grossglockner
Monetary Unit: schilling

Azerbaijan
Page/Location: 45/H4
Area: 33,436 sq. mi.
86,600 sq. km.
Population: 7,735,918
Capital: Baku
Largest City: Baku
Highest Point: Bazardyuzyu
Monetary Unit: manat

Bahamas
Page/Location: 104/B2
Area: 5,382 sq. mi.
13,939 sq. km.
Population: 262,034
Capital: Nassau
Largest City: Nassau
Highest Point: 207 ft. (63 m)
Monetary Unit: Bahamian dollar

Bahrain
Page/Location: 52/F3
Area: 240 sq. mi.
622 sq. km.
Population: 603,318
Capital: Manama
Largest City: Manama
Highest Point: Jabal Dukhān
Monetary Unit: Bahraini dinar

Bangladesh
Page/Location: 60/E3
Area: 55,598 sq. mi.
144,000 sq. km.
Population: 125,340,261
Capital: Dhākā
Largest City: Dhākā
Highest Point: Keokradong
Monetary Unit: taka

Barbados
Page/Location: 104/G4
Area: 166 sq. mi.
430 sq. km.
Population: 257,731
Capital: Bridgetown
Largest City: Bridgetown
Highest Point: Mt. Hillaby
Monetary Unit: Barbadian dollar

Belarus
Page/Location: 18/F3
Area: 80,154 sq. mi.
207,600 sq. km.
Population: 10,439,916
Capital: Minsk
Largest City: Minsk
Highest Point: Dzerzhinskaya
Monetary Unit: Belarusian ruble

Belgium
Page/Location: 30/C2
Area: 11,781 sq. mi.
30,513 sq. km.
Population: 10,203,683
Capital: Brussels
Largest City: Brussels
Highest Point: Botrange
Monetary Unit: Belgian franc

Belize
Page/Location: 102/D2
Area: 8,867 sq. mi.
22,966 sq. km.
Population: 224,663
Capital: Belmopan
Largest City: Belize City
Highest Point: Victoria Peak
Monetary Unit: Belize dollar

Benin
Page/Location: 79/F4
Area: 43,483 sq. mi.
112,620 sq. km.
Population: 5,342,000
Capital: Porto-Novo
Largest City: Cotonou
Highest Point: Nassoukou
Monetary Unit: CFA franc

Bhutan
Page/Location: 62/E2
Area: 18,147 sq. mi.
47,000 sq. km.
Population: 1,865,191
Capital: Thimphu
Largest City: Thimphu
Highest Point: Kula Kangri
Monetary Unit: ngultrum

Bolivia
Page/Location: 106/F7
Area: 424,163 sq. mi.
1,098,582 sq. km.
Population: 7,669,868
Capital: La Paz; Sucre
Largest City: La Paz
Highest Point: Nevado Ancohuma
Monetary Unit: boliviano

Bosnia and Herzegovina
Page/Location: 40/C3
Area: 19,940 sq. mi.
51,645 sq. km.
Population: 2,607,734
Capital: Sarajevo
Largest City: Sarajevo
Highest Point: Maglič
Monetary Unit: dinar

Botswana
Page/Location: 82/D5
Area: 231,803 sq. mi.
600,370 sq. km.
Population: 1,500,765
Capital: Gaborone
Largest City: Gaborone
Highest Point: Tsodilo Hills
Monetary Unit: pula

Brazil
Page/Location: 105/D3
Area: 3,286,470 sq. mi.
8,511,965 sq. km.
Population: 164,511,366
Capital: Brasília
Largest City: São Paulo
Highest Point: Pico da Neblina
Monetary Unit: real

Brunei
Page/Location: 66/D2
Area: 2,226 sq. mi.
5,765 sq. km.
Population: 307,616
Capital: Bandar Seri Begawan
Largest City: Bandar Seri Begawan
Highest Point: Bukit Pagon
Monetary Unit: Brunei dollar

Bulgaria
Page/Location: 41/G4
Area: 42,823 sq. mi.
110,912 sq. km.
Population: 8,652,745
Capital: Sofia
Largest City: Sofia
Highest Point: Musala
Monetary Unit: lev

Burkina Faso
Page/Location: 79/E3
Area: 105,869 sq. mi.
274,200 sq. km.
Population: 10,891,159
Capital: Ouagadougou
Largest City: Ouagadougou
Highest Point: 2,405 ft. (733 m)
Monetary Unit: CFA franc

Burundi
Page/Location: 82/E1
Area: 10,747 sq. mi.
27,835 sq. km.
Population: 6,052,614
Capital: Bujumbura
Largest City: Bujumbura
Highest Point: 8,760 ft. (2,670 m)
Monetary Unit: Burundi franc

Cambodia
Page/Location: 65/D3
Area: 69,898 sq. mi.
181,036 sq. km.
Population: 11,163,861
Capital: Phnom Penh
Largest City: Phnom Penh
Highest Point: Phnum Aoral
Monetary Unit: new riel

Cameroon
Page/Location: 76/H7
Area: 183,568 sq. mi.
475,441 sq. km.
Population: 14,677,510
Capital: Yaoundé
Largest City: Douala
Highest Point: Mt. Cameroon
Monetary Unit: CFA franc

Canada
Page/Location: 86
Area: 3,851,787 sq. mi.
9,976,139 sq. km.
Population: 29,123,194
Capital: Ottawa
Largest City: Toronto
Highest Point: Mt. Logan
Monetary Unit: Canadian dollar

Cape Verde
Page/Location: 74/K9
Area: 1,557 sq. mi.
4,033 sq. km.
Population: 393,843
Capital: Praia
Largest City: Praia
Highest Point: 9,282 ft. (2,829 m)
Monetary Unit: Cape Verde escudo

Central African Republic
Page/Location: 77/J6
Area: 240,533 sq. mi.
622,980 sq. km.
Population: 3,342,051
Capital: Bangui
Largest City: Bangui
Highest Point: Mt. Kayagangiri
Monetary Unit: CFA franc

Chad
Page/Location: 77/J4
Area: 495,752 sq. mi.
1,283,998 sq. km.
Population: 7,166,023
Capital: N'Djamena
Largest City: N'Djamena
Highest Point: Emi Koussi
Monetary Unit: CFA franc

Chile
Page/Location: 109/B3
Area: 292,257 sq. mi.
756,946 sq. km.
Population: 14,508,168
Capital: Santiago
Largest City: Santiago
Highest Point: Nevado Ojos del Salado
Monetary Unit: Chilean peso

China
Page/Location: 48/J6
Area: 3,705,386 sq. mi.
9,596,960 sq. km.
Population: 1,221,591,778
Capital: Beijing
Largest City: Shanghai
Highest Point: Mt. Everest
Monetary Unit: yuan

Colombia
Page/Location: 106/D3
Area: 439,513 sq. mi.
1,138,339 sq. km.
Population: 37,418,290
Capital: Bogotá
Largest City: Bogotá
Highest Point: Pico Cristóbal Colón
Monetary Unit: Colombian peso

Comoros
Page/Location: 74/G6
Area: 838 sq. mi.
2,170 sq. km.
Population: 589,797
Capital: Moroni
Largest City: Moroni
Highest Point: Karthala
Monetary Unit: Comorian franc

Congo, Dem. Rep. of the
Page/Location: 74/E5
Area: 905,563 sq. mi.
2,345,410 sq. km.
Population: 47,440,362
Capital: Kinshasa
Largest City: Kinshasa
Highest Point: Margherita Peak
Monetary Unit: zaire

Congo, Rep. of the
Page/Location: 74/D5
Area: 132,046 sq. mi.
342,000 sq. km.
Population: 2,583,198
Capital: Brazzaville
Largest City: Brazzaville
Highest Point: Lékéti Mts.
Monetary Unit: CFA franc

Costa Rica
Page/Location: 103/F4
Area: 19,730 sq. mi.
51,100 sq. km.
Population: 3,534,174
Capital: San José
Largest City: San José
Highest Point: Cerro Chirripó Grande
Monetary Unit: Costa Rican colón

Côte d'Ivoire
Page/Location: 78/D5
Area: 124,504 sq. mi.
322,465 sq. km.
Population: 14,986,218
Capital: Yamoussoukro
Largest City: Abidjan
Highest Point: Mt. Nimba
Monetary Unit: CFA franc

Croatia
Page/Location: 40/C3
Area: 22,050 sq. mi.
57,110 sq. km.
Population: 5,026,995
Capital: Zagreb
Largest City: Zagreb
Highest Point: Veliki Troglav
Monetary Unit: Croatian kuna

Cuba
Page/Location: 103/F1
Area: 42,803 sq. mi.
110,860 sq. km.
Population: 10,999,041
Capital: Havana
Largest City: Havana
Highest Point: Pico Turquino
Monetary Unit: Cuban peso

Cyprus
Page/Location: 49/C2
Area: 3,571 sq. mi.
9,250 sq. km.
Population: 752,808
Capital: Nicosia
Largest City: Nicosia
Highest Point: Olympus
Monetary Unit: Cypriot pound

Czech Republic
Page/Location: 27/H4
Area: 30,387 sq. mi.
78,703 sq. km.
Population: 10,318,958
Capital: Prague
Largest City: Prague
Highest Point: Sněžka
Monetary Unit: Czech koruna

Denmark
Page/Location: 20/C5
Area: 16,629 sq. mi.
43,069 sq. km.
Population: 5,268,775
Capital: Copenhagen
Largest City: Copenhagen
Highest Point: Yding Skovhøj
Monetary Unit: Danish krone

Djibouti
Page/Location: 77/P5
Area: 8,494 sq. mi.
22,000 sq. km.
Population: 434,116
Capital: Djibouti
Largest City: Djibouti
Highest Point: Moussa Ali
Monetary Unit: Djibouti franc

Dominica
Page/Location: 104/F4
Area: 290 sq. mi.
751 sq. km.
Population: 83,226
Capital: Roseau
Largest City: Roseau
Highest Point: Morne Diablotin
Monetary Unit: EC dollar

Dominican Republic
Page/Location: 104/D3
Area: 18,815 sq. mi.
48,730 sq. km.
Population: 8,228,151
Capital: Santo Domingo
Largest City: Santo Domingo
Highest Point: Pico Duarte
Monetary Unit: Dominican peso

Ecuador
Page/Location: 106/C4
Area: 109,483 sq. mi.
283,561 sq. km.
Population: 11,690,535
Capital: Quito
Largest City: Guayaquil
Highest Point: Chimborazo
Monetary Unit: sucre

Egypt
Page/Location: 77/L2
Area: 386,659 sq. mi.
1,001,447 sq. km.
Population: 64,791,891
Capital: Cairo
Largest City: Cairo
Highest Point: Mt. Catherine
Monetary Unit: Egyptian pound

El Salvador
Page/Location: 102/D3
Area: 8,124 sq. mi.
21,040 sq. km.
Population: 5,661,827
Capital: San Salvador
Largest City: San Salvador
Highest Point: Santa Ana
Monetary Unit: Salvadoran colón

Equatorial Guinea
Page/Location: 76/G7
Area: 10,831 sq. mi.
28,052 sq. km.
Population: 442,516
Capital: Malabo
Largest City: Malabo
Highest Point: Pico de Santa Isabel
Monetary Unit: CFA franc

Eritrea
Page/Location: 52/C5
Area: 46,842 sq. mi.
121,320 sq. km.
Population: 3,589,687
Capital: Asmara
Largest City: Asmara
Highest Point: Soira
Monetary Unit: nafka

Estonia
Page/Location: 42/E4
Area: 17,413 sq. mi.
45,100 sq. km.
Population: 1,444,721
Capital: Tallinn
Largest City: Tallinn
Highest Point: Munamägi
Monetary Unit: kroon

Ethiopia
Page/Location: 77/N6
Area: 435,184 sq. mi.
1,127,127 sq. km.
Population: 58,732,577
Capital: Addis Ababa
Largest City: Addis Ababa
Highest Point: Ras Dashen Terara
Monetary Unit: birr

Fiji
Page/Location: 68/G6
Area: 7,055 sq. mi.
18,272 sq. km.
Population: 792,441
Capital: Suva
Largest City: Suva
Highest Point: Tomaniivi
Monetary Unit: Fijian dollar

Finland
Page/Location: 20/H2
Area: 130,128 sq. mi.
337,032 sq. km.
Population: 5,109,148
Capital: Helsinki
Largest City: Helsinki
Highest Point: Kahperusvaara
Monetary Unit: markka

France
Page/Location: 32/D3
Area: 211,208 sq. mi.
547,030 sq. km.
Population: 58,470,421
Capital: Paris
Largest City: Paris
Highest Point: Mont Blanc
Monetary Unit: French franc

Gabon
Page/Location: 76/H7
Area: 103,346 sq. mi.
267,666 sq. km.
Population: 1,190,159
Capital: Libreville
Largest City: Libreville
Highest Point: Mt. Iboundji
Monetary Unit: CFA franc

Gambia, The
Page/Location: 78/B3
Area: 4,363 sq. mi.
11,300 sq. km.
Population: 1,248,085
Capital: Banjul
Largest City: Banjul
Highest Point: 98 ft. (30 m)
Monetary Unit: dalasi

Georgia
Page/Location: 45/G4
Area: 26,911 sq. mi.
69,700 sq. km.
Population: 5,174,642
Capital: T'bilisi
Largest City: T'bilisi
Highest Point: Kazbek
Monetary Unit: lari

Germany
Page/Location: 26/E3
Area: 137,803 sq. mi.
356,910 sq. km.
Population: 84,068,216
Capital: Berlin
Largest City: Berlin
Highest Point: Zugspitze
Monetary Unit: Deutsche mark

Ghana
Page/Location: 79/E4
Area: 92,099 sq. mi.
238,536 sq. km.
Population: 18,100,703
Capital: Accra
Largest City: Accra
Highest Point: Afadjoto
Monetary Unit: new cedi

Greece
Page/Location: 39/G3
Area: 50,944 sq. mi.
131,945 sq. km.
Population: 10,583,126
Capital: Athens
Largest City: Athens
Highest Point: Mt. Olympus
Monetary Unit: drachma

World Flags and Reference Guide

Grenada
Page/Location: 104/F5
Area: 133 sq. mi.
344 sq. km.
Population: 95,537
Capital: St. George's
Largest City: St. George's
Highest Point: Mt. St. Catherine
Monetary Unit: East Caribbean dollar

Guatemala
Page/Location: 102/D3
Area: 42,042 sq. mi.
108,889 sq. km.
Population: 11,558,407
Capital: Guatemala
Largest City: Guatemala
Highest Point: Tajumulco
Monetary Unit: quetzal

Guinea
Page/Location: 78/C4
Area: 94,925 sq. mi.
245,856 sq. km.
Population: 7,405,375
Capital: Conakry
Largest City: Conakry
Highest Point: Mt. Nimba
Monetary Unit: Guinea franc

Guinea-Bissau
Page/Location: 78/B3
Area: 13,948 sq. mi.
36,125 sq. km.
Population: 1,178,584
Capital: Bissau
Largest City: Bissau
Highest Point: 689 ft. (210 m)
Monetary Unit: Guinea-Bissau peso

Guyana
Page/Location: 106/G2
Area: 83,000 sq. mi.
214,970 sq. km.
Population: 706,116
Capital: Georgetown
Largest City: Georgetown
Highest Point: Mt. Roraima
Monetary Unit: Guyana dollar

Haiti
Page/Location: 103/H2
Area: 10,694 sq. mi.
27,697 sq. km.
Population: 6,611,407
Capital: Port-au-Prince
Largest City: Port-au-Prince
Highest Point: Pic la Selle
Monetary Unit: gourde

Honduras
Page/Location: 102/E3
Area: 43,277 sq. mi.
112,087 sq. km.
Population: 5,751,384
Capital: Tegucigalpa
Largest City: Tegucigalpa
Highest Point: Cerro de las Minas
Monetary Unit: lempira

Hungary
Page/Location: 40/D2
Area: 35,919 sq. mi.
93,030 sq. km.
Population: 9,935,774
Capital: Budapest
Largest City: Budapest
Highest Point: Kékes
Monetary Unit: forint

Iceland
Page/Location: 20/N7
Area: 39,768 sq. mi.
103,000 sq. km.
Population: 272,550
Capital: Reykjavík
Largest City: Reykjavík
Highest Point: Hvannadalshnúkur
Monetary Unit: króna

India
Page/Location: 62/C3
Area: 1,269,339 sq. mi.
3,287,588 sq. km.
Population: 967,612,804
Capital: New Delhi
Largest City: Calcutta
Highest Point: Nanda Devi
Monetary Unit: Indian rupee

Indonesia
Page/Location: 67/E4
Area: 741,096 sq. mi.
1,919,440 sq. km.
Population: 209,774,138
Capital: Jakarta
Largest City: Jakarta
Highest Point: Puncak Jaya
Monetary Unit: rupiah

Iran
Page/Location: 51/H3
Area: 636,293 sq. mi.
1,648,000 sq. km.
Population: 67,540,002
Capital: Tehrān
Largest City: Tehrān
Highest Point: Qolleh-ye Damāvand
Monetary Unit: Iranian rial

Iraq
Page/Location: 50/E3
Area: 168,753 sq. mi.
437,072 sq. km.
Population: 22,219,289
Capital: Baghdad
Largest City: Baghdad
Highest Point: Haji Ibrahim
Monetary Unit: Iraqi dinar

Ireland
Page/Location: 21/A4
Area: 27,136 sq. mi.
70,282 sq. km.
Population: 3,555,500
Capital: Dublin
Largest City: Dublin
Highest Point: Carrantuohill
Monetary Unit: Irish pound

Israel
Page/Location: 49/D3
Area: 8,019 sq. mi.
20,770 sq. km.
Population: 5,534,672
Capital: Jerusalem
Largest City: Tel Aviv-Yafo
Highest Point: Har Meron
Monetary Unit: new Israeli shekel

Italy
Page/Location: 18/E4
Area: 116,303 sq. mi.
301,225 sq. km.
Population: 57,534,088
Capital: Rome
Largest City: Rome
Highest Point: Monte Rosa
Monetary Unit: Italian lira

Jamaica
Page/Location: 103/G2
Area: 4,243 sq. mi.
10,990 sq. km.
Population: 2,615,582
Capital: Kingston
Largest City: Kingston
Highest Point: Blue Mountain Pk.
Monetary Unit: Jamaican dollar

Japan
Page/Location: 55/M4
Area: 145,882 sq. mi.
377,835 sq. km.
Population: 125,716,637
Capital: Tokyo
Largest City: Tokyo
Highest Point: Fujiyama
Monetary Unit: yen

Jordan
Page/Location: 49/E4
Area: 34,445 sq. mi.
89,213 sq. km.
Population: 4,324,638
Capital: Ammān
Largest City: Ammān
Highest Point: Jabal Ramm
Monetary Unit: Jordanian dinar

Kazakhstan
Page/Location: 46/G5
Area: 1,049,150 sq. mi.
2,717,300 sq. km.
Population: 16,898,572
Capital: Astana
Largest City: Almaty
Highest Point: Khan-Tengri
Monetary Unit: Kazakstani tenge

Kenya
Page/Location: 77/M7
Area: 224,960 sq. mi.
582,646 sq. km.
Population: 28,803,085
Capital: Nairobi
Largest City: Nairobi
Highest Point: Mt. Kenya
Monetary Unit: Kenya shilling

Kiribati
Page/Location: 69/H5
Area: 277 sq. mi.
717 sq. km.
Population: 82,449
Capital: Tarawa
Largest City: —
Highest Point: Banaba Island
Monetary Unit: Australian dollar

Korea, North
Page/Location: 58/D2
Area: 46,540 sq. mi.
120,539 sq. km.
Population: 24,317,004
Capital: P'yŏngyang
Largest City: P'yŏngyang
Highest Point: Paektu-san
Monetary Unit: North Korean won

Korea, South
Page/Location: 58/D4
Area: 38,023 sq. mi.
98,480 sq. km.
Population: 45,948,811
Capital: Seoul
Largest City: Seoul
Highest Point: Halla-san
Monetary Unit: South Korean won

Kuwait
Page/Location: 51/F4
Area: 6,880 sq. mi.
17,820 sq. km.
Population: 2,076,805
Capital: Kuwait
Largest City: Kuwait
Highest Point: 951 ft. (290 m)
Monetary Unit: Kuwaiti dinar

Kyrgyzstan
Page/Location: 46/H5
Area: 76,641 sq. mi.
198,500 sq. km.
Population: 4,540,185
Capital: Bishkek
Largest City: Bishkek
Highest Point: Pik Pobedy
Monetary Unit: som

Laos
Page/Location: 65/C2
Area: 91,428 sq. mi.
236,800 sq. km.
Population: 5,116,959
Capital: Vientiane
Largest City: Vientiane
Highest Point: Phou Bia
Monetary Unit: new kip

Latvia
Page/Location: 42/E4
Area: 24,749 sq. mi.
64,100 sq. km.
Population: 2,437,649
Capital: Riga
Largest City: Riga
Highest Point: Gaizina Kalns
Monetary Unit: Latvian let

Lebanon
Page/Location: 49/D3
Area: 4,015 sq. mi.
10,399 sq. km.
Population: 3,858,736
Capital: Beirut
Largest City: Beirut
Highest Point: Qurnat as Sawdā'
Monetary Unit: Lebanese pound

Lesotho
Page/Location: 80/E3
Area: 11,720 sq. mi.
30,355 sq. km.
Population: 2,007,814
Capital: Maseru
Largest City: Maseru
Highest Point: Thabana-Ntlenyana
Monetary Unit: loti

Liberia
Page/Location: 78/C4
Area: 43,000 sq. mi.
111,370 sq. km.
Population: 2,602,068
Capital: Monrovia
Largest City: Monrovia
Highest Point: Mt. Wuteve
Monetary Unit: Liberian dollar

Libya
Page/Location: 77/J2
Area: 679,358 sq. mi.
1,759,537 sq. km.
Population: 5,648,359
Capital: Tripoli
Largest City: Tripoli
Highest Point: Picco Bette
Monetary Unit: Libyan dinar

Liechtenstein
Page/Location: 37/F3
Area: 61 sq. mi.
158 sq. km.
Population: 31,461
Capital: Vaduz
Largest City: Vaduz
Highest Point: Grauspitz
Monetary Unit: Swiss franc

Lithuania
Page/Location: 42/D5
Area: 25,174 sq. mi.
65,200 sq. km.
Population: 3,635,932
Capital: Vilnius
Largest City: Vilnius
Highest Point: Nevaišiy
Monetary Unit: litas

Luxembourg
Page/Location: 31/F4
Area: 999 sq. mi.
2,587 sq. km.
Population: 422,474
Capital: Luxembourg
Largest City: Luxembourg
Highest Point: Ardennes Plateau
Monetary Unit: Luxembourg franc

Macedonia (F.Y.R.O.M.)
Page/Location: 39/G2
Area: 9,781 sq. mi.
25,333 sq. km.
Population: 2,113,866
Capital: Skopje
Largest City: Skopje
Highest Point: Korab
Monetary Unit: denar

Madagascar
Page/Location: 81/H8
Area: 226,657 sq. mi.
587,041 sq. km.
Population: 14,061,627
Capital: Antananarivo
Largest City: Antananarivo
Highest Point: Maromokotro
Monetary Unit: Malagasy franc

Malawi
Page/Location: 82/F3
Area: 45,747 sq. mi.
118,485 sq. km.
Population: 9,609,081
Capital: Lilongwe
Largest City: Blantyre
Highest Point: Mulanje Mts.
Monetary Unit: Malawi kwacha

Malaysia
Page/Location: 67/C2
Area: 127,316 sq. mi.
329,750 sq. km.
Population: 20,376,235
Capital: Kuala Lumpur
Largest City: Kuala Lumpur
Highest Point: Gunung Kinabalu
Monetary Unit: ringgit

Maldives
Page/Location: 48/G9
Area: 115 sq. mi.
298 sq. km.
Population: 280,391
Capital: Male
Largest City: Male
Highest Point: 20 ft. (6 m)
Monetary Unit: rufiyaa

Mali
Page/Location: 76/E4
Area: 478,764 sq. mi.
1,240,000 sq. km.
Population: 9,945,383
Capital: Bamako
Largest City: Bamako
Highest Point: Hombori Tondo
Monetary Unit: CFA franc

Malta
Page/Location: 38/D5
Area: 122 sq. mi.
316 sq. km.
Population: 379,365
Capital: Valletta
Largest City: Sliema
Highest Point: 830 ft. (253 m)
Monetary Unit: Maltese lira

Marshall Islands
Page/Location: 68/G3
Area: 70 sq. mi.
181 sq. km.
Population: 60,652
Capital: Majuro
Largest City: —
Highest Point: 20 ft. (6 m)
Monetary Unit: U.S. dollar

Mauritania
Page/Location: 76/C4
Area: 397,953 sq. mi.
1,030,700 sq. km.
Population: 2,411,317
Capital: Nouakchott
Largest City: Nouakchott
Highest Point: Kediet Ijill
Monetary Unit: ouguiya

Mauritius
Page/Location: 81/S15
Area: 718 sq. mi.
1,860 sq. km.
Population: 1,154,272
Capital: Port Louis
Largest City: Port Louis
Highest Point: 2,713 ft. (827 m)
Monetary Unit: Mauritian rupee

Mexico
Page/Location: 84/G7
Area: 761,601 sq. mi.
1,972,546 sq. km.
Population: 97,563,374
Capital: Mexico
Largest City: Mexico
Highest Point: Citlaltépetl
Monetary Unit: new Mexican peso

Micronesia
Page/Location: 68/D4
Area: 271 sq. mi.
702 sq. km.
Population: 122,950
Capital: Palikir
Largest City: —
Highest Point: —
Monetary Unit: U.S. dollar

Moldova
Page/Location: 41/J2
Area: 13,012 sq. mi.
33,700 sq. km.
Population: 4,475,232
Capital: Chişinău
Largest City: Chişinău
Highest Point: 1,408 ft. (429 m)
Monetary Unit: leu

Monaco
Page/Location: 33/G5
Area: 0.7 sq. mi.
1.9 sq. km.
Population: 31,892
Capital: Monaco
Largest: —
Highest Point: —
Monetary Unit: French franc

Mongolia
Page/Location: 54/D2
Area: 606,163 sq. mi.
1,569,962 sq. km.
Population: 2,538,211
Capital: Ulaanbaatar
Largest City: Ulaanbaatar
Highest Point: Tavan Bogd Uul
Monetary Unit: tughrik

Morocco
Page/Location: 76/C1
Area: 172,414 sq. mi.
446,550 sq. km.
Population: 30,391,423
Capital: Rabat
Largest City: Casablanca
Highest Point: Jebel Toubkal
Monetary Unit: Moroccan dirham

Mozambique
Page/Location: 82/G4
Area: 309,494 sq. mi.
801,590 sq. km.
Population: 18,165,476
Capital: Maputo
Largest City: Maputo
Highest Point: Monte Binga
Monetary Unit: metical

Myanmar (Burma)
Page/Location: 63/G3
Area: 261,969 sq. mi.
678,500 sq. km.
Population: 46,821,943
Capital: Rangoon
Largest City: Rangoon
Highest Point: Hkakabo Razi
Monetary Unit: kyat

Namibia
Page/Location: 82/C5
Area: 318,694 sq. mi.
825,418 sq. km.
Population: 1,727,183
Capital: Windhoek
Largest City: Windhoek
Highest Point: Brandberg
Monetary Unit: Namibian dollar

Nauru
Page/Location: 68/F5
Area: 7.7 sq. mi.
20 sq. km.
Population: 10,390
Capital: Yaren (district)
Largest City: —
Highest Point: 230 ft. (70 m)
Monetary Unit: Australian dollar

Nepal
Page/Location: 62/D2
Area: 54,663 sq. mi.
141,577 sq. km.
Population: 22,641,061
Capital: Kāthmāndu
Largest City: Kāthmāndu
Highest Point: Mt. Everest
Monetary Unit: Nepalese rupee

Netherlands
Page/Location: 28/B5
Area: 14,413 sq. mi.
37,330 sq. km.
Population: 15,653,091
Capital: The Hague; Amsterdam
Largest City: Amsterdam
Highest Point: Vaalserberg
Monetary Unit: Netherlands guilder

New Zealand
Page/Location: 71/Q10
Area: 103,736 sq. mi.
268,676 sq. km.
Population: 3,587,275
Capital: Wellington
Largest City: Auckland
Highest Point: Mt. Cook
Monetary Unit: New Zealand dollar

Nicaragua
Page/Location: 103/E3
Area: 49,998 sq. mi.
129,494 sq. km.
Population: 4,386,399
Capital: Managua
Largest City: Managua
Highest Point: Pico Mogotón
Monetary Unit: gold cordoba

Niger
Page/Location: 76/G4
Area: 489,189 sq. mi.
1,267,000 sq. km.
Population: 9,388,859
Capital: Niamey
Largest City: Niamey
Highest Point: Bagzane
Monetary Unit: CFA franc

Nigeria
Page/Location: 76/G6
Area: 356,668 sq. mi.
923,770 sq. km.
Population: 107,129,469
Capital: Abuja
Largest City: Lagos
Highest Point: Dimlang
Monetary Unit: naira

Norway
Page/Location: 20/C3
Area: 125,053 sq. mi.
323,887 sq. km.
Population: 4,404,456
Capital: Oslo
Largest City: Oslo
Highest Point: Glittertjnden
Monetary Unit: Norwegian krone

Oman
Page/Location: 53/G4
Area: 82,031 sq. mi.
212,460 sq. km.
Population: 2,264,590
Capital: Muscat
Largest City: Muscat
Highest Point: Jabal ash Shām
Monetary Unit: Omani rial

Pakistan
Page/Location: 53/H3
Area: 310,403 sq. mi.
803,944 sq. km.
Population: 132,185,299
Capital: Islāmābād
Largest City: Karāchi
Highest Point: K2 (Godwin Austen)
Monetary Unit: Pakistani rupee

Palau
Page/Location: 68/C4
Area: 177 sq. mi.
458 sq. km.
Population: 17,240
Capital: Koror
Largest City: Koror
Highest Point: 699 ft. (213m)
Monetary Unit: U.S. dollar

Panama
Page/Location: 103/F4
Area: 30,193 sq. mi.
78,200 sq. km.
Population: 2,693,417
Capital: Panamá
Largest City: Panamá
Highest Point: Barú
Monetary Unit: balboa

World Flags and Reference Guide

Papua New Guinea
Page/Location: 68/D5
Area: 178,259 sq. mi.
461,690 sq. km.
Population: 4,496,221
Capital: Port Moresby
Largest City: Port Moresby
Highest Point: Mt. Wilhelm
Monetary Unit: kina

Paraguay
Page/Location: 105/D5
Area: 157,047 sq. mi.
406,752 sq. km.
Population: 5,651,634;
Capital: Asunción
Largest City: Asunción
Highest Point: Sierra de Amambay
Monetary Unit: guaraní

Peru
Page/Location: 106/C5
Area: 496,222 sq. mi.
1,285,215 sq. km.
Population: 24,949,512
Capital: Lima
Largest City: Lima
Highest Point: Nevado Huascarán
Monetary Unit: nuevo sol

Philippines
Page/Location: 48/M8
Area: 115,830 sq. mi.
300,000 sq. km.
Population: 76,103,564
Capital: Manila
Largest City: Manila
Highest Point: Mt. Apo
Monetary Unit: Philippine peso

Poland
Page/Location: 27/K2
Area: 120,725 sq. mi.
312,678 sq. km.
Population: 38,700,291
Capital: Warsaw
Largest City: Warsaw
Highest Point: Rysy
Monetary Unit: zloty

Portugal
Page/Location: 34/A3
Area: 35,549 sq. mi.
92,072 sq. km.
Population: 9,867,654
Capital: Lisbon
Largest City: Lisbon
Highest Point: Serra da Estrela
Monetary Unit: Portuguese escudo

Qatar
Page/Location: 52/F3
Area: 4,247 sq. mi.
11,000 sq. km.
Population: 665,485
Capital: Doha
Largest City: Doha
Highest Point: Dukhān Heights
Monetary Unit: Qatari riyal

Romania
Page/Location: 41/F3
Area: 91,699 sq. mi.
237,500 sq. km.
Population: 21,399,114
Capital: Bucharest
Largest City: Bucharest
Highest Point: Moldoveanul
Monetary Unit: leu

Russia
Page/Location: 46/H3
Area: 6,592,812 sq. mi.
17,075,400 sq. km.
Population: 147,987,101
Capital: Moscow
Largest City: Moscow
Highest Point: El'brus
Monetary Unit: Russian ruble

Rwanda
Page/Location: 82/E1
Area: 10,169 sq. mi.
26,337 sq. km.
Population: 7,737,537
Capital: Kigali
Largest City: Kigali
Highest Point: Karisimbi
Monetary Unit: Rwanda franc

Saint Kitts and Nevis
Page/Location: 104/F3
Area: 104 sq. mi.
269 sq. km.
Population: 41,803
Capital: Basseterre
Largest City: Basseterre
Highest Point: Mt. Misery
Monetary Unit: East Caribbean dollar

Saint Lucia
Page/Location: 104/F4
Area: 238 sq. mi.
616 sq. km.
Population: 159,639
Capital: Castries
Largest City: Castries
Highest Point: Mt. Gimie
Monetary Unit: East Caribbean dollar

Saint Vincent and the Grenadines
Page/Location: 104/F4
Area: 131 sq. mi.
340 sq. km.
Population: 119,092
Capital: Kingstown
Largest City: Kingstown
Highest Point: Soufrière
Monetary Unit: East Caribbean dollar

Samoa
Page/Location: 69/H6
Area: 1,104 sq. mi.
2,860 sq. km.
Population: 219,509
Capital: Apia
Largest City: Apia
Highest Point: Mt. Silisili
Monetary Unit: tala

San Marino
Page/Location: 33/K5
Area: 23.4 sq. mi.
60.6 sq. km.
Population: 24,714
Capital: San Marino
Largest City: San Marino
Highest Point: Monte Titano
Monetary Unit: Italian lira

São Tomé and Príncipe
Page/Location: 76/G7
Area: 371 sq. mi.
960 sq. km.
Population: 147,865
Capital: São Tomé
Largest City: São Tomé
Highest Point: Pico de São Tomé
Monetary Unit: dobra

Saudi Arabia
Page/Location: 104/F3
Area: 756,981 sq. mi.
1,960,582 sq. km.
Population: 20,087,965
Capital: Riyadh
Largest City: Riyadh
Highest Point: Jabal Sawdā'
Monetary Unit: Saudi riyal

Senegal
Page/Location: 78/B3
Area: 75,954 sq. mi.
196,720 sq. km.
Population: 9,403,546
Capital: Dakar
Largest City: Dakar
Highest Point: Fouta Djallon
Monetary Unit: CFA franc

Seychelles
Page/Location: 74/H5
Area: 176 sq. mi.
455 sq. km.
Population: 78,142
Capital: Victoria
Largest City: Victoria
Highest Point: Morne Seychellois
Monetary Unit: Seychelles rupee

Sierra Leone
Page/Location: 78/B4
Area: 27,699 sq. mi.
71,740 sq. km.
Population: 4,891,546
Capital: Freetown
Largest City: Freetown
Highest Point: Loma Mansa
Monetary Unit: leone

Singapore
Page/Location: 66/B3
Area: 244 sq. mi.
632.6 sq. km.
Population: 3,461,929
Capital: Singapore
Largest City: Singapore
Highest Point: Bukit Timah
Monetary Unit: Singapore dollar

Slovakia
Page/Location: 27/K4
Area: 18,924 sq. mi.
49,013 sq. km.
Population: 5,393,016
Capital: Bratislava
Largest City: Bratislava
Highest Point: Gerlachovský Štít
Monetary Unit: Slovak koruna

Slovenia
Page/Location: 40/B3
Area: 7,898 sq. mi.
20,456 sq. km.
Population: 1,945,998
Capital: Ljubljana
Largest City: Ljubljana
Highest Point: Triglav
Monetary Unit: tolar

Solomon Islands
Page/Location: 68/E6
Area: 11,500 sq. mi.
29,785 sq. km.
Population: 462,855
Capital: Honiara
Largest City: Honiara
Highest Point: Mt. Makarakomburu
Monetary Unit: Solomon Islands dollar

Somalia
Page/Location: 77/Q6
Area: 246,200 sq. mi.
637,658 sq. km.
Population: 9,940,232
Capital: Mogadishu
Largest City: Mogadishu
Highest Point: Shimber Berris
Monetary Unit: Somali shilling

South Africa
Page/Location: 80/C3
Area: 471,008 sq. mi.
1,219,912 sq. km.
Population: 42,327,458
Capital: Cape Town; Pretoria
Largest City: Johannesburg
Highest Point: Injasuti
Monetary Unit: rand

Spain
Page/Location: 34/C2
Area: 194,881 sq. mi.
504,742 sq. km.
Population: 39,244,195
Capital: Madrid
Largest City: Madrid
Highest Point: Pico de Teide
Monetary Unit: peseta

Sri Lanka
Page/Location: 62/D6
Area: 25,332 sq. mi.
65,610 sq. km.
Population: 18,762,075
Capital: Colombo
Largest City: Colombo
Highest Point: Pidurutalagala
Monetary Unit: Sri Lanka rupee

Sudan
Page/Location: 77/L5
Area: 967,494 sq. mi.
2,505,809 sq. km.
Population: 32,594,128
Capital: Khartoum
Largest City: Omdurman
Highest Point: Jabal Marrah
Monetary Unit: Sudanese pound

Suriname
Page/Location: 107/G3
Area: 63,039 sq. mi.
163,270 sq. km.
Population: 443,446
Capital: Paramaribo
Largest City: Paramaribo
Highest Point: Juliana Top
Monetary Unit: Suriname guilder

Swaziland
Page/Location: 81/E2
Area: 6,705 sq. mi.
        17,366 sq. km.
Population: 1,031,600
Capital: Mbabane; Lobamba
Largest City: Mbabane
Highest Point: Emlembe
Monetary Unit: lilangeni

Sweden
Page/Location: 20/E3
Area: 173,665 sq. mi.
        449,792 sq. km.
Population: 8,946,193
Capital: Stockholm
Largest City: Stockholm
Highest Point: Kebnekaise
Monetary Unit: krona

Switzerland
Page/Location: 36/D4
Area: 15,943 sq. mi.
        41,292 sq. km.
Population: 7,248,984
Capital: Bern
Largest City: Zürich
Highest Point: Dufourspitze
Monetary Unit: Swiss franc

Syria
Page/Location: 50/D3
Area: 71,498 sq. mi.
        185,180 sq. km.
Population: 16,137,899
Capital: Damascus
Largest City: Damascus
Highest Point: Jabal ash Shaykh
Monetary Unit: Syrian pound

Taiwan
Page/Location: 61/J3
Area: 13,971 sq. mi.
        36,185 sq. km.
Population: 21,655,515
Capital: T'aipei
Largest City: T'aipei
Highest Point: Yü Shan
Monetary Unit: new Taiwan dollar

Tajikistan
Page/Location: 46/H6
Area: 55,251 sq. mi.
        143,100 sq. km.
Population: 6,013,855
Capital: Dushanbe
Largest City: Dushanbe
Highest Point: Communism Peak
Monetary Unit: Tajikistani ruble

Tanzania
Page/Location: 82/F2
Area: 364,699 sq. mi.
        945,090 sq. km.
Population: 29,460,753
Capital: Dar es Salaam
Largest City: Dar es Salaam
Highest Point: Kilimanjaro
Monetary Unit: Tanzanian shilling

Thailand
Page/Location: 65/C3
Area: 198,455 sq. mi.
        513,998 sq. km.
Population: 59,450,818
Capital: Bangkok
Largest City: Bangkok
Highest Point: Doi Inthanon
Monetary Unit: baht

Togo
Page/Location: 79/F4
Area: 21,927 sq. mi.
        56,790 sq. km.
Population: 4,735,610
Capital: Lomé
Largest City: Lomé
Highest Point: Mt. Agou
Monetary Unit: CFA franc

Tonga
Page/Location: 69/H7
Area: 289 sq. mi.
        748 sq. km.
Population: 107,335
Capital: Nuku'alofa
Largest City: Nuku'alofa
Highest Point: Kao Island
Monetary Unit: pa'anga

Trinidad and Tobago
Page/Location: 104/F5
Area: 1,980 sq. mi.
        5,128 sq. km.
Population: 1,273,141
Capital: Port-of-Spain
Largest City: Port-of-Spain
Highest Point: El Cerro del Aripo
Monetary Unit: Trin. & Tobago dollar

Tunisia
Page/Location: 76/G1
Area: 63,170 sq. mi.
        163,610 sq. km.
Population: 9,183,097
Capital: Tūnis
Largest City: Tūnis
Highest Point: Jabal ash Sha'nabī
Monetary Unit: Tunisian dinar

Turkey
Page/Location: 50/C2
Area: 301,382 sq. mi.
        780,580 sq. km.
Population: 63,528,225
Capital: Ankara
Largest City: Istanbul
Highest Point: Mt. Ararat
Monetary Unit: Turkish lira

Turkmenistan
Page/Location: 46/F6
Area: 188,455 sq. mi.
        488,100 sq. km.
Population: 4,225,351
Capital: Ashgabat
Largest City: Ashgabat
Highest Point: Rize
Monetary Unit: manat

Tuvalu
Page/Location: 68/G5
Area: 9.78 sq. mi.
        25.33 sq. km.
Population: 10,297
Capital: Funafuti
Largest City: —
Highest Point: 16 ft. (5 m)
Monetary Unit: Australian dollar

Uganda
Page/Location: 77/M7
Area: 91,076 sq. mi.
        235,887 sq. km.
Population: 20,604,874
Capital: Kampala
Largest City: Kampala
Highest Point: Margherita Peak
Monetary Unit: Ugandan shilling

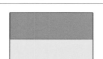

Ukraine
Page/Location: 44/D2
Area: 233,089 sq. mi.
        603,700 sq. km.
Population: 50,684,635
Capital: Kiev
Largest City: Kiev
Highest Point: Goverla
Monetary Unit: hryvnia

United Arab Emirates
Page/Location: 52/F4
Area: 29,182 sq. mi.
        75,581 sq. km.
Population: 2,262,309
Capital: Abu Dhabi
Largest City: Dubayy
Highest Point: Hajar Mts.
Monetary Unit: Emirian dirham

United Kingdom
Page/Location: 21
Area: 94,399 sq. mi.
        244,493 sq. km.
Population: 58,610,182
Capital: London
Largest City: London
Highest Point: Ben Nevis
Monetary Unit: pound sterling

United States
Page/Location: 88
Area: 3,618,765 sq. mi.
        9,372,610 sq. km.
Population: 267,954,767
Capital: Washington, D.C.
Largest City: New York
Highest Point: Mt. McKinley
Monetary Unit: U.S. dollar

Uruguay
Page/Location: 109/E3
Area: 68,039 sq. mi.
        176,220 sq. km.
Population: 3,261,707
Capital: Montevideo
Largest City: Montevideo
Highest Point: Cerro Catedral
Monetary Unit: Uruguayan peso

Uzbekistan
Page/Location: 46/G5
Area: 172,741 sq. mi.
        447,400 sq. km.
Population: 23,860,452
Capital: Tashkent
Largest City: Tashkent
Highest Point: Khodzha-Pir'yakh
Monetary Unit: som

Vanuatu
Page/Location: 68/F6
Area: 5,700 sq. mi.
        14,763 sq. km.
Population: 181,358
Capital: Port-Vila
Largest City: Port-Vila
Highest Point: Tabwemasana
Monetary Unit: vatu

Vatican City
Page/Location: 38/C2
Area: 0.17 sq. mi.
        0.44 sq. km.
Population: 830
Capital: —
Largest City: —
Highest Point: —
Monetary Unit: Vatican lira

Venezuela
Page/Location: 106/E2
Area: 352,143 sq. mi.
        912,050 sq. km.
Population: 22,396,407
Capital: Caracas
Largest City: Caracas
Highest Point: Pico Bolívar
Monetary Unit: bolívar

Vietnam
Page/Location: 65/D2
Area: 127,243 sq. mi.
        329,560 sq. km.
Population: 75,123,880
Capital: Hanoi
Largest City: Ho Chi Minh City
Highest Point: Fan Si Pan
Monetary Unit: new dong

Yemen
Page/Location: 52/E5
Area: 203,849 sq. mi.
        527,970 sq. km.
Population: 13,972,477
Capital: Sanaa
Largest City: Aden
Highest Point: Nabī Shu'ayb
Monetary Unit: Yemeni rial

Yugoslavia
Page/Location: 40/E3
Area: 39,517 sq. mi.
        102,350 sq. km.
Population: 10,655,317
Capital: Belgrade
Largest City: Belgrade
Highest Point: Đaravica
Monetary Unit: Yugoslav new dinar

Zambia
Page/Location: 82/E3
Area: 290,586 sq. mi.
        752,618 sq. km.
Population: 9,349,975
Capital: Lusaka
Largest City: Lusaka
Highest Point: Sunzu
Monetary Unit: Zambian kwacha

Zimbabwe
Page/Location: 82/E4
Area: 150,803 sq. mi.
        390,580 sq. km.
Population: 11,423,175
Capital: Harare
Largest City: Harare
Highest Point: Inyangani
Monetary Unit: Zimbabwe dollar

World Statistics

ELEMENTS OF THE SOLAR SYSTEM

	Mean Distance from Sun: in Miles	in Kilometers	Period of Revolution around Sun	Period of Rotation on Axis	Equatorial Diameter in Miles	in Kilometers	Surface Gravity (Earth = 1)	Mass (Earth = 1)	Mean Density (Water = 1)	Number of Satellites
Mercury	35,990,000	57,900,000	87.97 days	58.7 days	3,032	4,880	0.38	0.055	5.4	0
Venus	67,240,000	108,200,000	224.70 days	243.7 days†	7,521	12,104	0.91	0.815	5.2	0
Earth	93,000,000	149,700,000	365.26 days	23h 56m	7,926	12,755	1.00	1.00	5.5	1
Mars	141,610,000	227,900,000	686.98 days	24h 37m	4,221	6,794	0.38	0.107	3.9	2
Jupiter	483,675,000	778,400,000	11.86 years	9h 55m	88,846	142,984	2.36	317.8	1.3	16
Saturn	886,572,000	1,426,800,000	29.46 years	10h 30m	74,898	120,536	0.92	95.2	0.7	18
Uranus	1,783,957,000	2,871,000,000	84.01 years	17h 14m†	31,763	51,118	0.89	14.5	1.3	15
Neptune	2,795,114,000	4,498,300,000	164.79 years	16h 6m	30,778	49,532	1.13	17.1	1.6	8
Pluto	3,670,000,000	5,906,400,000	247.70 years	6.4 days†	1,413	2,274	0.07	0.002	2.1	1

† Retrograde motion

Source: NASA, National Space Science Data Center

DIMENSIONS OF THE EARTH

	Area in: Sq. Miles	Sq. Kilometers
Superficial area	196,939,000	510,072,000
Land surface	57,506,000	148,940,000
Water surface	139,433,000	361,132,000

	Distance in: Miles	Kilometers
Equatorial circumference	24,902	40,075
Polar circumference	24,860	40,007
Equatorial diameter	7,926.4	12,756.4
Polar diameter	7,899.8	12,713.6
Equatorial radius	3,963.2	6,378.2
Polar radius	3,949.9	6,356.8

Volume of the Earth	2.6×10^{11} cubic miles	10.84×10^{11} cubic kilometers
Mass or weight	6.6×10^{21} short tons	6.0×10^{21} metric tons
Maximum distance from Sun	94,600,000 miles	152,000,000 kilometers
Minimum distance from Sun	91,300,000 miles	147,000,000 kilometers

OCEANS AND MAJOR SEAS

	Area in: Sq. Miles	Sq. Kms.	Greatest Depth in: Feet	Meters
Pacific Ocean	63,855,000	166,241,000	36,198	11,033
Atlantic Ocean	31,744,000	82,217,000	28,374	8,648
Indian Ocean	28,417,000	73,600,000	25,344	7,725
Arctic Ocean	5,427,000	14,056,000	17,880	5,450
Caribbean Sea	970,000	2,512,300	24,720	7,535
Mediterranean Sea	969,000	2,509,700	16,896	5,150
South China Sea	895,000	2,318,000	15,000	4,600
Bering Sea	875,000	2,266,250	15,800	4,800
Gulf of Mexico	600,000	1,554,000	12,300	3,750
Sea of Okhotsk	590,000	1,528,100	11,070	3,370
East China Sea	482,000	1,248,400	9,500	2,900
Yellow Sea	480,000	1,243,200	350	107
Sea of Japan	389,000	1,007,500	12,280	3,740
Hudson Bay	317,500	822,300	846	258
North Sea	222,000	575,000	2,200	670
Black Sea	185,000	479,150	7,365	2,245
Red Sea	169,000	437,700	7,200	2,195
Baltic Sea	163,000	422,170	1,506	459

THE CONTINENTS

	Area in: Sq. Miles	Sq. Kms.	Percent of World's Land
Asia	17,128,500	44,362,815	29.5
Africa	11,707,000	30,321,130	20.2
North America	9,363,000	24,250,170	16.2
South America	6,879,725	17,818,505	11.9
Antarctica	5,405,000	14,000,000	9.4
Europe	4,057,000	10,507,630	7.0
Australia	2,967,893	7,686,850	5.1

MAJOR SHIP CANALS

	Length in: Miles	Kms.	Minimum Depth in: Feet	Meters
Volga-Baltic, Russia	225	362	–	–
Baltic-White Sea, Russia	140	225	16	5
Suez, Egypt	100.76	162	42	13
Albert, Belgium	80	129	16.5	5
Moscow-Volga, Russia	80	129	18	6
Volga-Don, Russia	62	100	–	–
Göta, Sweden	54	87	10	3
Kiel (Nord-Ostsee), Germany	53.2	86	38	12
Panama Canal, Panama	50.72	82	41.6	13
Houston Ship, U.S.A.	50	81	36	11

LARGEST ISLANDS

	Area in: Sq. Miles	Sq. Kms.
Greenland	840,000	2,175,600
New Guinea	305,000	789,950
Borneo	286,000	740,740
Madagascar	226,656	587,040
Baffin, Canada	195,928	507,454
Sumatra, Indonesia	164,000	424,760
Honshu, Japan	88,000	227,920
Great Britain	84,400	218,896
Victoria, Canada	83,896	217,290
Ellesmere, Canada	75,767	196,236
Celebes, Indonesia	72,986	189,034
South I., New Zealand	58,393	151,238
Java, Indonesia	48,842	126,501
North I., New Zealand	44,187	114,444
Cuba	42,803	110,860
Newfoundland, Canada	42,031	108,860
Luzon, Philippines	40,420	104,688
Iceland	39,768	103,000
Mindanao, Philippines	36,537	94,631
Ireland	32,589	84,406
Hokkaidô, Japan	30,436	78,829
Sakhalin, Russia	29,500	76,405

	Area in: Sq. Miles	Sq. Kms.
Hispaniola, Haiti & Dom. Rep.	29,399	76,143
Banks, Canada	27,038	70,028
Ceylon, Sri Lanka	25,332	65,610
Tasmania, Australia	24,600	63,710
Svalbard, Norway	23,957	62,049
Devon, Canada	21,331	55,247
Novaya Zemlya (north isl.), Russia	18,600	48,200
Marajó, Brazil	17,991	46,597
Tierra del Fuego, Chile & Argentina	17,900	46,360
Alexander, Antarctica	16,700	43,250
Axel Heiberg, Canada	16,671	43,178
Melville, Canada	16,274	42,150
Southhampton, Canada	15,913	41,215
New Britain, Papua New Guinea	14,100	36,519
Taiwan, China	13,836	35,835
Kyushu, Japan	13,770	35,664
Hainan, China	13,127	33,999
Prince of Wales, Canada	12,872	33,338
Spitsbergen, Norway	12,355	31,999
Vancouver, Canada	12,079	31,285
Timor, Indonesia	11,527	29,855
Sicily, Italy	9,926	25,708

	Area in: Sq. Miles	Sq. Kms.
Somerset, Canada	9,570	24,786
Sardinia, Italy	9,301	24,090
Shikoku, Japan	6,860	17,767
New Caledonia, France	6,530	16,913
Nordaustlandet, Norway	6,409	16,599
Samar, Philippines	5,050	13,080
Negros, Philippines	4,906	12,707
Palawan, Philippines	4,550	11,785
Panay, Philippines	4,446	11,515
Jamaica	4,232	10,961
Hawaii, United States	4,038	10,458
Viti Levu, Fiji	4,010	10,386
Cape Breton, Canada	3,981	10,311
Mindoro, Philippines	3,759	9,736
Kodiak, Alaska, U.S.A.	3,670	9,505
Cyprus	3,572	9,251
Puerto Rico, U.S.A.	3,435	8,897
Corsica, France	3,352	8,682
New Ireland, Papua New Guinea	3,340	8,651
Crete, Greece	3,218	8,335
Anticosti, Canada	3,066	7,941
Wrangel, Russia	2,819	7,301

PRINCIPAL MOUNTAINS

	Height in: Feet	Meters
Everest, Nepal-China	29,028	8,848
K2 (Godwin Austen), Pakistan-China	28,250	8,611
Kanchenjunga, Nepal-India	28,208	8,598
Lhotse, Nepal-China	27,923	8,511
Makalu, Nepal-China	27,789	8,470
Dhaulagiri, Nepal	26,810	8,172
Nanga Parbat, Pakistan	26,660	8,126
Annapurna, Nepal	26,504	8,078
Nanda Devi, India	25,645	7,817
Rakaposhi, Pakistan	25,550	7,788
Kongur Shan, China	25,325	7,719
Tirich Mir, Pakistan	25,230	7,690
Gongga Shan, China	24,790	7,556
Ismail Samani Peak, Tajikistan	24,590	7,495
Pobedy Peak, Kyrgyzstan	24,406	7,439
Chomo Lhari, Bhutan-China	23,997	7,314
Muztag, China	23,891	7,282
Cerro Aconcagua, Argentina	22,831	6,959
Ojos del Salado, Chile-Argentina	22,572	6,880
Bonete, Chile-Argentina	22,546	6,872
Tupungato, Chile-Argentina	22,310	6,800

	Height in: Feet	Meters
Pissis, Argentina	22,241	6,779
Mercedario, Argentina	22,211	6,770
Huascarán, Peru	22,205	6,768
Llullaillaco, Chile-Argentina	22,057	6,723
Nevada Ancohuma, Bolivia	21,489	6,550
Chimborazo, Ecuador	20,561	6,267
McKinley, Alaska	20,320	6,194
Logan, Yukon, Canada	19,524	5,951
Cotopaxi, Ecuador	19,347	5,897
Kilimanjaro, Tanzania	19,340	5,895
El Misti, Peru	19,101	5,822
Pico Cristóbal Colón, Colombia	18,947	5,775
Huila, Colombia	18,865	5,750
Citlaltépetl (Orizaba), Mexico	18,700	5,700
Damavand, Iran	18,605	5,671
El'brus, Russia	18,510	5,642
St. Elias, Alaska, U.S.A.-Yukon, Canada	18,008	5,489
Dykh-tau, Russia	17,070	5,203
Batian (Kenya), Kenya	17,058	5,199
Ararat, Turkey	16,946	5,165
Vinson Massif, Antarctica	16,864	5,140

	Height in: Feet	Meters
Margherita (Ruwenzori), Africa	16,795	5,119
Kazbek, Georgia-Russia	16,558	5,047
Puncak Jaya, Indonesia	16,503	5,030
Blanc, France	15,771	4,807
Klyuchevskaya Sopka, Russia	15,584	4,750
Fairweather, Br. Col., Canada	15,300	4,663
Dufourspitze (Mte. Rosa), Italy-Switzerland	15,203	4,634
Ras Dashen, Ethiopia	15,157	4,620
Matterhorn, Switzerland	14,691	4,478
Whitney, California, U.S.A.	14,494	4,418
Elbert, Colorado, U.S.A.	14,433	4,399
Rainier, Washington, U.S.A.	14,410	4,392
Shasta, California, U.S.A.	14,162	4,317
Pikes Peak, Colorado, U.S.A.	14,110	4,301
Finsteraarhorn, Switzerland	14,022	4,274
Mauna Kea, Hawaii, U.S.A.	13,796	4,205
Mauna Loa, Hawaii, U.S.A.	13,677	4,169
Jungfrau, Switzerland	13,642	4,158
Grossglockner, Austria	12,457	3,797
Fujiyama, Japan	12,389	3,776
Cook, New Zealand	12,349	3,764

LONGEST RIVERS

	Length in: Miles	Kms.
Nile, Africa	4,145	6,671
Amazon, S. America	4,007	6,448
Mississippi-Missouri-Red Rock, U.S.A.	3,710	5,971
Chang Jiang (Yangtze), China	3,500	5,633
Ob'-Irtysh, Russia-Kazakhstan	3,362	5,411
Yenisey-Angara, Russia	3,100	4,989
Huang He (Yellow), China	2,950	4,747
Congo (Zaire), Africa	2,780	4,474
Amur-Shilka-Onon, Asia	2,744	4,416
Lena, Russia	2,734	4,400
Mackenzie-Peace-Finlay, Canada	2,635	4,241
Paraná-La Plata, S. America	2,630	4,232
Mekong, Asia	2,610	4,200
Niger, Africa	2,580	4,152
Missouri-Red Rock, U.S.A.	2,564	4,125
Yenisey, Russia	2,500	4,028
Mississippi, U.S.A.	2,348	3,778
Murray-Darling, Australia	2,310	3,718
Volga, Russia	2,290	3,685
Madeira, S. America	2,013	3,240
Purus, S. America	1,995	3,211
Yukon, Alaska-Canada	1,979	3,185
Zambezi, Africa	1,950	3,138
São Francisco, Brazil	1,930	3,106
St. Lawrence, Canada-U.S.A.	1,900	3,058

	Length in: Miles	Kms.
Rio Grande, Mexico-U.S.A.	1,885	3,034
Syrdar'ya-Naryn, Asia	1,859	2,992
Indus, Asia	1,800	2,897
Danube, Europe	1,775	2,857
Brahmaputra, Asia	1,700	2,736
Tocantins, Brazil	1,677	2,699
Salween, Asia	1,675	2,696
Euphrates, Asia	1,650	2,655
Xi (Si), China	1,650	2,655
Amu Darya, Asia	1,616	2,601
Nelson-Saskatchewan, Canada	1,600	2,575
Orinoco, S. America	1,600	2,575
Paraguay, S. America	1,584	2,549
Kolyma, Russia	1,562	2,514
Ganges, Asia	1,550	2,494
Ural, Russia-Kazakhstan	1,509	2,428
Japurá, S. America	1,500	2,414
Arkansas, U.S.A.	1,450	2,334
Colorado, U.S.A.-Mexico	1,450	2,334
Negro, S. America	1,400	2,253
Dnepr, Russia-Belarus-Ukraine	1,368	2,202
Orange, Africa	1,350	2,173
Irrawaddy, Myanmar	1,325	2,132
Brazos, U.S.A.	1,309	2,107
Ohio-Allegheny, U.S.A.	1,306	2,102

	Length in: Miles	Kms.
Kama, Russia	1,252	2,031
Don, Russia	1,222	1,967
Red, U.S.A.	1,222	1,966
Columbia, U.S.A.-Canada	1,214	1,953
Tigris, Asia	1,181	1,901
Darling, Australia	1,160	1,867
Angara, Russia	1,135	1,827
Sungari, Asia	1,130	1,819
Pechora, Russia	1,124	1,809
Snake, U.S.A.	1,038	1,670
Churchill, Canada	1,000	1,609
Pilcomayo, S. America	1,000	1,609
Uruguay, S. America	994	1,600
Platte-N. Platte, U.S.A.	990	1,593
Ohio, U.S.A.	981	1,578
Magdalena, Colombia	956	1,538
Pecos, U.S.A.	926	1,490
Oka, Russia	918	1,477
Canadian, U.S.A.	906	1,458
Colorado, Texas, U.S.A.	894	1,439
Dniester, Ukraine-Moldova	876	1,410
Fraser, Canada	850	1,369
Rhine, Europe	820	1,319
Northern Dvina, Russia	809	1,302
Ottawa, Canada	790	1,271

PRINCIPAL NATURAL LAKES

	Area in: Sq. Miles	Sq. Kms.	Max. Depth in: Feet	Meters
Caspian Sea, Asia	143,243	370,999	3,264	995
Lake Superior, U.S.A.-Canada	31,820	82,414	1,329	405
Lake Victoria, Africa	26,628	69,215	270	82
Lake Huron, U.S.A.-Canada	23,010	59,596	748	228
Lake Michigan, U.S.A.	22,400	58,016	923	281
Aral Sea, Kazakhstan-Uzbekistan	15,830	41,000	213	65
Lake Tanganyika, Africa	12,650	32,764	4,700	1,433
Lake Baykal, Russia	12,162	31,500	5,316	1,620
Great Bear Lake, Canada	12,096	31,328	1,356	413
Lake Nyasa (Malawi), Africa	11,555	29,928	2,320	707
Great Slave Lake, Canada	11,031	28,570	2,015	614
Lake Erie, U.S.A.-Canada	9,940	25,745	210	64
Lake Winnipeg, Canada	9,417	24,390	60	18
Lake Ontario, U.S.A.-Canada	7,540	19,529	775	244
Lake Balkhash, Kazakhstan	7,081	18,340	87	27
Lake Ladoga, Russia	6,900	17,871	738	225
Lake Maracaibo, Venezuela	5,120	13,261	100	31
Lake Chad, Africa*	10,000 – 4,000	25,900 – 10,360	25	8
Lake Onega, Russia	3,761	9,741	377	115

	Area in: Sq. Miles	Sq. Kms.	Max. Depth in: Feet	Meters
Lake Eyre, Australia*	3,500-0	9,000-0	–	–
Lake Titicaca, Peru-Bolivia	3,200	8,288	1,000	305
Lake Nicaragua, Nicaragua	3,100	8,029	230	70
Lake Athabasca, Canada	3,064	7,936	400	122
Reindeer Lake, Canada*	2,568	6,651	–	–
Lake Turkana (Rudolf), Africa	2,463	6,379	240	73
Ysyk-Köl, Kyrgyzstan	2,425	6,281	2,303	702
Lake Torrens, Australia*	2,230	5,776	–	–
Vänern, Sweden	2,156	5,584	328	100
Nettilling Lake, Canada*	2,140	5,543	–	–
Lake Winnipegosis, Canada	2,075	5,374	38	12
Lake Mobutu Sese Seko (Albert), Africa	2,075	5,374	160	49
Kariba Lake, Zambia-Zimbabwe	2,050	5,310	295	90
Lake Nipigon, Canada	1,872	4,848	540	165
Lake Mweru, Dem. Rep. of the Congo-Zambia	1,800	4,662	60	18
Lake Manitoba, Canada	1,799	4,659	12	4
Lake Taymyr, Russia	1,737	4,499	85	26
Lake Khanka, China-Russia	1,700	4,403	33	10
Lake Kioga, Uganda	1,700	4,403	25	8
Lake of the Woods, U.S.A.-Canada	1,679	4,349	70	21

* Area and depth figures subject to great seasonal variations.

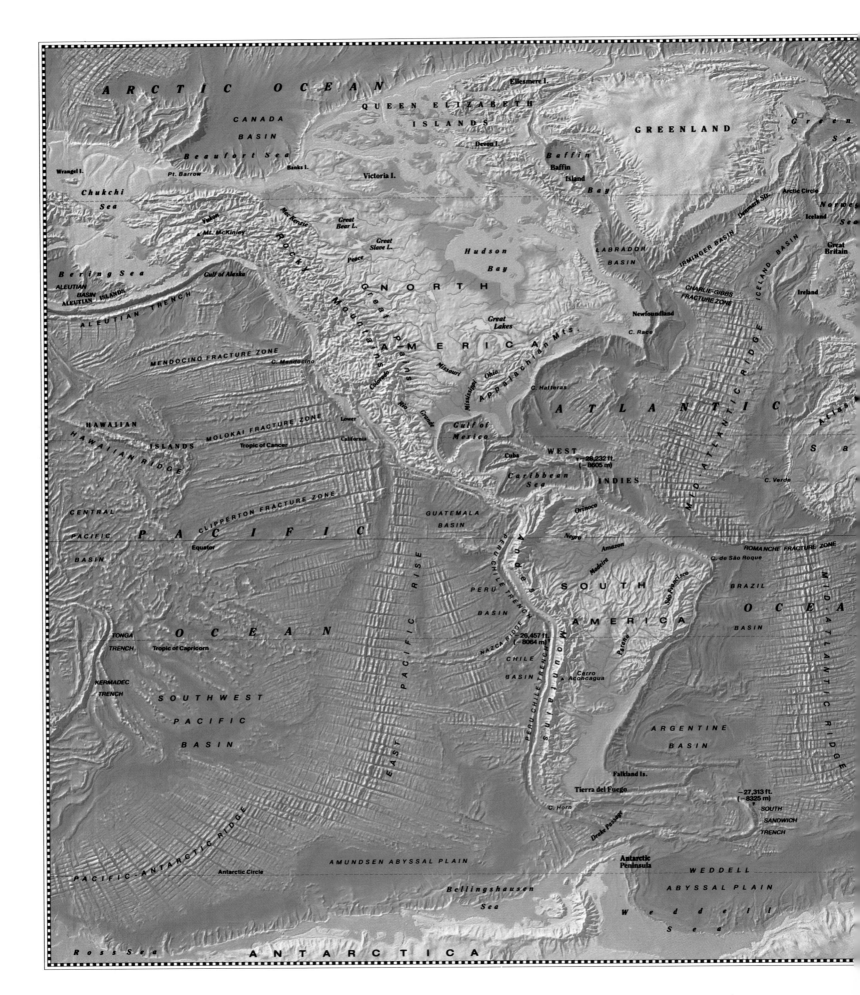

ARCTIC OCEAN

CANADA
BASIN

QUEEN ELIZABETH
ISLANDS

Ellesmere I.

GREENLAND

Green

Beaufort Sea

Devon I.

Baffin
Bay

Baffin
Island

Wrangel I.

Pt. Barrow

Banks I.

Victoria I.

*Chukchi
Sea*

Arctic Circle

Narwe

Bering Sea

Yukon

Mt. McKinley

ROCKY

Mac Kenzie

Great
Bear L.

Great
Slave L.

Hudson

Bay

LABRADOR
BASIN

IRMINGER BASIN

Denmark Str.

Iceland

ICELAND BASIN

Norwe

*Great
Britain*

Gulf of Alaska

ALEUTIAN
BASIN
ALEUTIAN ISLANDS

ALEUTIAN TRENCH

Peace

NORTH

Great
Lakes

Newfoundland

C. Race

CHARLIE-GIBBS
FRACTURE ZONE

Ireland

MENDOCINO FRACTURE ZONE

C. Mendocino

Mountains

Great

A-M-E-R-I-C-A

Missouri

Ohio

Appalachian Mts.

C. Hatteras

ATLANTIC

HAWAIIAN

MOLOKAI FRACTURE ZONE

Colorado

Plains

Lower

Rio

Grande

Mississippi

Gulf of
Mexico

C

HAWAIIAN RIDGE
ISLANDS

Tropic of Cancer

California

WEST

Cuba

–28,232 ft.
(– 8605 m)

Atlas

S e a

CENTRAL

CLIPPERTON FRACTURE ZONE

PACIFIC

PACIFIC

GUATEMALA
BASIN

*Caribbean
Sea*

INDIES

Orinoco

C. Verde

MID-ATLANTIC RIDGE

ROMANCHE FRACTURE ZONE

BASIN

Equator

PACIFIC

Negro

Amazon

C. de São Roque

BRAZIL

MID-ATLANTIC

TONGA
TRENCH

Tropic of Capricorn

OCEAN

PERU
BASIN

PERU-CHILE TRENCH

Madeira

SOUTH

São Francisco

BASIN

OCEA

RIDGE

KERMADEC
TRENCH

NAZCA RIDGE

CHILE
BASIN

–26,457 ft.
(– 8064 m)

SUBLAIR Mountains

Andes

AMERICA

Patagu

SOUTHWEST

EAST PACIFIC RISE

Cerro
Aconcagua

ARGENTINE

PACIFIC

BASIN

BASIN

Falkland Is.

–27,313 ft.
(– 8325 m)

Tierra del Fuego

SOUTH
SANDWICH
TRENCH

PACIFIC-ANTARCTIC RIDGE

C. Horn

Drake Passage

Antarctic
Peninsula

WEDDELL

AMUNDSEN ABYSSAL PLAIN

Antarctic Circle

ABYSSAL PLAIN

*Bellingshausen
Sea*

W e d d e l l

S e a

Ross Sea

ANTARCTICA

World

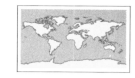

▼ −17,881 ft.
(−5450 m)

ARCTIC   OCEAN

FRANZ JOSEF LAND   SEVERNAYA
ZEMLYA

NEW SIBERIAN IS.

SVALBARD

WEGIAN

NOVAYA
ZEMLYA

Kara
Sea

Laptev

Sea

Wrangel I.

Nordkapp

Barents
Sea

Baltic Sea

Kjölen

L. Ladoga

S   i   b   e   r   i   a

Bering
Sea

ALEUTIAN
BASIN

ALEUTIAN   ISLANDS

Ob.

Yenisei

Lena

Angara

Kamchatka
Pen.

EUROPE

Volga

Dnieper

Ural Mountains

Irtysh

Ob.

Lena

Aldan

A   S   I   A

Sea of
Okhotsk

Sakhalin

Amur

KURIL-KAMCHATKA TRENCH

ALEUTIAN TRENCH

Danube

Black Sea

Caspian Sea

Aral
Sea

L. Balkhash

L. Baykal

Gobi

Sea of
Honshu
Japan

JAPAN
TRENCH

NORTHWEST

PACIFIC

BASIN

terranean Sea

Euphrates

Kunlun

Huang

East
China
Sea

Nile

Red Sea

Himalaya

Mt. Everest

Chang

PACIFIC

RICA

Indus

Ganges

Taiwan

Tropic of Cancer

ara

Arabian
Sea

ARABIAN
BASIN

Bay
of
Bengal

Salween

Mekong

South
China
Sea

Luzon

PHILIPPINE

BASIN

MARIANA IS.

MARIANA

TRENCH

Challenger Deep
−36,198 ft.
(−11,033 m)

MARSHALL IS.

CENTRAL

PACIFIC

BASIN

CARLSBERG
RIDGE

C. Comorin

Ceylon

CEYLON
PLAIN

Borneo

Mindanao

CAROLINE IS.

Victoria

Kilimanjaro

SOMALI
BASIN

CENTRAL

INDIAN

RIDGE

Sumatra

JAVA TRENCH

Java

24,443 ft.
(−7450 m)

Celebes

New Guinea

MELANESIAN

BASIN

Equator

OCEAN

Congo

INDIAN

OLA

Zambezi

Madagascar

I   N   D   I   A   N

NINETYEAST RIDGE

Coral
Sea

Great Barrier Reef

Fiji Is.

RIDGE

Orange

OCEAN

SOUTHEAST INDIAN RIDGE

Tropic of Capricorn

CAPE
Good Hope

BROKEN
PLATEAU

AUSTRALIA

Tasman
Sea

North Cape

North I.

BASIN

HAS RIDGE

C. Leeuwin

S. AUSTRALIA BASIN

Tasmania

South I.

SOUTHWEST INDIAN RIDGE

KERGUELEN
PLATEAU

SOUTHEAST INDIAN RIDGE

SOUTHEAST INDIAN RIDGE

ENDERBY ABYSSAL PLAIN

AUSTRALIAN-ANTARCTIC BASIN

Antarctic Circle

C. Adare

Amery
Ice Shelf

Ross Sea

A   N   T   A   R   C   T   I   C   A

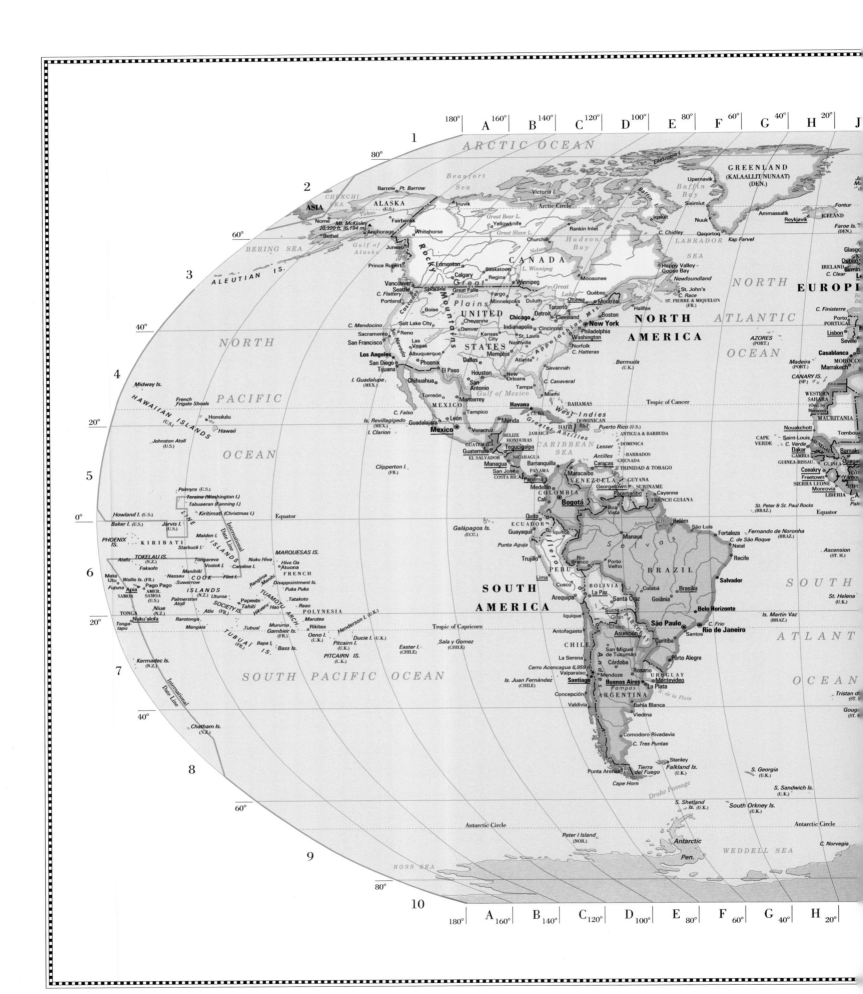

World

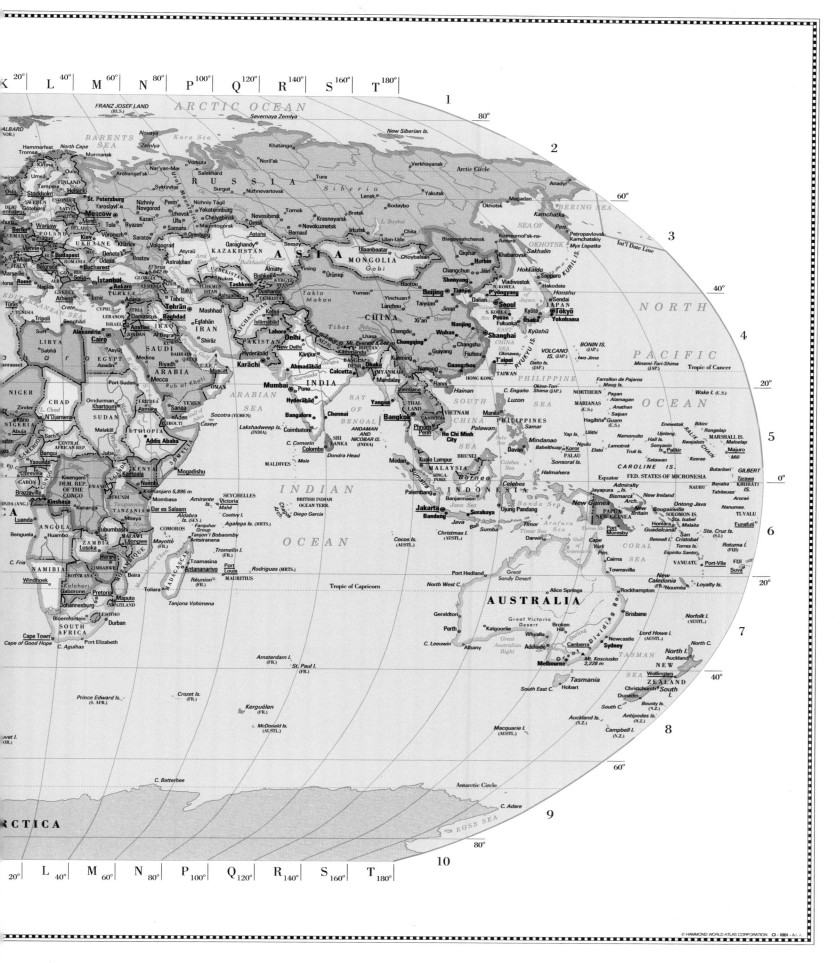

POPULATION OF CITIES AND TOWNS

⊛ OVER 5,000,000 ● 500,000 - 1,999,999
● 2,000,000 - 4,999,999 ○ UNDER 500,000

SCALE 1:81,700,000 ROBINSON PROJECTION STANDARD PARALLELS 38°N AND 38°S

MILES 0 — 1000 — 2000 — 3000 — 4000
KILOMETERS 0 — 1000 — 2000 — 3000 — 4000

AREA OF OPTIMIZATION

AREA OF OPTIMIZATION

The red band which surrounds this map defines the "Area of Optimization." Within this bounding curve is the most accurate conformal map that can be made of the region. Outside the optimized area, distortion increases rapidly, and tears or other irregularities in the grid may occur.

GREENLAND
(KALAALLIT NUNAAT)
(DENMARK)

Arctic Circle

Denmark Strait

Jan Mayen
(NOR.)

NORWEGIAN

SEA

BARENTS

SEA

Novaya
Zemlya

North Cape

Mys Kanin Nos
Kanin
Pen.

ICELAND

Hammerfest
Vadsø
Tromsø
Vesterålen
Narvik
Kiruna
Kebnekaise 2,111 m
Gällivare
Harstad
Lofoten
Bodø
Murmansk
Monchegorsk
Apatity
Kola
Pen.
White Sea
Severodvinsk
Kem'
Medvezh'yegorsk
Onega
Archangel

ATLANTIC OCEAN

Faroe Is.
(DEN.)
Tórshavn

Shetland
Is.

NORTH
SEA

FINLAND

Kajaani
Oulu
Vaasa
Tampere
Lahti
Turku
Helsinki
St. Petersburg

SWEDEN
Östersund
Sundsvall
Gävle
Uppsala
Stockholm

NORWAY
Bergen
Oslo
Stavanger

DENMARK
Copenhagen

GERMANY

UNITED KINGDOM
London

IRELAND
Dublin

FRANCE
Paris

SPAIN
Madrid

PORTUGAL
Lisbon

ITALY
Rome

POLAND
Warsaw

UKRAINE
Kiev

BELARUS
Minsk

ATLANTIC OCEAN

MEDITERRANEAN SEA

AFRICA

ALGERIA

MOROCCO

TUNISIA

GREECE
Athens

TURKEY

SCALE 1:17,500,000 OPTIMAL CONFORMAL PROJECTION

MILES
KILOMETERS

POPULATION OF CITIES AND TOWNS
☐ OVER 3,000,000
☐ 1,000,000 - 2,999,999
● 500,000 - 999,999
● 100,000 - 499,999
○ UNDER 100,000

© Copyright by HAMMOND WORLD ATLAS CORPORATION CD-1002-A

Europe

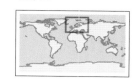

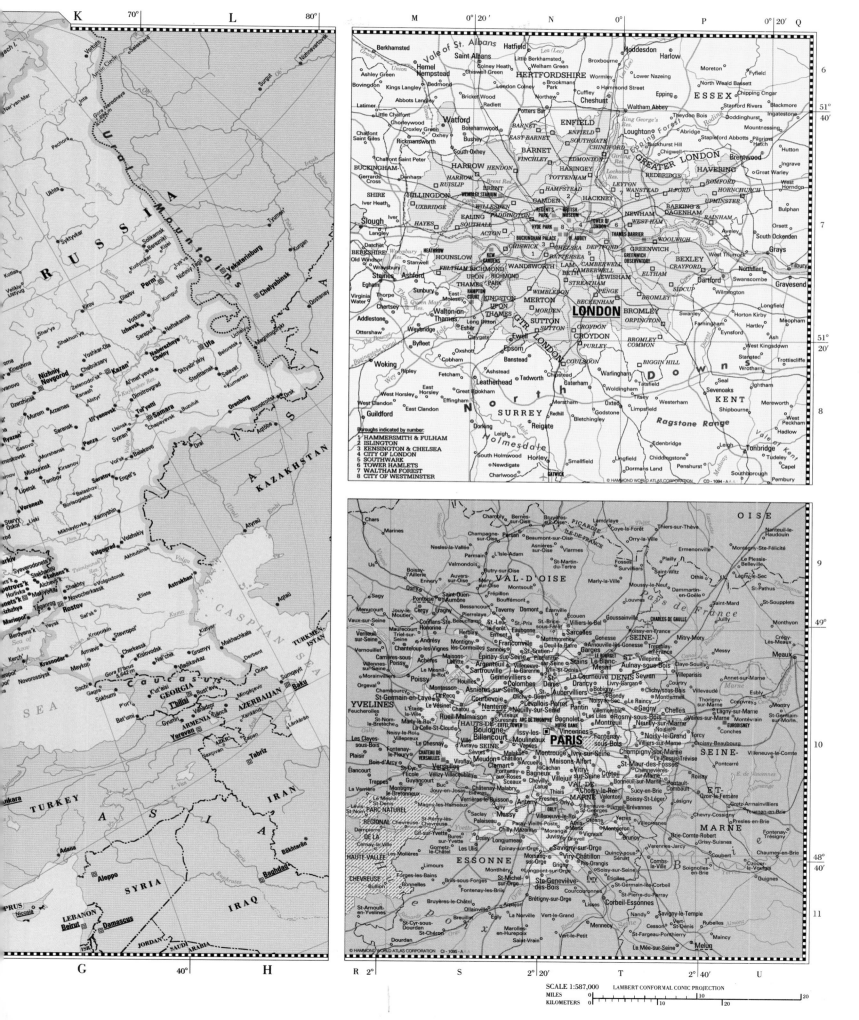

SCALE 1:587,000   LAMBERT CONFORMAL CONIC PROJECTION

Scandinavia and Finland, Iceland

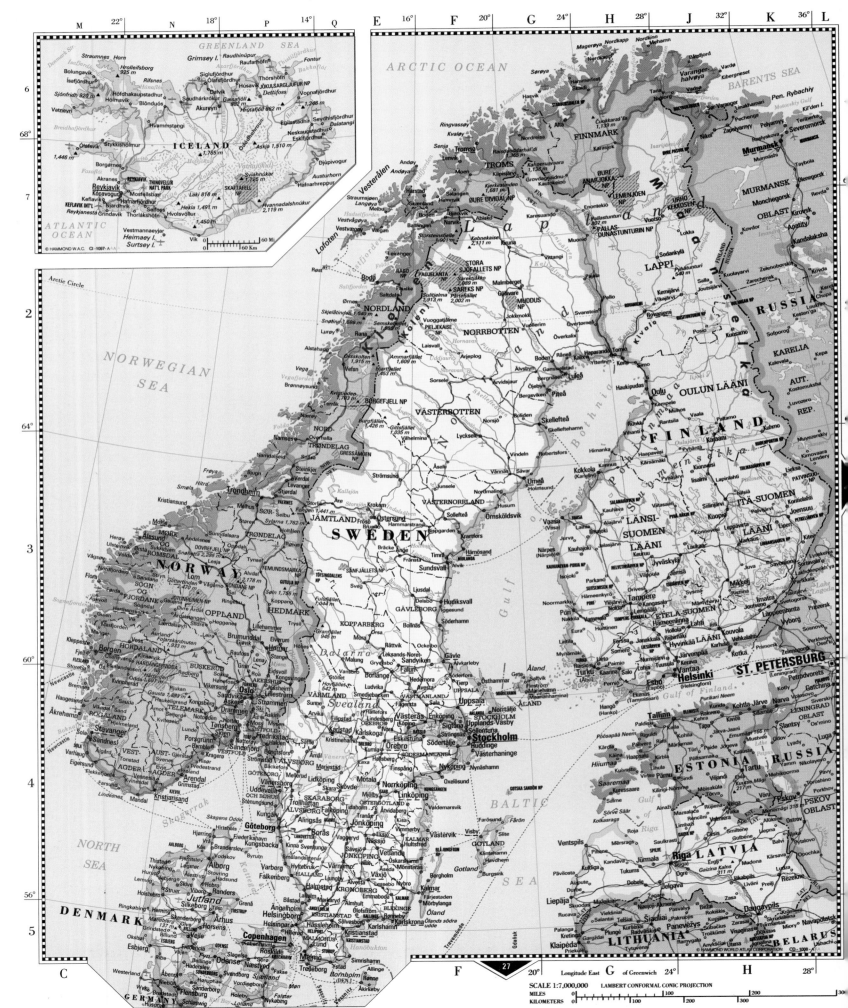

SCALE 1:3,500,000   LAMBERT CONFORMAL CONIC PROJECTION
MILES
KILOMETERS

Northeastern Ireland, Northern England and Wales

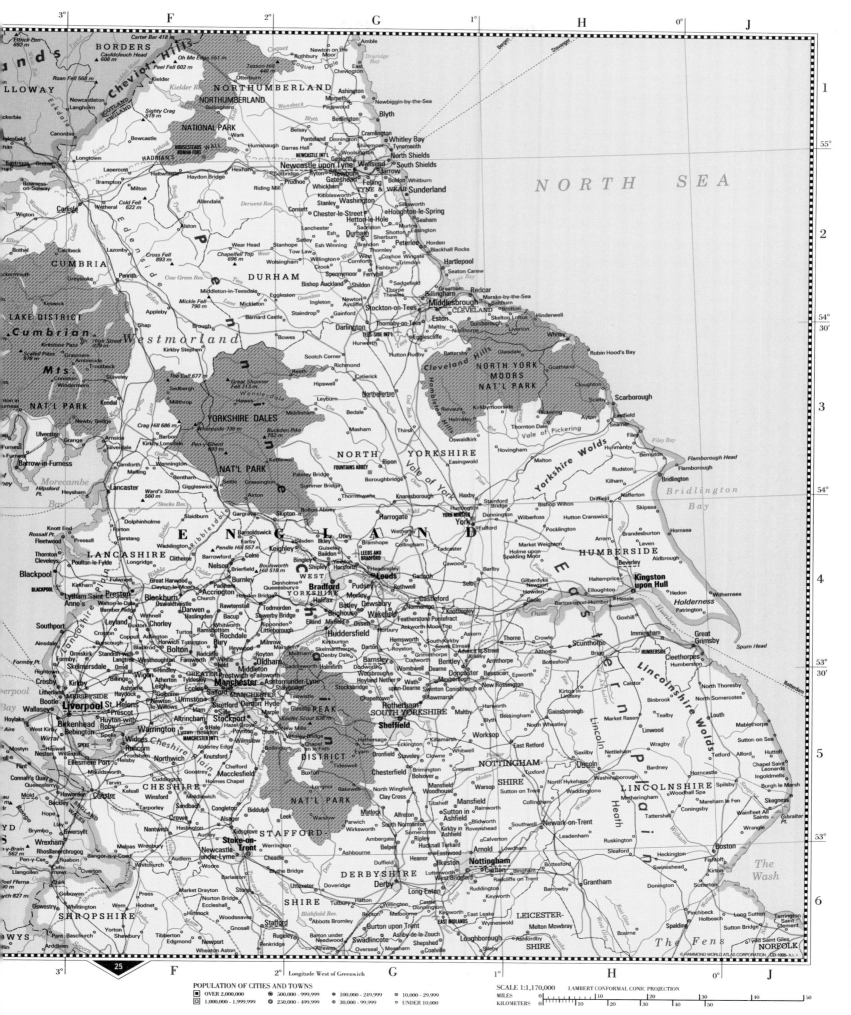

NORTH SEA

POPULATION OF CITIES AND TOWNS
- ▪ OVER 2,000,000
- ◻ 1,000,000 - 1,999,999
- ⦿ 500,000 - 999,999
- ⊙ 250,000 - 499,999
- ◉ 100,000 - 249,999
- ⦿ 30,000 - 99,999
- ⊙ 10,000 - 29,999
- ○ UNDER 10,000

Longitude West of Greenwich

SCALE 1:1,170,000   LAMBERT CONFORMAL CONIC PROJECTION

MILES
0   10   20   30   40   50

KILOMETERS
0   10   20   30   40   50

© HAMMOND WORLD ATLAS CORPORATION CD-1005-AAA

Southern England and Wales

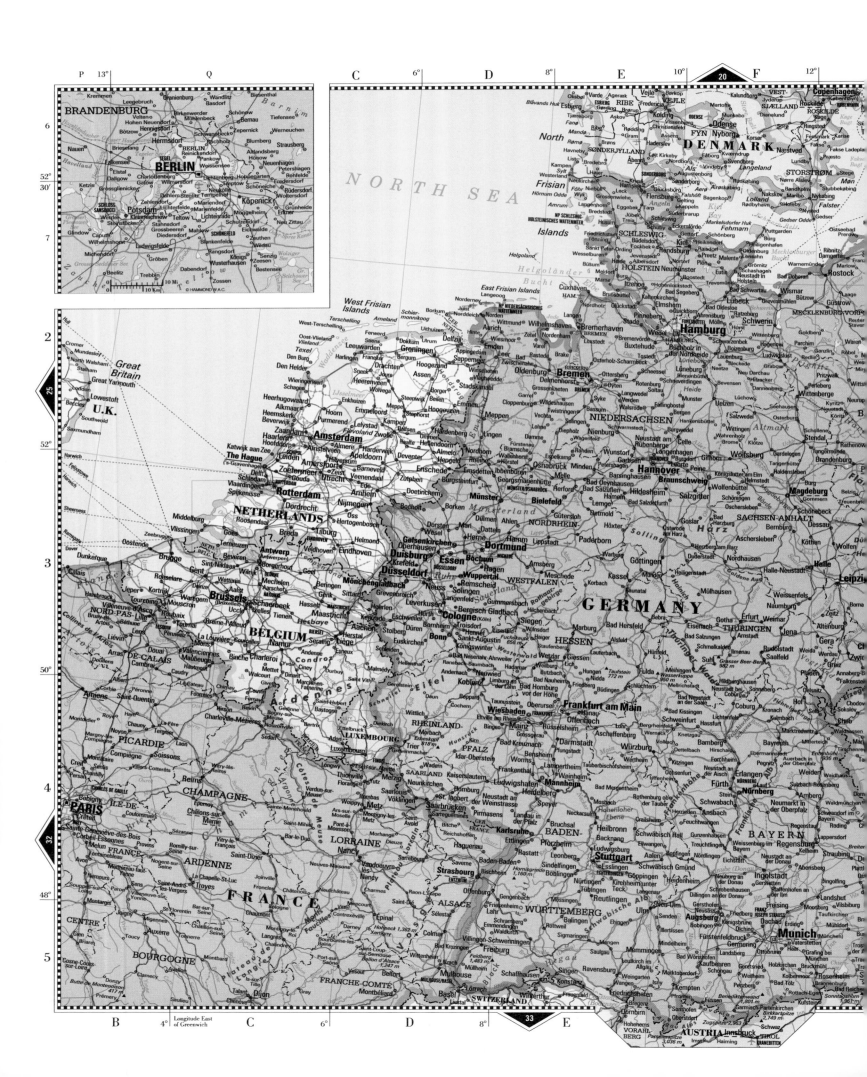

North Central Europe

POPULATION OF CITIES AND TOWNS

■ OVER 2,000,000	● 500,000 - 999,999	● 100,000 - 249,999	● 10,000 - 29,999
▣ 1,000,000 - 1,999,999	● 250,000 - 499,999	● 30,000 - 99,999	○ UNDER 10,000

SCALE 1:3,500,000   LAMBERT CONFORMAL CONIC PROJECTION

MILES

KILOMETERS

GERMANY

NIEDERSACHSEN · **NORDRHEIN-WESTFALEN** · **HESSEN** · **THÜRINGEN** · **SCHLESWIG-HOLSTEIN** · **MECKLENBURG-VORPOMMERN** · **SACHSEN-ANHALT** · **BREMEN** · **HAMBURG**

Helgoländer Bucht · Frisian Islands · Ostfriesland · Münsterland · Sauerland · Lüneburger Heide · Teutoburger Wald · Wiehengebirge · Wesergebirge · Eggegebirge · Rothaargebirge · Harz · Ith Hills · Solling · Hainich

Brocken 1,142 m · Bruchberg 928 m · Meissner 750 m · Grosser Ahrensberg 522 m · Hohegrass 615 m · Wüstegarten 675 m · Wilseder Berg 169 m · 367 m · 405 m · 290 m · 468 m

Hamburg · Bremen · Hannover · Braunschweig · Oldenburg · Osnabrück · Münster · Dortmund · Wuppertal · Bielefeld · Paderborn · Hildesheim · Göttingen · Kassel · Wolfsburg · Salzgitter · Celle · Lüneburg · Cuxhaven · Bremerhaven · Wilhelmshaven · Emden · Leer · Meppen · Lingen · Rheine

POPULATION OF CITIES AND TOWNS

■	OVER 2,000,000
◻	1,000,000 – 1,999,999
●	500,000 – 999,999
◉	250,000 – 499,999
●	100,000 – 249,999
●	30,000 – 99,999
●	10,000 – 29,999
○	UNDER 10,000

SCALE 1:1,170,000   LAMBERT CONFORMAL CONIC PROJECTION

MILES 0 10 20 30 40 50

KILOMETERS 0 10 20 30 40 50

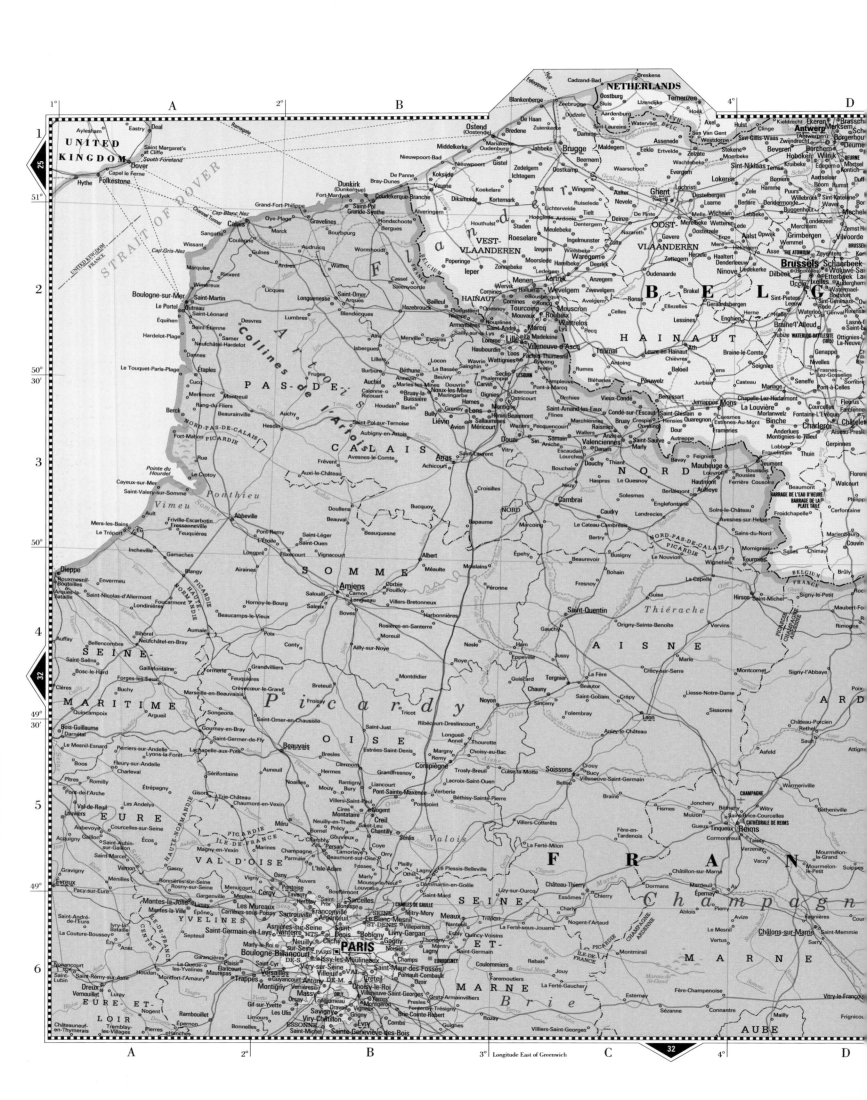

Belgium, Northern France, Western Germany

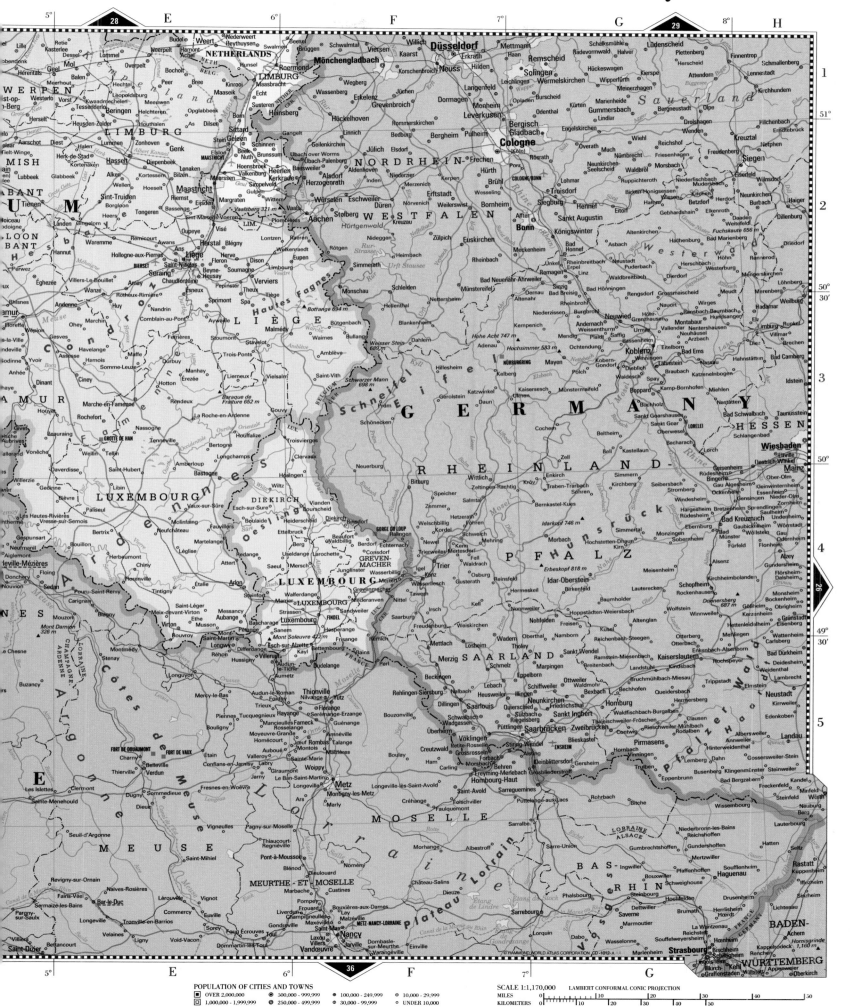

POPULATION OF CITIES AND TOWNS

■ OVER 2,000,000	● 500,000 - 999,999	● 100,000 - 249,999	○ 10,000 - 29,999
▣ 1,000,000 - 1,999,999	● 250,000 - 499,999	○ 30,000 - 99,999	○ UNDER 10,000

SCALE 1:1,170,000   LAMBERT CONFORMAL CONIC PROJECTION

MILES 0 — 10 — 20 — 30 — 40 — 50

KILOMETERS 0 — 10 — 20 — 30 — 40 — 50

West Central Europe

POPULATION OF CITIES AND TOWNS

■ OVER 2,000,000	● 500,000 - 999,999
□ 1,000,000 - 1,999,999	● 250,000 - 499,999

- ● 100,000 - 249,999
- ● 30,000 - 99,999
- ● 10,000 - 29,999
- ○ UNDER 10,000

SCALE 1:3,500,000   LAMBERT CONFORMAL CONIC PROJECTION

MILES   0   50   100   150

KILOMETERS   0   50   100   150

© HAMMOND WORLD ATLAS CORPORATION   CI - 1018 - A-A

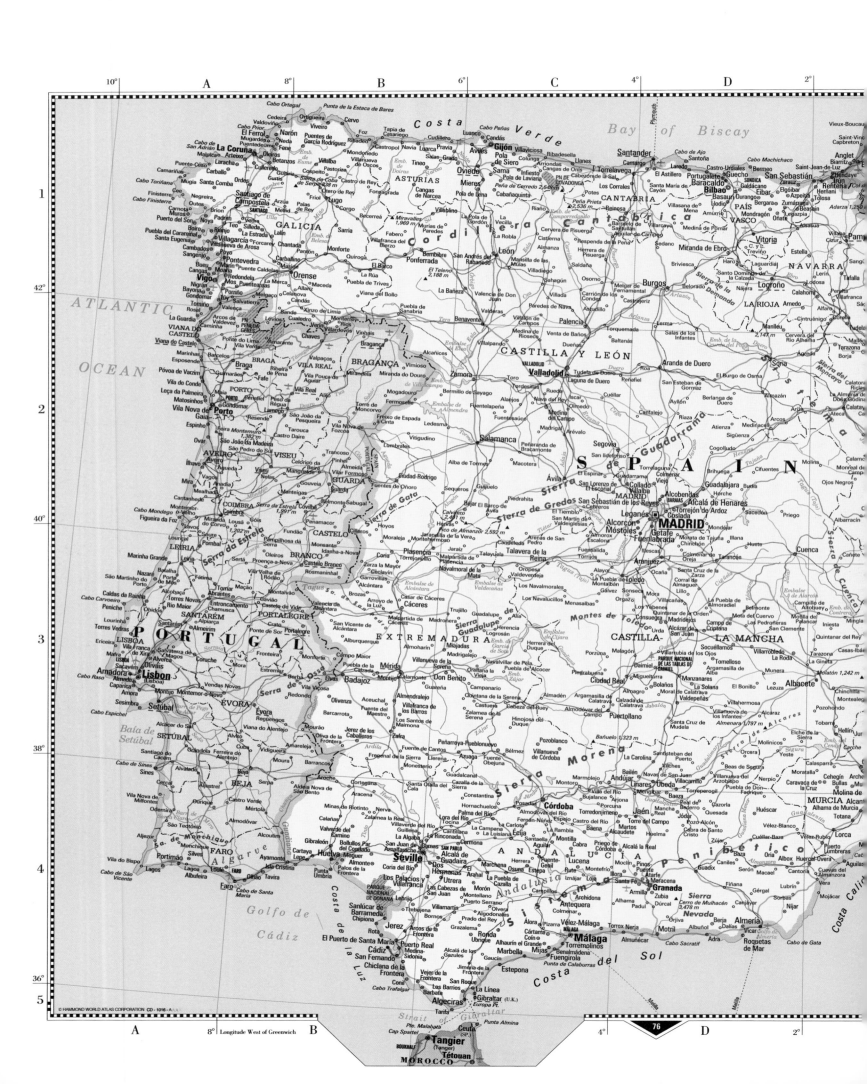

Spain, Portugal

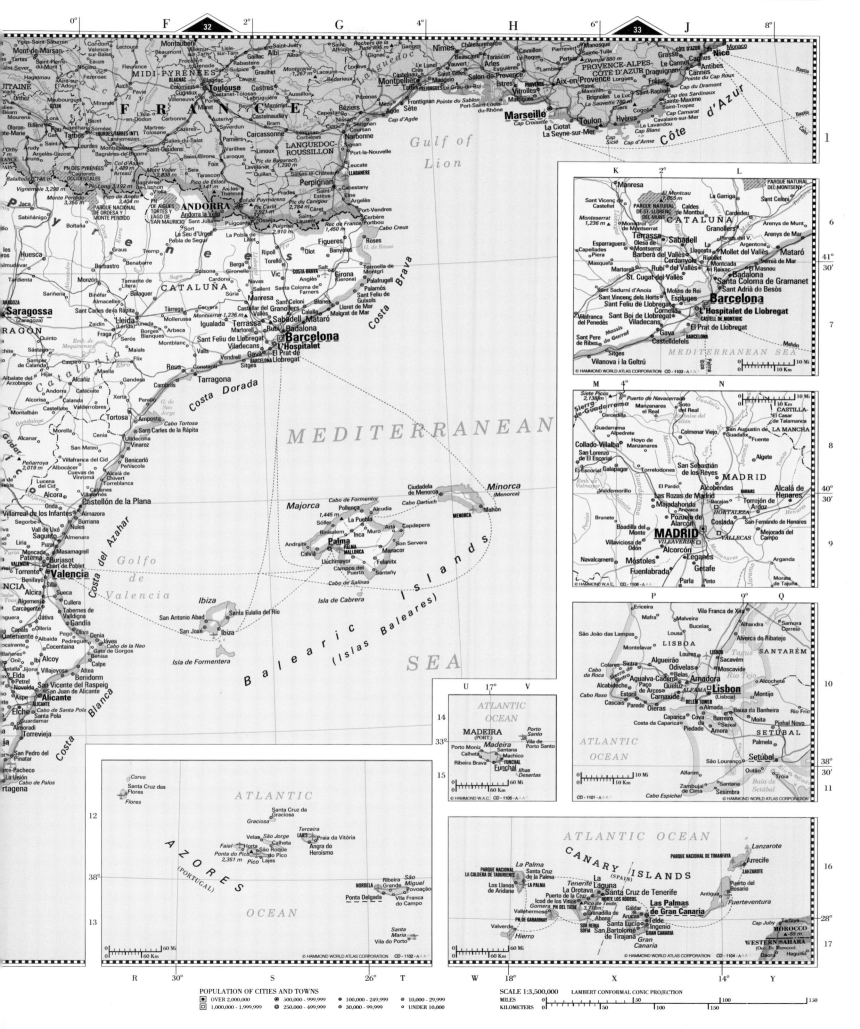

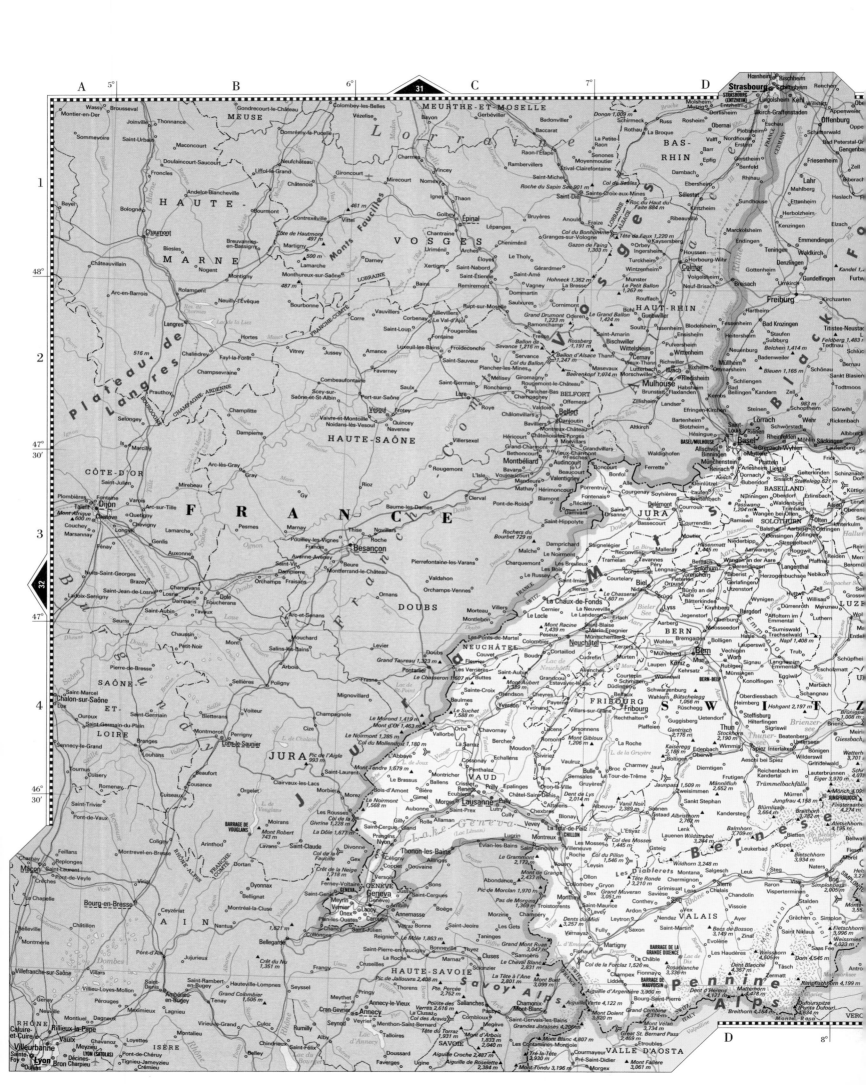

Central Alps Region

POPULATION OF CITIES AND TOWNS

☐ OVER 2,000,000   ● 500,000 - 999,999   ● 100,000 - 249,999   ○ 10,000 - 29,999

☐ 1,000,000 - 1,999,999   ● 250,000 - 499,999   ● 30,000 - 99,999   ○ UNDER 10,000

SCALE 1:1,170,000   LAMBERT CONFORMAL CONIC PROJECTION

MILES

KILOMETERS

© HAMMOND WORLD ATLAS CORPORATION CC-1018-A

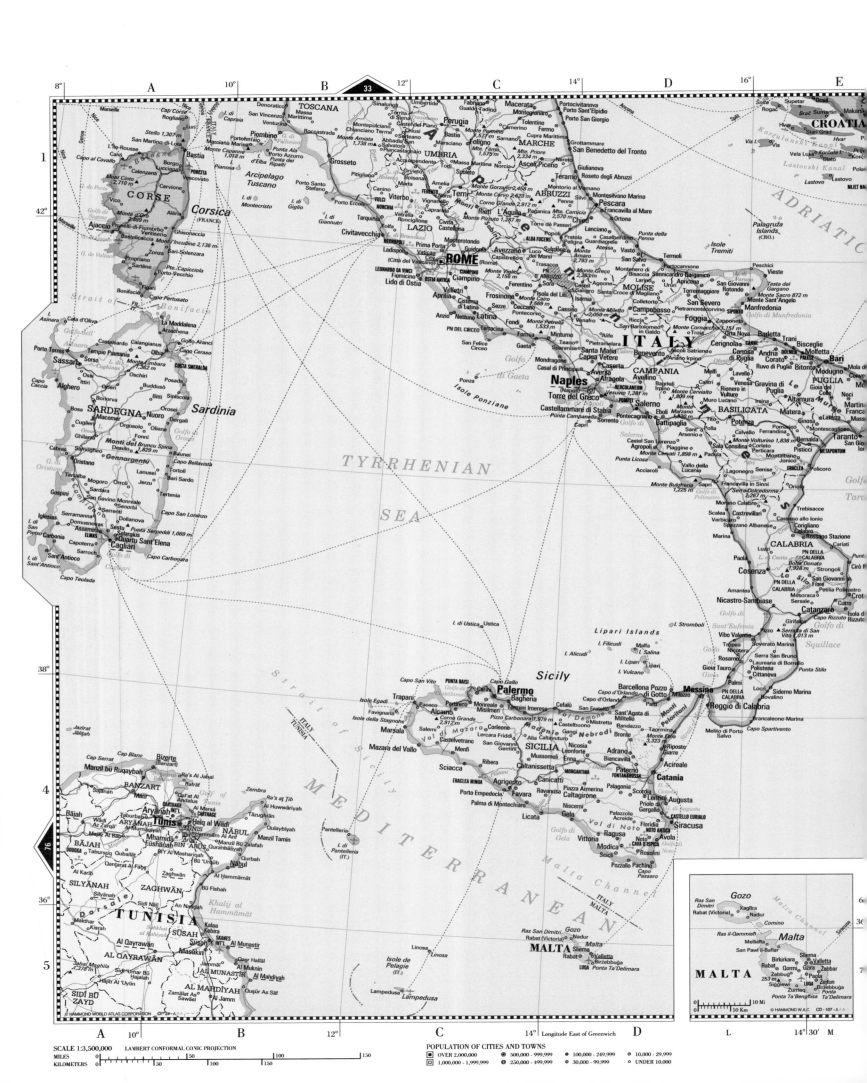

SCALE 1:3,500,000   LAMBERT CONFORMAL CONIC PROJECTION

MILES   0   50   100   150

KILOMETERS 0   50   100   150

POPULATION OF CITIES AND TOWNS

| ■ OVER 2,000,000 | ● 500,000 - 999,999 | ● 100,000 - 249,999 | ○ 10,000 - 29,999 |
| ◻ 1,000,000 - 1,999,999 | ◉ 250,000 - 499,999 | ○ 30,000 - 99,999 | ∘ UNDER 10,000 |

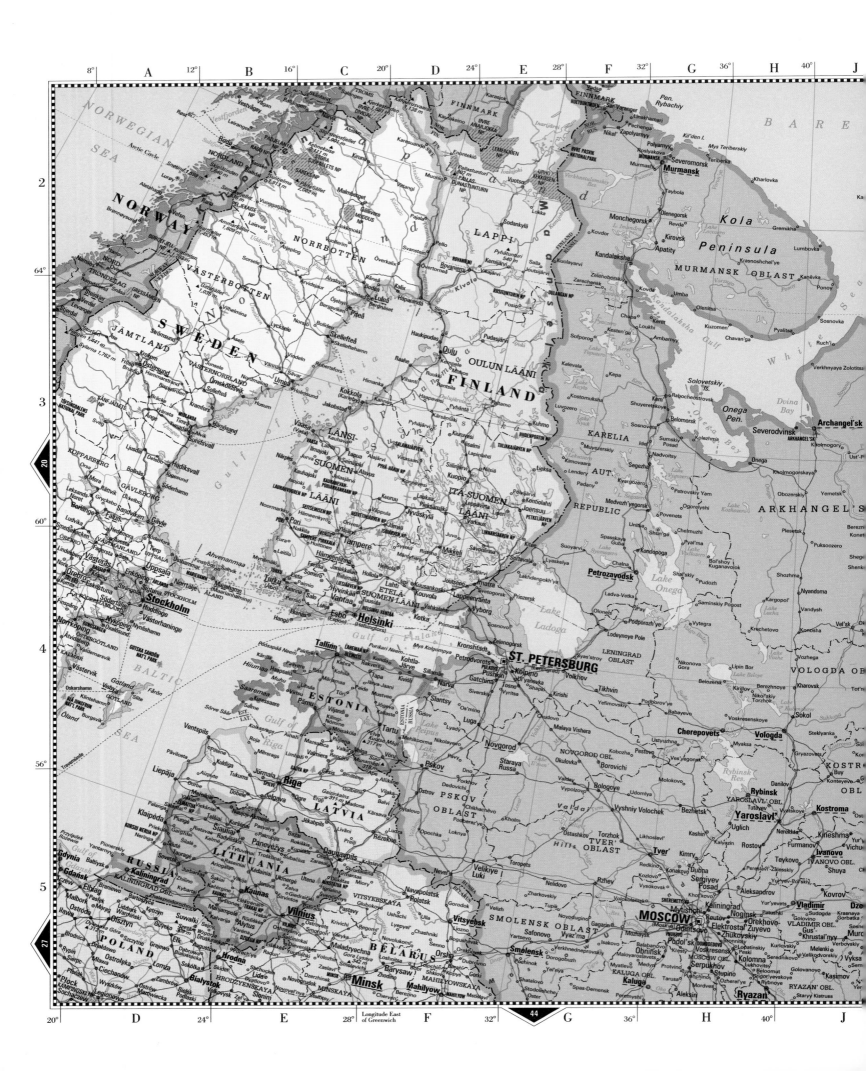

Northeastern Europe

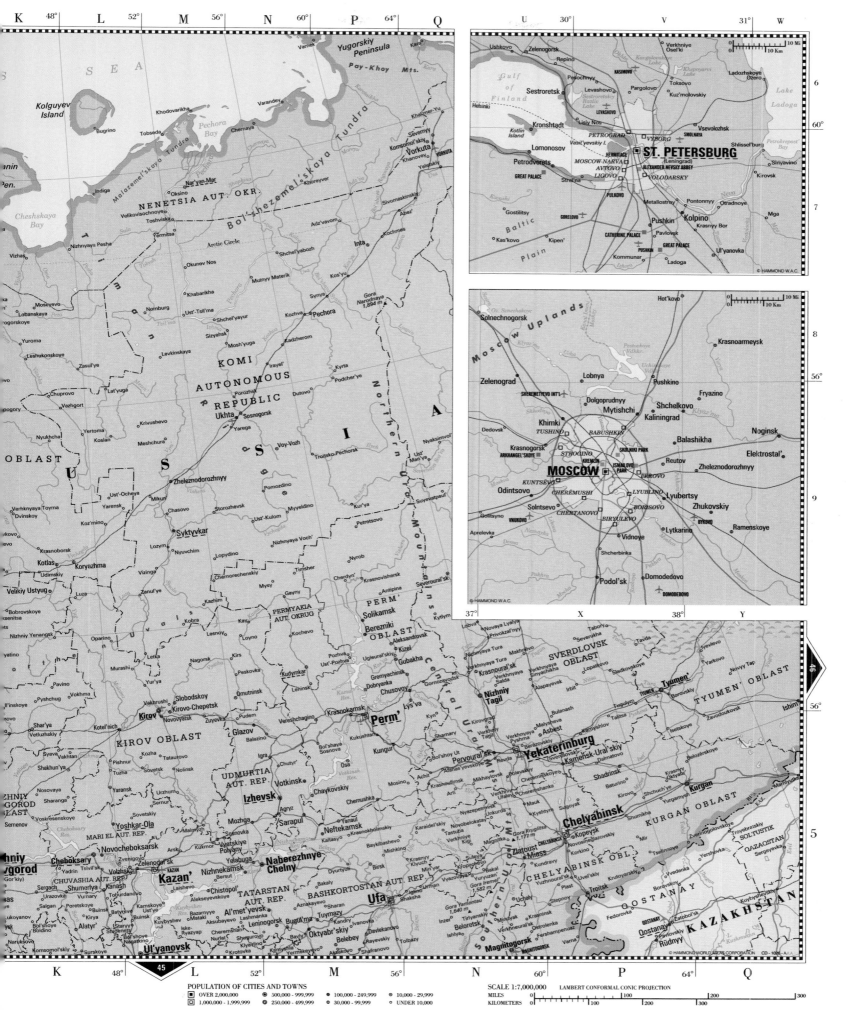

POPULATION OF CITIES AND TOWNS
- ■ OVER 2,000,000
- ▣ 1,000,000 - 1,999,999
- ● 500,000 - 999,999
- ● 250,000 - 499,999
- ● 100,000 - 249,999
- ● 30,000 - 99,999
- ● 10,000 - 29,999
- ● UNDER 10,000

SCALE 1:7,000,000   LAMBERT CONFORMAL CONIC PROJECTION

MILES 0   100   200   300
KILOMETERS 0   100   200   300

Southeastern Europe

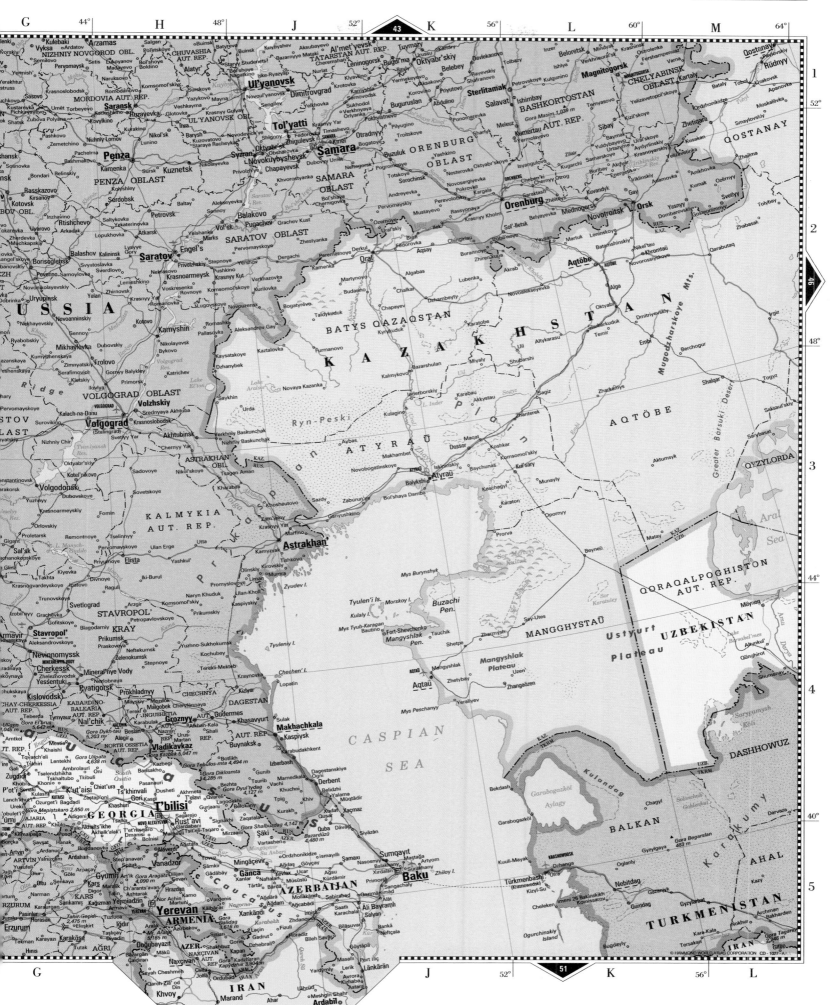

Russia and Neighboring Countries

RUSSIA
(Administrative divisions are named only when they differ from their respective capitals.)

1. ADYGEA AUT. REP.
2. KARACHAY-CHERKESSIA AUT. REP.
3. KABARDINO-BALKARIA AUT. REP.
4. NORTH OSSETIA AUT. REP.
5. INGUSHETIA AUT. REP.
6. CHECHNYA AUT. REP.
7. DAGESTAN AUT. REP.
8. MORDOVIA AUT. REP.
9. CHUVASHIA AUT. REP.
10. MARI EL AUT. REP.
11. TATARSTAN AUT. REP.
12. BASHKORTOSTAN AUT. REP.
13. UDMURTIA AUT. REP.
14. PERMYAKIA AUT. OKRUG
15. KHAKASSIA AUT. REP.
16. UST'-ORDA AUT. OKRUG
17. AGA AUT. OKRUG

© HAMMOND WORLD ATLAS CORPORATION CD-1029-A-A-A

POPULATION OF CITIES AND TOWNS

■ OVER 2,000,000   ● 500,000 - 999,999   ○ 50,000 - 99,999
▣ 1,000,000 - 1,999,999   ● 100,000 - 499,999   ○ UNDER 50,000

SCALE 1:21,000,000   LAMBERT CONFORMAL CONIC PROJECTION

MILES 0   300   600   900
KILOMETERS 0   300   600   900

Asia

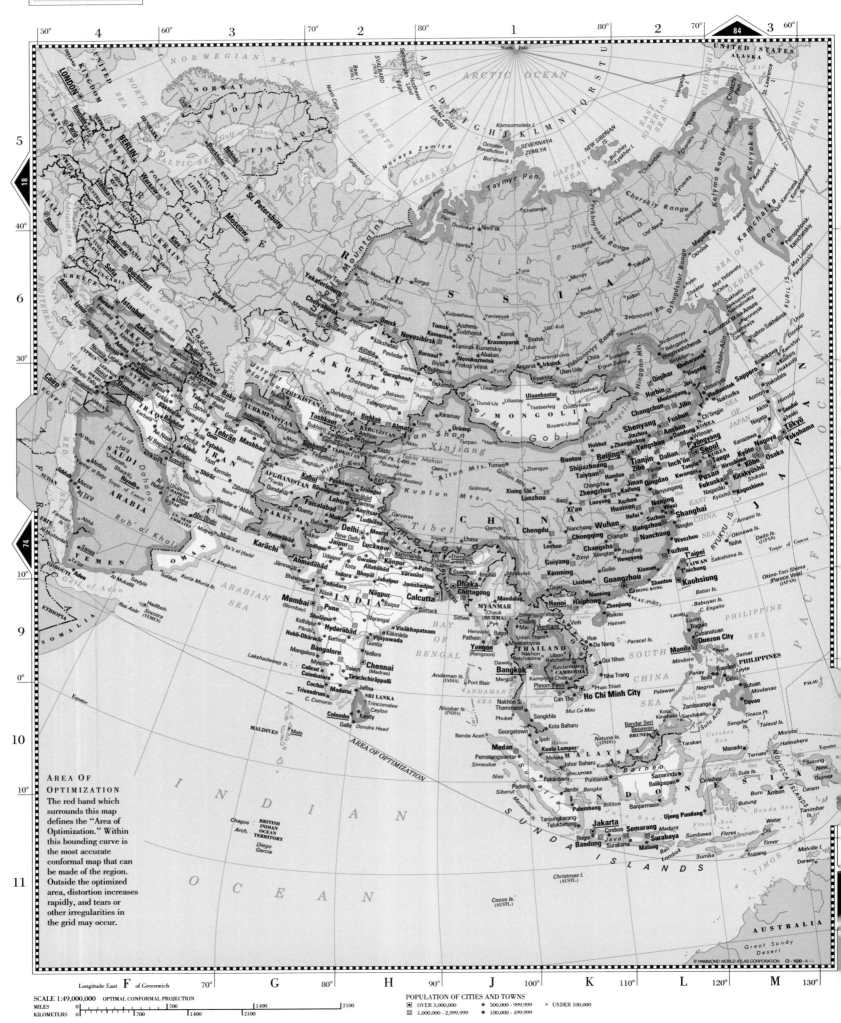

Eastern Mediterranean Region

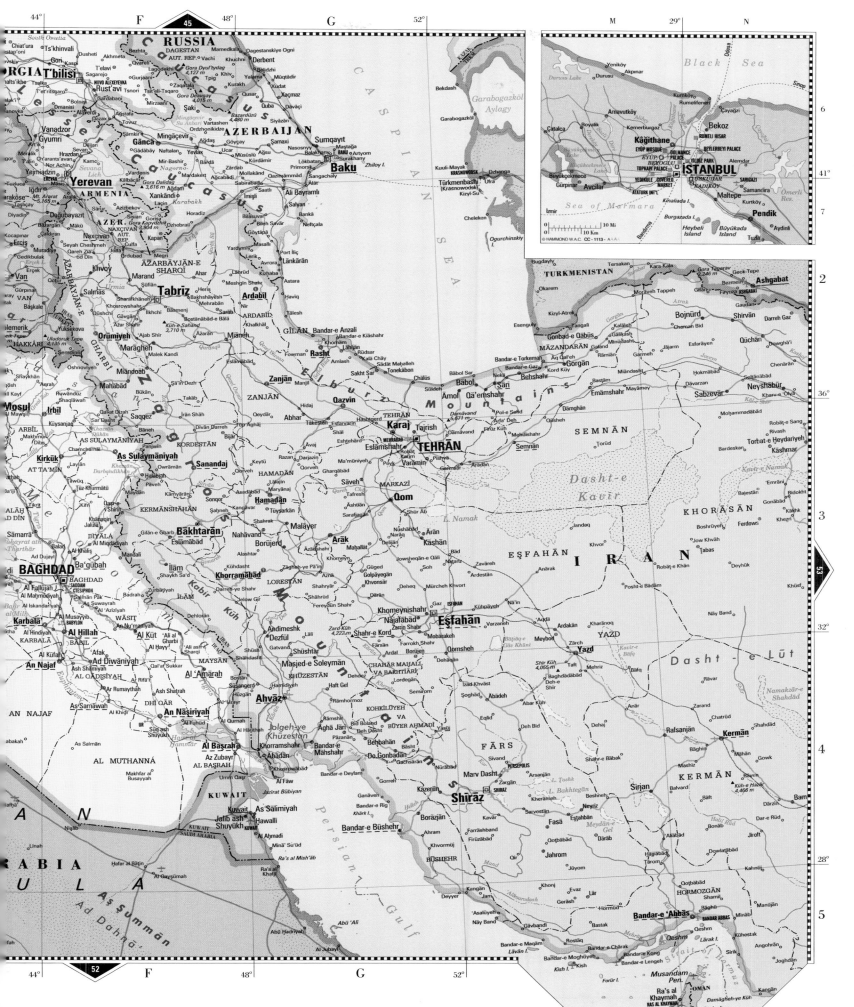

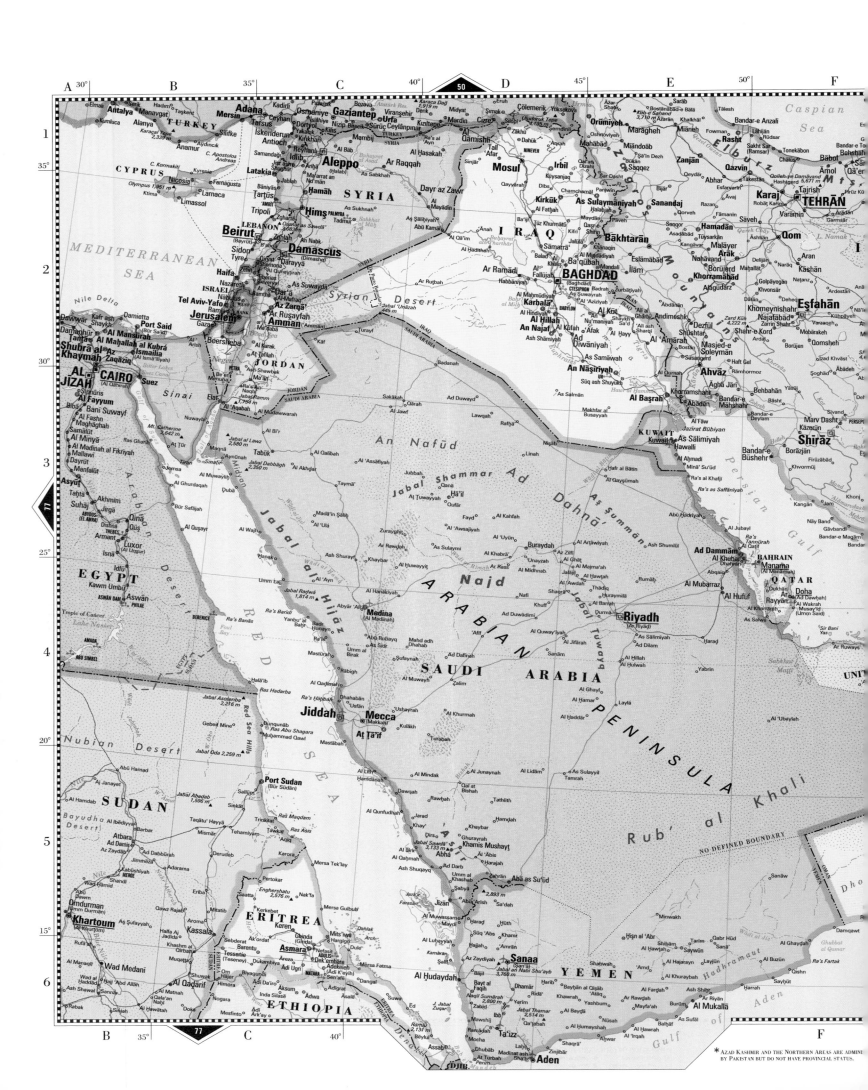

Southwestern Asia

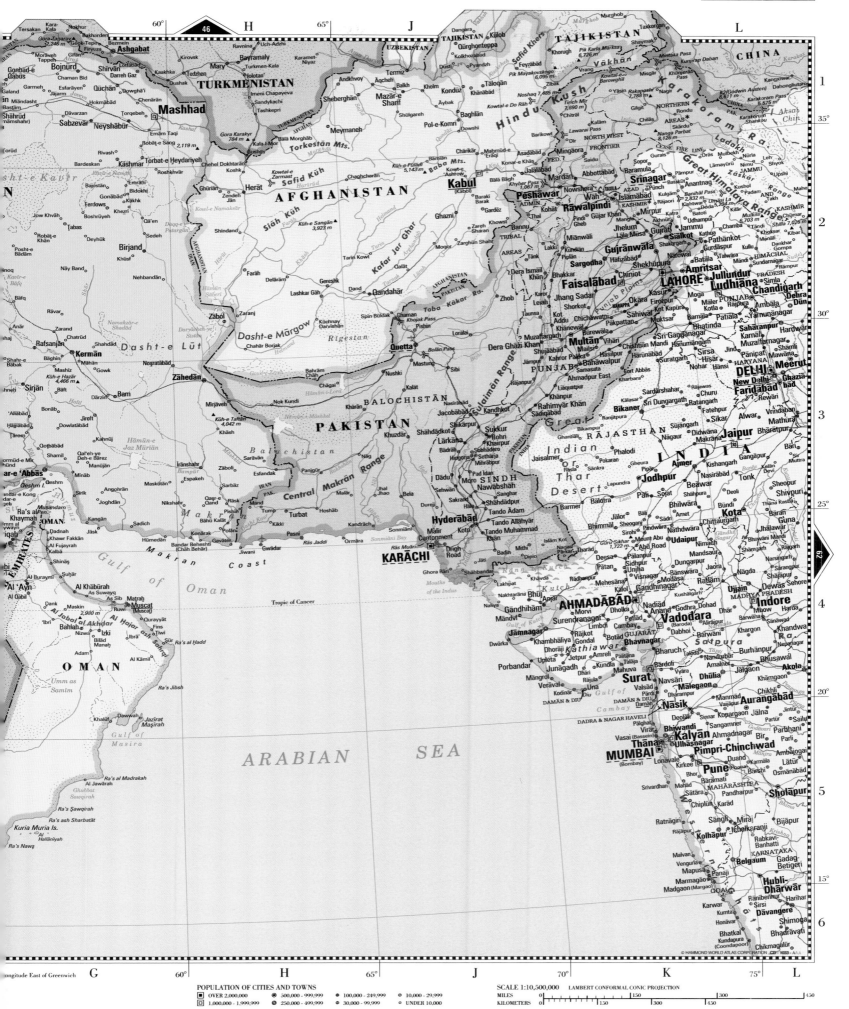

POPULATION OF CITIES AND TOWNS

- ■ OVER 2,000,000
- ■ 1,000,000 - 1,999,999
- ● 500,000 - 999,999
- ● 250,000 - 499,999
- ● 100,000 - 249,999
- ● 30,000 - 99,999
- ● 10,000 - 29,999
- ○ UNDER 10,000

SCALE 1:10,500,000 LAMBERT CONFORMAL CONIC PROJECTION

MILES
KILOMETERS

© HAMMOND WORLD ATLAS CORPORATION

Eastern Asia

38°

SŎRAKSAN NAT'L PARK
Inje
Yangyang
ODAESAN
NAT'L PARK
Hongch'ŏn
KANGOWŎN - DO
Kangnŭng
T'aebaek Mts
▲ Nogwak-san 1,321 m
Paektok-san 1,350 m
Samch'ŏk
Wŏnju
P'yŏngch'ang
Yŏngwŏl

2

Chech'ŏn
CH'UNGCH'ŎNG-
BUKTO
Ulchin
Ch'ungju
Yŏngju
Andong
SOUTH
KYŎNGSANG-
BUKTO
Yŏng-yang
Andong Lake
CHUWANG-SAN NAT'L PARK
Yŏngdŏk

58

Sangju
Ch'ŏngsong
Ŭisŏng
Yŏngdŏk

KOREA

36°

Sŏnsan
Kimch'ŏn
P'algong-san 1,192 m
TAEGU-
JIKHALSI
TAEGU
Kumi
Hwayang
Kyŏngsan
SILLA TOMBS
KYŎNGJU NAT'L PARK
PULGUK-SA

Kaji-san 1,240 m
Kyŏngju
Changgi-ap

SOUTH
KYŎNGSANG-
NAMDO
Miryang
Samnangjin
Yŏngch'ŏn
Ulsan

Ch'angwŏn
Ŭiryŏng
ULSAN
KIMHAE

Masan
Kosŏng
Chinhae
Kimhae
PUSAN-JIKHALSI
UNITED NATIONS MEMORIAL CEM.

3

Ch'ungmu
Shinhyŏn
HALLYŎ HAESANG
NAT'L PARK
Koje Island
PUSAN

Kara-saki
Kamitsushima

SOUTH KOREA
JAPAN
Cheju
Tsu Island

 ULLŬNG I.
(S. KOREA)

Liancourt Rocks
(Sovereignty Disputed)

SEA   OF   JAPAN

OKI
ISLANDS
Dōgo
Saigō
OKI
Dōzen
DAISEN-OKI
NAT'L PARK

Komatsu
Kaga
Mikuni
Sakai
FUKUI
Sabae
Takefu
FU

DAISEN-OKI
NAT'L PARK
Sakaiminato
Jizō-zaki
Hino-misaki
Hirata
Taisha
YONAGO
Yonago
TOTTORI
Tottori
Hyō-no-sen 1,510 m
Toyo'oka
Miya
Obama
Tsuruga
Mihama

SAN'IN KAIGIN
NATIONAL PARK
Kyōga-misaki
Waskasa
Bay

Iwami
Matsue
Izumo
IZUMO
Shinji L.
Wakasa
Maizuru
CHŪBU
Nagahama
Imazu
Maihara

Oda
Gōtsu
SHIMANE
Tsuyama
Fukuchiyama
Ayabe
KYŌTO KINKI
Hikone
Yo

Hamada
Niimi
Dai-sen 1,711 m
Sonobe
Kameoka
Moriyama
NAGAOKAKYŌ

34°

Masuda
Shōbara
Miyoshi
Takahashi
Asahi
KYŌTO
ŌTSU
SHIGA
Biwa
Yo

HIROSHIMA
Fuchū
Ibara
Sōja
KORAKUEN GARDEN
Kurashiki
OKAYAMA
Akō
HIMEJI CASTLE
Himeji
KŌBE
Akashi
Nishiwaki
Sanda
Shimamoto
HYŌGO
Takatsuki
Hirakata

Mi-shima
CHŪGOKU Mts
Kanmuri-yama 1,339 m
Hiroshima
PEACE MEMORIAL PARK
HIROSHIMA
Takehara
Mihara
Onomichi
Fukuyama
Kasaoka
CHŪGOKU
Tonosho
Marugame
Sakaide
TAKAMATSU
Naruto
OSAKA
Kishiwada
Izumi
NARA
Gose
Hashimoto

YAMAGUCHI
Yamaguchi
Ōtake
Kure
SETO-NAIKAI
NAT'L PARK
Kan'onji
Zentsūji
KAGAWA
Kojima
Harima
Sea
Awaji
Sumoto
Izumi-Sano
ŌSAKA
Kashihara
YOSHINO-
KUMANO NAT'L
Hakken-san 1,915 m

Shimonoseki
Hōfu
Tokuyama
Iwakuni
Hōjō
Imabari
Niihama
Saijō
Ikeda
TOKUSHIMA
Wakayama
Arida
Kainan

Onoda
Ube
UBE
Kudamatsu
Yanai
Sea of lyo
Matsuyama
MATSUYAMA
Tokushima
WAKAYAMA
Shingū

4

Kitakyūshū
KITAKYŪSHŪ
Yukuhashi
Nakatsu
Sea of Suo
CHŪGOKU
KYŪSHŪ
NAT'L PARK
EHIME
KŌCHI
TOKUSHIMA
Anan
Gobō
Tanabe
Kumano

Fukuoka
Nogata
Tagawa
Usa
Nagahama
Yawatahama
Ishizuchi-san 1,982 m
Tsurugi-san 1,955 m
NANKI

FUKUOKA
Iizuka
Amagi
ŌITA
Beppu
Uwajima
Yoshida
Ōzu
Ino
KŌCHI
Aki
Nachi-Katsuura
Ō-shima
Shio-no-misaki

Hirado
Karatsu
Tosu
SAGA
Kurume
Ōita
ŌITA
Hiji
Mie
Uchiko
Susaki
Tosa
Muroto

Imari
Saga
Kashima
Ōkawa
Yamaga
Usuki
Tsukumi
Yawatahama
Kubokawa
Tosa Bay
Muroto-zaki

GOTŌ
ISLANDS
Nakadōri
KAMIGOTŌ
Sasebo
Ōmuta
ASO NAT'L PARK
Kuni-san 1,787 m
Saiki
Nakamura
Shikoku

SAIKAI
NAT'L PARK
NAGASAKI
Ōmura
KUMAMOTO
Aso-san 1,592 m
Tsukumi
Sukumo
Tosashimizu
Shimanto

Nagasaki
NAGASAKI PEACE PARK
Isahaya
Kumamoto
KUMAMOTO
Mie
Okino-
shima
Ashizuri-misaki

Fukue
FUKUE
Shimabara
Hondo
Taketa
Nobeoka

Fukue
Kyūshū Highlands

32°

Amakusa
Sea
UNZEN-AMAKUSA
NATIONAL PARK
Hondo
Yatsushiro
Kunimi-dake 1,739 m
Mimi
PACIFIC

Ushibuka
Minamata
Hitoyoshi
MIYAZAKI
Hyūga
OCEAN

Kami-
Koshiki I.
Akune
Izumi
Ōkuchi
Saito
Takanabe

Shimo-
Koshiki
I.
Sendai
Kushikino
Kobayashi
Kirishima-yama
1,700 m
Sadowara
MIYAZAKI

5

Makurazaki
KAGOSHIMA
Kagoshima
Kokubu
Miyazaki

EAST

Kagoshima
KAGOSHIMA
Tarumizu
Kushima
Nichinan

CHINA

Nomo-misaki
Kaseda
Kanoya
Kōyama
Kushima
Kyūshū

SEA

Kuro-
shima
Iō-
shima
Makizaki
Ōsumi Pen.
YAKU NAT'L PARK
Satā-misaki

Ōsumi Strait

Kuchinoerabu
Naka
Naha
Mage-
shima
Nishino'omote
Tanega

ŌSUMI ISLANDS
Kamiyaku
Yaku

KIRISHIMA-YAKU NAT'L PARK

Central and Southern Japan

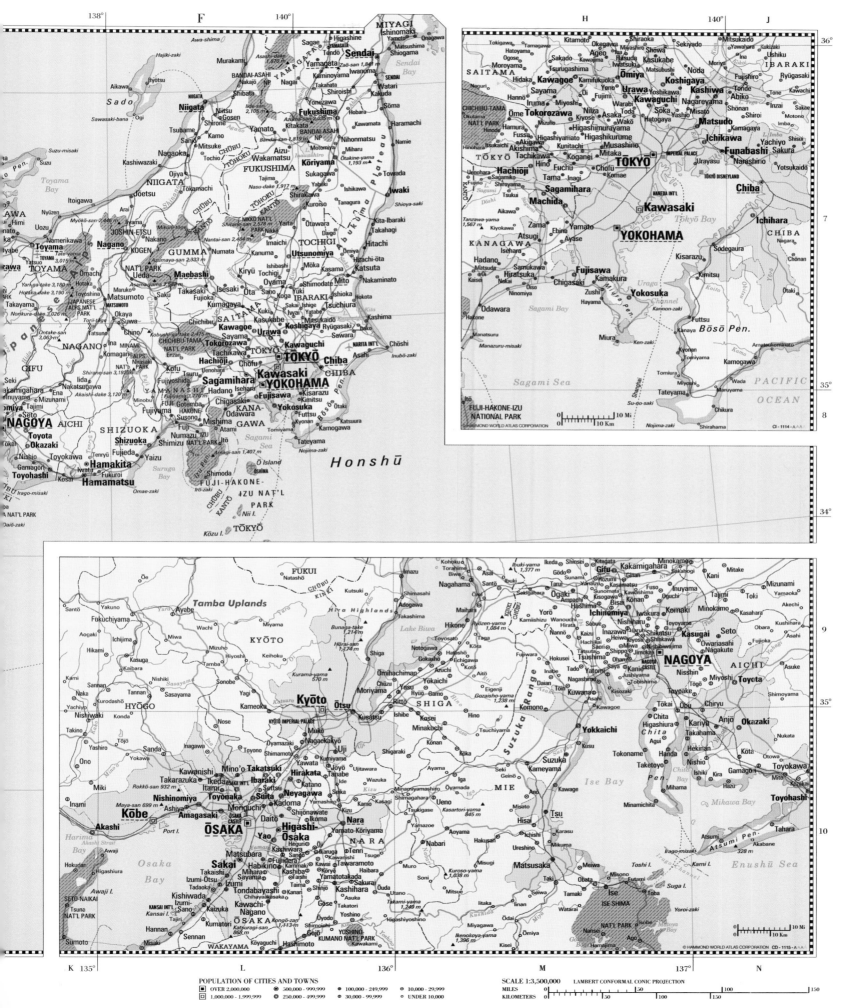

SCALE 1:3,500,000   LAMBERT CONFORMAL CONIC PROJECTION

Korea

SCALE 1:3,500,000   LAMBERT CONFORMAL CONIC PROJECTION

Longitude East of Greenwich

POPULATION OF CITIES AND TOWNS

■ OVER 2,000,000	● 500,000 - 999,999	● 100,000 - 249,999	○ 10,000 - 29,999
▣ 1,000,000 - 1,999,999	● 250,000 - 499,999	● 30,000 - 99,999	○ UNDER 10,000

© HAMMOND W.A.C. CD   © HAMMOND WORLD ATLAS CORPORATION

Northeastern China

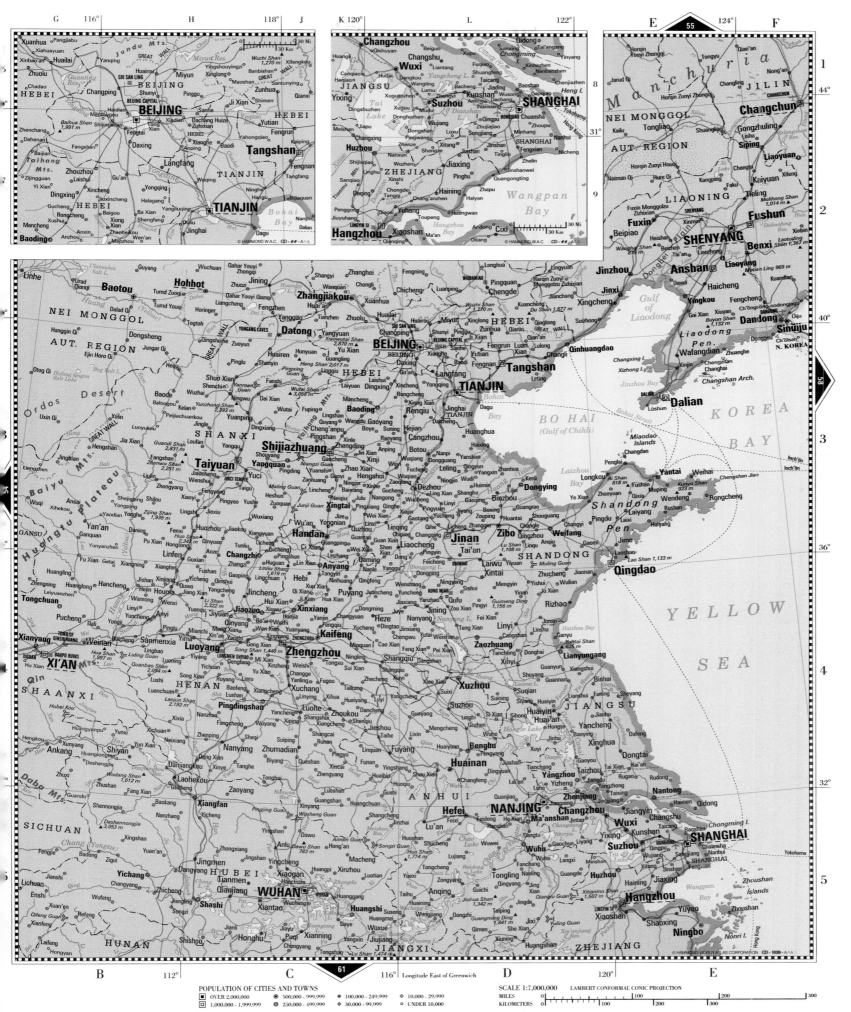

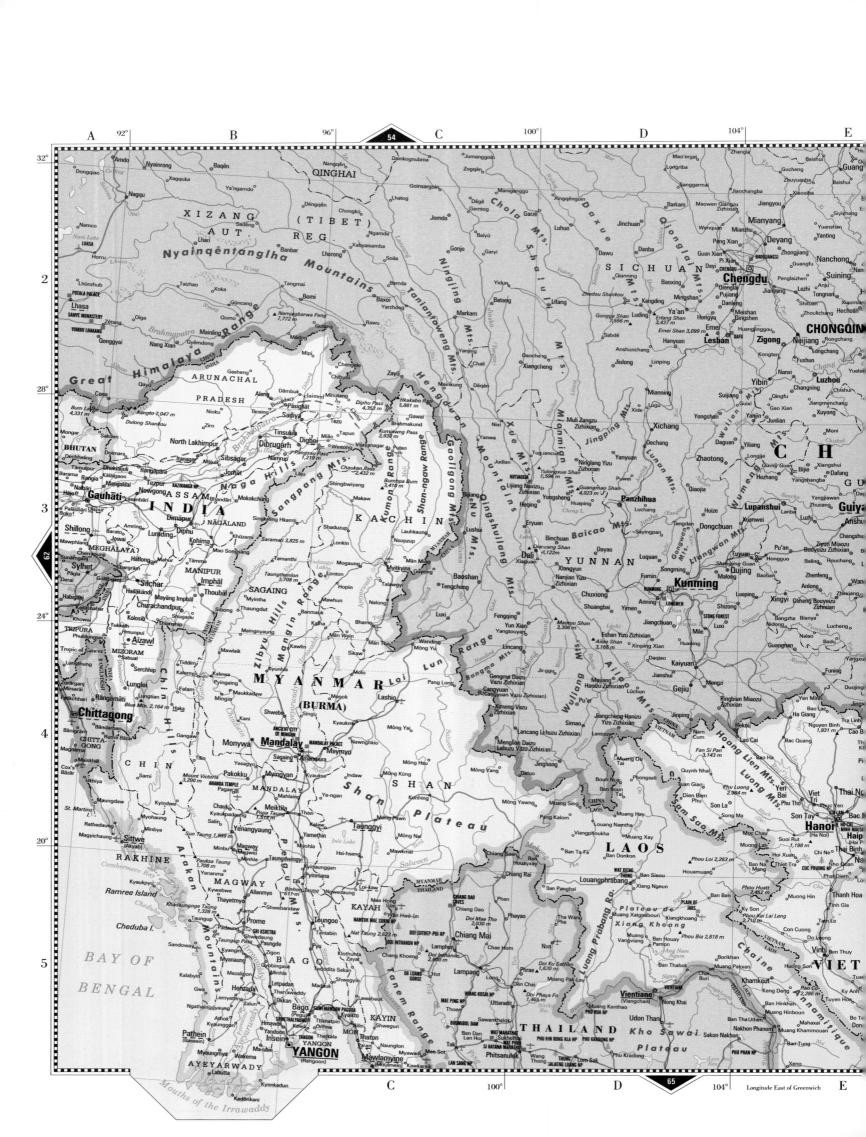

Southeastern China, Northern Indochina

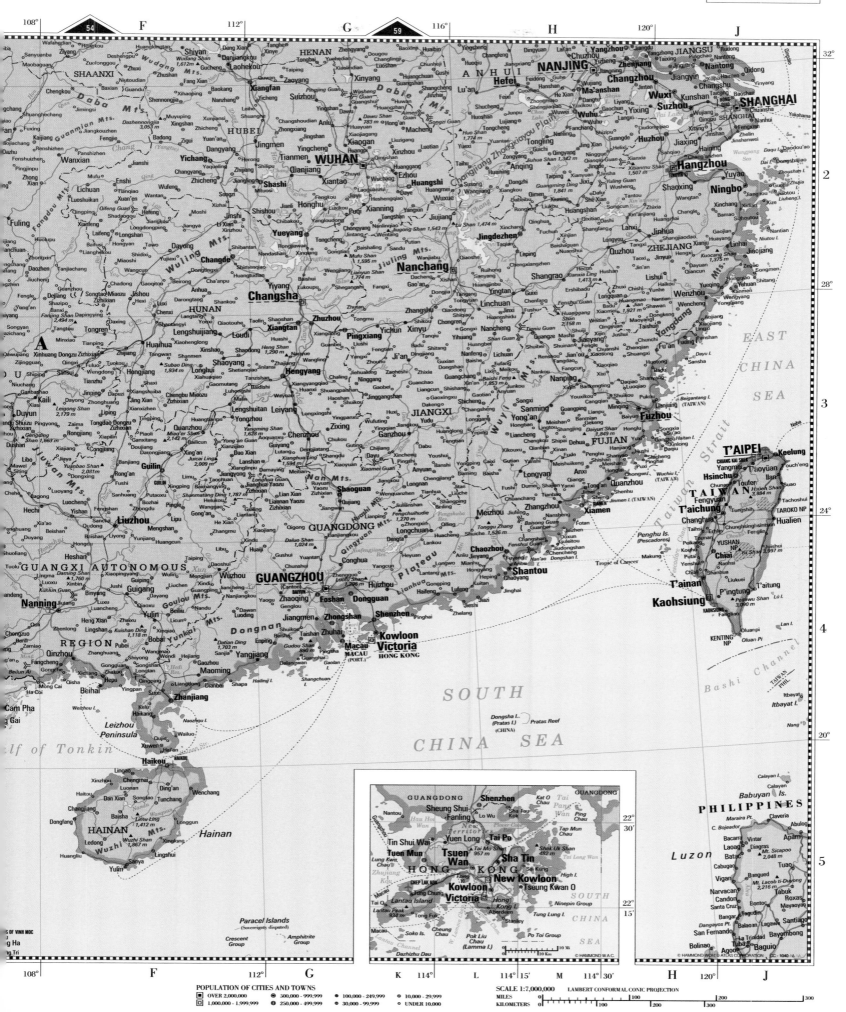

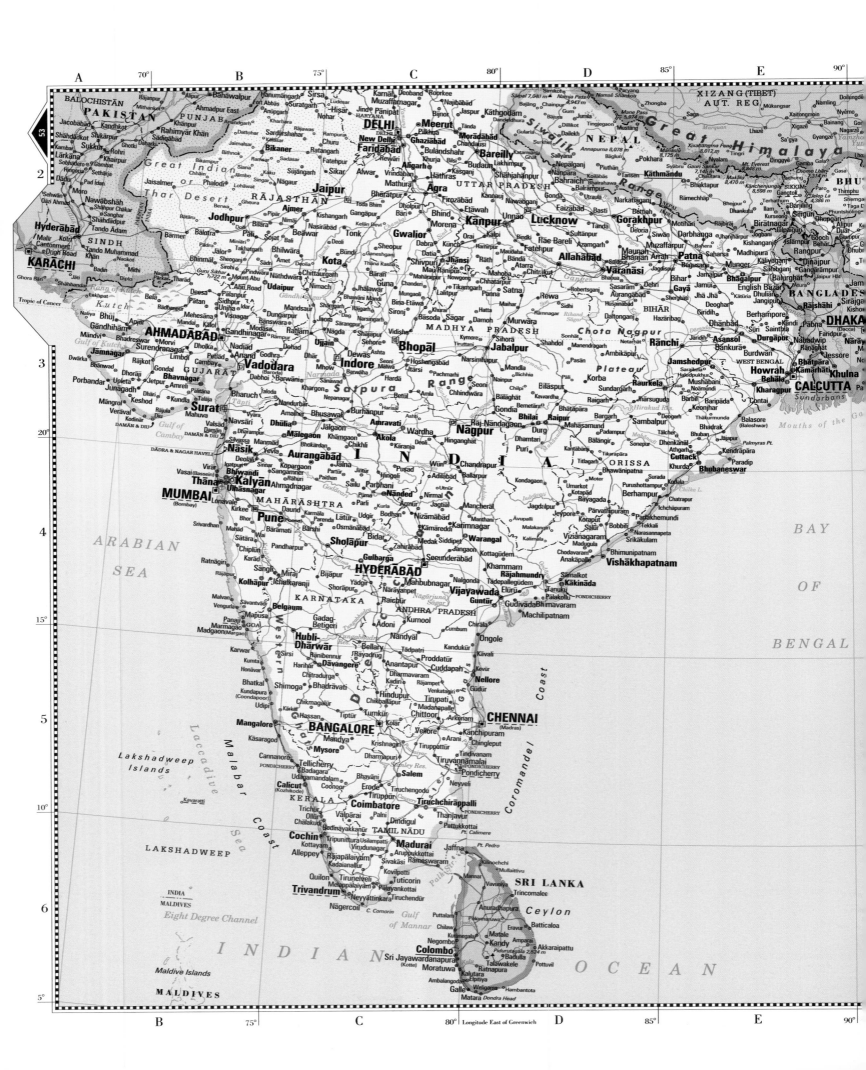

Southern Asia

POPULATION OF CITIES AND TOWNS

■ OVER 2,000,000	● 500,000 - 999,999
▣ 1,000,000 - 1,999,999	⊗ 250,000 - 499,999

⊛ 100,000 - 249,999	○ 10,000 - 29,999
⊗ 30,000 - 99,999	· UNDER 10,000

SCALE 1:10,500,000   LAMBERT CONFORMAL CONIC PROJECTION

MILES 0   150   300   450

KILOMETERS 0   150   300

Punjab Plain, Southern India

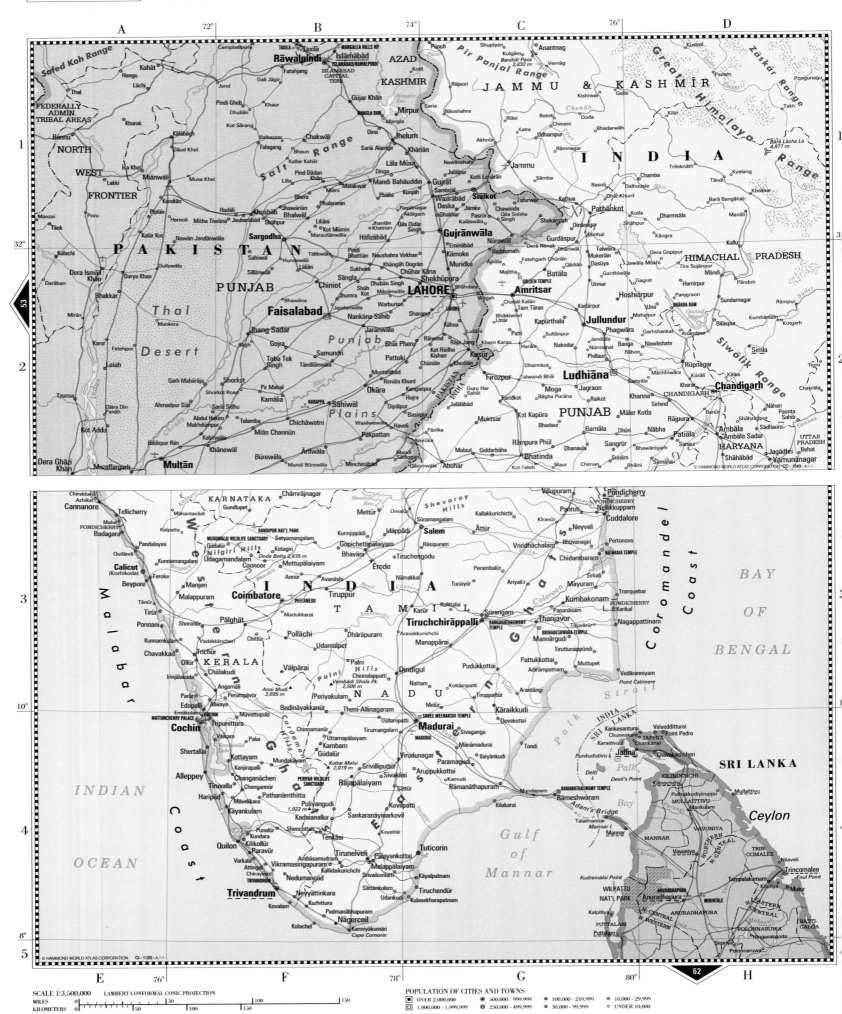

Indochina

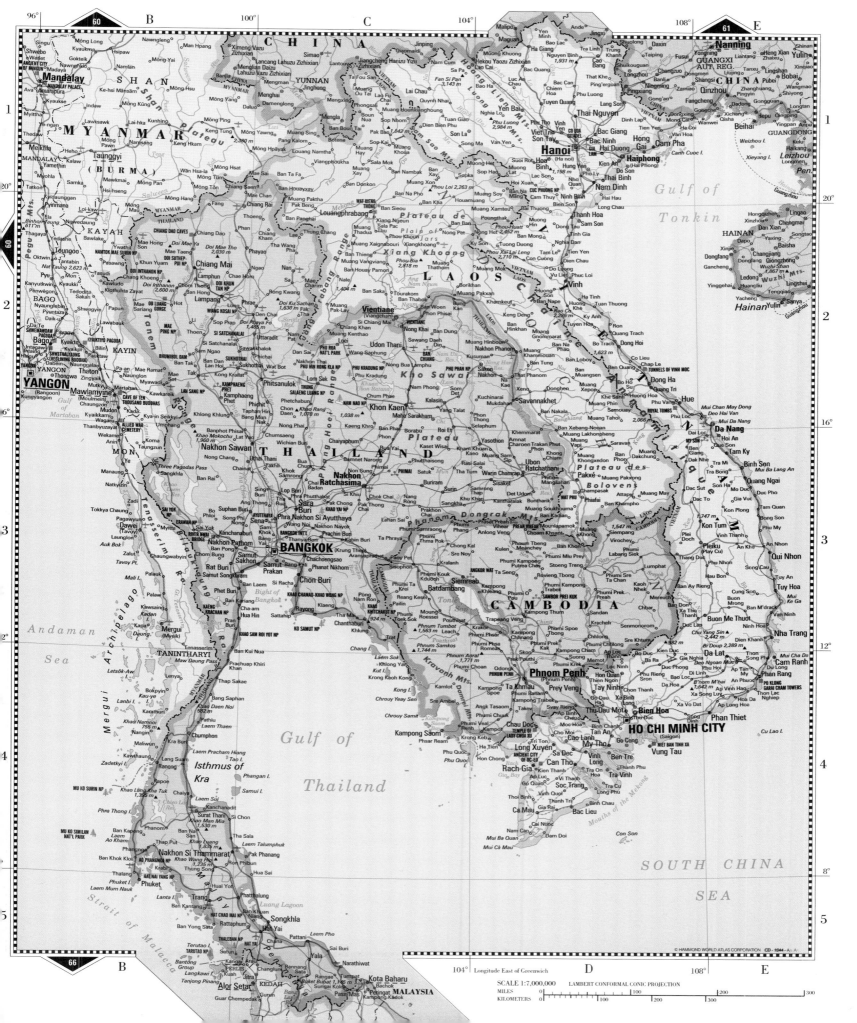

95°   A   100°   B   105°   C   110°   D   115°

Andaman

Mergui
Archipelago

Mergui
(Myeik)

Tenasserim

**MYANMAR
(BURMA)**

Letsôk-Aw I.

Lenya

Bokpyin

Khao Daen Noi
592 m

Khao Namnol
755 m

Zadetkyi I.

Ranong

Kapoe

Kra Buri

Isthmus of
Kra

Chumphon

Pathiu

Prachuap Khiri
Khan

Hua Hin

Cha-am
Sattahip

Bang Saphan

Rayong

THAILAND

Chanthaburi

Tha Mai

Krel

Reang Kesei

Krakor

Batdambang

Chang L.

Pouthisat

Phnum Tumbôt
1,563 m

Leach

Pursat

Phnum Sâmkos
1,744 m

Kampong
Thum

Kampong
Chhnang

Kampong
Cham

Sênmônôrôm

Ban Don

Krông Kaôh
Kong

Chrouy Samit

Kampong Saom

Kampot

Phnom Penh
(Phnum Pénh)

Phnum Aôral
1,771 m

Takêv

Prey Veng

Sway Riêng

Chau Doc

Kampong Saom

Phu Quoc I.

Long Xuyen

Rach Gia

Kien Thanh

Thoi Binh

Ca Mau

Bac Lieu

Soc Trang

Tra Vinh

Can Tho

Sa Dec

Vinh Long

My Tho

Go Cong

Tra Cu

Mûi Cà Mau

Con Son

Mouths of the Mekong

SOUTH CHIN

SEA

Spratly I

(Sovereignty)

Phu Quoc I.

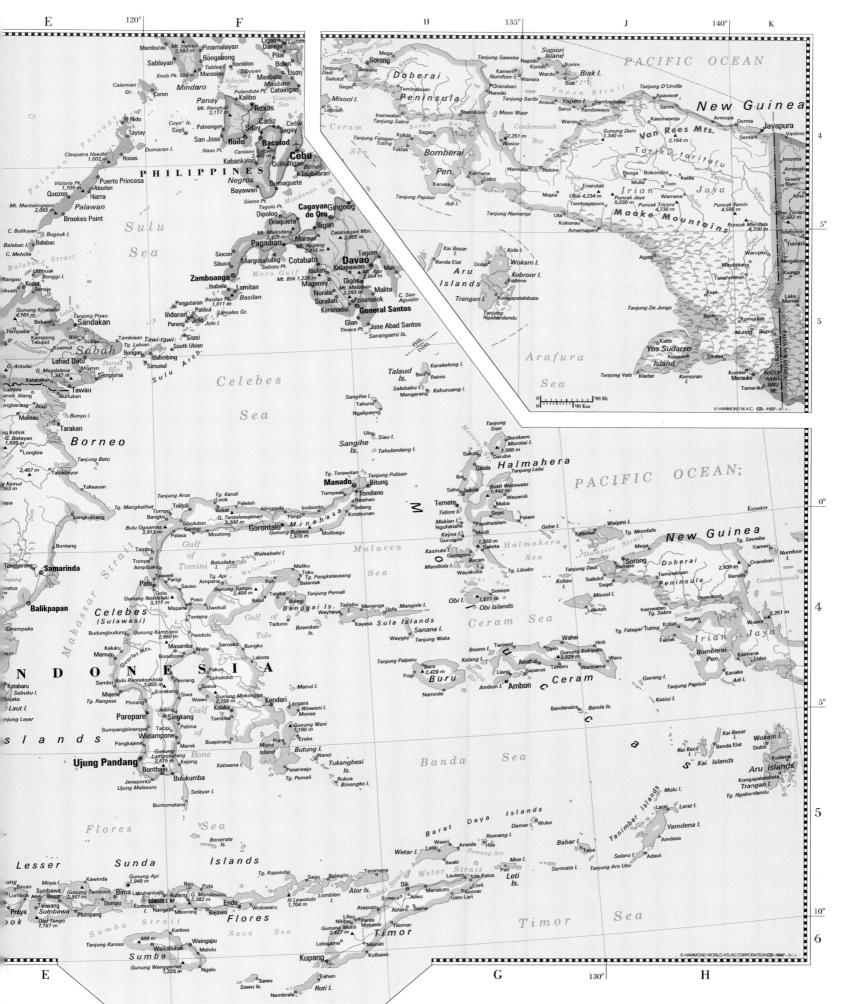

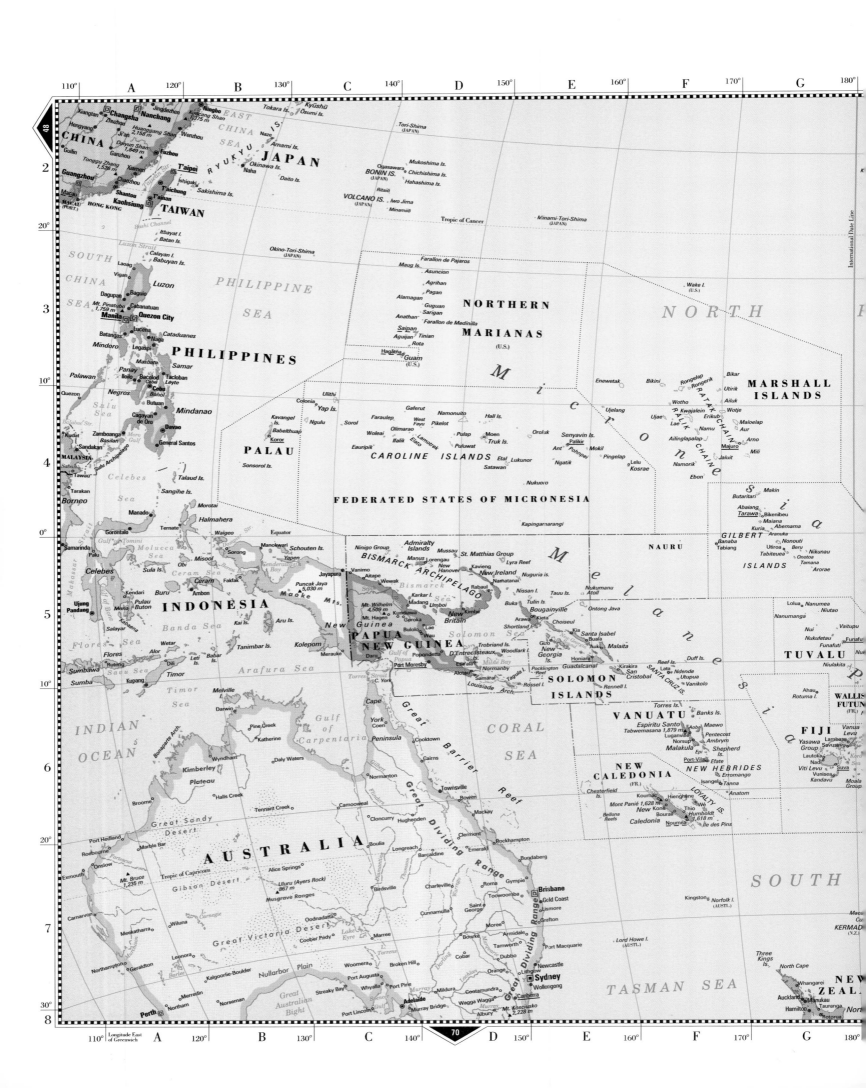

Central Pacific Ocean

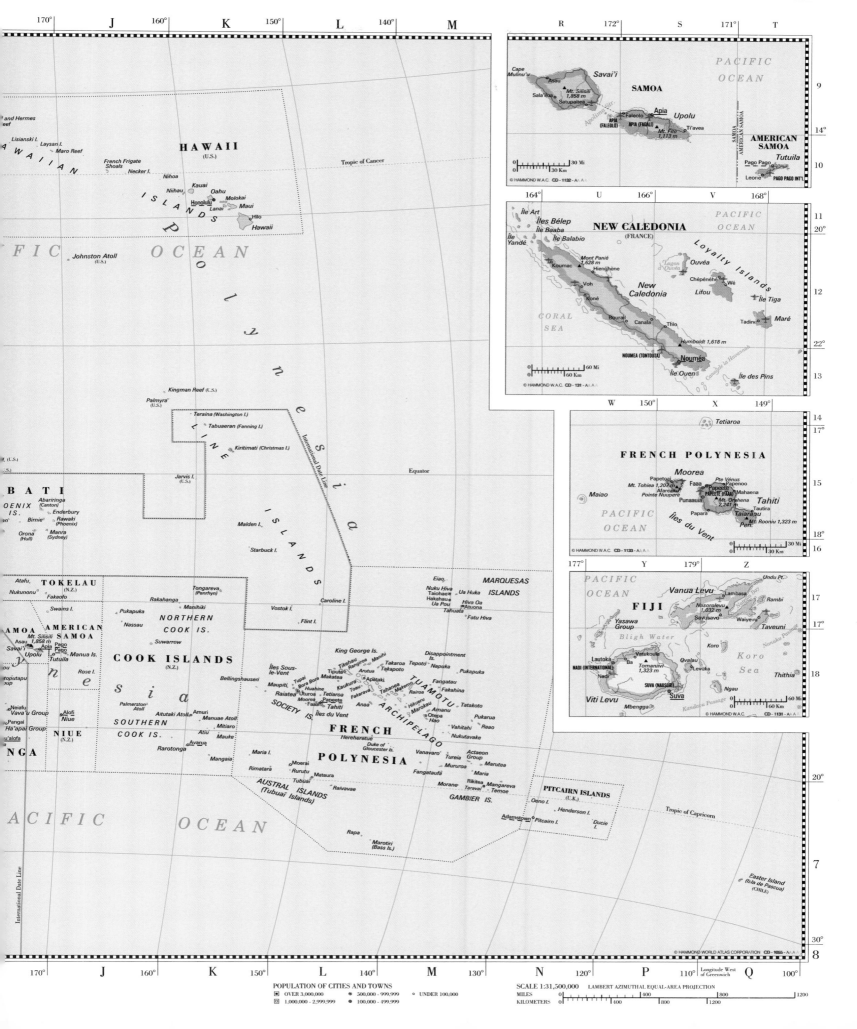

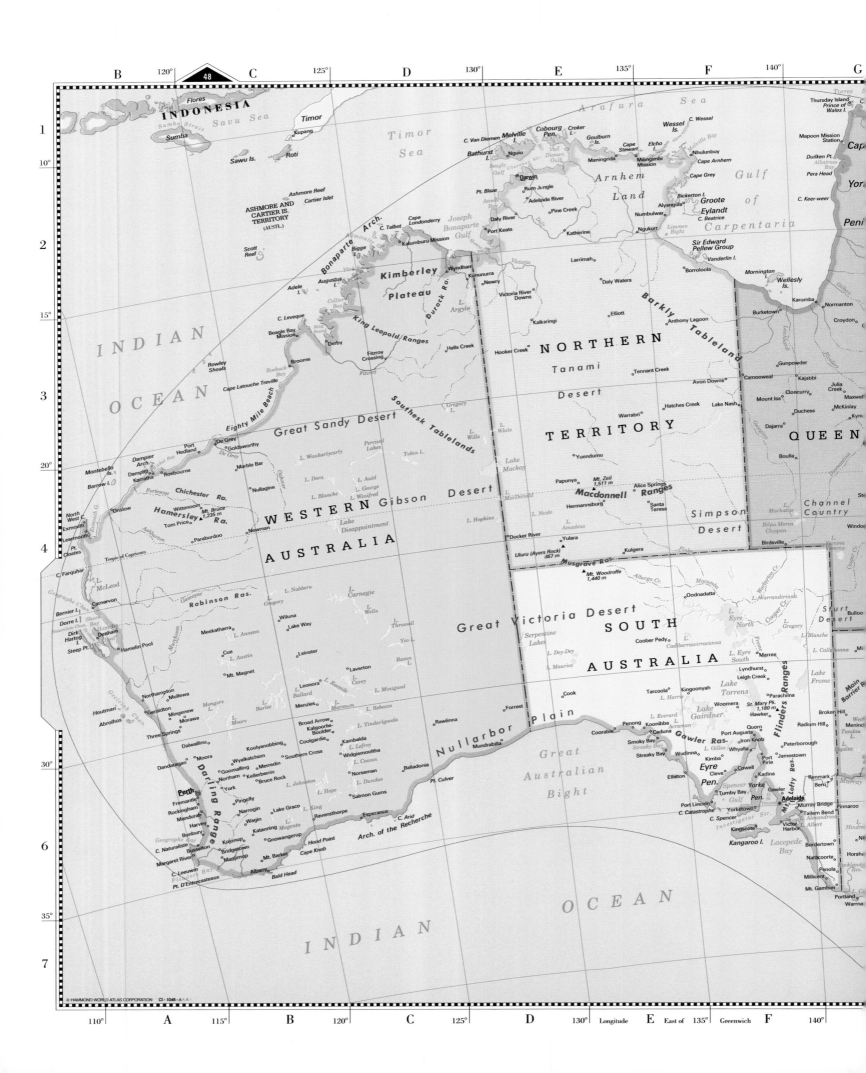

Northeastern Australia

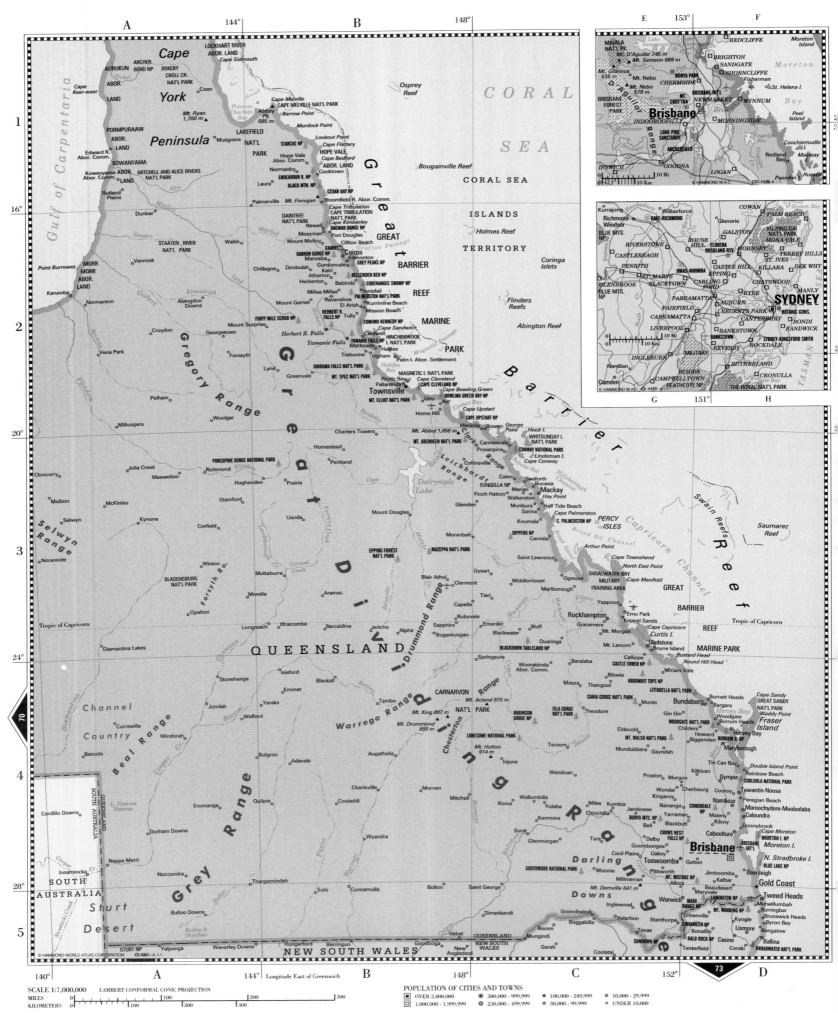

Southeastern Australia

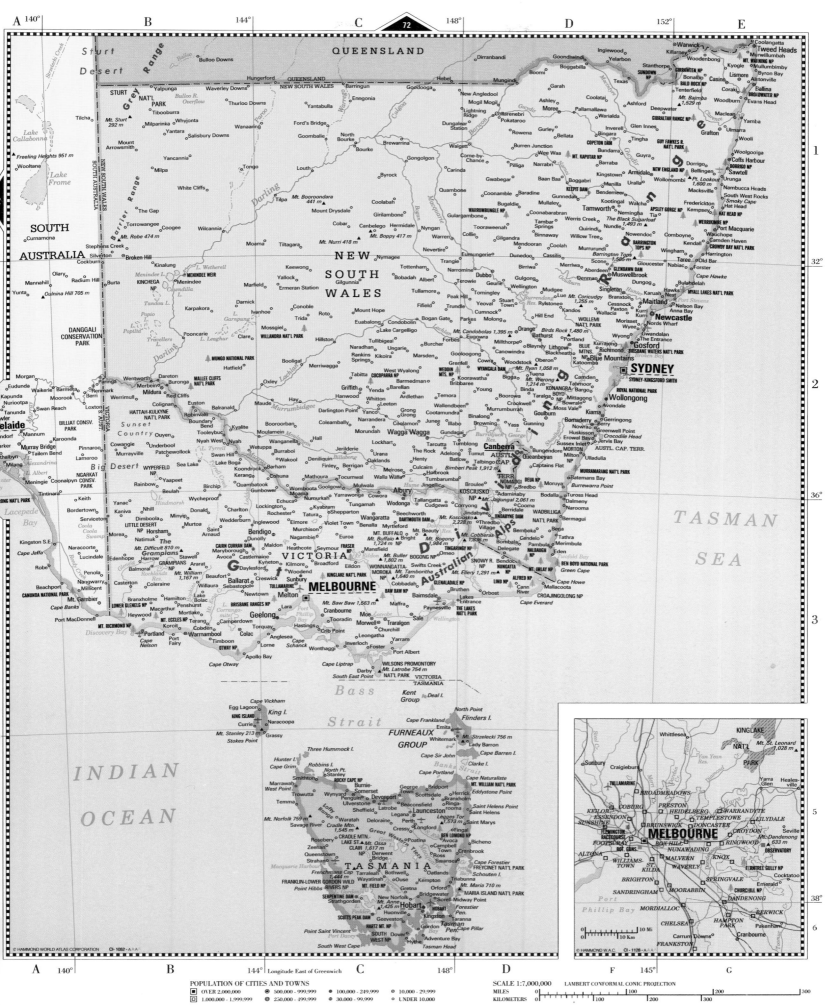

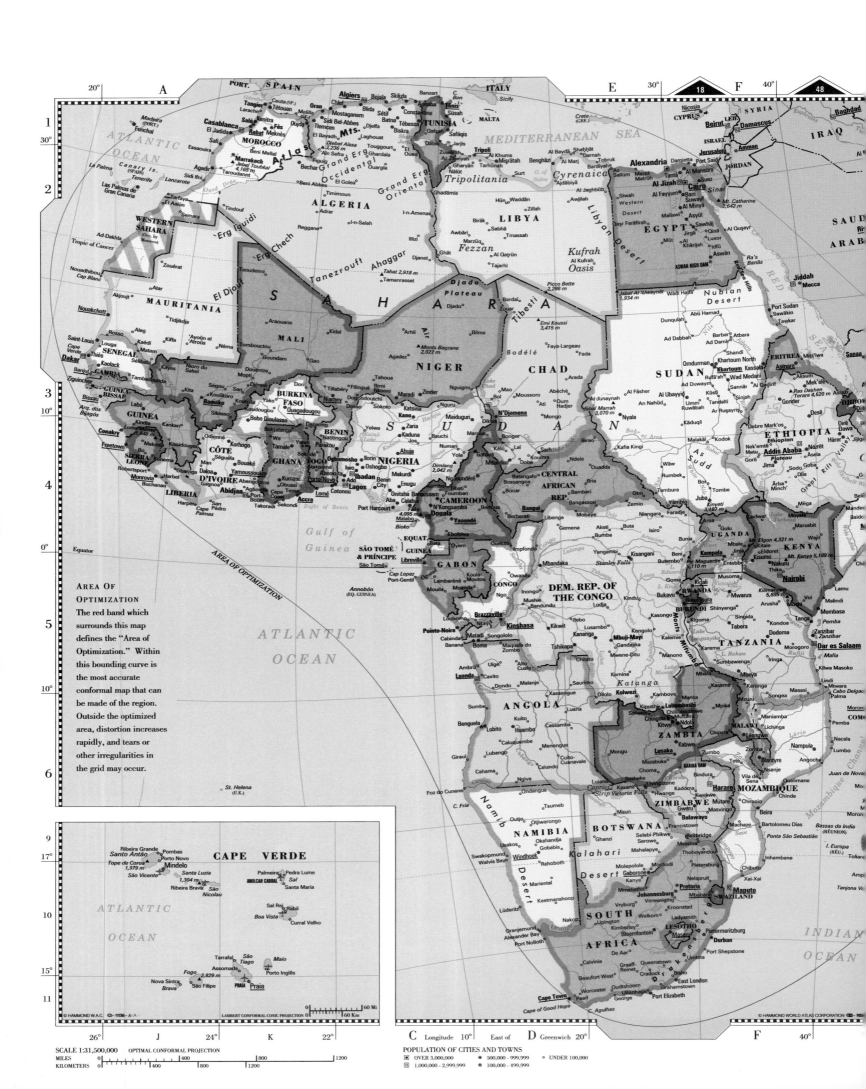

AREA OF
OPTIMIZATION
The red band which
surrounds this map
defines the "Area of
Optimization." Within
this bounding curve is
the most accurate
conformal map that can
be made of the region.
Outside the optimized
area, distortion increases
rapidly, and tears or
other irregularities in
the grid may occur.

CAPE VERDE

SCALE 1:31,500,000   OPTIMAL CONFORMAL PROJECTION

MILES
KILOMETERS

© HAMMOND W.A.C.

LAMBERT CONFORMAL CONIC PROJECTION

POPULATION OF CITIES AND TOWNS
◻ OVER 3,000,000   ⊛ 500,000 - 999,999   ○ UNDER 100,000
◻ 1,000,000 - 2,999,999 • 100,000 - 499,999

Africa

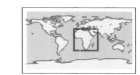

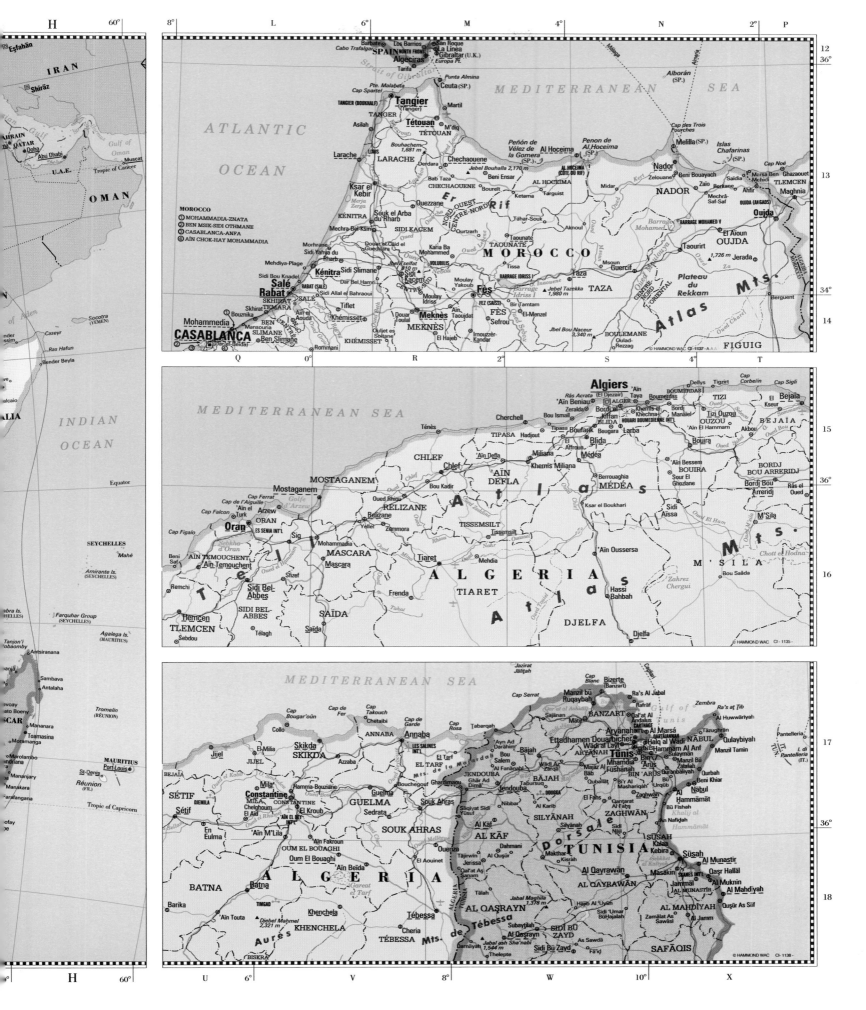

Northern Africa

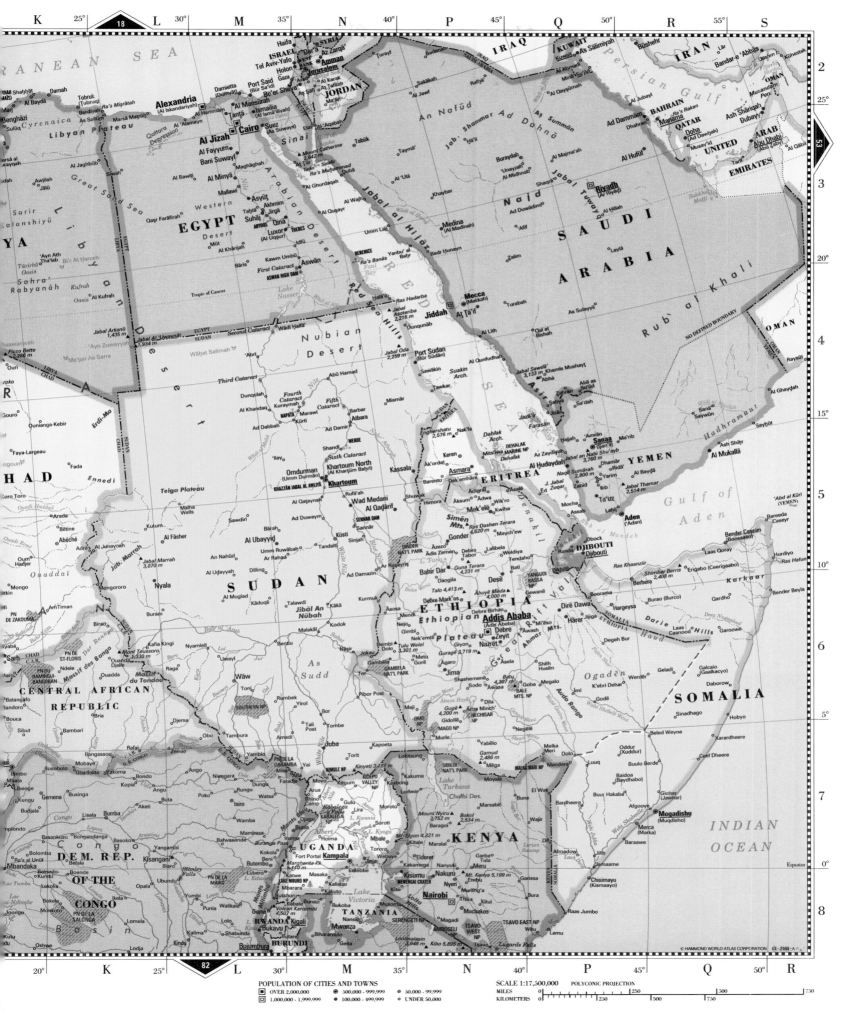

POPULATION OF CITIES AND TOWNS

■ OVER 2,000,000	● 500,000 - 999,999	● 50,000 - 99,999
▣ 1,000,000 - 1,999,999	● 100,000 - 499,999	○ UNDER 50,000

SCALE 1:17,500,000   POLYCONIC PROJECTION

MILES 0 — 250 — 500 — 750
KILOMETERS 0 — 250 — 500 — 750

© HAMMOND WORLD ATLAS CORPORATION   GL-2100-A

ATLANTIC

OCEAN

SCALE 1:7,000,000   POLYCONIC PROJECTION
MILES   0   100   200   300
KILOMETERS 0   100   200   300

© HAMMOND WORLD ATLAS CORPORATION Q · 1058 - A ·

Southern West Africa

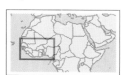

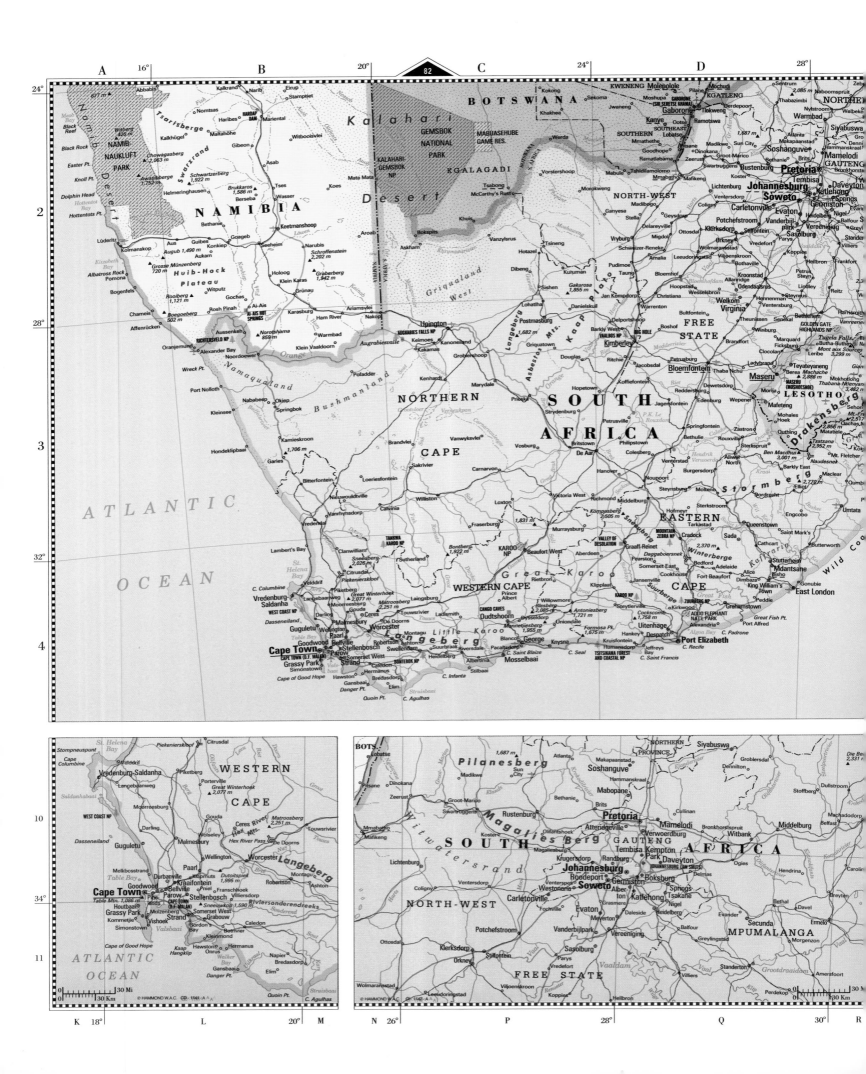

A   16°   B   20°   82   C   24°   D   28°

BOTSWANA

Meob Bay
Black Reef
677 m
Abbabis
Kalkrand
Narib
Eirup
Stampriet
Kokong
Sekoma
Pilane
Mochudi
2,085 m
Naboomspruit
NORTHE

KWENENG Molepolole

Black Rock
Witberg 426 m
Wilberg
NAMIB-NAUKLUFT PARK
Chowagasberg 2,063 m
Helmeringhausen
Hottentot Bay
Hottentots Pt.

NAMIBIA

Kalahari

Desert

GEMSBOK NATIONAL PARK

MABUASEHUBE GAME RES.

KGALAGADI

KALAHARI-GEMSBOK NP

Luderitz
Kolmanskop

ATLANTIC

OCEAN

NORTHERN

CAPE

SOUTH

AFRICA

WESTERN CAPE

FREE STATE

LESOTHO

EASTERN

CAPE

Cape Town
Port Elizabeth

Cape of Good Hope
C. Agulhas

WESTERN CAPE

St. Helena Bay
Cape Columbine
Vredenburg-Saldanha
Langebaanweg
WEST COAST NP
Dassenelland
Guguletu
Cape Town
Table Mtn. 1,086 m
Grassy Park
Houtbaai
Simonstown
Cape of Good Hope

ATLANTIC OCEAN

0   30 Mi
0   30 Km
© HAMMOND W.A.C. CD- 1141 -A

K   18°   L   20°   M

BOTS
Lobatse

NORTHERN PROVINCE

1,687 m
Atlanta
Siyabuswa
Groblersdal
Die Be
2,331 m

Pilanesberg
Soshanguve
Makapaanstad
Dennilton
Dullstroom

Sun City
Hammanskraal
Stoffberg
Belfast

Pretoria
Mamelodi
Bronkhorstspruit
Middelburg
Witbank

GAUTENG
SOUTH
AFRICA

Johannesburg
Soweto

NORTH-WEST

FREE STATE

MPUMALANGA

0   30 Mi
0   30 Km
© HAMMOND W.A.C. CD- 1142 -A

N   26°   P   28°   Q   30°

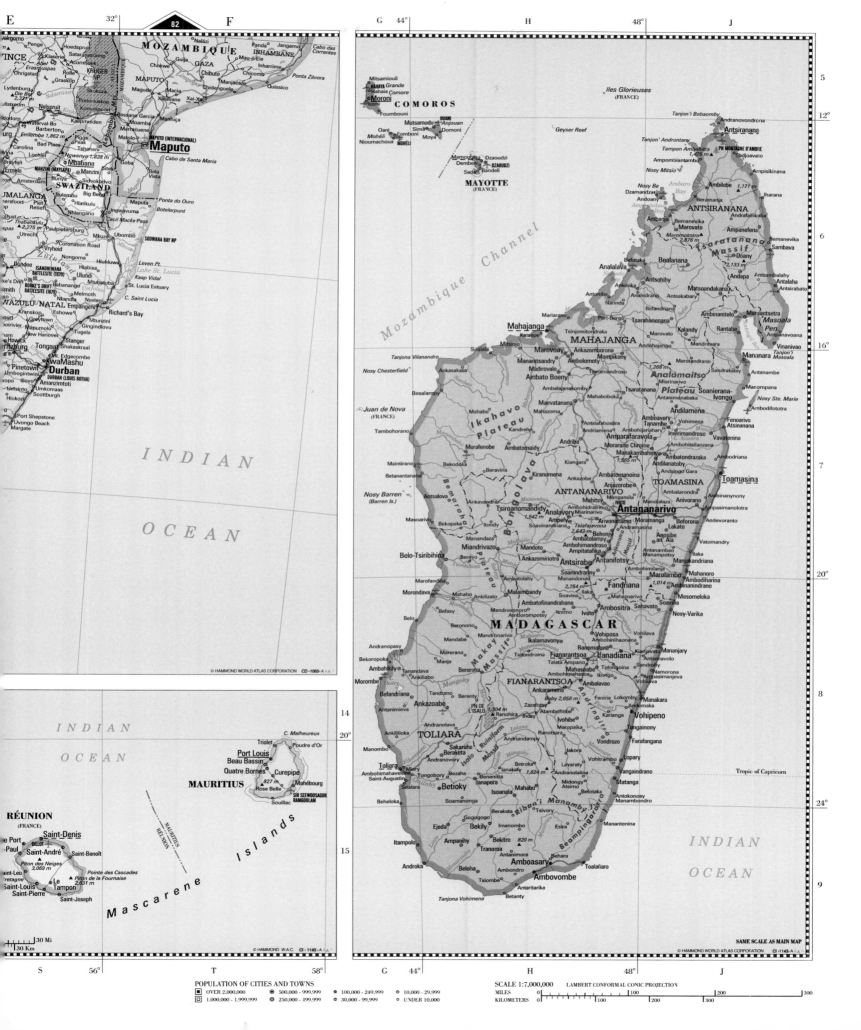

POPULATION OF CITIES AND TOWNS

■ OVER 2,000,000   ◉ 500,000 - 999,999   ● 100,000 - 249,999   ⊙ 10,000 - 29,999
▣ 1,000,000 - 1,999,999   ◍ 250,000 - 499,999   ○ 30,000 - 99,999   ○ UNDER 10,000

SCALE 1:7,000,000   LAMBERT CONFORMAL CONIC PROJECTION

MILES   0   100   200   300
KILOMETERS   0   100   200   300

Southern Africa

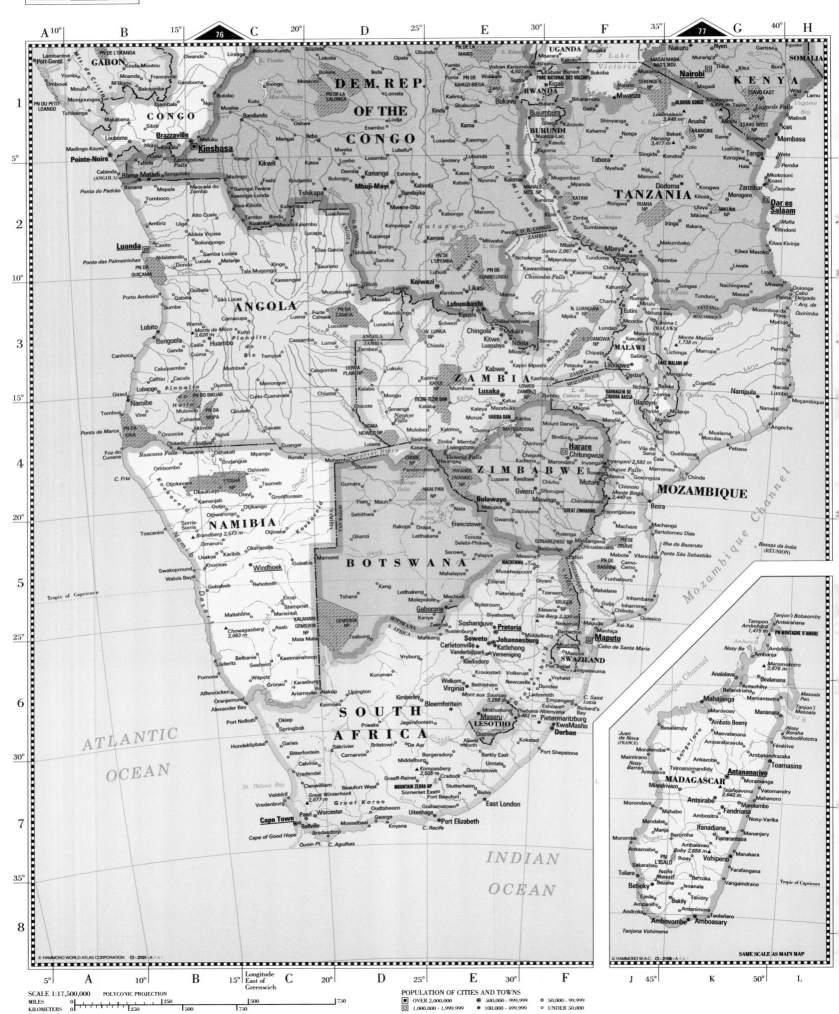

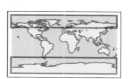

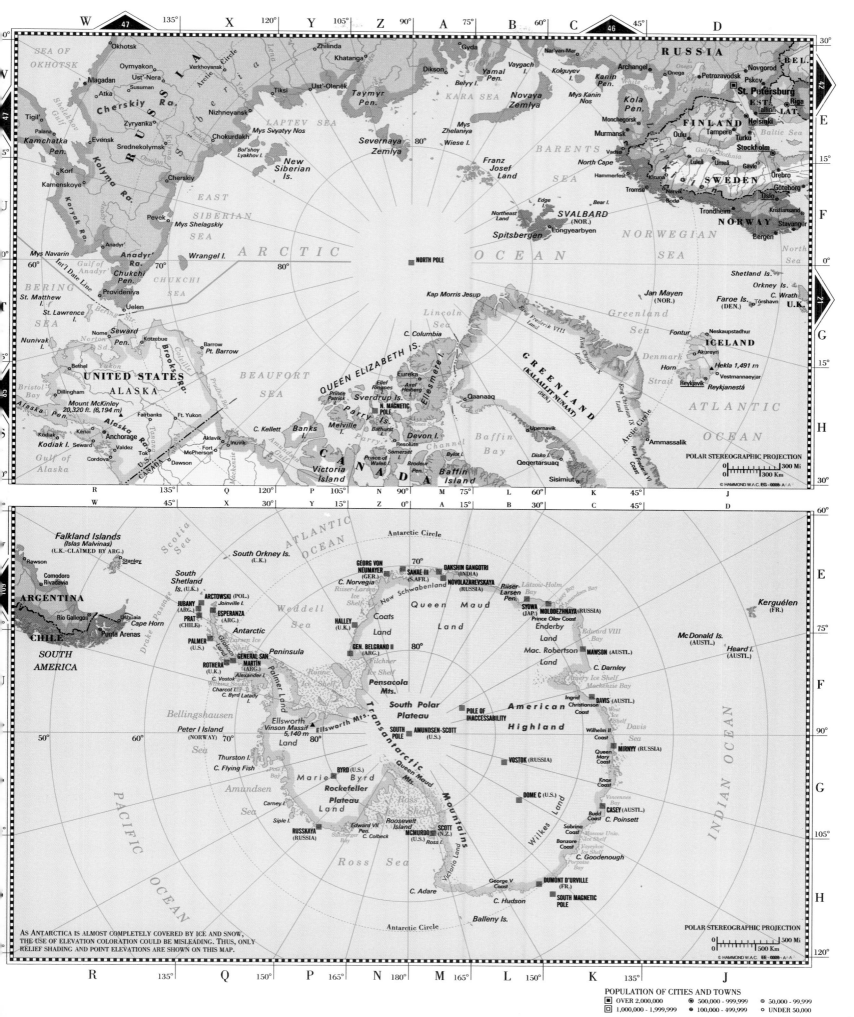

POLAR STEREOGRAPHIC PROJECTION

© HAMMOND W.A.C. EG–0009–A·A·A

AS ANTARCTICA IS ALMOST COMPLETELY COVERED BY ICE AND SNOW,
THE USE OF ELEVATION COLORATION COULD BE MISLEADING. THUS, ONLY
RELIEF SHADING AND POINT ELEVATIONS ARE SHOWN ON THIS MAP.

POLAR STEREOGRAPHIC PROJECTION

© HAMMOND W.A.C. EE–0009–A·A·A

POPULATION OF CITIES AND TOWNS

| ■ OVER 2,000,000 | ● 500,000 - 999,999 | ◦ 50,000 - 99,999 |
| □ 1,000,000 - 1,999,999 | ● 100,000 - 499,999 | ◦ UNDER 50,000 |

North America

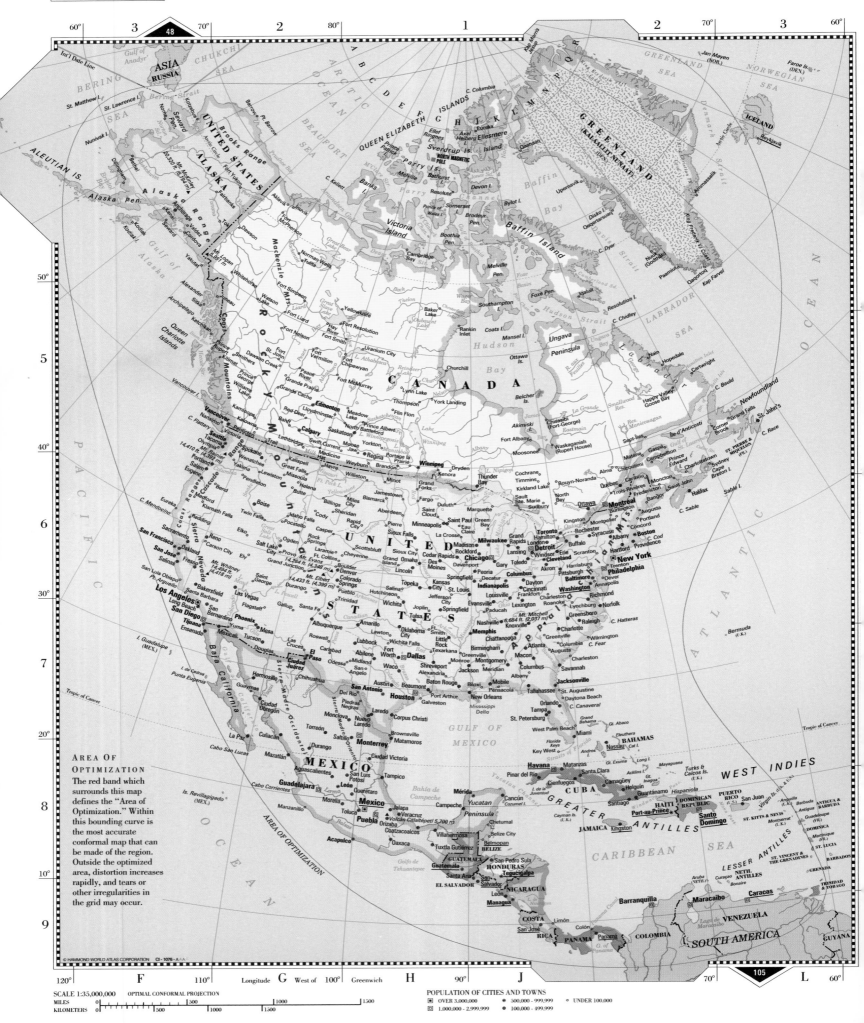

AREA OF OPTIMIZATION

The red band which surrounds this map defines the "Area of Optimization." Within this bounding curve is the most accurate conformal map that can be made of the region. Outside the optimized area, distortion increases rapidly, and tears or other irregularities in the grid may occur.

SCALE 1:35,000,000   OPTIMAL CONFORMAL PROJECTION

MILES 0   500   1000   1500
KILOMETERS 0   500   1000   1500

POPULATION OF CITIES AND TOWNS

⊡ OVER 3,000,000	• 500,000 - 999,999	○ UNDER 100,000
⊠ 1,000,000 - 2,999,999	• 100,000 - 499,999	

Alaska

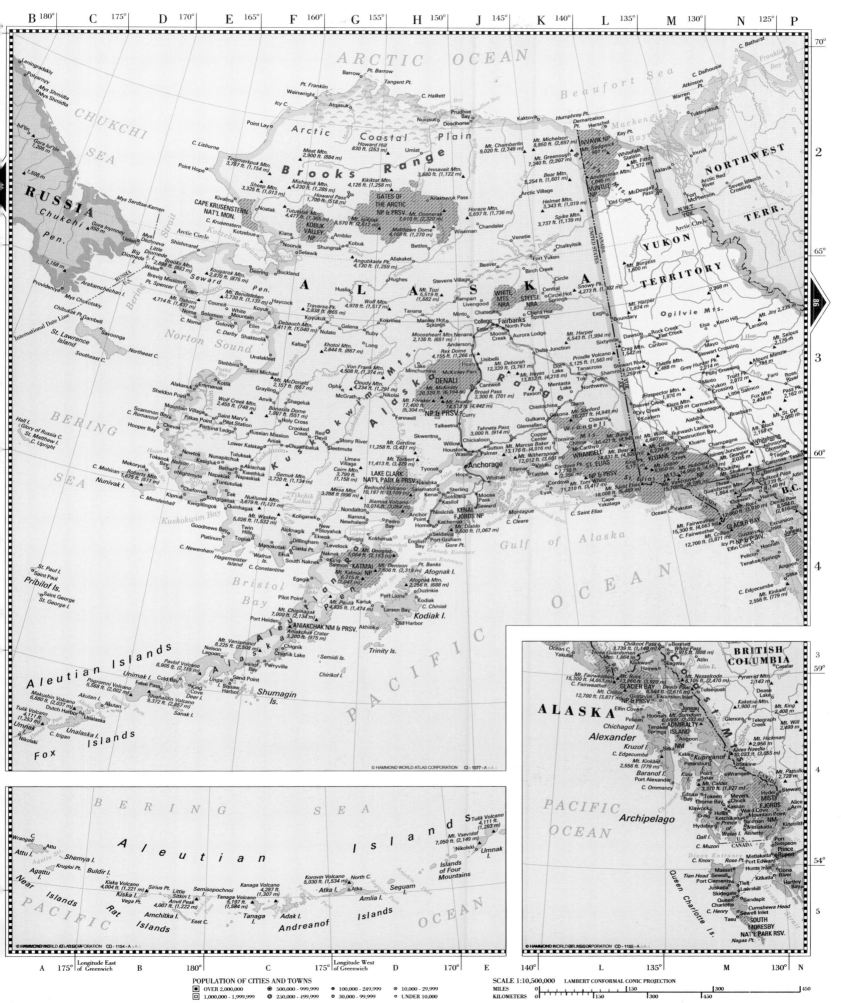

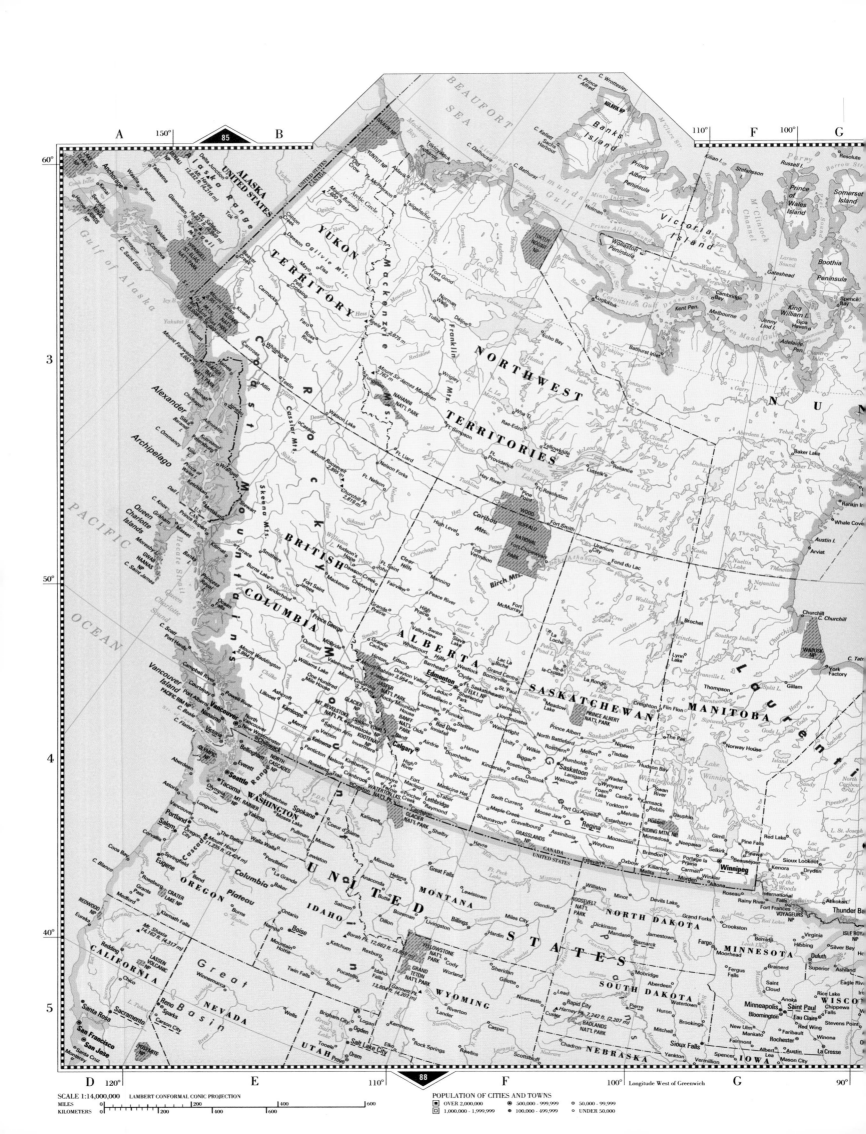

Canada

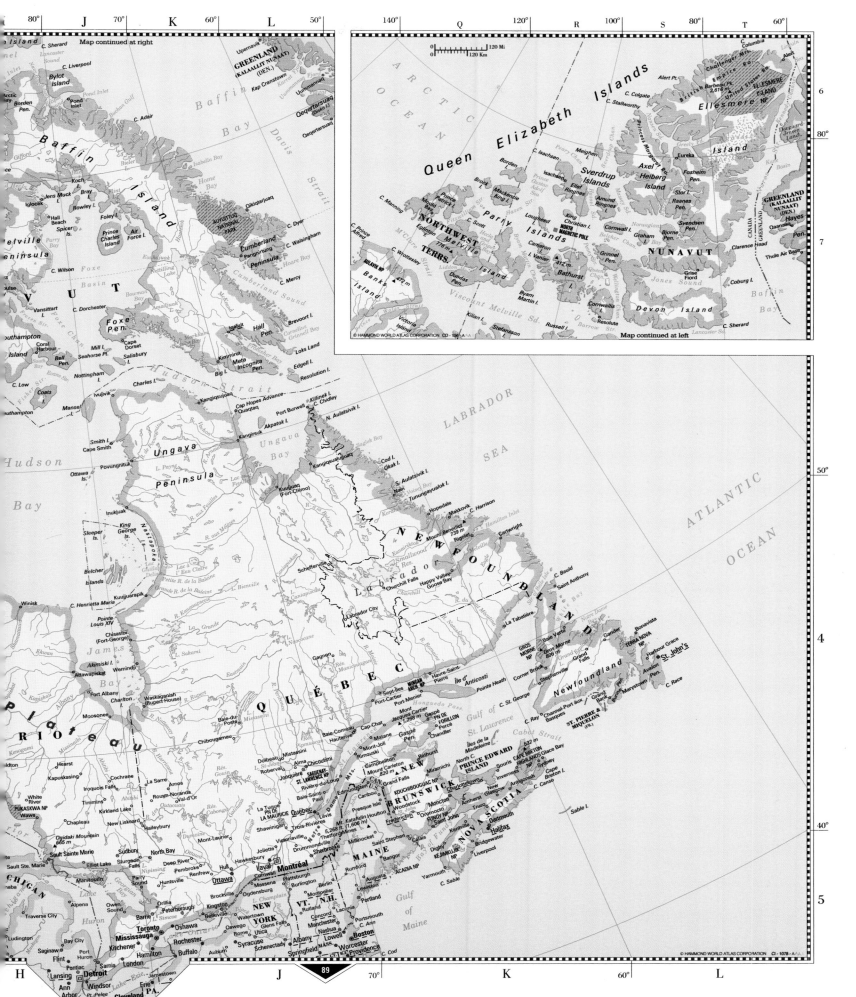

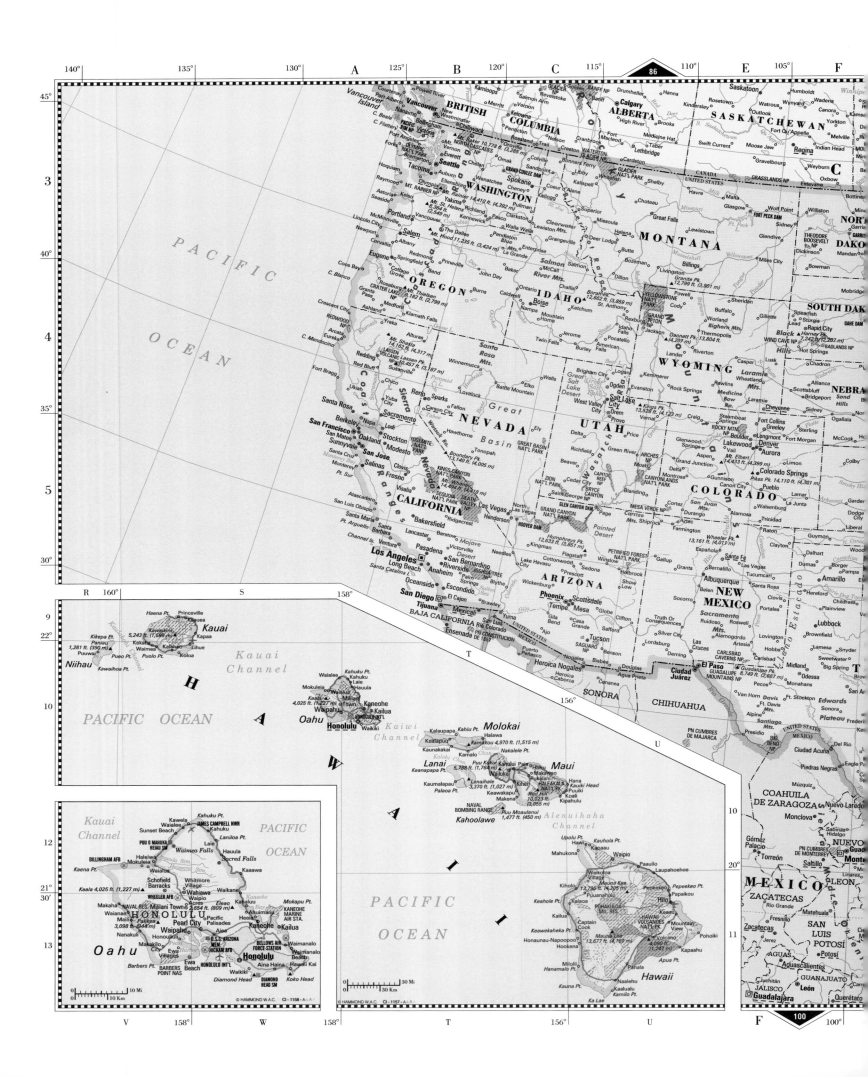

United States

Southwestern Canada, Northwestern United States

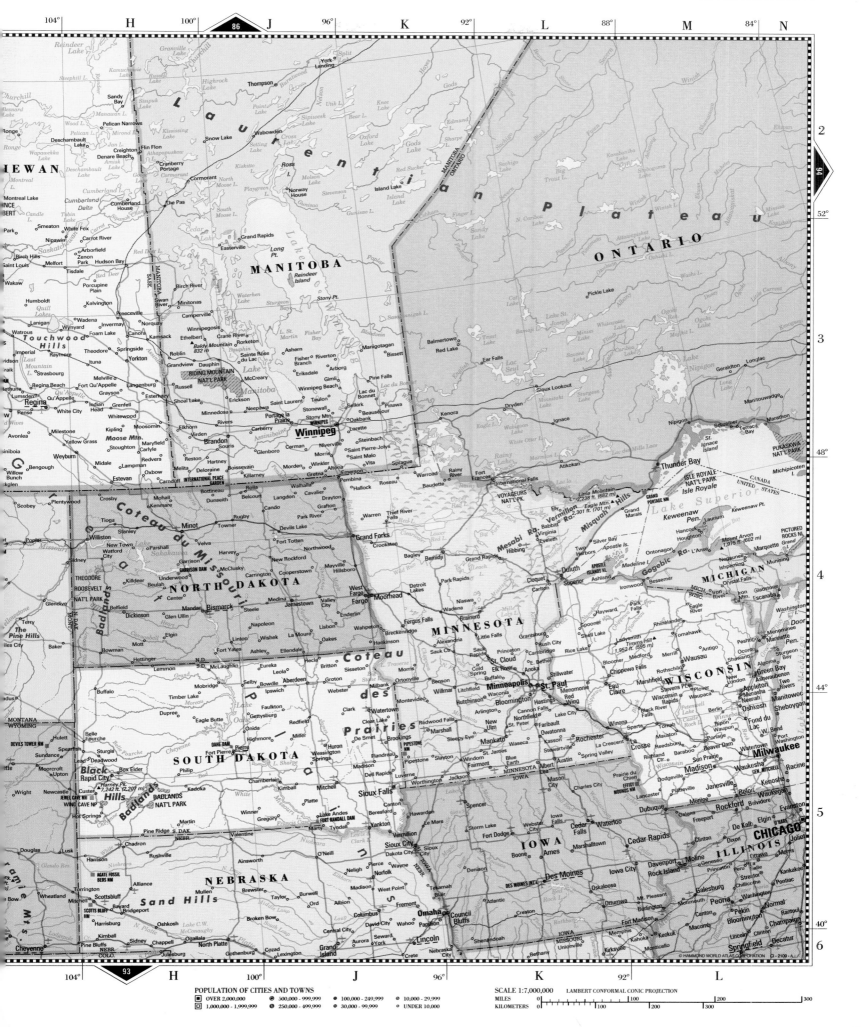

Southwestern United States

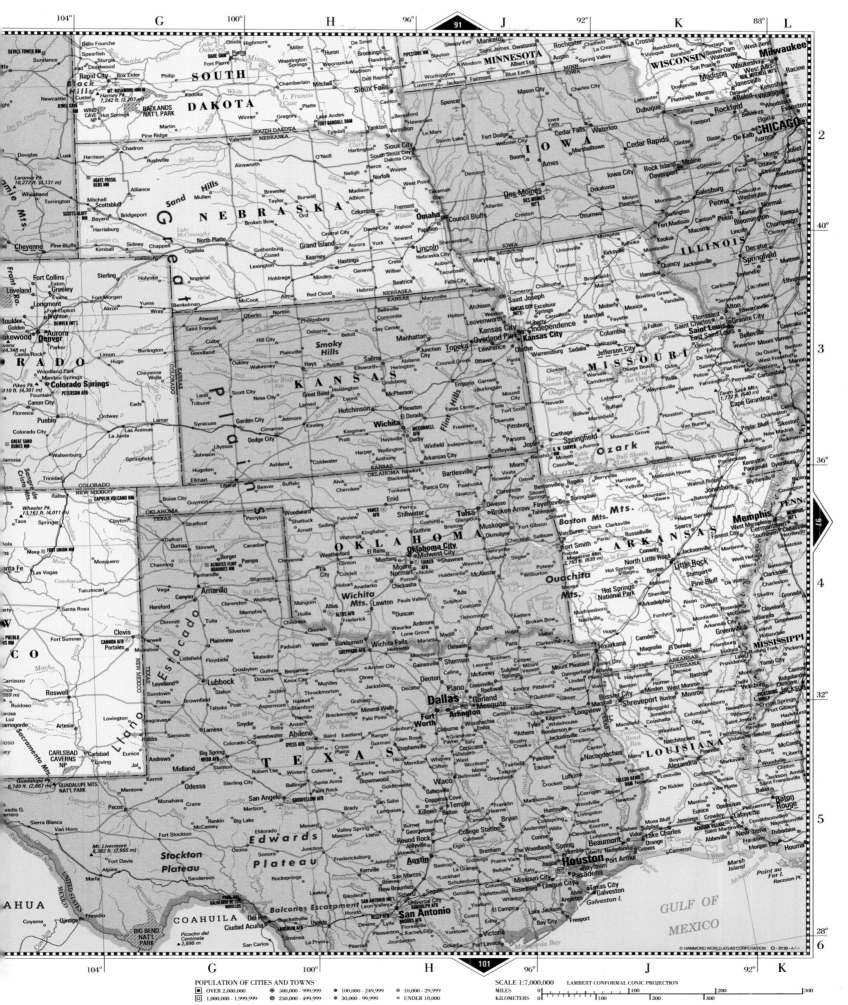

POPULATION OF CITIES AND TOWNS

■ OVER 2,000,000   ● 500,000 - 999,999   ● 100,000 - 249,999   ○ 10,000 - 29,999
□ 1,000,000 - 1,999,999   ● 250,000 - 499,999   ○ 30,000 - 99,999   ○ UNDER 10,000

SCALE 1:7,000,000   LAMBERT CONFORMAL CONIC PROJECTION

MILES   0   100   200   300

KILOMETERS   0   100   200   300

Southeastern Canada, Northeastern United States

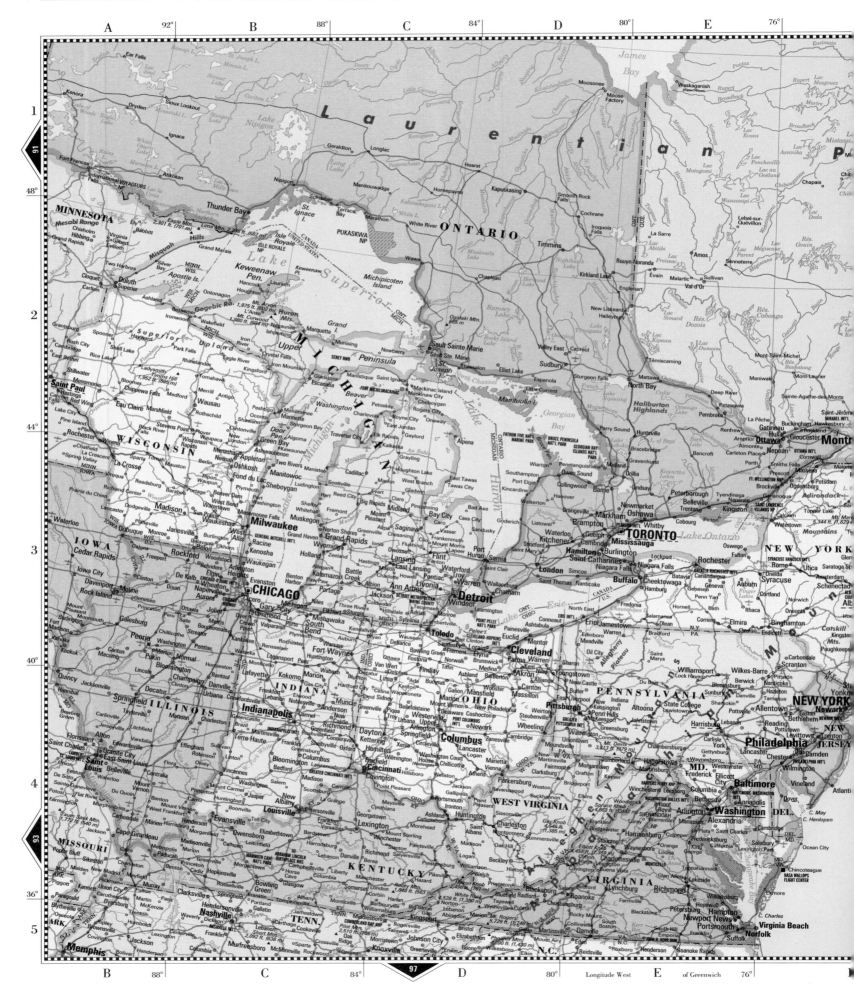

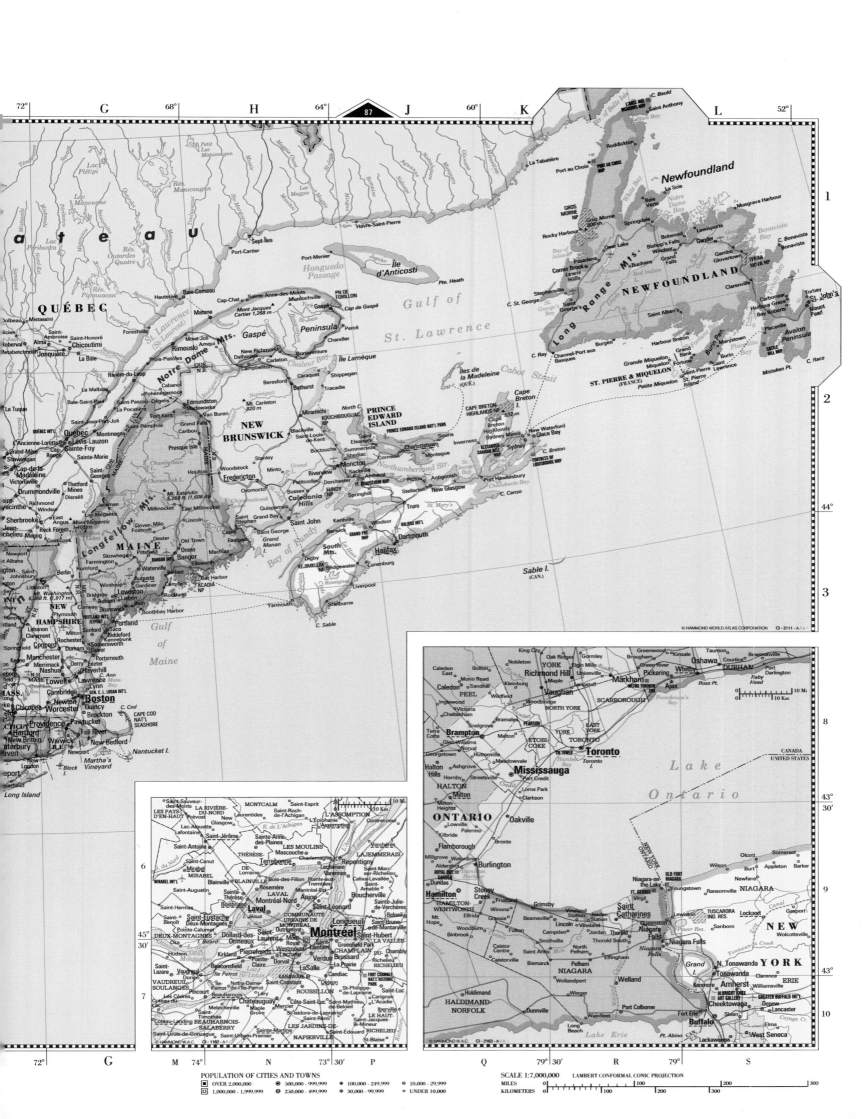

POPULATION OF CITIES AND TOWNS

| ■ OVER 2,000,000 | ● 500,000 - 999,999 | ● 100,000 - 249,999 | ● 10,000 - 29,999 |
| ▣ 1,000,000 - 1,999,999 | ● 250,000 - 499,999 | ● 30,000 - 99,999 | ○ UNDER 10,000 |

SCALE 1:7,000,000   LAMBERT CONFORMAL CONIC PROJECTION

MILES 0 ─────── 100 ─── 200 ─── 300

KILOMETERS 0 ─────── 100 ─── 200 ─── 300

Southeastern United States

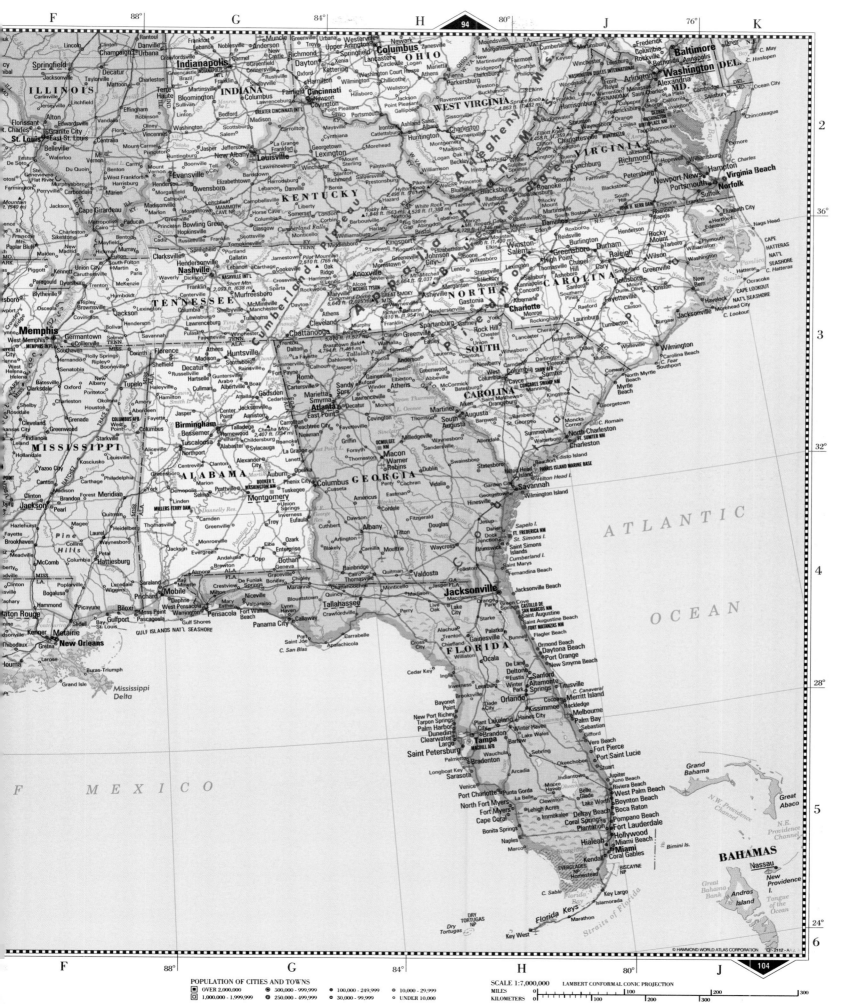

POPULATION OF CITIES AND TOWNS

| ■ OVER 2,000,000 | ● 500,000 - 999,999 | ◉ 100,000 - 249,999 | ○ 10,000 - 29,999 |
| ◘ 1,000,000 - 1,999,999 | ● 250,000 - 499,999 | ◌ 30,000 - 99,999 | ○ UNDER 10,000 |

SCALE 1:7,000,000   LAMBERT CONFORMAL CONIC PROJECTION

MILES
KILOMETERS

Los Angeles, New York, Philadelphia, Washington

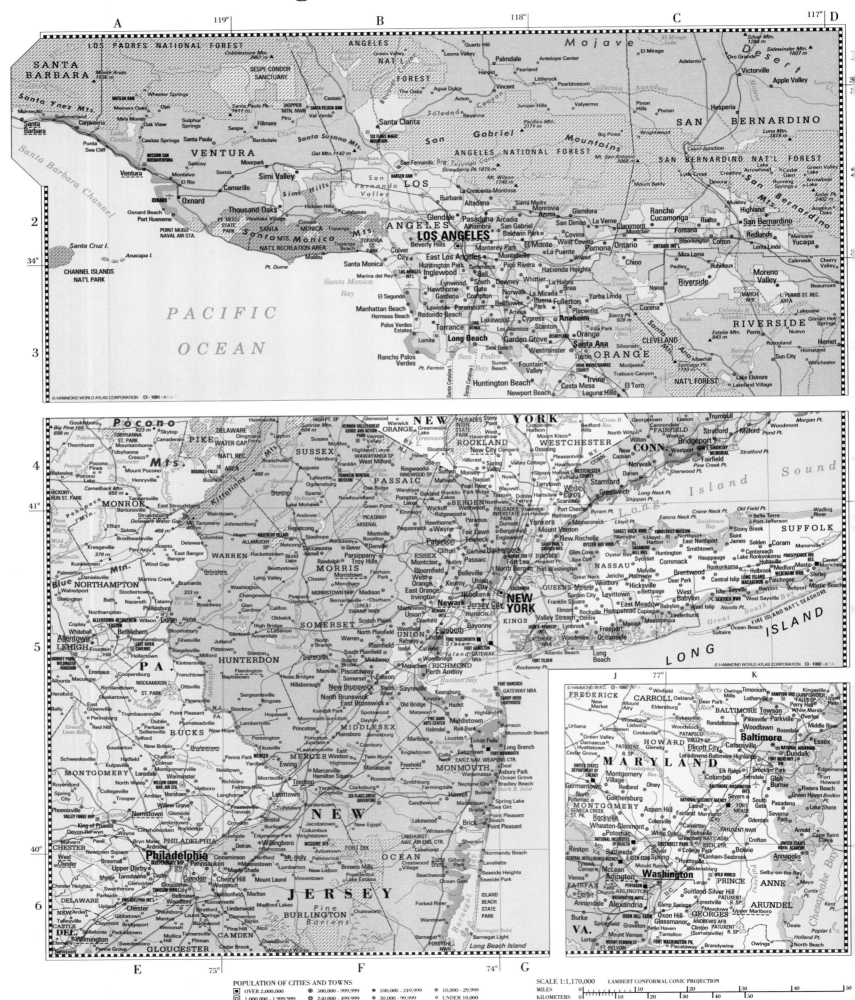

POPULATION OF CITIES AND TOWNS

■ OVER 2,000,000	● 500,000 - 999,999	● 100,000 - 249,999	○ 10,000 - 29,999
▣ 1,000,000 - 1,999,999	● 250,000 - 499,999	● 30,000 - 99,999	○ UNDER 10,000

SCALE 1:1,170,000   LAMBERT CONFORMAL CONIC PROJECTION

Seattle, San Francisco, Detroit, Chicago

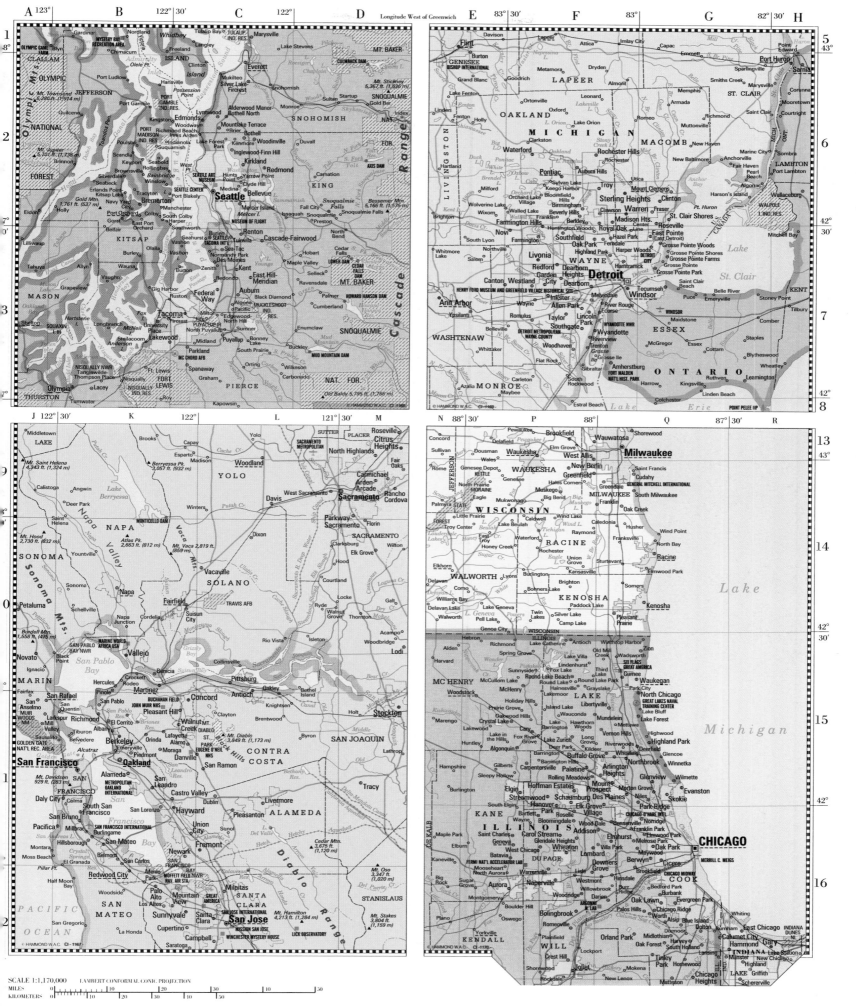

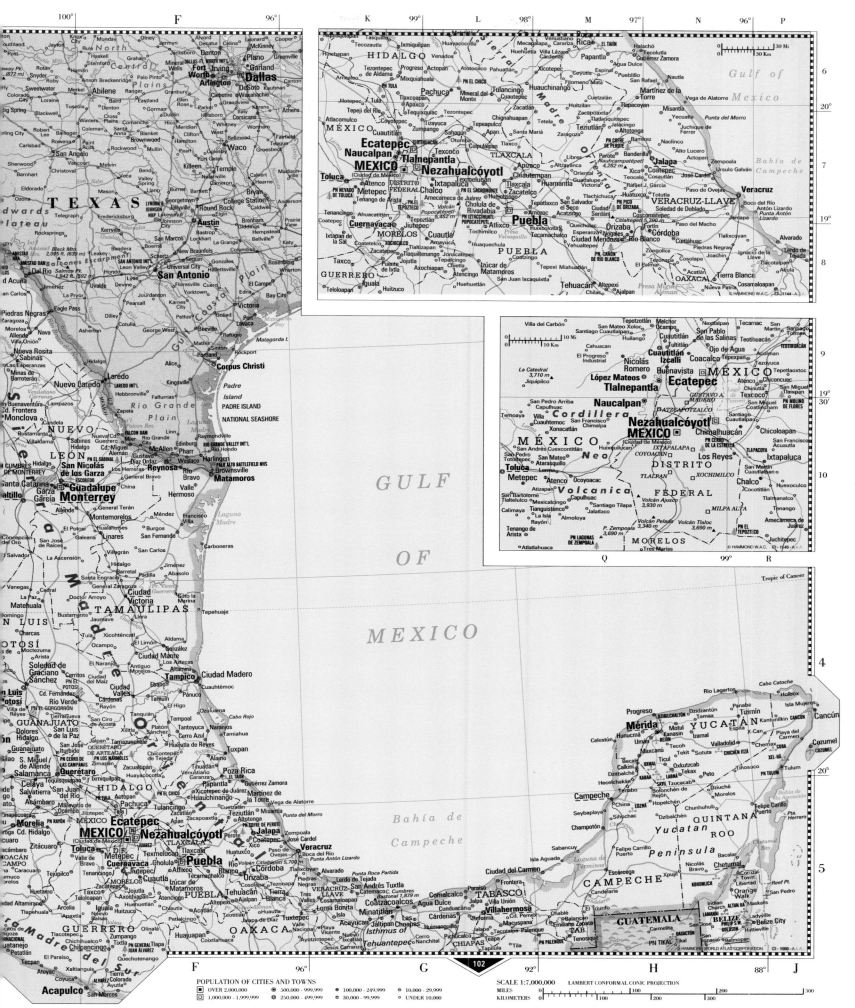

A 100° B 96° C 92° D 88° Tropic of

GULF OF MEXICO

El Limón Xicohténcatl Aldama
Corritos Ocampo Cd. Mante Xicohténcatl González
Cd. Mante González Altamira
El Naranjo Antiguo Los Aztecas
Ciudad Morelos
SAN LUIS POTOSÍ Cd. Valles **Tampico Ciudad Madero**
Ciudad PN EL POTOSÍ Cd. Valles Cuauhtémoc Arrecife
Fernández Tamuin Pánuco Alacrán
Río Verde Cárdenas Ébano
Rayón El Higo
San Ciro Ozuluama
1 GUANAJUATO de Acosta Tanquián Naranjos
San Luis Jalpan Xilitla Tantoyuca Tamiahua
de la Paz Tamazunchale Chicontepec Río Lagartos Cabo Catoche
QUERÉTARO Zimapán Cerro Azul I. Contoy
DE ARTEAGA PN LOS Huejutla de Tuxpan Progreso DZIBILCHALTÚN Dzidzantún Panaba Holbox Isla Mujeres
Querétaro MÁRMOLES Reyes Celestún Hunucmá Motul Temax Tizimín CANCÚN
Zacualtipán Poza Rica Maxcanú Umán Kanasín Izamal Espita Kantunilkin **Cancún**
San Juan HIDALGO Actopan Papantla **Mérida** Valladolid X-Can Playa del
del Río PN TULA Huauchinango Agua Dulce Calkiní UXMAL YUCATÁN Ticul Oxkutzcab CHICHÉN ITZÁ Chemax Carmen
20° Pachuca Tulancingo Tlapacoyan Heceichakán KABAH Tekax Peto COBÁ Punta Molas
MÉXICO Zacualpan Teziutlán Misantla Punta del Morro Tenabo LABNÁ SAYIL Tzucacab Tihosuco COZUMEL Cozumel
Ecatepec Apizaco Perote Xico Zempoala Campeche Hopelchén Dziuché PN TULUM Isla del Cozumel
MÉXICO **Nezahualcóyotl** Tlaxcala Apizaco José Cardel Seybaplaya China EDZNÁ Chunhuhub Bahía de la Ascensión XEL-HÁ Tulum
Toluca Texmelucan TLAXCALA Veracruz Champotón Sihochac Dzibalchén Yucatán Felipe Carrillo Puerto Punta Celarain
Metepec Cholula **Puebla** **VERACRUZ** Boca del Río Sabancuy QUINTANA ROO Punta Herrero
Cuernavaca Jiutepec Atlixco Orizaba Volcán Citlaltépetl 5,700 m Isla Aguada Laguna de
MORELOS Cuautla LLAVE Córdoba Alvarado I. del Carmen **Peninsula** Bahía del Espíritu Santo
Taxco Izúcar de Río Tlacotalpan Ciudad del Carmen Felipe Carrillo Términos Bacalar
Iguala Atencingo Matamoros Blanca Catemaco Frontera Puerto Escárcega Nicolás Chetumal
Nueva PUEBLA Tehuacán Altepexi Tierra Blanca San Andrés Tuxtla C. Cumbres Paraíso CAMPECHE Bravo Banco
2 Balsas Ajalpan Tres Valles Cosamaloapan Bastonal 1,879 m Agua TABASCO Jalpa Villa Unión Xpujil Orange Walk Chinchorro
Tlacotepec PN GEN. Teotitlán Huautla Coatzacoalcos Dulce **Villahermosa** Candelaria Ambergris Cay
Zumpango JUAN ÁLVAREZ Olinalá Tuxtepec Loma Minatitlán Cárdenas Chablé San Pedro
Chilpancingo Tlapa Chilapa Valle Nacional Bonita Isla Acayucan Jalapa PEMEX Balancán KOHUNLICH
MÉXICO Huajuapan Playa Vicente Comalcalco Teapa Emiliano Zapata MEX. Belize
Tixtla Ayotzintepec Nuevo Ixcatlán Hormiguillo Macuspana Palenque GUAT. LAMANAÍ PHILIP S.W. GOLDSON
Sierra Colorada Coixtlahuaca Jesús Carranza Cerro Reforma Tacotalpa Tenosique PN PALENQUE UAXACTÚN ALTUN HA Maskall
Acapulco MONTE ALBÁN Nanchital Pichucalco Tila OAXACTÚN Indian Church Hattieville BELIZE
San Zaachila **Oaxaca** Cerro Zempoaltepec Raudales Yajalón PN TIKAL TIKAL Baldy Beacon Belize
ÁLVAREZ Marcos Zimatlán 3,395 m Malpaso Tapilula 421 m YAXCHILÁN Hill Belmopan City
Copala OAXACA San Pablo MITLA Matías Romero Copainalá Bochil Ocosingo PN LAGUNAS La Libertad Victoria Pk. Colson Pt.
Cuajinicuilapa Huitzco Ocotlán **Isthmus of** Chiapa de Ixtlán Simojovel DE MONTEBELLO Flores Dangriga 1,120 m Turneffe
Pinotepa Ejutla Tuxtla Corzo San Cristóbal de las Casas Dolores Maya Beach Islands
Nacional Miahuatlán **Tehuantepec** **Gutiérrez** Teopisca CHIAPAS Lago Petén Itzá Independence Glover's
16° 2,515 m **Tuxtla** Las Rosas Las Margaritas Monkey River Reef
PN LAGUNAS DE CHACAHUA Tehuantepec Union **Gutiérrez** Comitán Ixcán PN LAGUNAS Lubantún
Nopala 3,139 m Juchitán de Tonalá Villa Flores Villa BONAMPAK DE MONTEBELLO San Maya
Puerto Escondido Huamelula Zaragoza Chahuites Arriaga Corzo La Trinitaria San Ignacio Gorda Punta Negra I. de Utila
Puerto Ángel Pochutla Salina Paredón Jaltenango Chicomuselo 3,834 m Cobán **San Pedro** Morales Livingston Punta Sal La Ceiba
Tres Picos Cruz de la Paz Barillas Carchá Puerto Cortés Trujillo
Golfo de Pijijiapan Mapastepec Acacoyagua Motozintla Santa Cruz Rabinal Los Amates Esparta La Masica Tela P. Bonito 2,435 m
Tehuantepec Huixtla del Quiché Salamá Gualán Villanueva **San Pedro Sula** Yoro Jocón Olanchito
Volcán Tacaná Chichicastenango Zacapa COPÁN El Progreso Santa Bárbara Monte Mucu
Tapachula Volcán Tajumulco 4,220 m **Guatemala** Jalapa Chiquimula Santa Rosa Florida Cerro Las Minas 2,849 m 2,152 m
3 Puerto Madero 3,139 m Quezaltenango Sololá LA AURORA Cucuyagua de Copán Lepaera San Francisco
Ciudad Hidalgo Retalhuleu Chimaltenango Antigua **Villa Nueva** Jutiapa La Esperanza **HONDURAS** de la Paz
Mazatenango **Guatemala** Cuilapa Siguatepeque
Nueva Concepción Escuintla Chiquimulilla Moyuta TAZUMAL Santa La Paz PN LA TIGRA Monte el Chile 2,2
Sonsonate Ahuachapán Santa Ana Chalatenango **Tegucigalpa** Talanga Morocelí
Volcán de Santa Ana Cojutepeque Cerro Las Minas El Paraíso
San Salvador Cojutepeque San Vicente Comayagua Curarén Yuscarán Danlí Murra
EL SALVADOR Zacatecoluca San Miguel Nacaome Sabanagrande Soto Pico Mo
12° Usulután San Lorenzo San Lucas San Sebastián 2,107 m
La Unión Marcovia Choluteca Nuevo de Oro
Punta Nueva Villa Estelí
San Juan Punta Cosigüina El Viejo Volcán San Cristóbal Nueva Isidro Larreynaga
Chinandega 1,745 m Chichigalpa de los Ra
Corinto León Telica
Managua
La Concepción
Diriamba

PACIFIC

OCEAN

© HAMMOND WORLD ATLAS CORPORATION CI-1067-A·A·A

B 96° Longitude West of Greenwich C 92° D 88°

SCALE 1:7,000,000 **LAMBERT CONFORMAL CONIC PROJECTION** **POPULATION OF CITIES AND TOWNS**
MILES 0 100 200 300 ■ OVER 2,000,000 ● 500,000 - 999,999 ● 100,000 - 249,999 ● 10,000 - 29,999
KILOMETERS 0 100 200 300 ▣ 1,000,000 - 1,999,999 ● 250,000 - 499,999 ○ 30,000 - 99,999 ○ UNDER 10,000

Eastern Caribbean, Bahamas

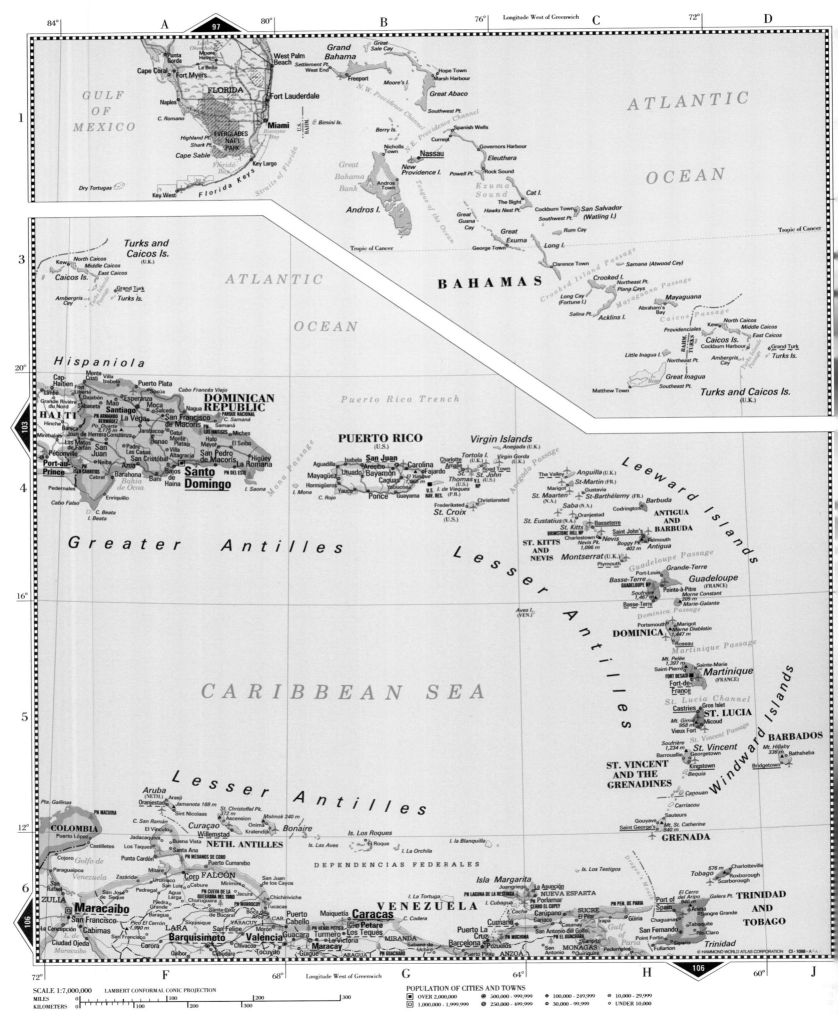

South America

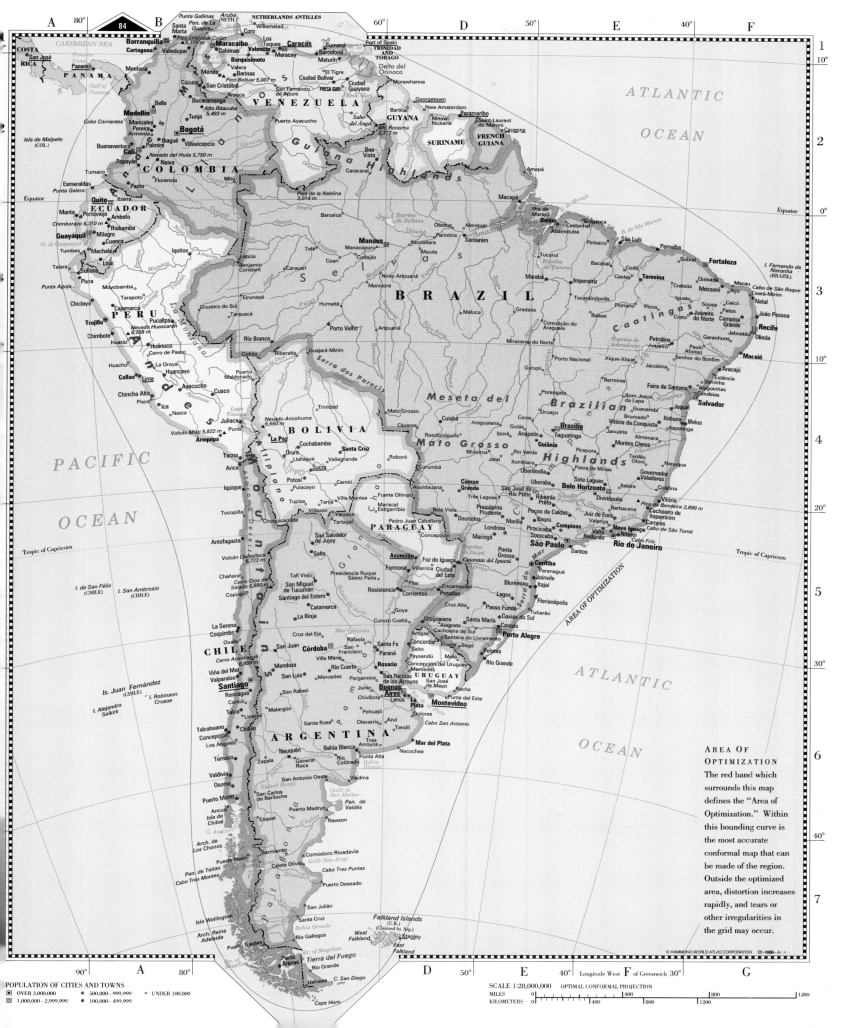

Northern South America

© HAMMOND WORLD ATLAS CORPORATION   CI - 2107 - A

POPULATION OF CITIES AND TOWNS

■ OVER 2,000,000 ● 500,000 - 999,999 ● 50,000 - 99,999
▣ 1,000,000 - 1,999,999 ● 100,000 - 499,999 ○ UNDER 50,000

SCALE 1:15,000,000   LAMBERT CONFORMAL CONIC PROJECTION

Southeastern Brazil

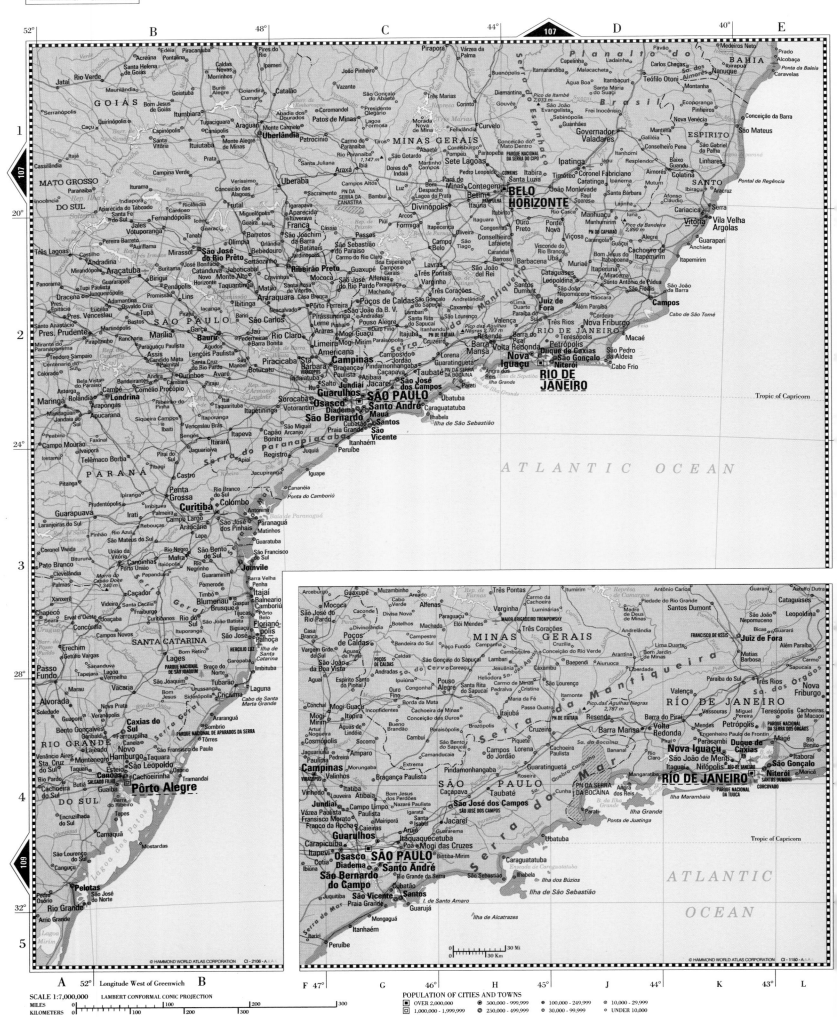

SCALE 1:7,000,000   LAMBERT CONFORMAL CONIC PROJECTION

POPULATION OF CITIES AND TOWNS

| ■ OVER 2,000,000 | ● 500,000 - 999,999 | ● 100,000 - 249,999 | ○ 10,000 - 29,999 |
| ▣ 1,000,000 - 1,999,999 | ● 250,000 - 499,999 | ● 30,000 - 99,999 | ○ UNDER 10,000 |

Southern South America

Falkland Islands
(Islas Malvinas)
(U.K. CLAIMED BY ARGENTINA)

West Falkland — East Falkland

S. Georgia I. (U.K.)

POPULATION OF CITIES AND TOWNS
- ■ OVER 2,000,000
- □ 1,000,000 - 1,999,999
- ● 500,000 - 999,999
- ● 100,000 - 499,999
- ● 50,000 - 99,999
- ○ UNDER 50,000

SCALE 1:15,000,000   LAMBERT CONFORMAL CONIC PROJECTION
MILES 0 ... 200 400 600
KILOMETERS 0 ... 200 400 600

© HAMMOND WORLD ATLAS CORPORATION   CI - 2105 - A

Index of the World

This index lists places and geographic features found in the atlas. Every name is followed by the country or area to which it belongs. Except for cities, towns, countries and cultural areas, all entries include a reference to feature type, such as province, river, island, peak, and so on. The page number and alpha-numeric code appear in blue to the right of each listing. The page number directs you to the largest scale map on which the name can be found. The code refers to the grid squares formed by the horizontal and vertical lines of latitude and longitude on each map. Following the letters from left to right, and the numbers from top to bottom, helps you to locate quickly the square containing the place or feature. Inset maps have their own alpha-numeric codes. Names that are accompanied by a point symbol are indexed to the symbol's location on the map. Other names are indexed to the initial letter of the name. The primary abbreviations used in this index are listed below.

Index Abbreviations

A Ab,Can	Alberta	**Gre.**	Greece
Afg.	Afghanistan	**Grld.**	Greenland
Afr.	Africa	**Gren.**	Grenada
Ak,US	Alaska	**Grsld.**	Grassland
Al,US	Alabama	**Guad.**	Guadeloupe
Alb.	Albania	**Guat.**	Guatemala
Alg.	Algeria	**Gui.**	Guinea
And.	Andorra	**Guy.**	Guyana
Ang.	Angola		
Angu.	Anguilla	**H Har.**	Harbor
Ant.	Antarctica	**Hi,US**	Hawaii
Anti.	Antigua and	**Hon.**	Honduras
	Barbuda	**Hts.**	Heights
Ar,US	Arkansas	**Hun.**	Hungary
Arch.	Archipelago		
Arg.	Argentina	**I Ia,US**	Iowa
Arm.	Armenia	**Ice.**	Iceland
Aru.	Aruba	**Id,US**	Idaho
ASam.	American Samoa	**Il,US**	Illinois
Ash.	Ashmore and Cartier	**IM**	Isle of Man
	Islands	**In,US**	Indiana
Aus.	Austria	**Indo.**	Indonesia
Austl.	Australia	**Int'l**	International
Az,US	Arizona	**Ire.**	Ireland
Azer.	Azerbaijan	**Isl., Isls.**	Island, Islands
Azor.	Azores	**Isr.**	Israel
		Isth.	Isthmus
B Bahm.	Bahamas, The	**It.**	Italy
Bahr.	Bahrain		
Bang.	Bangladesh	**J Jam.**	Jamaica
Bar.	Barbados	**Jor.**	Jordan
BC,Can	British Columbia		
Bela.	Belarus	**K Kaz.**	Kazakhstan
Belg.	Belgium	**Kiri.**	Kiribati
Belz.	Belize	**Ks,US**	Kansas
Ben.	Benin	**Kuw.**	Kuwait
Berm.	Bermuda	**Ky,US**	Kentucky
Bhu.	Bhutan	**Kyr.**	Kyrgyzstan
Bol.	Bolivia		
Bosn.	Bosnia and	**L La,US**	Louisiana
	Herzegovina	**Lat.**	Latvia
Bots.	Botswana	**Lcht.**	Liechtenstein
Braz.	Brazil	**Leb.**	Lebanon
Bru.	Brunei	**Les.**	Lesotho
Bul.	Bulgaria	**Libr.**	Liberia
Burk.	Burkina Faso	**Lith.**	Lithuania
Buru.	Burundi	**Lux.**	Luxembourg
BVI	British Virgin Islands		
		M Ma,US	Massachusetts
C Ca,US	California	**Madg.**	Madagascar
CAfr.	Central African	**Madr.**	Madeira
	Republic	**Malay.**	Malaysia
Camb.	Cambodia	**Mald.**	Maldives
Camr.	Cameroon	**Malw.**	Malawi
Can.	Canada	**Mart.**	Martinique
Can.	Canal	**May.**	Mayotte
Canl.	Canary Islands	**Mb,Can**	Manitoba
Cap.	Capital	**Md,US**	Maryland

Cap. Terr.	Capital Territory	**Me,US**	Maine
Cay.	Cayman Islands	**Mex.**	Mexico
C.d'Iv.	Côte d'Ivoire	**Mi,US**	Michigan
Chan.	Channel	**Micr.**	Micronesia, Federated
Chl.	Channel Islands		States of
Co,US	Colorado	**Mn,US**	Minnesota
Col.	Colombia	**Mo,US**	Missouri
Com.	Comoros	**Mol.**	Moldova
Cont.	Continent	**Mon.**	Monument
CpV.	Cape Verde Islands	**Mona.**	Monaco
CR	Costa Rica	**Mong.**	Mongolia
Cr.	Creek	**Monts.**	Montserrat
Cro.	Croatia	**Mor.**	Morocco
Ct,US	Connecticut	**Moz.**	Mozambique
Cyp.	Cyprus	**Mrsh.**	Marshall Islands
Czh.	Czech Republic	**Mrta.**	Mauritania
		Mrts.	Mauritius
D DC,US	District of Columbia	**Ms,US**	Mississippi
De,US	Delaware	**Mt.**	Mount
Den.	Denmark	**Mt,US**	Montana
Depr.	Depression	**Mtn., Mts.**	Mountain, Mountains
Des.	Desert		
Dist.	District	**N NAm.**	North America
Djib.	Djibouti	**Namb.**	Namibia
Dom.	Dominica	**NAnt.**	Netherlands Antilles
Dpcy.	Dependency	**Nat'l**	National
D.R.Congo	Democratic Republic	**NB,Can**	New Brunswick
	of the Congo	**NC,US**	North Carolina
DRep.	Dominican Republic	**NCal.**	New Caledonia
		ND,US	North Dakota
E Ecu.	Ecuador	**Ne,US**	Nebraska
Eng,UK	England	**Neth.**	Netherlands
EqG.	Equatorial Guinea	**Nf,Can**	Newfoundland
Erit.	Eritrea	**Nga.**	Nigeria
ESal.	El Salvador	**NH,US**	New Hampshire
Est.	Estonia	**NI,UK**	Northern Ireland
Eth.	Ethiopia	**Nic.**	Nicaragua
Eur.	Europe	**NJ,US**	New Jersey
		NKor.	North Korea
F Falk.	Falkland Islands	**NM,US**	New Mexico
Far.	Faroe Islands	**NMar.**	Northern Mariana
Fed. Dist.	Federal District		Islands
Fin.	Finland	**Nor.**	Norway
Fl,US	Florida	**NP**	National Park
Fr.	France	**NS,Can**	Nova Scotia
FrG.	French Guiana	**Nv,US**	Nevada
FrPol.	French Polynesia	**NW,Can**	Northwest Territories
FYROM	Former Yugoslav Rep.	**NY,US**	New York
	of Macedonia	**NZ**	New Zealand
G Ga,US	Georgia	**O Oh,US**	Ohio
Gam.	Gambia, The	**Ok,US**	Oklahoma
Gaza	Gaza Strip	**On,Can**	Ontario
GBis.	Guinea-Bissau	**Or,US**	Oregon
Geo.	Georgia		
Ger.	Germany	**P Pa,US**	Pennsylvania
Gha.	Ghana	**PacUS**	Pacific Islands, U.S.
Gib.	Gibraltar	**Pak.**	Pakistan

Pan.	Panama	**Sur.**	Suriname
Par.	Paraguay	**Sval.**	Svalbard
PE,Can	Prince Edward Island	**Swaz.**	Swaziland
Pen.	Peninsula	**Swe.**	Sweden
Phil.	Philippines	**Swi.**	Switzerland
Phys. Reg.	Physical Region		
Pitc.	Pitcairn Islands	**T Tah.**	Tahiti
Plat.	Plateau	**Tai.**	Taiwan
PNG	Papua New Guinea	**Taj.**	Tajikistan
Pol.	Poland	**Tanz.**	Tanzania
Port.	Portugal	**Terr.**	Territory
PR	Puerto Rico	**Thai.**	Thailand
Prov.	Province	**Tn,US**	Tennessee
Pt.	Point	**Tok.**	Tokelau
		Trin.	Trinidad and Tobago
Q Qu,Can	Quebec	**Trkm.**	Turkmenistan
		Trks.	Turks and Caicos
R Rec.	Recreation(al)		Islands
Reg.	Region	**Turk.**	Turkey
Rep.	Republic	**Tuv.**	Tuvalu
Res.	Reservoir, Reservation	**Tx,US**	Texas
Reun.	Réunion		
RI,US	Rhode Island	**U UAE**	United Arab Emirates
Riv.	River	**Ugan.**	Uganda
Rom.	Romania	**UK**	United Kingdom
Rsv.	Reserve	**Ukr.**	Ukraine
Rus.	Russia	**Uru.**	Uruguay
Rwa.	Rwanda	**US**	United States
		USVI	U.S. Virgin Islands
S SAfr.	South Africa	**Ut,US**	Utah
Sam.	Samoa	**Uzb.**	Uzbekistan
SAm.	South America		
SaoT.	São Tomé and	**V Va,US**	Virginia
	Príncipe	**Val.**	Valley
SAr.	Saudi Arabia	**Van.**	Vanuatu
Sc,UK	Scotland	**VatC.**	Vatican City
SC,US	South Carolina	**Ven.**	Venezuela
SD,US	South Dakota	**Viet.**	Vietnam
Sen.	Senegal	**Vol.**	Volcano
Sey.	Seychelles	**Vt,US**	Vermont
Sing.	Singapore		
Sk,Can	Saskatchewan	**W Wa,US**	Washington
SKor.	South Korea	**Wal,UK**	Wales
SLeo.	Sierra Leone	**Wall.**	Wallis and Futuna
Slov.	Slovenia	**WBnk.**	West Bank
Slvk.	Slovakia	**Wi,US**	Wisconsin
SMar.	San Marino	**WSah.**	Western Sahara
Sol.	Solomon Islands	**WV,US**	West Virginia
Som.	Somalia	**Wy,US**	Wyoming
Sp.	Spain		
Spr., Sprs.	Spring, Springs	**Y Yem.**	Yemen
SrL.	Sri Lanka	**Yk,Can**	Yukon Territory
StH.	Saint Helena	**Yugo.**	Yugoslavia
Str.	Strait		
StK.	Saint Kitts and Nevis	**Z Zam.**	Zambia
StL.	Saint Lucia	**Zim.**	Zimbabwe
StV.	Saint Vincent and the		
	Grenadines		

A

Aachen, Ger. 31/F2
Aalen, Ger. 33/J2
Aalsmeer, Neth. 28/B4
Aalst, Belg. 30/D2
Aalten, Neth. 28/D5
Aalter, Belg. 28/A6
Aarau, Swi. 36/E3
Aarschot, Belg. 28/B7
Aba, Nga. 79/G5
Abā as Su'ūd, SAr. 52/D5
Ābādān, Iran 51/G4
Ābādeh, Iran 51/H4
Abaeté, Braz. 108/C1
Abaetetuba, Braz. 107/J4
Abakan, Rus. 46/K4
Abancay, Peru 106/D6
Abashiri, Japan 55/N3
Abasolo, Mex. 101/E4
Abay, Kaz. 46/H5
Abaza, Rus. 46/K4
Abbeville, La, US 93/J5
Abbeville, Fr. 30/A3
Abbottābād, Pak. 53/K2
Abdulino, Rus. 45/K1
Abéché, Chad 77/K5
Abengourou, C.d'Iv. 78/E5
Åbenrå, Den. 26/E1
Abeokuta, Nga. 79/F5
Aberdare, Wal, UK 24/C3
Abhá, SAr. 52/D5
Abhar, Iran 51/G2
Abidjan, C.d'Iv. 78/D5
Abilene, Tx, US 93/H4
Abingdon, Eng, UK 25/E3
Abnūb, Egypt 50/B5
Åbo (Turku), Fin. 42/D3
Abomey, Ben. 79/F5
Abony, Hun. 40/D2
Abu Dhabi (cap.), UAE 53/F4
Abū Ḩammād, Egypt 49/B4
Abū Ḩummuş, Egypt 49/B4
Abū Kabīr, Egypt 49/B4
Abū Kamāl, Syria 50/E3
Abuja (cap.), Nga. 79/G4
Abulog, Phil. 61/J5
Acadia National Park, Me, US 95/G2
Acámbaro, Mex. 101/E4
Acaponeta, Mex. 100/D4
Acapulco de Juárez, Mex. 102/B2
Acarigua, Ven. 106/E2
Acatzingo, Mex. 101/M7
Acayucan, Mex. 102/C2
Accra (cap.), Gha. 79/E5
Accrington, Eng, UK 23/F4
Acheng, China 55/K2
Achern, Ger. 31/H6
Achinsk, Rus. 46/K4
Acireale, It. 38/D4
Aconcagua (peak), Arg.,Chile 109/B3
Acopiara, Braz. 107/L5
Acqui Terme, It. 33/H4
Actopan, Mex. 101/L6
Açu, Braz. 107/L5
Ad Damīr, Sudan 52/B5
Ad Dammām, SAr. 52/F3
Ad Dilinjāt, Egypt 49/B4
Ad Dīwānīyah, Iraq 51/F4
Ad Duwaym, Sudan 77/M5
Ad-Dakhla, Mor. 76/B3
Ada, Ok, US 93/H4
Adamantina, Braz. 108/B2
Adams (mt.), Wa, US 90/C4
Adamstown (cap.), Pitc. 69/M7
'Adan, Yem. 52/D6
Adana, Turk. 49/D1
Adapazarı, Turk. 41/K5
Addis Ababa (cap.), Eth. 77/N6
Addison, Il, US 99/P16
Adekeieh (Ādī K'eyih), Erit. 52/C6
Adelaide, Austl. 73/A2
Aden (gulf) 52/E6
Adilābād, India 62/C4
Adirondack (mts.), NY, US 94/F2
Adıyaman, Turk. 50/D2
Adjud, Rom. 41/H2
Adliswil, Swi. 37/E3
Ado Ekiti, Nga. 79/G5
Ado Odo, Nga. 79/F5
Ādoni, India 62/C4
Adra, Sp. 34/D4
Adrano, It. 38/D4
Adrar, Alg. 76/E2
Adrian, Mi, US 94/C3
Adriatic (sea), It. 40/B4
Ādwa, Eth. 52/C6
Aegean (sea), Gre.,Turk. 39/J3
'Afak, Iraq 51/F3
Afghanistan (ctry.) 53/H2
Afragola, It. 38/D2
Africa (cont.) 74/*
'Afula, Isr. 49/G6
Afyon, Turk. 44/D5
Agadez, Niger 79/G2
Agadir, Mor. 76/D1
Agartala, India 63/F3
Agboville, C.d'Iv. 78/D5
Ağdam, Azer. 45/H5
Agde, Fr. 32/E5
Agen, Fr. 32/D4
Āghā Jārī, Iran 51/G4
Agoo, Phil. 61/J5
Āgra, India 62/C2
Agrigento, It. 38/C4
Agrínion, Gre. 39/G3
Agryz, Rus. 43/M4
Agua Dulce, Mex. 102/C2
Agua Prieta, Mex. 92/E5
Aguachica, Col. 103/H4
Aguadilla, PR 104/E3
Aguaí, Braz. 108/G7
Agualva-Cacém, Port. 35/P10
Aguascalientes, Mex. 100/E4
Agudos, Braz. 108/B2
Aguilares, Arg. 109/C2
Aguilas, Sp. 34/E4
Agüimes, Canl. 35/X17
Agustín Codazzi, Col. 103/H4
Ahar, Iran 45/H5
Ahaus, Ger. 28/E4
Ahlat, Turk. 50/E2
Ahlen, Ger. 29/E5
Ahmadābād, India 62/B3
Ahmadnagar, India 62/B4
Ahmadpur East, Pak. 62/B2
Ahrensburg, Ger. 29/H1
Ahuachapán, ESal. 102/D3
Ahvāz, Iran 51/G4
Aichach, Ger. 37/H1
Aiken, SC, US 97/H3
'Aïn Beïda, Alg. 76/G1
'Aïn Sefra, Alg. 76/E1
Aina Haina, Hi, US 88/W13
Airdrie, Ab, Can. 90/E3
Aiud, Rom. 41/F2
Aix-en-Provence, Fr. 32/F5
Aíyion, Gre. 39/H3
Aīzawl, India 60/B4
Aizu-Wakamatsu, Japan 57/F2
Ajaccio, Fr. 38/A2
Ajalpan, Mex. 101/M8
Ajax, On, Can. 95/U8
Ajdābiyā, Libya 77/K1
Ajka, Hun. 40/C2
Ajmer, India 62/B2
Akashi, Japan 56/D3
Akçaabat, Turk. 44/F4
Akçakale, Turk. 50/D2
Akhalts'ikhe, Geo. 45/G4
Akharnaí, Gre. 39/N8
Akhisar, Turk. 44/C5
Akhmīm, Egypt 50/B5
Akhtubinsk, Rus. 45/H2
Aki, Japan 56/C4
Akita, Japan 55/N4
Akjoujt, Mrta. 78/B2
Akkaraipattu, SrL. 62/D6
'Akko, Isr. 49/D3
Akō, Japan 56/D3
Akola, India 62/C3
Åkrehamn, Nor. 20/C4
Akron, Oh, US 94/D3
Aksaray, Turk. 50/C2
Akşehir, Turk. 50/B2
Aksu, China 46/J5
Akune, Japan 56/B4
Akure, Nga. 79/G5
Akyazı, Turk. 41/K5
Al Aḩmadī, Kuw. 51/G4
Al 'Amārah, Iraq 51/F4
Al 'Aqabah, Jor. 49/D5
Al 'Ayn, UAE 53/G4
Al 'Azīzīyah, Libya 76/H1
Al Bāb, Syria 50/D2
Al Badrashayn, Egypt 49/B5
Al Bājūr, Egypt 49/B4
Al Başrah, Iraq 51/F4
Al Bayḑā, Libya 77/K1
Al Fāsher, Sudan 77/L5
Al Fashn, Egypt 50/B4
Al Fatḩah, Iraq 51/E3
Al Fāw, Iraq 51/G4
Al Fayyūm, Egypt 50/B4
Al Ḩammām, Egypt 50/B4
Al Ḩammāmāt, Tun. 38/B4
Al Ḩasakah, Syria 50/E2
Al Ḩawāmidīyah, Egypt 49/B5
Al Ḩayy, Iraq 51/F3
Al Ḩillah, Iraq 51/F3
Al Hindīyah, Iraq 51/F3
Al Hoceima, Mor. 76/E1
Al Ḩudaydah, Yem. 52/D6
Al Hufūf, SAr. 52/E3
Al Iskandarīyah, Egypt 49/A4
Al Ismā'īlīyah, Egypt 49/C4
Al Jamm, Tun. 38/B5
Al Jīzah, Egypt 49/B4
Al Junaynah, Sudan 77/K5
Al Kāf, Tun. 76/G1
Al Karak, Jor. 49/D4
Al Khābūrah, Oman 53/G4
Al Khalīl (Hebron), WBnk. 49/D4
Al Khānkah, Egypt 49/B4
Al Khārijah, Egypt 77/M2
Al Kharṭūm Baḩrī (Khartoum North), Sudan 77/M4
Al Khubar, SAr. 52/F3
Al Khums, Libya 76/H1
Al Kiswah, Syria 49/E3
Al Kūfah, Iraq 51/F3
Al Kūt, Iraq 51/F3
Al Lādhiqīyah (Latakia), Syria 49/D2
Al Madīnah, SAr. 52/C4
Al Madīnah al Fikrīyah, Egypt 50/B5
Al Maḩallah al Kubrá, Egypt 49/B4
Al Mahdīyah, Tun. 38/B5
Al Maḩmūdīyah, Egypt 49/B4
Al Manşūrah, Egypt 49/B4
Al Manzilah, Egypt 49/B4
Al Marāghah, Egypt 50/B5
Al Marj, Libya 77/K1
Al Marsá, Tun. 38/B4
Al Maţarīyah, Egypt 49/C4
Al Mawşil (Mosul), Iraq 51/E2
Al Mayādin, Syria 50/E3
Al Minyā, Egypt 50/B4
Al Mubarraz, SAr. 52/E4
Al Mukallā, Yem. 52/E6
Al Muknīn, Tun. 38/B5
Al Munastīr, Tun. 38/B5
Al Musayyib, Iraq 51/F3
Al Qaḑārif, Sudan 52/C6
Al Qāmishlī, Syria 50/E2
Al Qanāţir al Khayrīyah, Egypt 49/B4
Al Qayrawān, Tun. 38/B5
Al Quşayr, Syria 49/E2
Al Ubayyiḑ, Sudan 77/M5
Al Wāsiţah, Egypt 49/B5
Alabama (state), US 97/G3
Alabaster, Al, US 97/G3
Alaca, Turk. 44/E4
Alagir, Rus. 45/H4
Alagoinhas, Braz. 107/L6
Alajuela, CR 103/E4
Alameda, Ca, US 99/K11
Alamo, Mex. 102/B1
Alamo, Ca, US 99/K11
Alamogordo, NM, US 93/F4
Alamosa, Co, US 93/F3
Åland (isl.), Fin. 20/G3
Alanya, Turk. 49/C1
Alaşehir, Turk. 50/B2
Alaska (pen.), US 85/F4
Alaska (gulf), US 85/J4
Alaska (state), US 85/G2
Alaska (range), Ak, US 85/H3
Alatyr', Rus. 45/H1
Alaverdi, Arm. 45/H4
Alba, It. 33/H4
Alba Iulia, Rom. 41/F2
Albacete, Sp. 34/E3
Albania (ctry.), Alb. 39/F2
Albany, Or, US 90/C4
Albany, Ga, US 97/G4
Albany (cap.), NY, US 94/F3
Albany, Ca, US 99/K11
Albemarle, NC, US 97/H3
Albenga, It. 33/H4
Albert (lake), D.R. Congo 77/M7
Albert Lea, Mn, US 91/K5
Alberta (prov.), Can. 86/E3
Alberton, SAfr. 80/Q13
Albertville, Al, US 97/G3
Albertville, Fr. 33/G4
Albi, Fr. 32/E5
Albina, Sur. 107/H2
Albion, Mi, US 94/C3
Alblasserdam, Neth. 28/B5
Ålborg, Den. 20/D4
Albufeira, Port. 34/A4
Albuquerque, NM, US 92/F4
Albury, Austl. 73/C3
Alcabideche, Port. 35/P10
Alcalá de Guadaira, Sp. 34/C4
Alcalá de Henares, Sp. 35/N9
Alcalá la Real, Sp. 34/D4
Alcamo, It. 38/C4
Alcantarilla, Sp. 34/E4
Alcázar de San Juan, Sp. 34/D3
Alcira, Sp. 35/E3
Alcobendas, Sp. 35/N8
Alcora, Sp. 35/E2
Alcorcón, Sp. 35/N9
Alcoy, Sp. 35/E3
Aldan, Rus. 47/N4
Aldershot, Eng, UK 25/F4
Alderwood Manor-Bothell North, Wa, US 99/C2
Aldine, Tx, US 93/J5
Aldridge, Eng, UK 25/E1
Aleg, Mrta. 78/B2
Alegrete, Braz. 109/E2
Aleksandrov, Rus. 42/H4
Aleksandrovsk, Rus. 43/N4
Aleksandrovsk-Sakhalinskiy, Rus. 55/N1
Aleksandrów Łódzki, Pol. 27/K3
Alekseyevka, Rus. 44/F2
Aleksin, Rus. 44/F1
Aleksinac, Yugo. 40/E4
Além Paraíba, Braz. 108/L6
Alençon, Fr. 32/D2
Alenquer, Braz. 107/H4
Alessandria, It. 33/H4
Ålesund, Nor. 20/C3
Aleutian (isls.), Ak, US 85/B5
Alexander (isl.), Ant. 83/V
Alexander (arch.), US 85/L4
Alexander City, Al, US 97/G3
Alexandria, La, US 93/J5
Alexandria, MN, US 91/K4
Alexandria, Rom. 41/G4
Alexandroúpolis, Gre. 41/G5
Aleysk, Rus. 46/J4
Alfeld, Ger. 29/G5
Alfenas, Braz. 108/H6
Alfreton, Eng, UK 23/G5
Alfter, Ger. 31/G2
Algeciras, Sp. 34/C4
Algemesí, Sp. 35/E3
Algeria (ctry.) 76/F2
Alghero, It. 38/A2
Algiers (cap.), Alg. 76/F1
Algonquin, Il, US 99/P14
Algueirão, Port. 35/P10
Algund (Lagundo), It. 37/H4
Alhama de Murcia, Sp. 34/E4
Alhaurín el Grande, Sp. 34/C4
'Alī al Gharbī, Iraq 51/F3
Ali Bayramlı, Azer. 51/G2
Aliağa, Turk. 44/C5
Alibeyköy, Turk. 41/J5
Alicante, Sp. 35/E3
Alice, Tx, US 96/D5
Alice Springs, Austl. 68/C7
Alīgarh, India 62/C2
Alingsås, Swe. 20/E4
Alīpur, Pak. 62/B2
Alīpur Duār, India 62/E2
Alirājpur, India 53/K4
Alkmaar, Neth. 28/B3
Allada, Ben. 79/F5
Allahābād, India 62/D2
Allanmyo, Myan. 60/B5
Allegheny (mts.), US 94/D4
Allen Park, Mi, US 99/F7
Allende, Mex. 101/E3
Allende, Mex. 96/C4
Allentown, Pa, US 94/F3
Alleppey, India 62/C6
Alliance, Ne, US 91/H5
Alliance, Oh, US 94/D3
Allschwil, Swi. 36/D2
Alma, Qu, Can. 95/G1
Alma, Mi, US 94/C3
Almada, Port. 35/P10
Almansa, Sp. 35/E3
Almaty, Kaz. 46/H5
Almazora, Sp. 35/E3
Almelo, Neth. 28/D4
Almenara, Braz. 107/K7
Almendralejo, Sp. 34/B3
Almere, Neth. 28/C4
Almería, Sp. 34/D4
Al'met'yevsk, Rus. 43/M5
Älmhult, Swe. 20/E4
Almonte, Sp. 34/B4
Almuñécar, Sp. 34/D4
Alofi, NZ 69/J6
Alor Setar, Malay. 65/C5
Alotau, PNG 68/E6
Alphen aan de Rijn, Neth. 28/B4
Alps (mts.), It. 33/G4
Alsdorf, Ger. 31/F2
Alsfeld, Ger. 33/H1
Alsip, Il, US 99/Q16
Alta, Nor. 20/G1
Alta Floresta, Braz. 107/G5
Alta Gracia, Arg. 109/D3
Altagracia, Nic. 102/E4
Altamira, Braz. 107/H4
Altamira, Mex. 102/B1
Altamonte Springs, Fl, US 97/H4
Altamura, It. 40/C5
Altay, Mong. 54/D2
Altay, China 54/B2
Altdorf, Swi. 37/E4
Altena, Ger. 29/E6
Altenburg, Ger. 26/G3
Alton, Il, US 93/K3
Alton, Eng, UK 25/F4
Altoona, Pa, US 94/E3
Altos, Braz. 107/K5
Altrincham, Eng, UK 23/F5
Altus, Ok, US 93/H4
Alushta, Ukr. 44/E3
Alvarado, Mex. 101/P8
Alverca, Port. 35/P10
Alvesta, Swe. 20/E4
Alvin, Tx, US 93/J5
Alvorada, Braz. 108/A4
Alytus, Lith. 27/N1
Alzey, Ger. 31/H4
Am Timan, Chad 77/K5
Amadora, Port. 35/P10
Amagasaki, Japan 55/M5
Amagi, Japan 56/B4
Amaliás, Gre. 39/G4
Amalner, India 62/C3
Amambaí, Braz. 109/E1
Amanzimtoti, SAfr. 81/E3
Amarillo, Tx, US 93/G4
Amasya, Turk. 44/E4
Amazon (riv.), Braz. 106/G4
Ambahikily, Madg. 81/G8
Ambajogai, India 53/L5
Ambāla, India 53/L2
Ambalavao, Madg. 81/H8
Ambanja, Madg. 81/J6
Ambato, Ecu. 106/C4
Ambato Boeny, Madg. 81/H7
Ambatofinandrahana, Madg. 81/H8
Ambatolampy, Madg. 81/H7
Ambatondrazaka, Madg. 81/J7
Amberg, Ger. 33/J2
Ambikāpur, India 62/D3
Ambinanindrano, Madg. 81/J8
Ambinanitelo, Madg. 81/J6
Amboasary, Madg. 81/H9
Amboavory, Madg. 81/J7
Ambodiharina, Madg. 81/J8
Ambohimandroso, Madg. 81/H7
Ambon, Indo. 67/G4
Ambositra, Madg. 81/H8
Ambovombe, Madg. 81/H9
Ameca, Mex. 100/D4
Amecameca de Juárez, Mex. 101/R10
American Fork, Ut, US 92/E2
Americana, Braz. 108/C2
Americus, Ga, US 97/G3
Amersfoort, Neth. 28/C4
Amersham, Eng, UK 25/F3
Amet, India 62/B2
Amherst, NY, US 95/V10
Amiens, Fr. 30/B4
Amla, India 62/C3
Amman (cap.), Jor. 49/D4
Āmol, Iran 51/H2
Amozoc, Mex. 101/L7
Ampanefena, Madg. 81/J6
Ampanihy, Madg. 81/H9
Amparafaravola, Madg. 81/J7
Amparai, SrL. 62/D6
Amparo, Braz. 108/G7
Ampitatafika, Madg. 81/H7
Amposta, Sp. 35/F2
Amravati, India 62/C3
Amreli, India 62/B3
Amritsar, India 53/K2
Amstelveen, Neth. 28/B4
Amsterdam, NY, US 94/F3
Amsterdam (cap.), Neth. 28/B4
Amstetten, Aus. 40/B1
Amu Darya (riv.), Trkm. 46/G5
Amursk, Rus. 55/M1
An Nabk, Syria 49/E2
An Nahūd, Sudan 77/L5
An Najaf, Iraq 51/F4
An Nāşirīyah, Iraq 51/F4
Anaco, Ven. 106/F2
Anaheim, Ca, US 92/C4
Anakāpalle, India 62/D4
Analalava, Madg. 81/H6
Analavory, Madg. 81/H7
Anamur, Turk. 49/C1
Anan, Japan 56/D4
Anand, India 62/B3
Anantapur, India 62/C5
Anantnag, India 53/L2
Anapa, Rus. 44/F3
Anápolis, Braz. 107/J7
Añatuya, Arg. 109/D2
Ancaster, On, Can. 95/T9
Anchorage, Ak, US 85/J3
Ancona, It. 40/A4
Ancud, Chile 109/B5
Anda, China 55/K2
Andalusia, Al, US 97/G4
Andaman (sea), Asia 63/F5
Andaman (isls.), India 63/F5
Andenne, Belg. 31/E3
Andernach, Ger. 31/G3
Anderson, In, US 97/G1
Anderson, SC, US 97/H3
Andes, Cordillera de los (mts.), SAm. 106/C4
Andijon, Uzb. 46/H5
Andilamena, Madg. 81/J7
Andilanatoby, Madg. 81/J7
Andīmeshk, Iran 51/G3
Andira, Braz. 108/B2
Andong, SKor. 56/A2
Andorra (ctry.) 35/F1
Andorra la Vella (cap.), And. 35/F1
Andover, Eng, UK 25/E4
Andradas, Braz. 108/G7
Andradina, Braz. 108/B2
Andria, It. 40/C5
Andriba, Madg. 81/H7
Androka, Madg. 81/H9
Andros (isl.), Bah. 97/J5
Andújar, Sp. 34/C3
Anegada Passage (chan.), NAm. 104/E3
Aného, Togo 79/F5
Angarsk, Rus. 54/E1
Ángel, Salto (falls), Ven. 106/F2
Ängelholm, Swe. 20/E4
Angers, Fr. 32/C3
Angkor (ruin), Camb. 65/C3
Anglesey (isl.), Wal, UK 22/D5
Anglet, Fr. 34/E1
Angleton, Tx, US 93/J5
Angol, Chile 109/B4
Angola, Afr. 82/B2
Angola (ctry.) 82/C3
Angoulême, Fr. 32/D4
Angra dos Reis, Braz. 108/J7
Angren, Uzb. 46/H5
Anjār, India 62/B3
Anjou, Qu, Can. 95/N6
Ankang, China 59/B4
Ankara (cap.), Turk. 44/E5
Ankazoabo, Madg. 81/H8
Anklam, Ger. 27/G2
Anlong, China 63/J2
Anlu, China 61/G2
Ann Arbor, Mi, US 99/E7
Annaba, Alg. 76/G1
Annaberg-Buchholz, Ger. 33/K1
Annapolis (cap.), Md, US 94/E4
Annecy, Fr. 36/C6
Annecy-le-Vieux, Fr. 36/C6
Annemasse, Fr. 36/C5
Anniston, Al, US 97/G3
Annonay, Fr. 32/F4
Anosibe an' Ala, Madg. 81/J7
Ans, Belg. 31/E2
Ansan, SKor. 58/F7
Ansbach, Ger. 33/J2
Ansfelden, Aus. 40/B1
Anshan, China 58/B2
Anshun, China 60/E3
Ansŏng, SKor. 58/D4
Antakya, Turk. 49/E1
Antalaha, Madg. 81/J6
Antalya, Turk. 49/B1
Antananarivo (cap.), Madg. 81/H7
Antanifotsy, Madg. 81/H7
Antarctic (pen.), Ant. 83/W
Antarctic Circle 83/Z
Antarctica (cont.) 83/*
Antequera, Sp. 34/C4
Antibes, Fr. 33/G5
Anticosti, Île d' (isl.), Qu, Can. 95/J1
Antigua and Barbuda (ctry.), Anti. 104/F3
Antigua Guatemala, Guat. 102/D3
Antioch, Ca, US 99/L11
Antofagasta, Chile 109/B1
Antony, Fr. 30/B6
Antrim, NI, UK 22/B2
Antsalova, Madg. 81/H7
Antsirabe, Madg. 81/H7
Antsiranana, Madg. 81/J6
Antwerpen, Belg. 28/B6
Anūpgarh, India 62/B2
Anuradhapura, SrL. 62/D6
Anyang, SKor. 58/F7
Anzhero-Sudzhensk, Rus. 46/J4
Anzio, It. 38/C2
Aomori, Japan 55/N3
Aosta, It. 33/G4
Apan, Mex. 101/L7
Aparecida, Braz. 108/C2
Aparri, Phil. 61/J5
Apartadó, Col. 103/G5
Apatin, Yugo. 40/D3
Apatity, Rus. 42/G2
Apatzingán de la Constitución, Mex. 100/E5
Apeldoorn, Neth. 28/C4
Apennines (mts.), It. 38/C1
Apia (cap.), Sam. 69/S9
Apizaco, Mex. 101/L7
Apóstoles, Arg. 109/E2
Appalachian (mts.), US 94/D4
Appenzell, Swi. 37/F3
Aprilia, It. 38/C2
Apsheronsk, Rus. 44/F3
Apucarana, Braz. 108/B2
Aqtaū, Kaz. 45/J4
Aqtöbe, Kaz. 45/L2
Aquidauana, Braz. 107/G8
Ar Ramādī, Iraq 51/E3
Ar Ramthā, Jor. 49/D3
Ar Rayyān, Qatar 52/F3
Ar Ruşayfah, Jor. 49/E3
Arabian (des.), Egypt 77/M2
Arabian (pen.), SAr. 52/D3
Arabian (sea), Asia 53/H5
Aracaju, Braz. 107/L6

112

Araca – Beala

Aracati, Braz. 107/L4
Araçatuba, Braz. 108/B2
Aracruz, Braz. 108/D1
Araçuaí, Braz. 107/K7
'Arad, Isr. 49/D4
Arad, Rom. 40/E2
Araguaína, Braz. 107/J5
Araguari, Braz. 108/B1
Arai, Japan 57/F2
Arāk, Iran 51/G3
Aral (sea), Kaz., Uzb. 46/G5
Aral, Kaz. 46/G5
Ārān, Iran 51/G3
Aranda de Duero, Sp. 34/D2
Arandelovac, Yugo. 40/E3
Arani, India 62/C5
Aranjuez, Sp. 34/D2
Arapiraca, Braz. 107/L5
Arapongas, Braz. 108/B2
Araranguá, Braz. 108/B4
Araraquara, Braz. 108/B2
Araras, Braz. 108/C2
Araripina, Braz. 107/K5
Arauca, Col. 106/D2
Araucária, Braz. 108/B3
Arawa, PNG 68/E5
Araxá, Braz. 108/C1
Ārba Minch', Eth. 77/N6
Arcata, Ca, US 90/B5
Archangel (Arkhangel'sk), Rus. 42/J2
Arches National Park, Ut, US 92/E3
Archman, Trkm. 45/L5
Arcos, Braz. 108/C2
Arcos de la Frontera, Sp. 34/C4
Arcoverde, Braz. 107/L5
Arctic (ocean) 84/A2
Arctic Circle 86/C2
Ardabīl, Iran 51/G2
Ardahan, Turk. 45/G4
Ardakān, Iran 51/H3
Arden-Arcade, Ca, US 99/M9
Ardeşen, Turk. 45/G4
Ardmore, Ok, US 93/H4
Arecibo, PR 104/E3
Areia Branca, Braz. 107/L4
Arendal, Nor. 20/D4
Arequipa, Peru 106/D7
Arezzo, It. 33/J5
Argentan, Fr. 32/C2
Argenteuil, Fr. 30/B6
Argentina (ctry.), Arg. 109/C4
Árgos, Gre. 39/H4
Århus, Den. 20/D4
Arica, Chile 106/D7
Arida, Japan 56/D3
Arima, Trin. 104/F5
Ariquemes, Braz. 106/F5
Arivonimamo, Madg. 81/H7
Arizona (state), US 92/D4
Arjona, Col. 103/H4
Arkadelphia, Ar, US 93/J4
Arkansas (state), US 96/E3
Arkansas (riv.), US 88/F3
Arkansas City, Ks, US 93/H3
Arkonam, India 62/C5
Arles, Fr. 32/F5
Arlington, Tx, US 93/H4
Arlington, Va, US 97/J2
Arlington Heights, Il, US 99/P15
Arlon, Belg. 31/E4
Armant, Egypt 52/B3
Armavir, Rus. 45/G3
Armenia, Col. 106/C3
Armenia (ctry.) 45/H5
Armentières, Fr. 30/B2
Armería, Mex. 100/E5
Armidale, Austl. 73/D1
Armūr, India 62/C4
Arnavutköy, Turk. 51/M6
Arnhem, Neth. 28/C5
Arnold, Eng, UK 23/G6
Arnsberg, Ger. 29/F6
Arnstadt, Ger. 33/J1
Arolsen, Ger. 29/G6
Arona, Canl. 35/X16
Arqalyq, Kaz. 46/G4
Arrah, India 62/D2
Arraiján, Pan. 103/G4
Arras, Fr. 30/B3
Arrecife, Canl. 35/Y16
Arriaga, Mex. 102/C2
Arroyo Grande, Ca, US 92/B4
Arsen'yev, Rus. 55/L3
Árta, Gre. 39/G3
Arteixo, Sp. 34/A1
Artem, Rus. 55/L3
Artemisa, Cuba 103/F1
Artesia, NM, US 93/F4
Artigas, Uru. 109/E3
Artvin, Turk. 45/G4
Arua, Ugan. 77/M7
Aruba (isl.), Neth. 104/D4
Arucas, Canl. 35/X16
Arujá, Braz. 108/G8
Aruppukkottai, India 62/C6
Arusha, Tanz. 82/G1
Arvayheer, Mong. 54/E2
Arvika, Swe. 20/E4
Arvin, Ca, US 92/C4
Aryānah, Tun. 38/B4
Arys', Kaz. 46/G5
Arzamas, Rus. 45/G1
Aş Şaff, Egypt 49/B5
As Sālimīyah, Kuw. 51/G4
As Salţ, Jor. 49/D3
As Samāwah, Iraq 51/F4
As Sanţah, Egypt 49/B4
As Sinbillāwayn, Egypt 49/B4
As Sulaymānīyah, Iraq 51/F3
As Suwaydā', Syria 49/E3
As Suways, Egypt 49/C4
Asahi, Japan 57/G3
Asahikawa, Japan 55/N3
Asansol, India 62/E3
Asbest, Rus. 43/P4
Aschaffenburg, Ger. 33/H2
Aschersleben, Ger. 26/F3
Ascoli Piceno, It. 40/A4
Āsela, Eth. 77/N6
Asenovgrad, Bul. 41/G4
Ash Shāriqah, UAE 53/G3
Ash Shaţrah, Iraq 51/F4
Ashdod, Isr. 49/F8
Asheboro, NC, US 97/J3
Asheville, NC, US 97/H3
Ashford, Eng, UK 25/G4
Ashgabat (cap.), Trkm. 51/J2
Ashington, Eng, UK 23/G1
Ashland, Or, US 90/C5
Ashland, Ky, US 97/H2
Ashland, Oh, US 94/D3
Ashmūn, Egypt 49/B4
Ashqelon, Isr. 49/F8
Ashta, India 62/C3
Ashtabula, Oh, US 94/D3
Ashton-in-Makerfield, Eng, UK 23/F5
Ashton-under-Lyne, Eng, UK 23/F5
Asia (cont.) 48/*
Asino, Rus. 46/J4
Aşkale, Turk. 45/G5
Asker, Nor. 20/D4
Asmara (cap.), Erit. 52/C5
Asnières-sur-Seine, Fr. 30/B6
Aspe, Sp. 35/E3
Asprópirgos, Gre. 39/N8
Assab, Erit. 52/D6
Asse, Belg. 31/D2
Assemini, It. 38/A3
Assen, Neth. 28/D3
Assiniboine (mt.), BC, Can. 90/E3
Assis, Braz. 108/B2
Astana (cap.), Kaz. 46/H4
Asten, Neth. 28/C6
Asti, It. 33/H4
Astorga, Braz. 108/B2
Astoria, Or, US 90/C4
Astrakhan', Rus. 45/J3
Asunción (cap.), Par. 109/E2
Aswān, Egypt 52/B4
Asyūţ, Egypt 52/B3
Aţ Ţafīlah, Jor. 49/D4
Aţ Ţā'if, SAr. 52/D4
At Tall, Syria 49/E3
At Tall al Kabīr, Egypt 49/B4
Atacama (des.), Chile 109/C2
Atakpamé, Togo 79/F5
Atami, Japan 57/F3
Atar, Mrta. 78/B1
Atarra, India 62/D2
Atascadero, Ca, US 92/B4
Atbara, Sudan 77/M4
Atbasar, Kaz. 46/G4
Atchison, Ks, US 93/J3
Atenco, Mex. 101/Q10
Ath, Belg. 30/C2
Athabasca (riv.), Ab, Can. 86/E3
Athabasca (lake), Ab,Sk, Can. 86/E3
Athens, Tx, US 93/J4
Athens, Ga, US 97/H3
Athens, Oh, US 97/H2
Athens, Al, US 97/G3
Athens, Tn, US 97/G3
Athens (cap.), Gre. 39/N9
Atherton, Eng, UK 23/F4
Ati, Chad 76/J5
Atibaia, Braz. 108/G8
Atkarsk, Rus. 45/H2
Atlanta (cap.), Ga, US 97/G3
Atlantic (ocean) 16/G3
Atlantic City, NJ, US 94/F4
Atlixco, Mex. 101/L8
Atoyac, Mex. 101/E5
Attendorn, Ger. 29/E6
Atteridgeville, SAfr. 80/Q12
Attu, Ak, US 85/A5
Atwater, Ca, US 92/B3
Atyraū, Kaz. 45/J3
Auburn, Ca, US 92/B3
Auburn, Al, US 97/G3
Auburn, In, US 94/C3
Auburn, Me, US 95/G2
Auburn, NY, US 94/E3
Auburn, Wa, US 99/C3
Auburn Hills, Mi, US 99/F6
Auch, Fr. 32/D5
Auckland, NZ 71/R10
Auderghem, Belg. 31/D2
Audincourt, Fr. 36/C3
Aue, Ger. 33/K1
Auer (Ora), It. 37/H5
Auerbach, Ger. 33/K1
Augsburg, Ger. 37/G1
Augusta, Ga, US 97/H3
Augusta (cap.), Me, US 95/G2
Augusta, It. 38/D4
Augustów, Pol. 27/M2
Auki, Sol. 68/F5
Aurangābād, India 62/C4
Aurangābād, India 62/D3
Aurich, Ger. 29/E2
Aurillac, Fr. 32/E4
Aurora, Co, US 93/F3
Aurora, Il, US 99/P16
Austin, Mn, US 91/K5
Austin (cap.), Tx, US 93/H5
Australia (cont.) 70/*
Australia (ctry.) 70/*
Austria (ctry.) 33/L3
Autlán de Navarro, Mex. 100/D5
Autun, Fr. 32/F3
Auxerre, Fr. 32/E3
Avaré, Braz. 108/B2
Aveiro, Port. 34/A2
Avellino, It. 40/B5
Avenal, Ca, US 92/B3
Aversa, It. 40/B5
Avesta, Swe. 42/C3
Avezzano, It. 38/C1
Avignon, Fr. 32/F5
Ávila de los Caballeros, Sp. 34/C2
Avilés, Sp. 34/C1
Avion, Fr. 30/B3
Avola, It. 38/D4
Awbārī, Libya 76/H2
Awka, Nga. 79/G5
Awsīm, Egypt 49/B4
Ayabe, Japan 56/D3
Ayacucho, Peru 106/D6
Ayagöz, Kaz. 46/J5
Ayamonte, Sp. 34/B4
Ayapel, Col. 103/H4
Aybastı, Turk. 44/F4
Aydın, Turk. 50/A2
Ayeyarwady (riv.), Myan. 63/G4
Aylesbury, Eng, UK 25/F3
Aylesford, Eng, UK 25/G4
Aytos, Bul. 41/H4
Ayvalık, Turk. 44/C5
Az Zabadānī, Syria 49/E3
Az Zaqāzīq, Egypt 49/B4
Az Zarqā', Jor. 49/E3
Az Zāwiyah, Libya 76/H1
Az Zubayr, Iraq 51/F4
Azamgarh, India 62/D2
A'zāz, Syria 49/E1
Azerbaijan (ctry.) 45/H4
Azogues, Ecu. 106/C4
Azores (dpcy.), Port. 35/R12
Azov, Rus. 44/F3
Azul, Arg. 109/E4
Azur, Côte d' (coast), Fr. 33/G5

B

Baar, Swi. 37/E3
Baarn, Neth. 28/C4
Babaeski, Turk. 41/H5
Babahoyo, Ecu. 106/C4
Bābil (Babylon) (ruin), Iraq 51/F3
Bābol, Iran 51/H2
Babruysk, Bela. 44/D1
Bac Giang, Viet. 65/D1
Bac Lieu, Viet. 65/D4
Bac Ninh, Viet. 65/D1
Bacabal, Braz. 107/K4
Bacarra, Phil. 61/J5
Bacău, Rom. 41/H2
Bačka Palanka, Yugo. 40/D3
Bačka Topola, Yugo. 40/D3
Backnang, Ger. 33/H2
Bacolod, Phil. 67/F1
Bad Driburg, Ger. 29/G5
Bad Dürkheim, Ger. 31/H5
Bad Harzburg, Ger. 29/H5
Bad Hersfeld, Ger. 33/H1
Bad Homburg vor der Höhe, Ger. 33/H1
Bad Honnef, Ger. 31/G2
Bad Kissingen, Ger. 26/F3
Bad Kreuznach, Ger. 31/G4
Bad Langensalza, Ger. 29/H6
Bad Mergentheim, Ger. 33/H2
Bad Munder am Deister, Ger. 29/G4
Bad Nauheim, Ger. 33/H1
Bad Neuenahr-Ahrweiler, Ger. 31/G2
Bad Neustadt an der Saale, Ger. 33/J1
Bad Oeynhausen, Ger. 29/F4
Bad Oldesloe, Ger. 26/F2
Bad Pyrmont, Ger. 29/G5
Bad Reichenhall, Ger. 40/A2
Bad Salzuflen, Ger. 29/F4
Bad Salzungen, Ger. 26/F3
Bad Schwartau, Ger. 26/F2
Bad Segeberg, Ger. 26/F2
Bad Tölz, Ger. 37/H2
Bad Waldsee, Ger. 37/F2
Bad Wildungen, Ger. 29/G6
Bad Zwischenahn, Ger. 29/F2
Badagara, India 62/C5
Badajoz, Sp. 34/B3
Badalona, Sp. 35/L7
Baden, Aus. 40/C1
Baden, Swi. 37/E3
Baden-Baden, Ger. 33/H2
Badīn, Pak. 62/A3
Badlands (plat.), SD, US 91/H5
Badlands National Park, SD, US 91/H5
Bādrāh, Pak. 53/J3
Badulla, SrL. 62/D6
Baena, Sp. 34/C4
Baesweiler, Ger. 31/F2
Baeza, Sp. 34/D4
Bafang, Camr. 79/H5
Baffin (isl.), Can. 87/H1
Bafia, Camr. 76/H7
Bafoussam, Camr. 79/H5
Bafra, Turk. 44/E4
Baganga, Phil. 67/G2
Bagé, Braz. 109/F3
Baghdad (cap.), Iraq 51/F3
Bagheria, It. 38/C3
Baghlān, Afg. 53/J1
Bagnols-sur-Cèze, Fr. 32/F4
Bago (Pegu), Myan. 65/B2
Baguio, Phil. 61/J5
Bahamas (ctry.), Bahm. 103/H1
Bahāwalpur, Pak. 62/B2
Bahçe, Turk. 50/D2
Bahía Blanca, Arg. 109/D4
Bahir Dar, Eth. 77/N5
Bahlah, Oman 53/G4
Bahraich, India 62/D2
Bahrain (ctry.), Bahr. 52/F3
Baia Mare, Rom. 41/F2
Baia Sprie, Rom. 41/F2
Băicoi, Rom. 41/G3
Baie-Comeau, Qu, Can. 95/G1
Baiersbronn, Ger. 37/E1
Baildon, Eng, UK 23/G4
Bailén, Sp. 34/D3
Băileşti, Rom. 41/F3
Bainbridge, Ga, US 97/G4
Baixa da Banheira, Port. 35/P10
Baixo Guandu, Braz. 108/D1
Baiyin, China 54/E4
Baja, Hun. 40/D2
Baja California (pen.), Mex. 92/D5
Bājah, Tun. 38/A4
Bakau, Gam. 78/A3
Baker, La, US 93/K5
Baker (mt.), Wa, US 90/C3
Baker City, Or, US 90/D4
Bakersfield, Ca, US 92/C4
Bakhchysaray, Ukr. 44/E3
Bakhmach, Ukr. 44/E2
Bākhtarān, Iran 51/F3
Baku (cap.), Azer. 45/J4
Balabac, Phil. 67/E2
Ba'labakk, Leb. 49/E2
Bālāghāt, India 62/D3
Balakhna, Rus. 43/J4
Balakovo, Rus. 45/H1
Bālāngīr, India 62/D3
Balaoan, Phil. 61/J5
Balashikha, Rus. 43/W9
Balashov, Rus. 45/G2
Balasore (Baleshwar), India 62/E3
Balassagyarmat, Hun. 40/D1
Balcarce, Arg. 109/E4
Balearic (isls.), Sp. 35/G3
Balen, Belg. 28/C6
Baley, Rus. 54/H1
Balıkesir, Turk. 44/C5
Balikpapan, Indo. 67/E4
Balimbing, Phil. 67/E2
Balingen, Ger. 37/E1
Balkan (mts.), Bul. 41/F4
Balkhash (lake), Kaz. 46/H5
Ballarat, Austl. 73/B3
Ballarpur, India 62/C4
Ballina, Austl. 73/E1
Ballymena, NI, UK 22/B2
Balmazújváros, Hun. 40/E2
Balneário Camboriú, Braz. 108/B3
Bālotra, India 62/B2
Balqash, Kaz. 46/H5
Balrāmpur, India 62/D2
Balş, Rom. 41/G3
Balsas, Braz. 107/J5
Bălţi, Mol. 41/H2
Baltic (sea), Eur. 18/E3
Balţīm, Egypt 49/B4
Baltimore, Md, US 97/J2
Baltiysk, Rus. 27/K1
Bālurghāt, India 62/E2
Balykshi, Kaz. 45/J3
Bam, Iran 51/J4
Bamako (cap.), Mali 78/D3
Bambari, CAfr. 77/K6
Bamberg, Ger. 33/J2
Bambuí, Braz. 108/C2
Bamenda, Camr. 79/H5
Banbury, Eng, UK 25/E2
Bāndā, India 62/D2
Banda Aceh, Indo. 66/A2
Bandar Seri Begawan (cap.), Bru. 66/D3
Bandar-e 'Abbās, Iran 51/J5
Bandar-e Anzalī, Iran 51/G2
Bandar-e Būshehr, Iran 51/G4
Bandar-e Māhshahr, Iran 51/G4
Bandeirantes, Braz. 108/B2
Bandırma, Turk. 41/H5
Bandundu, D.R. Congo 82/C1
Bandung, Indo. 66/C5
Banes, Cuba 103/H1
Banff National Park, Can. 90/E3
Banfora, Burk. 78/D4
Bangalore, India 62/C5
Bangangté, Camr. 79/H5
Bangar, Phil. 61/J5
Bangassou, CAfr. 77/K7
Bangkok (cap.), Thai. 65/C3
Bangkok, Bight of (bay), Thai. 63/H5
Bangladesh (ctry.) 62/E3
Bangor, Me, US 95/G2
Bangor, NI, UK 22/C2
Bangued, Phil. 61/J5
Bangui (cap.), CAfr. 77/J7
Banhā, Egypt 49/B4
Banī Mazār, Egypt 50/B4
Banikoara, Ben. 79/F4
Bāniyās, Syria 49/D2
Banja Luka, Bosn. 40/C3
Banjarmasin, Indo. 66/D4
Banjul (cap.), Gam. 78/A3
Bānkurā, India 62/E3
Bannu, Pak. 53/K2
Banská Bystrica, Slvk. 27/K4
Banstead, Eng, UK 25/F4
Bānswāra, India 62/B3
Banyoles, Sp. 35/G1
Banyuwangi, Indo. 66/D5
Banzart (Bizerte), Tun. 38/A4
Baoding, China 59/G7
Baoji, China 54/F5
Baoshan, China 60/C3
Baotou, China 59/B2
Bāqa el Gharbiyya, Isr. 49/G7
Ba'qūbah, Iraq 51/F3
Bar, Yugo. 40/D4
Bar-le-Duc, Fr. 31/E6
Barabai, Indo. 66/E4
Barabinsk, Rus. 46/H4
Baraboo, Wi, US 91/L5
Baracaldo, Sp. 34/D1
Baracoa, Cuba 103/H1
Baramula, India 53/K2
Bāran, India 62/C2
Baranavichy, Bela. 44/C1
Baranoa, Col. 103/H4
Barão de Cocais, Braz. 108/D1
Barbacena, Braz. 108/D2
Barbados (ctry.), Bar. 104/G4
Barbastro, Sp. 35/F1
Barbate de Franco, Sp. 34/C4
Barberà del Vallès, Sp. 35/L6
Barberton, Oh, US 94/D3
Barbil, India 62/E3
Barcellona Pozzo di Gotto, It. 38/D3
Barcelona, Ven. 106/F1
Barcelona, Sp. 35/L7
Bardejov, Slvk. 27/L4
Bārdoli, India 53/K4
Bareilly, India 62/C2
Barendrecht, Neth. 28/B5
Barentu, Erit. 52/C5
Bargarh, India 62/D3
Bari, It. 40/C5
Barika, Alg. 76/G1
Barillas, Guat. 102/D3
Barinas, Ven. 106/D2
Baripāda, India 62/E3
Bariri, Braz. 108/B2
Barisāl, Bang. 62/F3
Barletta, It. 40/C5
Bārmer, India 62/B2
Barnāla, India 53/L2
Barnaul, Rus. 46/J4
Barneveld, Neth. 28/C4
Barnsley, Eng, UK 23/G4
Barnstaple, Eng, UK 24/B4
Barpeta, India 62/F2
Barquisimeto, Ven. 106/E1
Barra, Braz. 107/K6
Barra Bonita, Braz. 108/B2
Barra Del Colorado, CR 103/F4
Barra do Corda, Braz. 107/J5
Barra do Garças, Braz. 107/H7
Barra do Piraí, Braz. 108/K7
Barra Mansa, Braz. 108/J7
Barranca, Peru 106/C6
Barrancabermeja, Col. 106/D2
Barranquilla, Col. 103/H4
Barreiras, Braz. 107/K6
Barretos, Braz. 108/B2
Barrie, On, Can. 94/E2
Barrington, Il, US 99/P15
Barroso, Braz. 108/D2
Barrow (pt.), Ak, US 85/G1
Barrow, Ak, US 85/G1
Barrow-in-Furness, Eng, UK 23/E3
Barry, Wal, UK 24/C4
Bārshi, India 62/C4
Barsinghausen, Ger. 29/G4
Barstow, Ca, US 92/C4
Bartica, Guy. 106/G2
Bartın, Turk. 41/L5
Bartlesville, Ok, US 93/J3
Bartlett, Il, US 99/P16
Bartolomé Masó, Cuba 103/G1
Bartoszyce, Pol. 27/L1
Bartow, Fl, US 97/H5
Barus, Indo. 66/A3
Baruun-Urt, Mong. 54/G2
Barwāha, India 62/C3
Barwāni, India 62/B3
Barysaw, Bela. 42/F5
Barysh, Rus. 45/H1
Basauri, Sp. 34/D1
Basel, Swi. 36/D2
Basildon, Eng, UK 25/G3
Basingstoke, Eng, UK 25/E4
Başkale, Turk. 51/F2
Bāsoda, India 62/C3
Bassano del Grappa, It. 33/J4
Bassari, Togo 79/F4
Basse-Terre, Fr. 104/F4
Bassein (Vasai), India 53/K5
Basseterre (cap.), StK. 104/F3
Bastī, India 62/D2
Bastia, Fr. 38/A1
Bastos, Braz. 108/B2
Basyūn, Egypt 49/B4
Bat Yam, Isr. 49/F7
Bata, EqG. 76/G7
Batac, Phil. 61/J5
Batāla, India 53/L2
Batangas, Phil. 68/B3
Batatais, Braz. 108/C2
Batavia, NY, US 94/E3
Batavia, Il, US 99/P16
Bataysk, Rus. 44/F3
Bătdambang, Camb. 65/C3
Bath, Me, US 95/G3
Bath, Eng, UK 24/D4
Bathurst, Austl. 73/D2
Batley, Eng, UK 23/G4
Batman, Turk. 50/E2
Batna, Alg. 76/G1
Baton Rouge (cap.), La, US 93/K5
Batouri, Camr. 76/H7
Batticaloa, SrL. 62/D6
Battipaglia, It. 40/B5
Battle Creek, Mi, US 94/C3
Batu Pahat, Malay. 66/B3
Bat'umi, Geo. 45/G4
Baturaja, Indo. 66/B4
Baturité, Braz. 107/L4
Batys Qazaqstan, Kaz. 46/E5
Baunatal, Ger. 29/G6
Baurú, Braz. 108/B2
Bautzen, Ger. 27/H3
Bawku, Gha. 79/E4
Bay City, Tx, US 93/J5
Bayamo, Cuba 103/G1
Bayamón, PR 104/E3
Bayanhongor, Mong. 54/E2
Bayawan, Phil. 67/F2
Bayburt, Turk. 44/G4
Baydhabo (Baidoa), Som. 77/P7
Bayeux, Braz. 107/M5
Bayeux, Fr. 32/C2
Baykal (lake), Rus. 46/L4
Bayombong, Phil. 61/J5
Bayonet Point, Fl, US 97/H4
Bayonne, Fr. 34/E1
Bayramaly, Trkm. 53/H1
Bayreuth, Ger. 33/J2
Baytown, Tx, US 93/J5
Baza, Sp. 34/D4
Beaconsfield, Qu, Can. 95/N7
Bealanana, Madg. 81/J6

113
Beatr – Bruss

Beatrice, Ne, US 93/H2
Beau Bassin, Mrts. 81/T15
Beaufort, SC, US 97/H3
Beaufort West, SAfr. 80/C4
Beaume, Fr. 32/F3
Beaumont, Tx, US 93/J5
Beauvais, Fr. 30/B5
Beāwar, India 62/B2
Bebedouro, Braz. 108/B2
Bebington, Eng, UK 23/E5
Bebra, Ger. 29/G7
Bečej, Yugo. 40/E3
Béchar, Alg. 76/E1
Beckingen, Ger. 31/F5
Beckley, WV, US 97/H2
Beckum, Ger. 29/F5
Bedburg, Ger. 28/D6
Bedford, In, US 97/G2
Bedford, Eng, UK 25/F2
Bedlington, Eng, UK 23/G1
Bedworth, Eng, UK 25/E2
Beek, Neth. 31/E2
Beenleigh, Austl. 72/D4
Be'er Sheva', Isr. 49/D4
Beerzel, Belg. 28/B6
Beeville, Tx, US 96/D4
Begusarai, India 62/E2
Behbahān, Iran 51/G4
Behshahr, Iran 51/H2
Bei'an, China 55/K2
Beihai, China 65/E1
Beijing (cap.), China 59/H7
Beipiao, China 59/E2
Beira, Moz. 82/F4
Beirut (cap.), Leb. 49/D3
Beja, Port. 34/B3
Bejaïa, Alg. 76/G1
Béjar, Sp. 34/C2
Bekasi, Indo. 66/C5
Békés, Hun. 40/E2
Békéscsaba, Hun. 40/E2
Bekily, Madg. 81/H9
Belā, India 62/D2
Bela Crkva, Yugo. 40/E3
Bela Vista, Braz. 107/G8
Belarus (ctry.) 18/F3
Belas, Port. 35/P10
Bełchatów, Pol. 27/K3
Belebey, Rus. 43/M5
Belém, Braz. 107/J4
Belen, Turk. 49/E1
Belev, Rus. 44/F1
Belfast (cap.), NI, UK 22/C2
Belfort, Fr. 36/C2
Belgaum, India 62/B4
Belgium (ctry.) 26/C3
Belgorod, Rus. 44/F2
Belgrade (cap.), Yugo. 40/E4
Beli Manastir, Cro. 40/D3
Belize (ctry.), Belz. 102/D2
Belize City, Belz. 102/D2
Bell Ville, Arg. 109/D3
Bella Vista, Arg. 109/E2
Bellary, India 62/C4
Belle Glade, Fl, US 97/H5
Bellefontaine, Oh, US 94/D3
Belleville, On, Can. 94/E2
Bellevue, Wa, US 99/C2
Bellingham, Wa, US 90/C3
Bellinzona, Swi. 37/F5
Bello, Col. 106/C2
Belluno, It. 33/K3
Bellville, SAfr. 80/L10
Belmont, Ca, US 99/K11
Belmopan (cap.), Belz. 102/D2
Belo Horizonte, Braz. 108/D1
Belo Jardim, Braz. 107/L5
Belo-Tsiribihina, Madg. 81/H7
Beloeil, Qu, Can. 95/P6
Belogorsk, Rus. 55/K1
Beloha, Madg. 81/H9
Beloit, Wi, US 91/L5
Belomorsk, Rus. 42/G2
Belorechensk, Rus. 44/F3
Beloretsk, Rus. 43/N5
Belovo, Rus. 46/J4
Belper, Eng, UK 23/G5
Belton, Tx, US 93/H5
Belvidere, Il, US 91/L5
Bembéréké, Ben. 79/F4
Bemetāra, India 62/D3
Bemmel, Neth. 28/C5
Ben Tre, Viet. 65/D4
Benalmádena, Sp. 34/C4
Benavente, Sp. 34/C1
Bend, Or, US 90/C4
Bendigo, Austl. 73/C3
Bene Beraq, Isr. 49/F7
Benešov, Czh. 33/L2
Benevento, It. 40/B5
Bengal, Bay of (gulf), Asia 62/E4
Benghāzī, Libya 76/K1
Bengkayang, Indo. 66/C3
Bengkulu, Indo. 66/B4
Benguela, Ang. 82/B3
Beni, D.R. Congo 77/L7
Beni Mellal, Mor. 76/D1
Benicarló, Sp. 35/F2
Benicia, Ca, US 99/K10
Benidorm, Sp. 35/E3
Benin (ctry.) 79/F4
Benin City, Nga. 79/G5
Benin, Bight of (bay), Afr. 76/F6
Bennettsville, SC, US 97/J3
Bennington, Vt, US 94/F3
Bensenville, Il, US 99/Q16
Bensheim, Ger. 33/H2
Bentley, Eng, UK 23/G4
Bento Gonçalves, Braz. 108/B4
Benton, Ar, US 93/J4
Benton Harbor, Mi, US 94/C3
Bentong, Malay. 66/B3
Benxi, China 58/B2
Beppu, Japan 56/B4
Beraketa, Madg. 81/H8
Berat, Alb. 40/D5
Berbera, Som. 77/Q5
Berbérati, CAfr. 76/J7
Berchem, Belg. 28/B6
Berck, Fr. 25/H6
Berdsk, Rus. 46/J4
Berdyans'k, Ukr. 44/F3
Berdychiv, Ukr. 44/D2
Berea, Ky, US 97/G2
Berehove, Ukr. 40/F1
Berekum, Gha. 79/E5
Berettyóújfalu, Hun. 40/E2
Berezniki, Rus. 43/N4
Bergama, Turk. 44/C5
Bergamo, It. 33/H4
Bergara, Sp. 34/D1
Bergen, Nor. 20/C3
Bergen, Ger. 27/G1
Bergen op Zoom, Neth. 28/B5
Bergerac, Fr. 32/D4
Bergheim, Ger. 31/F2
Bergisch Gladbach, Ger. 31/G2
Bergkamen, Ger. 29/E5
Bergneustadt, Ger. 29/E6
Bergum, Neth. 28/D2
Berhampore, India 62/E3
Berhampur, India 62/D4
Bering (sea), Asia, NAm. 47/U4
Bering (str.), Rus., US 85/E3
Beringen, Belg. 28/C6
Berkel, Neth. 28/B5
Berkeley, Ca, US 99/K11
Berkhamsted, Eng, UK 25/F3
Berkley, Mi, US 99/F6
Berkovitsa, Bul. 41/F4
Berleburg, Ger. 29/F6
Berlin, NH, US 95/G2
Berlin (cap.), Ger. 27/G2
Bermejo, Bol. 109/D1
Bermeo, Sp. 34/D1
Bern (cap.), Swi. 36/D4
Bernal, Peru 106/B5
Bernburg, Ger. 26/F3
Beroun, Czh. 33/L2
Berovo, FYROM 40/F5
Bertoua, Camr. 76/H7
Berwick, Pa, US 94/E3
Berwyn, Il, US 99/Q16
Besançon, Fr. 36/C3
Beslan, Rus. 45/H4
Bessacarr, Eng, UK 23/G5
Bessemer, Al, US 97/G3
Best, Neth. 28/C5
Bet She'an, Isr. 49/D3
Bet Shemesh, Isr. 49/F8
Bethesda, Md, US 97/J2
Bethlehem, Pa, US 94/F3
Béthune, Fr. 30/B2
Betim, Braz. 108/C1
Betioky, Madg. 81/H8
Bettiah, India 62/D2
Betūl, India 62/C3
Beuningen, Neth. 28/C5
Beveren, Belg. 28/B6
Beverley, Eng, UK 23/H4
Beverly Hills, Mi, US 99/F6
Beverungen, Ger. 29/G5
Beverwijk, Neth. 28/B4
Bexbach, Ger. 31/G5
Bexhill, Eng, UK 25/G5
Beypazarı, Turk. 41/K5
Beyşehir, Turk. 50/B2
Bezhetsk, Rus. 42/H4
Béziers, Fr. 32/E5
Bhabua, India 62/D2
Bhadrak, India 62/E3
Bhadreswar, India 62/A3
Bhāgalpur, India 62/E2
Bhakkar, Pak. 53/K2
Bhaktapur, Nepal 62/E2
Bhānwad, India 62/A3
Bharātpur, India 62/C2
Bharuch, India 62/B3
Bhātāpāra, India 62/D3
Bhatinda, India 53/K2
Bhatkal, India 62/B5
Bhātpāra, India 62/E3
Bhavāni, India 62/C5
Bhavnagar, India 62/B3
Bhawāni Mandi, India 62/C3
Bhawānipatna, India 62/D4
Bhilai, India 62/D3
Bhīlwāra, India 62/B2
Bhīmavaram, India 62/D4
Bhimunipatnam, India 62/D4
Bhind, India 62/C2
Bhiwandi, India 62/B4
Bhopāl, India 62/C3
Bhor, India 62/B4
Bhuban, India 62/E3
Bhubaneswar, India 62/E3
Bhusawal, India 62/C3
Bhutan (ctry.) 62/E2
Biafra, Bight of (bay), Camr. 76/G7
Biała Podlaska, Pol. 27/M2
Białogard, Pol. 27/J2
Białystok, Pol. 27/M2
Biancavilla, It. 38/D4
Biarritz, Fr. 34/E1
Bibā, Egypt 50/B4
Biberach an der Riss, Ger. 37/F1
Bicester, Eng, UK 25/E3
Bida, Nga. 79/G4
Bīdar, India 62/C4
Biddeford, Me, US 95/G3
Biddulph, Eng, UK 23/F5
Biel, Swi. 36/D3
Bielawa, Pol. 27/J3
Bielefeld, Ger. 29/F4
Biella, It. 33/H4
Bielsk Podlaski, Pol. 27/M2
Bielsko-Biała, Pol. 27/K4
Bien Hoa, Viet. 65/D4
Big Rapids, Mi, US 94/C3
Big Spring, Tx, US 93/G4
Biga, Turk. 41/H5
Bignona, Sen. 78/A3
Biguaçu, Braz. 108/B3
Bihać, Bosn. 40/B3
Bīhar, India 62/E2
Bijeljina, Bosn. 40/D3
Bijelo Polje, Yugo. 40/D4
Bijnor, India 62/C2
Bīkaner, India 62/B2
Bikin, Rus. 55/L2
Bila Tserkva, Ukr. 44/D2
Bilāra, India 62/B2
Bilāspur, India 62/D3
Bilbao, Sp. 34/D1
Bilbays, Egypt 49/B4
Bilecik, Turk. 44/D4
Biłgoraj, Pol. 27/M3
Bilhorod-Dnistrovs'kyy, Ukr. 41/K2
Billingham, Eng, UK 23/G2
Billings, Mt, US 90/F4
Biloxi, Ms, US 97/F4
Bilqas Qism Awwal, Egypt 49/B4
Bilsi, India 62/C2
Bilzen, Belg. 31/E2
Bima, Indo. 67/E5
Bimbo, CAfr. 77/J7
Bin 'Arūs, Tun. 38/B4
Bina-Etāwa, India 62/C3
Binche, Belg. 31/D3
Bindki, India 62/D2
Bindura, Zim. 82/F4
Bingen, Ger. 31/G4
Bingerville, C.d'Iv. 78/E5
Binghamton, NY, US 94/F3
Bingley, Eng, UK 23/G4
Bingöl, Turk. 50/E2
Binh Son, Viet. 65/E3
Binjai, Indo. 66/A3
Biograd, Cro. 40/B4
Bīr, India 53/L5
Birāk, Libya 76/H2
Birao, CAfr. 77/K5
Birātnagar, Nepal 62/E2
Birecik, Turk. 50/D2
Birigui, Braz. 108/B2
Biritiba-Mirim, Braz. 108/G8
Bīrjand, Iran 53/G2
Birkenhead, Eng, UK 23/E5
Bîrlad, Rom. 41/H2
Birmingham, Al, US 97/G3
Birmingham, Eng, UK 25/E2
Birmingham, Mi, US 99/F6
Birni Nkonni, Niger 79/G3
Birobijan, Rus. 55/L2
Birsk, Rus. 43/M5
Biscay (bay), Fr.,Sp. 34/C1
Bisceglie, It. 40/C5
Bischheim, Fr. 31/G6
Bishkek (cap.), Kyr. 46/H5
Bishop Auckland, Eng, UK 23/G2
Bishop's Stortford, Eng, UK 25/G3
Biskra, Alg. 76/G1
Bislig, Phil. 67/G2
Bismarck (arch.), PNG 68/D5
Bismarck (cap.), ND, US 91/H4
Bismil, Turk. 50/E2
Bissau (cap.), GBis. 78/B4
Bistrița, Rom. 41/G2
Bitlis, Turk. 50/E2
Bitola, FYROM 40/E5
Bitonto, It. 40/C5
Bitung, Indo. 67/G3
Bixby, Ok, US 96/E3
Biyalā, Egypt 49/B4
Biysk, Rus. 46/J4
Bjelovar, Cro. 40/C3
Black (sea), Eur.,Asia 41/J4
Blackburn, Eng, UK 23/F4
Blackfoot, Id, US 90/E5
Blackpool, Eng, UK 23/E4
Blagnac, Fr. 32/D5
Blagoevgrad, Bul. 41/F4
Blagoveshchensk, Rus. 55/K1
Blainville, Qu, Can. 95/N6
Blaj, Rom. 41/F2
Blanc (peak), Fr. 36/C6
Blanca, Costa (coast), Sp. 35/E4
Blanes, Sp. 35/G2
Blankenberge, Belg. 30/C1
Blansko, Czh. 33/M2
Blantyre, Malw. 82/G4
Blenheim, NZ 71/R11
Blida, Alg. 76/F1
Blieskastel, Ger. 31/G5
Bloemendaal, Neth. 28/B4
Bloemfontein, SAfr. 80/D3
Blois, Fr. 32/D3
Blomberg, Ger. 29/G5
Bloomingdale, Il, US 99/P16
Bloomington, Il, US 91/L5
Bloomington, In, US 97/G2
Bloomsburg, Pa, US 94/E3
Blora, Indo. 66/D5
Blue Island, Il, US 99/Q16
Blue Mountains, Austl. 73/D2
Blue Ridge (mts.), US 97/H3
Bluefield, WV, US 97/H2
Bluefields, Nic. 103/F4
Bluffton, In, US 94/C3
Blumenau, Braz. 108/B3
Blyth, Eng, UK 23/G1
Blytheville, Ar, US 93/K4
Bo, SLeo. 78/C5
Boa Esperança, Braz. 108/C2
Boa Vista, Braz. 106/F3
Boaco, Nic. 102/E3
Boadilla del Monte, Sp. 35/N9
Bobbili, India 62/D4
Bobigny, Fr. 30/B6
Bobingen, Ger. 37/G1
Böblingen, Ger. 33/H2
Bobo Dioulasso, Burk. 78/D4
Bobrov, Rus. 44/G2
Boca Raton, Fl, US 97/H5
Bocaiúva, Braz. 107/K7
Bocas del Toro, Pan. 103/F4
Bochnia, Pol. 27/L4
Bocholt, Ger. 28/D5
Bochum, Ger. 29/E6
Bodaybo, Rus. 47/M4
Bodegraven, Neth. 28/B4
Boden, Swe. 42/D2
Bodensee (Constance) (lake), Swi 37/F2
Bodhan, India 62/C4
Bodināyakkanūr, India 62/C5
Bodø, Nor. 20/E2
Bodrum, Turk. 50/A2
Bogalusa, La, US 97/F4
Bogandé, Burk. 79/E3
Bogatynia, Pol. 27/H3
Boğazlıyan, Turk. 44/E5
Bognor Regis, Eng, UK 25/F5
Bogor, Indo. 66/C5
Bogotá (cap.), Col. 106/D3
Bohicon, Ben. 79/F5
Boiro, Sp. 34/A1
Boisbriand, Qu, Can. 95/N6
Boise (cap.), Id, US 90/D5
Bojnūrd, Iran 51/J2
Boksburg, SAfr. 80/Q13
Bol, Chad 76/H5
Bolesławiec, Pol. 27/H3
Bolgatanga, Gha. 79/E4
Bolinao, Phil. 61/H5
Bolingbrook, Il, US 99/P16
Bolívar, Arg. 109/D4
Bolívar (peak), Ven. 106/D2
Bolivia (ctry.), Bol. 106/F7
Bologna, It. 33/J4
Bologoye, Rus. 42/G4
Bolton, Eng, UK 23/F4
Bolu, Turk. 44/D4
Bolvadin, Turk. 50/B2
Bolzano, It. 37/H5
Bom Despacho, Braz. 108/C1
Bom Jesus da Lapa, Braz. 107/K6
Bom Jesus do Itabapoana, Braz. 108/D2
Boma, D.R. Congo 82/B2
Bomaderry, Austl. 73/D2
Bon (cape), Tun. 38/B4
Bondoukou, C.d'Iv. 78/E4
Bondowoso, Indo. 66/D5
Bönen, Ger. 29/E5
Bongabong, Phil. 67/F1
Bongao, Phil. 67/E3
Bongor, Chad 76/J5
Bonita Springs, Fl, US 97/H5
Bonn, Ger. 31/G2
Bonthain, Indo. 67/E5
Bontoc, Phil. 61/J5
Bonyhád, Hun. 40/D2
Boone, Ia, US 91/K5
Boosaaso (Bender Cassim), Som. 77/Q5
Bootle, Eng, UK 23/E5
Boppard, Ger. 31/G3
Bor, Rus. 43/K4
Bor, Turk. 50/C2
Bor, Yugo. 40/F3
Borås, Swe. 20/E4
Borāzjān, Iran 51/G4
Borča, Yugo. 40/E3
Bordeaux, Fr. 32/C4
Borehamwood, Eng, UK 25/F3
Borger, Tx, US 93/G4
Borgerhout, Belg. 28/B6
Borghorst, Ger. 29/E4
Borisoglebsk, Rus. 45/G2
Borken, Ger. 28/D5
Borlänge, Swe. 20/E3
Borna, Ger. 26/G3
Borne, Neth. 28/D4
Bornem, Belg. 28/B6
Borneo (isl.), Asia 67/E3
Bornheim, Ger. 31/G2
Borovichi, Rus. 42/G4
Borşa, Rom. 41/F2
Borssele, Neth. 28/A6
Borūjerd, Iran 51/G3
Boryslav, Ukr. 27/M4
Borzya, Rus. 54/H1
Bosanska Dubica, Bosn. 40/C3
Bosanska Gradiška, Bosn. 40/C3
Bosanska Krupa, Bosn. 40/C3
Bosanski Brod, Bosn. 40/D3
Bosanski Petrovac, Bosn. 40/C3
Bosanski Šamac, Bosn. 40/D3
Bose, China 61/E4
Boskoop, Neth. 28/B4
Bosnia and Herzegovina (ctry.) 40/C3
Bosporus (str.), Turk. 44/D4
Bosporus (riv.), Turk. 51/N6
Bossangoa, CAfr. 76/J6
Bossier City, La, US 93/J4
Boston, Eng, UK 23/H6
Boston (cap.), Ma, US 95/G3
Botād, India 53/K4
Botevgrad, Bul. 41/F4
Bothell, Wa, US 99/C2
Bothnia (gulf), Swe., Fin 20/F3
Botoşani, Rom. 41/H2
Botou, China 59/D3
Botswana (ctry.) 82/D5
Bottrop, Ger. 28/D5
Botucatu, Braz. 108/B2
Bouaflé, C.d'Iv. 78/D5
Bouaké, C.d'Iv. 78/D5
Bouar, CAfr. 76/J6
Boucherville, Qu, Can. 95/P6
Bouguenais, Fr. 32/C3
Bouira, Alg. 76/F1
Boukoumbé, Ben. 79/F4
Boulder, Co, US 93/F2
Boulder City, Nv, US 92/D4
Boulogne-Billancourt, Fr. 30/B6
Boulogne-sur-Mer, Fr. 25/H5
Bourg-en-Bresse, Fr. 36/B5
Bourg-lès-Valence, Fr. 32/F4
Bourges, Fr. 32/E3
Bourgoin-Jallieu, Fr. 32/F4
Bournemouth, Eng, UK 25/E5
Bowling Green, Ky, US 97/G2
Bowling Green, Oh, US 94/D3
Boxmeer, Neth. 28/C5
Boxtel, Neth. 28/C5
Boyabat, Turk. 44/E4
Boynton Beach, Fl, US 97/H5
Bozoum, CAfr. 76/J6
Bozova, Turk. 50/D2
Bozüyük, Turk. 44/D5
Bozyazı, Turk. 49/C1
Bra, It. 33/G4
Bracknell, Eng, UK 25/F4
Brad, Rom. 41/F2
Bradenton, Fl, US 97/H5
Bradford, Pa, US 94/E3
Bradford, Eng, UK 23/G4
Braga, Port. 34/A2
Bragado, Arg. 109/D4
Bragança, Braz. 107/J4
Bragança, Port. 34/B2
Bragança Paulista, Braz. 108/G7
Brahmaputra (riv.), India 63/F2
Brăila, Rom. 41/H3
Braine-l'Alleud, Belg. 31/D2
Braine-le-Comte, Belg. 31/D2
Braintree, Eng, UK 25/G3
Brake, Ger. 29/F2
Brakel, Ger. 29/G5
Brampton, On, Can. 95/T8
Bramsche, Ger. 29/F4
Brandenburg, Ger. 26/G2
Brandon, Fl, US 97/H5
Brandon, Ms, US 97/F3
Braniewo, Pol. 27/K1
Brantford, On, Can. 95/S9
Branzoll (Bronzolo), It. 37/H4
Brasília (cap.), Braz. 107/J7
Braşov, Rom. 41/G3
Brasschaat, Belg. 28/B6
Bratislava (cap.), Slvk. 40/C1
Bratsk, Rus. 47/L4
Brattleboro, Vt, US 95/F3
Braulio Carrillo, CR 103/F4
Braunau am Inn, Aus. 33/K2
Braunschweig, Ger. 29/H4
Brava, Costa (coast), Sp. 35/G2
Brawley, Ca, US 92/D4
Bray, Ire. 22/B5
Brazil (ctry.), Braz. 105/D3
Brazzaville (cap.), Congo 82/C1
Brčko, Bosn. 40/D3
Breaza, Rom. 41/G3
Brecht, Belg. 28/B6
Břeclav, Czh. 33/M2
Breda, Neth. 28/B5
Bregenz, Aus. 37/F3
Bremen, Ger. 29/F2
Bremerhaven, Ger. 29/F1
Bremerton, Wa, US 99/B2
Bremervörde, Ger. 29/G2
Brenham, Tx, US 93/H5
Brentwood, Eng, UK 25/G3
Brescia, It. 33/J4
Bressuire, Fr. 32/C3
Brest, Bela. 27/M2
Brest, Fr. 32/A2
Breves, Braz. 107/H4
Brewer, Me, US 95/G2
Brežice, Slov. 40/B3
Bria, CAfr. 77/K6
Bridgend, Wal, UK 24/C3
Bridgeport, Ct, US 94/F3
Bridgetown (cap.), Bar. 104/G4
Bridgwater, Eng, UK 24/D4
Bridlington, Eng, UK 23/H3
Brieg Brzeg, Pol. 27/J3
Brielle, Neth. 28/B5
Brigham City, Ut, US 90/E5
Brighouse, Eng, UK 23/G4
Brighton, Co, US 93/F3
Brighton, Eng, UK 25/F5
Brikama, Gam. 78/A3
Brilon, Ger. 29/F6
Brindisi, It. 40/C5
Brisbane, Austl. 72/F6
Bristol, Tn, US 97/H2
Bristol, Eng, UK 24/D4
Bristol (chan.), Eng,Wal, UK 24/B4
British Columbia (prov.), Can. 86/D3
Brive-la-Gaillarde, Fr. 32/D4
Brno, Czh. 33/M2
Broadstairs, Eng, UK 25/H4
Brockton, Ma, US 95/G3
Brodnica, Pol. 27/K2
Broken Arrow, Ok, US 93/J3
Broken Hill, Austl. 73/B1
Bromsgrove, Eng, UK 24/D2
Bron, Fr. 36/A6
Bronte, It. 38/D4
Brooke's Point, Phil. 67/E2
Brookfield, Il, US 99/Q16
Brookfield, Wi, US 99/P13
Brookhaven, Ms, US 93/K5
Brooks (range), US 85/F2
Brossard, Qu, Can. 95/P7
Brownfield, Tx, US 93/G4
Brownhills, Eng, UK 25/E1
Brownsville, Tn, US 97/F3
Brownsville, Tx, US 96/D5
Bruay-la-Buissière, Fr. 30/B3
Bruchsal, Ger. 33/H2
Brugge, Belg. 30/C1
Brühl, Ger. 31/F2
Brumado, Braz. 107/K6
Brummen, Neth. 28/D4
Brumunddal, Nor. 20/D3
Brunei (ctry.) 66/D2
Brunssum, Neth. 31/E2
Brunswick, Oh, US 94/D3
Brunswick, Me, US 95/G3
Brunswick, Ga, US 97/H4
Brusque, Braz. 108/B3
Brussels (cap.), Belg. 31/D2

114

Bryan – Chicl

Bryan, Tx, US 93/H5
Bryansk, Rus. 44/E1
Bryce Canyon National Park, Ut, US 92/D3
Brynmawr, Wal, UK 24/C3
Brzesko, Pol. 27/L4
Buala, Sol. 68/E5
Bucak, Turk. 50/B2
Bucaramanga, Col. 106/D2
Buchanan, Libr. 78/C5
Bucharest (cap.), Rom. 41/H4
Buchholz in der Nordheide, Ger. 29/G2
Bückeburg, Ger. 29/G4
Buckley, Wal, UK 23/E5
Bucyrus, Oh, US 94/D3
Budaörs, Hun. 40/D2
Budapest (cap.), Hun. 40/D2
Budaun, India 62/C2
Büdingen, Ger. 33/H1
Buea, Camr. 76/G7
Buenaventura, Col. 106/C3
Buenavista, Mex. 101/Q9
Buenos Aires (cap.), Arg. 109/E3
Buffalo, NY, US 95/V10
Buffalo Grove, Il, US 99/Q15
Buftea, Rom. 41/G3
Buga, Col. 106/C3
Bugaba, Pan. 103/F4
Bugojno, Bosn. 40/C3
Bugul'ma, Rus. 43/M5
Buguruslan, Rus. 45/K1
Bühl, Ger. 37/E2
Buhuşi, Rom. 41/H2
Bujumbura (cap.), Buru. 82/E1
Bukavu, D.R. Congo 82/E1
Bukhoro, Uzb. 46/G6
Bukittinggi, Indo. 66/B4
Bukoba, Tanz. 82/F1
Bulan, Phil. 67/F1
Bulancak, Turk. 44/F4
Bulandshahr, India 62/C2
Bulawayo, Zim. 82/E5
Bulgaria (ctry.) 41/G4
Bullhead City, Az, US 92/D4
Bulukumba, Indo. 67/F5
Bumba, D.R. Congo 77/K7
Bundaberg, Austl. 72/D4
Bünde, Ger. 29/F4
Būndi, India 62/C2
Bunia, D.R. Congo 77/M7
Bunschoten, Neth. 28/C4
Bunya Park, Austl. 72/E6
Buon Me Thuot, Viet. 65/E3
Būr Sa'īd (Port Said), Egypt 49/C4
Būr Sūdān, Sudan 52/C5
Buraydah, SAr. 52/D3
Burbank, Ca, US 92/C4
Burbank, Il, US 99/Q16
Burdur, Turk. 50/B2
Burdwān, India 62/E3
Büren, Ger. 29/F5
Būrewāla, Pak. 53/K2
Burg, Ger. 26/F2
Burgdorf, Ger. 29/H4
Burgess Hill, Eng, UK 25/F5
Burghausen, Ger. 40/A1
Burgos, Sp. 34/D1
Burgstall (Postal), It. 37/H4
Burgsteinfurt, Ger. 29/E4
Burgwedel, Ger. 29/G3
Burhaniye, Turk. 44/C5
Burhānpur, India 62/C3
Burien, Wa, US 99/C3
Buriram, Thai. 65/C3
Burjasot, Sp. 35/E3
Burkburnett, Tx, US 93/H4
Burkina Faso (ctry.) 79/E3
Burlingame, Ca, US 99/K11
Burlington, Ia, US 91/L5
Burlington, NC, US 97/J2
Burlington, On, Can. 95/T9
Burnham-on-Sea, Eng, UK 24/D4
Burnie-Somerset, Austl. 73/C4
Burnley, Eng, UK 23/F4
Burntwood, Eng, UK 25/E1
Burrel, Alb. 40/D5
Burriana, Sp. 35/E3
Bursa, Turk. 44/D4
Burscheid, Ger. 29/E6
Burton, Mi, US 99/E6
Burton upon Trent, Eng, UK 23/G6
Burundi (ctry.) 82/E1
Bury, Eng, UK 23/F4
Bury Saint Edmunds, Eng, UK 25/G2
Bushey, Eng, UK 25/F3
Busko-Zdrój, Pol. 27/L3
Bussum, Neth. 28/C4
Busto Arsizio, It. 33/H4
Butare, Rwa. 82/E1
Butembo, D.R. Congo 77/L7
Butiá, Braz. 108/B4
Butler, Pa, US 94/E3
Butte-Silver Bow County, Mt, US 90/E4
Butterworth, Malay. 66/B2
Butuan, Phil. 67/G2
Buturlinovka, Rus. 45/G2
Butzbach, Ger. 33/H1
Buxtehude, Ger. 29/G2
Buxton, Eng, UK 23/G5
Buy, Rus. 42/J4
Buyant-Uhaa, Mong. 54/G3
Buynaksk, Rus. 45/H4
Büyükçekmece, Turk. 51/M6
Buzău, Rom. 41/H3
Buzuluk, Rus. 45/K1
Bydgoszcz, Pol. 27/J2
Bykhov, Bela. 44/D1
Bytom, Pol. 27/K3
Bytów, Pol. 27/J1

C

Ca Mau, Viet. 65/D4
Caazapá, Par. 109/E2
Cabaiguán, Cuba 103/G1
Cabañaquinta, Sp. 34/C1
Cabanatuan, Phil. 68/B3
Cabimas, Ven. 106/D1
Cabinda, Ang. 82/B2
Cabo Frio, Braz. 108/D2
Cabo San Lucas, Mex. 100/C4
Cabo San Lucas (cape), Mex. 100/C4
Cabot (str.), NS,NF, Can. 87/K4
Cabra, Sp. 34/C4
Cabugao, Phil. 61/J5
Caçador, Braz. 108/B3
Čačak, Yugo. 40/E4
Caçapava, Braz. 108/H8
Cáceres, Braz. 106/G7
Cáceres, Sp. 34/B3
Cacheu, GBis. 78/A3
Cachoeira do Sul, Braz. 108/A4
Cachoeira Paulista, Braz. 108/H7
Cachoeirinha, Braz. 108/B4
Cachoeiro de Itapemirim, Braz. 108/D2
Čadca, Slvk. 27/K4
Cadillac, Mi, US 94/C2
Cadiz, Phil. 67/F1
Cádiz, Sp. 34/B4
Cádiz, Golfo de (gulf), Port.,Sp. 34/B4
Caen, Fr. 32/C2
Caerphilly, Wal, UK 24/C3
Cagliari, It. 38/A3
Cagnes-sur-Mer, Fr. 33/G5
Caguas, PR 104/E3
Cahors, Fr. 32/D4
Cahul, Mol. 41/J3
Caibarién, Cuba 103/G1
Caicó, Braz. 107/L5
Caieiras, Braz. 108/G8
Cairns, Austl. 72/B2
Cairo, Ga, US 97/G4
Cairo (cap.), Egypt 49/B5
Cajamarca, Peru 106/C5
Calabar, Nga. 79/H5
Calabozo, Ven. 106/E2
Calafat, Rom. 40/F4
Calahorra, Sp. 34/E1
Calais, Fr. 30/A2
Calama, Chile 109/C1
Călăraşi, Rom. 41/H3
Calatayud, Sp. 34/E2
Calbayog, Phil. 67/F1
Calcutta, India 62/E3
Caldas da Rainha, Port. 34/A3
Caldas Novas, Braz. 108/B1
Caledon, On, Can. 95/T8
Caleta Olivia, Arg. 109/C6
Calexico, Ca, US 92/D4
Calgary, Ab, Can. 90/E3
Cali, Col. 106/C3
Calicut (Kozhikode), India 62/C5
California (state), US 92/B3
California (gulf), Mex. 92/D5
Callao, Peru 106/C6
Callaway, Fl, US 97/G4
Callosa de Segura, Sp. 35/E3
Caloundra, Austl. 72/D4
Calpulálpan, Mex. 101/L7
Caltagirone, It. 38/D4
Caltanissetta, It. 38/D4
Caluire-et-Cuire, Fr. 36/A6
Calumet City, Il, US 99/Q16
Calviá, Sp. 35/G3
Calvillo, Mex. 100/E4
Cam Pha, Viet. 65/D1
Cam Ranh, Viet. 65/E4
Camaçari, Braz. 107/L6
Camagüey, Cuba 103/G1
Camaiore, It. 33/J5
Camajuaní, Cuba 103/G1
Camaquã, Braz. 108/B4
Camargo, Sp. 34/D1
Camas, Sp. 34/B4
Cambará, Braz. 108/B2
Cambé, Braz. 108/B2
Cambodia (ctry.) 65/D3
Cambrai, Fr. 30/C3
Cambridge, Oh, US 94/D3
Cambridge, Md, US 97/J2
Cambridge, Ma, US 95/G3
Cambridge, On, Can. 95/S9
Cambridge, Eng, UK 25/G2
Cambrils, Sp. 35/F2
Camden, NJ, US 94/F4
Cameroon (ctry.), Camr. 76/H7
Cametá, Braz. 107/J4
Camiri, Bol. 106/F8
Camoapa, Nic. 102/E3
Camocim, Braz. 107/K4
Campbell, Ca, US 99/L12
Campbell River, BC, Can. 90/B3
Campbellsville, Ky, US 97/G2
Campeche, Mex. 102/D2
Campeche (bay), Mex. 101/G5
Campina Grande, Braz. 107/L5
Campinas, Braz. 108/F7
Campo Belo, Braz. 108/C2
Campo de la Cruz, Col. 103/H4
Campo Formoso, Braz. 107/K6
Campo Grande, Braz. 107/H8
Campo Largo, Braz. 108/B3
Campo Limpo Paulista, Braz. 108/G8
Campo Maior, Braz. 107/K4
Campo Mourão, Braz. 108/A3
Campoalegre, Col. 106/C3
Campobasso, It. 40/B5
Campos do Jordão, Braz. 108/H7
Campos dos Goytacazes, Braz. 108/D2
Campos Novos, Braz. 108/B3
Çan, Turk. 41/H5
Can Tho, Viet. 65/D4
Canada (ctry.) 86/*
Cañada de Gómez, Arg. 109/D3
Çanakkale, Turk. 41/H5
Canandaigua, NY, US 94/E3
Cananea, Mex. 92/E5
Canary (isls.) 76/B2
Cañas, CR 102/E4
Canaveral (cape), Fl, US 97/H4
Canavieiras, Braz. 107/L7
Canberra (cap.), Austr. 73/D2
Cancún, Mex. 102/E1
Candeias, Braz. 107/L6
Cândido Mota, Braz. 108/B2
Candon, Phil. 61/J5
Canela, Braz. 108/B4
Cangas, Sp. 34/A1
Cangas de Narcea, Sp. 34/B1
Cangzhou, China 59/D3
Canicatti, It. 38/C4
Canindé, Braz. 107/L4
Çankırı, Turk. 44/E4
Cannanore, India 62/C5
Cannes, Fr. 33/G5
Cannock, Eng, UK 24/D1
Canoas, Braz. 108/B4
Canoinhas, Braz. 108/B3
Canosa di Puglia, It. 40/C5
Cantaura, Ven. 106/F2
Canterbury, Eng, UK 25/H4
Canton, Il, US 91/L5
Canton, Ms, US 93/K4
Canton, Oh, US 94/D3
Canton, Mi, US 99/E7
Cantù, It. 33/H4
Canvey Island, Eng, UK 25/G3
Canyon, Tx, US 93/G4
Canyonlands National Park, Ut, US 92/E3
Cao Bang, Viet. 65/D1
Cao Lanh, Viet. 65/D4
Cap-de-la-Madeleine, Qu, Can. 95/F2
Cap-Haïtien, Haiti 103/H2
Capanema, Braz. 107/J4
Capannori, It. 33/J5
Capão Bonito, Braz. 108/B3
Caparica, Port. 35/P10
Cape Breton (isl.), Can. 95/J2
Cape Coast, Gha. 79/E5
Cape Cod Nat'l Seashore, Ma, US 95/G3
Cape Coral, Fl, US 97/H5
Cape Girardeau, Mo, US 93/K3
Cape Hatteras Nat'l Seashore, NC, US 97/K3
Cape Town (cap.), SAfr. 80/L10
Cape Verde (ctry.) 74/J9
Cape York (pen.), Austl. 70/G2
Capelinha, Braz. 108/D1
Capitão Poço, Braz. 107/J4
Čapljina, Bosn. 40/C4
Capua, It. 40/B5
Caracal, Rom. 41/G3
Caracas (cap.), Ven. 106/E1
Caraguatatuba, Braz. 108/H8
Carangola, Braz. 108/D2
Caransebeş, Rom. 40/F3
Carapicuíba, Braz. 108/G8
Caratinga, Braz. 108/D1
Caravaca de la Cruz, Sp. 34/E3
Carazinho, Braz. 109/F2
Carballo, Sp. 34/A1
Carbondale, Pa, US 94/F3
Carbonia, It. 38/A3
Carcagente, Sp. 35/E3
Carcassonne, Fr. 32/E5
Cárdenas, Mex. 102/C2
Cárdenas, Mex. 102/B1
Cárdenas, Cuba 103/F1
Cardiff (cap.), Wal, UK 24/C4
Carei, Rom. 40/F2
Cariacica, Braz. 108/D2
Cariaco, Ven. 104/F5
Cariamanga, Ecu. 106/C4
Caribbean (sea) 84/J8
Caribou, Me, US 95/G2
Caripito, Ven. 104/F5
Carletonville, SAfr. 80/P13
Carlisle, Pa, US 94/E3
Carlisle, Eng, UK 23/F2
Carlos M. De Cespedes, Cuba 103/G1
Carlsbad, NM, US 93/F4
Carlton, Eng, UK 23/G6
Carmagnola, It. 33/G4
Carmichael, Ca, US 99/M9
Carmo do Paranaíba, Braz. 108/C1
Carmona, Sp. 34/C4
Carnaxide, Port. 35/P10
Carnot, CAfr. 76/J7
Carol Stream, Il, US 99/P16
Carolina, PR 104/E3
Caroline (isls), Micr. 68/D4
Carouge, Swi. 36/C5
Carpathian (mts.), Eur. 27/J4
Carpentaria (gulf), Austl. 70/F2
Carpentersville, Il, US 99/P15
Carpentras, Fr. 32/F4
Carpi, It. 33/J4
Carrara, It. 33/J4
Carrickfergus, NI, UK 22/C2
Carrollton, Ga, US 97/G3
Çarşamba, Turk. 44/F4
Carson City (cap.), Nv, US 92/C3
Cartagena, Col. 103/H4
Cartagena, Sp. 35/E4
Cartago, Col. 106/C3
Cartago, CR 103/F4
Cartersville, Ga, US 97/G3
Carthage, Mo, US 93/J3
Carthage (Qarţājannah) (ruin), Tun. 38/B4
Caruaru, Braz. 107/L5
Carúpano, Ven. 106/F1
Carvin, Fr. 30/B3
Cary, NC, US 97/J3
Cary, Il, US 99/P15
Casa Branca, Braz. 108/F6
Casa Grande, Az, US 92/E4
Casablanca, Mor. 76/D1
Casal di Principe, It. 38/D2
Casale Monferrato, It. 33/H4
Casarano, It. 39/F2
Cascade (range), Wa, US 90/C5
Cascade-Fairwood, Or, US 99/C3
Cascais, Port. 35/P10
Cascavel, Braz. 107/L4
Cascavel, Braz. 109/F1
Cascina, It. 33/J5
Caserta, It. 40/B5
Casilda, Arg. 109/D3
Casper, Wy, US 91/G5
Caspian (sea), Asia 46/E5
Cassilândia, Braz. 108/B1
Cassino, It. 40/A5
Castanhal, Braz. 107/J4
Castaños, Mex. 96/C5
Castel del Piano, It. 38/C1
Castellammare di Stabia, It. 40/B5
Castellar del Vallès, Sp. 35/G2
Castelldefels, Sp. 35/K7
Castellón de la Plana, Sp. 35/E3
Castelo Branco, Port. 34/B3
Castelvetrano, It. 38/C4
Castilla, Peru 106/B5
Castleford, Eng, UK 23/G4
Castres, Fr. 32/E5
Castricum, Neth. 28/B3
Castries (cap.), StL. 104/F4
Castro, Chile 109/B5
Castro, Braz. 108/B3
Castro Valley, Ca, US 99/K11
Castrop-Rauxel, Ger. 29/E5
Castrovillari, It. 38/E3
Catacamas, Hon. 102/E3
Cataguases, Braz. 108/L6
Cataiñgan, Phil. 67/F1
Catalão, Braz. 108/C1
Catamarca, Arg. 109/C2
Catanduva, Braz. 108/B2
Catania, It. 38/D4
Catanzaro, It. 38/E3
Catarman, Phil. 67/F1
Catemaco, Mex. 102/C2
Caterham and Warlingham, Eng, UK 25/F4
Cativá, Pan. 103/G4
Caucaia, Braz. 107/L4
Caucasia, Col. 103/H5
Caucasus (mts.), Geo. 45/G4
Cauquenes, Chile 109/B4
Cavaillon, Fr. 32/F5
Caxambu, Braz. 108/J6
Caxias, Braz. 107/K4
Caxias do Sul, Braz. 108/B4
Cayce, SC, US 97/H3
Çayeli, Turk. 45/G4
Cayenne (cap.), FrG. 107/H3
Cayman (isls.), UK 103/F2
Cazin, Bosn. 40/B3
Ceará-Mirim, Braz. 107/L5
Cebu, Phil. 67/F1
Ceccano, It. 38/C2
Cecina, It. 33/J5
Cedar City, Ut, US 92/D3
Cegléd, Hun. 40/D2
Celaya, Mex. 101/E4
Celebes (isl.), Indo. 67/E4
Celebes (sea), Asia 67/F3
Celina, Oh, US 94/C3
Celle, Ger. 29/H3
Centenario, Arg. 109/C4
Center Point, Al, US 97/G3
Cento, It. 33/J4
Central African Republic (ctry.) 77/J6
Central Siberian (plat.), Rus. 47/L3
Centralia, Il, US 93/K3
Centralia, Wa, US 90/C4
Cerdanyola del Vallès, Sp. 35/L7
Ceres, Braz. 107/J7
Ceres, SAfr. 80/L10
Cereté, Col. 103/H4
Cergy, Fr. 30/B5
Cerignola, It. 40/B5
Çerkezköy, Turk. 41/J5
Çermik, Turk. 50/D2
Cernavodă, Rom. 41/J3
Cerro Azul, Mex. 102/B1
Cerro de Pasco, Peru 106/C6
Cervia, It. 33/K4
Cesena, It. 33/K4
Cesenatico, It. 33/K4
Cēsis, Lat. 42/E4
České Budějovice, Czh. 33/L2
Çeşme, Turk. 39/K3
Cetinje, Yugo. 40/D4
Ceuta, Sp. 34/C5
Ceyhan, Turk. 49/D1
Ceylânpınar, Turk. 50/E2
Ceylon (isl.), SrL. 62/D6
Chachapoyas, Peru 106/C5
Chachoengsao, Thai. 65/C3
Chad (lake), Afr. 76/H5
Chad (ctry.) 77/J4
Chālakudi, India 62/C5
Chalatenango, ESal. 102/D3
Chalco, Mex. 101/R10
Chalfont Saint Peter, Eng, UK 25/F3
Challans, Fr. 32/C3
Chalon-sur-Saône, Fr. 36/A4
Châlons-sur-Marne, Fr. 31/D6
Chālūs, Iran 51/G2
Cham, Ger. 33/K2
Chaman, Pak. 53/J2
Chamba, India 53/L2
Chambas, Cuba 103/G1
Chambersburg, Pa, US 94/E4
Chambéry, Fr. 32/F4
Chambly, Qu, Can. 95/P7
Champaign, Il, US 91/L5
Champlain (lake), Can.,US 94/F2
Champotón, Mex. 102/D2
Champs-sur-Marne, Fr. 30/B6
Chandausi, India 62/C2
Chanderi, India 62/C3
Chandīgarh, India 53/L2
Chandrapur, India 62/C4
Changchun, China 59/F2
Changde, China 61/F2
Changhua, Tai. 61/J3
Changhŭng, SKor. 58/D5
Changsha, China 61/G2
Changshu, China 59/L8
Changshun, China 61/E3
Changsŏng, SKor. 58/D5
Changsŭngp'o, SKor. 58/E5
Ch'angwŏn, SKor. 56/A3
Changzhi, China 59/C3
Changzhou, China 59/K8
Chanthaburi, Thai. 65/C3
Chanute, Ks, US 93/J3
Chapala, Mex. 100/E4
Chapayevsk, Rus. 45/J1
Chapecó, Braz. 108/A3
Chapel Hill, NC, US 97/J3
Chapeltown, Eng, UK 23/G5
Charata, Arg. 109/D2
Chārīkār, Afg. 53/J1
Chärjew, Trkm. 46/G6
Charleroi, Belg. 31/D3
Charleston, Il, US 97/F2
Charleston, SC, US 97/J3
Charleston (cap.), WV, US 94/D4
Charleville-Mézières, Fr. 31/D4
Charlotte, NC, US 97/H3
Charlotte Amalie, USVI 104/E3
Charlottetown (cap.), PE, Can. 95/J2
Chartres, Fr. 32/D2
Chascomús, Arg. 109/E4
Château-Thierry, Fr. 30/C5
Châteaudun, Fr. 32/D2
Châteauguay, Qu, Can. 95/N7
Châteauroux, Fr. 32/D3
Châtelet, Belg. 31/D3
Châtellerault, Fr. 32/D3
Chatham, NB, Can. 95/H2
Chatham, On, Can. 94/D3
Chatham, Eng, UK 25/G4
Chatrapur, India 62/E4
Chattanooga, Tn, US 97/G3
Chau Doc, Viet. 65/D4
Chaudfontaine, Belg. 31/E2
Chauk, Myan. 60/B4
Chaumont, Fr. 36/B1
Chaykovskiy, Rus. 43/M4
Cheb, Czh. 33/K1
Cheboksary, Rus. 43/K4
Chech'ŏn, SKor. 56/A2
Cheektowaga, NY, US 95/V10
Chegdomyn, Rus. 55/L1
Chegutu, Zim. 82/F4
Cheju, SKor. 55/K5
Chełm, Pol. 27/M3
Chełmno, Pol. 27/K2
Chelmsford, Eng, UK 25/G3
Chełmża, Pol. 27/K2
Cheltenham, Eng, UK 24/D3
Chelyabinsk, Rus. 43/P5
Chemnitz, Ger. 26/G3
Chennai (Madras), India 62/D5
Chenôve, Fr. 36/A3
Chenzhou, China 61/G3
Cherbourg, Fr. 32/C2
Cherchell, Alg. 76/F1
Cheremkhovo, Rus. 54/E1
Cherepovets, Rus. 42/H4
Cherkasy, Ukr. 44/E2
Cherkessk, Rus. 45/G3
Chernihiv, Ukr. 44/D2
Chernivtsi, Ukr. 41/G1
Chernushka, Rus. 43/N4
Cherven Bryag, Bul. 41/G4
Chervonohrad, Ukr. 27/N3
Chesapeake (bay), US 89/L4
Chesham, Eng, UK 25/F3
Cheshunt, Eng, UK 25/F3
Chester, Pa, US 94/F4
Chester, Eng, UK 23/F5
Chester-le-Street, Eng, UK 23/G2
Chesterfield, Eng, UK 23/G5
Chetumal, Mex. 102/D2
Cheyenne (cap.), Wy, US 91/G5
Chhatarpur, India 62/C3
Chhindwāra, India 62/C3
Chiai, Tai. 61/J4
Chiang Mai, Thai. 65/B2
Chiapa de Corzo, Mex. 102/C2
Chiat'ura, Geo. 45/G4
Chiautempan, Mex. 101/L7
Chiavari, It. 33/H4
Chiba, Japan 57/G3
Chibuto, Moz. 81/F2
Chicago, Il, US 99/Q16
Chicago Heights, Il, US 99/Q16
Chicago Ridge, Il, US 99/Q16
Chīchāwatni, Pak. 53/K2
Chichester, Eng, UK 25/F5
Chichibu, Japan 57/F3
Chichicastenango, Guat. 102/D3
Chichigalpa, Nic. 102/E3
Chickasha, Ok, US 93/H4
Chiclana de la Frontera, Sp. 34/B4

116

Dayto – Evans

Daytona Beach, Fl, US 97/H4
De Aar, SAfr. 80/D3
De Bilt, Neth. 28/C4
De Kalb, Il, US 91/L5
De Land, Fl, US 97/H4
De Ridder, La, US 93/J5
Dead (sea), Isr.,Jor. 49/D4
Deal, Eng, UK 25/H4
Deán Funes, Arg. 109/D3
Dearborn, Mi, US 99/F7
Dearborn Heights, Mi, US 99/F7
Death Valley National Park, US 92/C3
Debar, FYROM 40/E5
Dębica, Pol. 27/L3
Dęblin, Pol. 27/L3
Debre Birhan, Eth. 77/N6
Debre Mark'os, Eth. 77/N5
Debre Tabor, Eth. 77/N5
Debre Zeyit, Eth. 77/N6
Debrecen, Hun. 40/E2
Decatur, Il, US 91/L6
Decatur, Al, US 97/G3
Decatur, Ga, US 97/G3
Děčín, Czh. 27/H3
Décines-Charpieu, Fr. 36/A6
Dédougou, Burk. 78/E3
Dedza, Malw. 82/F3
Deerfield, Il, US 99/P15
Defiance, Oh, US 94/C3
Deggendorf, Ger. 33/K2
Dehra Dūn, India 53/L2
Dehri, India 62/D3
Deinze, Belg. 28/A7
Dej, Rom. 41/F2
Dekemhare (Dek'emhāre), Erit. 52/C5
Del Rio, Tx, US 93/G5
Delano, Ca, US 92/C4
Delaware, Oh, US 94/D3
Delaware (bay), NJ, US 94/F4
Delaware (state), US 94/F4
Delaware (riv.), US 94/F3
Delbrück, Ger. 29/F5
Delčevo, FYROM 40/F5
Delémont, Swi. 36/D3
Delft, Neth. 28/B4
Delfzijl, Neth. 28/D2
Delhi, India 62/C2
Delmenhorst, Ger. 29/F2
Delphi (Dhelfoí) (ruin), Gre. 39/H3
Delray Beach, Fl, US 97/H5
Deltona, Fl, US 97/H4
Deming, NM, US 100/D1
Demirci, Turk. 44/D5
Demmin, Ger. 26/G2
Demopolis, Al, US 97/G3
Den Helder, Neth. 28/B3
Denain, Fr. 30/C3
Denali National Park and Preserve, Ak, US 85/H3
Denderleeuw, Belg. 31/D2
Dendermonde, Belg. 28/B6
Denia, Sp. 35/F3
Denison, Tx, US 93/H4
Denizli, Turk. 50/B2
Denmark (ctry.) 20/C5
Denpasar, Indo. 66/E5
Denton, Tx, US 93/H4
Denton, Tx, US 96/D3
Denton, Eng, UK 23/F5
Denver (cap.), Co, US 93/F3
Deoband, India 62/C2
Deogarh, India 62/D3
Deoghar, India 62/E3
Deolāli, India 62/B4
Deoria, India 62/D2
Depew, NY, US 95/V10
Depok, Indo. 66/C5
Dera Ghāzi Khān, Pak. 53/K2
Dera Ismā'īl Khān, Pak. 53/K2
Derbent, Rus. 45/J4
Derby, Ks, US 93/H3
Derby, Eng, UK 23/G6
Derry, NH, US 95/G3
Derventa, Bosn. 40/C3
Des Moines (cap.), Ia, US 93/J2
Des Moines, Wa, US 99/C3
Des Plaines, Il, US 99/Q15
Descalvado, Braz. 108/C2
Desē, Eth. 77/N5
Desoto, Tx, US 101/F1
Despatch, SAfr. 80/D4
Dessau, Ger. 26/G3
Destelbergen, Belg. 28/A6
Detmold, Ger. 29/F5
Detroit, Mi, US 99/F7
Deurne, Belg. 28/B6
Deurne, Neth. 28/C6
Deux-Montagnes, Qu, Can. 95/N6
Deva, Rom. 40/F3
Develi, Turk. 50/C2
Deventer, Neth. 28/D4
Devils Lake, ND, US 91/J3
Devonport, Austl. 73/C4
Devrek, Turk. 41/K5
Dewās, India 62/C3
Dewsbury, Eng, UK 23/G4
Deyang, China 60/E2
Dezfūl, Iran 51/G3
Dezhou, China 59/D3
Dhaka (cap.), Bang. 62/F3
Dhamtari, India 62/D3
Dhānbād, India 62/E3
Dhankutā, Nepal 62/E2
Dhār, India 62/C3
Dharampur, India 62/B3
Dhāri, India 62/B3
Dharmapuri, India 62/C5
Dharmavaram, India 62/C5
Dhekialjuli, India 60/B3
Dhenkānāl, India 62/E3
Dholka, India 62/B3
Dholpur, India 62/C2
Dhorāji, India 62/B3
Dhubri, India 62/E2
Dhūlia, India 62/B3
Dhuliān, India 62/E3
Dhupgāri, India 62/E2
Diadema, Braz. 108/G8
Diamantina, Braz. 108/D1
Diapaga, Burk. 79/F3
Didam, Neth. 28/D5
Didcot, Eng, UK 25/E3
Dīdwāna, India 53/K3
Diébougou, Burk. 78/E4
Diekirch, Lux. 31/F4
Diemen, Neth. 28/B4
Diepenbeek, Belg. 31/E2
Diepholz, Ger. 29/F3
Dieppe, Fr. 30/A4
Diest, Belg. 28/C7
Dietikon, Swi. 37/E3
Diffa, Niger 76/H5
Digboi, India 60/B3
Digne-les-Bains, Fr. 33/G4
Digos, Phil. 67/G2
Dijon, Fr. 36/A3
Dikirnis, Egypt 49/B4
Diksmuide, Belg. 30/B1
Dilbeek, Belg. 31/D2
Dili, Indo. 67/G5
Dillenburg, Ger. 31/H2
Dillingen, Ger. 31/F5
Dillingen an der Donau, Ger. 26/F4
Dilsen, Belg. 28/C6
Dimāpur, India 60/B3
Dimbokro, C.d'Iv. 78/D5
Dimitrovgrad, Rus. 45/J1
Dimitrovgrad, Yugo. 41/F4
Dimitrovgrad, Bul. 41/G4
Dimona, Isr. 49/D4
Dinājpur, Bang. 62/E2
Dinar, Turk. 50/B2
Dindigul, India 62/C5
Dingolfing, Ger. 33/K2
Dingras, Phil. 61/J5
Dinslaken, Ger. 28/D5
Dinuba, Ca, US 92/C3
Diourbel, Sen. 78/A3
Diphu, India 60/B3
Dipolog, Phil. 67/F2
Dirē Dawa, Eth. 77/P6
Diriamba, Nic. 102/E4
Dishnā, Egypt 52/B3
Dispur, India 60/A3
Distrito Federal (fed. dist.), Mex. 101/K7
Disūq, Egypt 49/B4
Diu, India 62/B3
Divinópolis, Braz. 108/C2
Divo, C.d'Iv. 78/D5
Divriği, Turk. 44/F5
Dixon, Il, US 91/L5
Dixon, Ca, US 99/L10
Diyarb Najm, Egypt 49/B4
Diyarbakır, Turk. 50/E2
Djamaa, Alg. 76/G1
Djelfa, Alg. 76/F1
Djibo, Burk. 79/E3
Djibouti (cap.), Djib. 77/P5
Djibouti (ctry.) 77/P5
Djougou, Ben. 79/F4
Dnipro (riv.), Ukr. 44/E3
Dniprodzerzhyns'k, Ukr. 44/E2
Dnipropetrovs'k, Ukr. 44/E2
Dnister (riv.), Eur. 44/D3
Do Gonbadān, Iran 51/G4
Do Son, Viet. 65/D1
Döbeln, Ger. 26/G3
Doboj, Bosn. 40/D3
Dobrich, Bul. 41/H4
Dobrush, Bela. 44/D1
Dobryanka, Rus. 43/N4
Dodge City, Ks, US 93/G3
Dodoma, Tanz. 82/G2
Doetinchem, Neth. 28/D5
Dogondoutchi, Niger 79/G3
Doğubayazıt, Turk. 45/H5
Doha (cap.), Qatar 52/F3
Dohad, India 62/B3
Dole, Fr. 36/B3
Dolgoprudnyy, Rus. 43/W9
Dollard-des-Ormeaux, Qu, Can. 95/N7
Dolores, Arg. 109/E4
Dolores, Guat. 102/D2
Dolton, Il, US 99/Q16
Dom Pedrito, Braz. 109/F3
Dombóvár, Hun. 40/D2
Dominica (ctry.), Dom. 104/F4
Dominican Republic (ctry.) 104/D3
Domodossola, It. 37/E5
Don Benito, Sp. 34/C3
Donaueschingen, Ger. 37/E2
Doncaster, Eng, UK 23/G4
Donets'k, Ukr. 44/F2
Dong Ha, Viet. 65/D2
Dong Hoi, Viet. 65/D2
Dongchuan, China 60/D3
Dongen, Neth. 28/B5
Dongguan, China 61/G4
Dongsheng, China 59/B3
Dongtai, China 59/E4
Dongying, China 59/D3
Donji Vakuf, Bosn. 40/C3
Dorchester, Eng, UK 24/D5
Dordrecht, Neth. 28/B5
Dori, Burk. 79/E3
Dorking, Eng, UK 25/F4
Dormagen, Ger. 28/D6
Dornbirn, Aus. 37/F3
Dorohoi, Rom. 41/H2
Dorsten, Ger. 28/D5
Dortmund, Ger. 29/E5
Dörtyol, Turk. 49/E1
Dorval, Qu, Can. 95/N7
Dos Hermanas, Sp. 34/C4
Dosso, Niger 79/F3
Dothan, Al, US 97/G4
Douai, Fr. 30/C3
Douala, Camr. 76/G7
Douarnenez, Fr. 32/A2
Douchy-les-Mines, Fr. 30/C3
Douglas, Az, US 100/C2
Douglas, Ga, US 97/H4
Douglas (cap.), IM, UK 22/D3
Dour, Belg. 30/C3
Dourados, Braz. 107/H8
Dover, Eng, UK 25/H4
Dover (cap.), De, US 94/F4
Dover (str.), Fr.,UK 32/D1
Downers Grove, Il, US 99/P16
Dracena, Braz. 108/B2
Drachten, Neth. 28/D2
Drăgăşani, Rom. 41/G3
Draguignan, Fr. 33/G5
Drake (passage) 109/C8
Dráma, Gre. 41/G5
Drammen, Nor. 20/D4
Draveil, Fr. 30/B6
Dresden, Ger. 27/G3
Dreux, Fr. 30/A6
Driebergen, Neth. 28/C4
Drigh Road, Pak. 62/A3
Drobeta-Turnu Severin, Rom. 40/F3
Drogheda, Ire. 22/B4
Drohobych, Ukr. 27/M4
Droitwich, Eng, UK 24/D2
Dronfield, Eng, UK 23/G5
Dronten, Neth. 28/C3
Drummondville, Qu, Can. 95/F2
Drunen, Neth. 28/C5
Druten, Neth. 28/C5
Drvar, Bosn. 40/C3
Dschang, Camr. 79/H5
Dubayy, UAE 53/G3
Dubbo, Austl. 73/D2
Dübendorf, Swi. 37/E3
Dublin, Ga, US 97/H3
Dublin (cap.), Ire. 22/B5
Dublin, Ca, US 99/L11
Dubna, Rus. 42/H4
Dubnica nad Váhom, Slvk. 27/K4
Dubno, Ukr. 44/C2
Dubrovnik, Cro. 40/D4
Dubuque, Ia, US 91/L5
Dudelange, Lux. 31/F5
Duderstadt, Ger. 29/H5
Dudinka, Rus. 46/J3
Dudley, Eng, UK 24/D1
Duffel, Belg. 28/B6
Duisburg, Ger. 28/D6
Duitama, Col. 106/D2
Duiven, Neth. 28/D5
Dülmen, Ger. 29/E5
Dumaguete, Phil. 67/F2
Dumas, Tx, US 93/G4
Dumfries, Sc, UK 22/E1
Dún Laoghaire, Ire. 22/B5
Dunaharaszti, Hun. 40/D2
Dunakeszi, Hun. 40/D2
Dunaújváros, Hun. 40/D2
Duncan, Ok, US 93/H4
Duncanville, Tx, US 96/D3
Dund-Us, Mong. 54/C2
Dundalk, Ire. 22/B4
Dundas, On, Can. 95/T9
Dunedin, Fl, US 97/H4
Dunedin, NZ 71/R12
Dungarpur, India 62/B3
Dunhua, China 55/K3
Dunhuang, China 54/C3
Dunkirk (Dunkerque), Fr. 30/B1
Dunkwa, Gha. 79/E5
Dunmurry, NI, UK 22/B2
Dunstable, Eng, UK 25/F3
Duque de Caxias, Braz. 108/K7
Durango, Co, US 92/F3
Durango, Mex. 96/B5
Durango, Sp. 34/D1
Durant, Ok, US 93/H4
Durazno, Uru. 109/E3
Durban, SAfr. 81/E3
Durbanville, SAfr. 80/L10
Düren, Ger. 31/F2
Durg, India 62/D3
Durgāpur, India 62/E3
Durham, NC, US 97/J3
Durham, NH, US 95/G3
Durham, Eng, UK 23/G2
Durrës, Alb. 40/D5
Dushanbe (cap.), Taj. 46/G6
Düsseldorf, Ger. 28/D6
Duyun, China 61/E3
Düzce, Turk. 41/K5
Düzici, Turk. 50/D2
Dwārka, India 62/A3
Dyat'kovo, Rus. 44/E1
Dyer, In, US 94/C3
Dzaoudzi (cap.), May. 81/H6
Dzerzhinsk, Rus. 42/J4
Dzhankoy, Ukr. 44/E3
Działdowo, Pol. 27/L2
Dzierżoniów, Pol. 27/J3
Dzuunmod, Mong. 54/F2

E

Eagle Pass, Tx, US 96/C4
Easley, SC, US 97/H3
East Chicago, In, US 99/R16
East China (sea), Asia 68/B2
East Detroit (East Pointe), Mi, US 99/G7
East Grinstead, Eng, UK 25/F4
East Hill-Meridian, Wa, US 99/C3
East Lansing, Mi, US 94/C3
East Liverpool, Oh, US 94/D3
East London, SAfr. 80/D4
East Point, Ga, US 97/G3
East Pointe (East Detroit), Mi, US 99/G7
East Retford, Eng, UK 23/H5
East Saint Louis, Il, US 93/K3
East Siberian (sea), Rus. 47/S2
Eastbourne, Eng, UK 25/G5
Eastern Ghats (mts.), India 62/C5
Eastleigh, Eng, UK 25/E5
Easton, Pa, US 94/F3
Eastwood, Eng, UK 23/G6
Eau Claire, Wi, US 91/L4
Ebano, Mex. 102/B1
Ebbw Vale, Wal, UK 24/C3
Eberswalde-Finow, Ger. 27/G2
Ebetsu, Japan 55/N3
Eboli, It. 40/B5
Ebolowa, Camr. 76/H7
Ecatepec, Mex. 101/Q9
Eccles, Eng, UK 23/F5
Échirolles, Fr. 32/F4
Echt, Neth. 28/C6
Écija, Sp. 34/C4
Eckernförde, Ger. 26/E1
Ecorse, Mi, US 99/F7
Ecuador (ctry.), Ecu. 106/C4
Ede, Nga. 79/G5
Ede, Neth. 28/C4
Edéa, Camr. 76/H7
Edegem, Belg. 28/B6
Eden, NC, US 97/J2
Edendale, SAfr. 81/E3
Edewecht, Ger. 29/E2
Edgewood-North Hill, Wa, US 99/C3
Édhessa, Gre. 40/F5
Edinburg, Tx, US 96/D5
Edirne, Turk. 41/H5
Edmonds, Wa, US 99/C2
Edmonton (cap.), Ab, Can. 90/E2
Edremit, Turk. 44/C5
Edwardsville, Il, US 93/K3
Eeklo, Belg. 28/A6
Effingham, Il, US 93/K3
Effon Alaiye, Nga. 79/G5
Eger, Hun. 40/E2
Egglescliffe, Eng, UK 23/G3
Egham, Eng, UK 25/F4
Eğridir, Turk. 50/B2
Egypt (ctry.) 77/L2
Ehingen, Ger. 37/F1
Eibar, Sp. 34/D1
Eibergen, Neth. 28/D4
Eidsvoll, Nor. 20/D3
Einbeck, Ger. 29/G5
Eindhoven, Neth. 28/C6
Eisenach, Ger. 29/H7
Eisenhüttenstadt, Ger. 27/H2
Eisenstadt, Aus. 40/C2
Eisenfeld, Ger. 31/G2
Eitorf, Ger. 31/G2
Ejea de los Caballeros, Sp. 35/E1
Ejeda, Madg. 81/H9
Ekeren, Belg. 28/B6
Ekibastuz, Kaz. 46/H4
Eksjö, Swe. 20/E4
El Aaiún, Mor. 76/C2
El Arahal, Sp. 34/C4
El Bagre, Col. 103/H5
El Banco, Col. 103/H4
El Bayadh, Alg. 76/F1
El Campo, Tx, US 93/H5
El Carmen de Bolívar, Col. 103/H4
El Centro, Ca, US 92/D4
El Cerrito, Ca, US 99/K11
El Dorado, Ar, US 93/J4
El Dorado, Ks, US 93/H3
El Ferrol, Sp. 34/A1
El Golea, Alg. 76/F1
El Grullo, Mex. 100/D5
El Jadida, Mor. 76/D1
El Nevado (peak), Arg. 109/C4
El Oued, Alg. 76/G1
El Paso, Tx, US 92/F5
El Pilar, Ven. 104/F5
El Prat de Llobregat, Sp. 35/L7
El Progreso, Hon. 102/E3
El Progreso, Guat. 102/D3
El Puerto de Santa María, Sp. 34/B4
El Rama, Nic. 103/E3
El Reno, Ok, US 93/H4
El Salto, Mex. 100/D4
El Salvador, Cuba 103/H1
El Salvador (ctry.), ESal. 102/D3
El Tigre, Ven. 106/F2
El Viejo, Nic. 102/E3
El'brus (peak), Rus. 45/G4
Élancourt, Fr. 30/A6
Elat, Isr. 49/D5
Elazığ, Turk. 50/D2
Elbasan, Alb. 40/E5
Elbe (riv.), Ger. 26/E2
Elbeuf, Fr. 32/D2
Elbląg, Pol. 27/K1
Elburg, Neth. 28/C4
Elche, Sp. 35/E3
Elda, Sp. 35/E3
Eldorado, Arg. 109/F2
Eldoret, Kenya 77/N7
Elefsís, Gre. 39/N8
Elektrostal', Rus. 43/X9
Elgin, Il, US 99/P15
Elgon (peak), Ugan. 77/M7
Elista, Rus. 45/H3
Elizabeth City, NC, US 97/J2
Elizabethton, Tn, US 97/H2
Elizabethtown, Ky, US 97/G2
Ełk, Pol. 27/M2
Elk City, Ok, US 93/H4
Elk Grove, Ca, US 99/M10
Elk Grove Village, Il, US 99/P16
Elk River, Mn, US 91/K4
Elk Silver, NM, US 100/D1
Elkhart, In, US 94/C3
Elko, Nv, US 90/E5
Ellensburg, Wa, US 90/C4
Ellesmere Port, Eng, UK 23/F5
Ellicott City, Md, US 94/E4
Ellwangen, Ger. 33/J2
Elmadağ, Turk. 44/E5
Elmhurst, Il, US 99/Q16
Elmina, Gha. 79/E5
Elmira, NY, US 94/E3
Elmshorn, Ger. 29/G1
Elmwood Park, Il, US 99/Q16
Elsdorf, Ger. 31/F2
Elst, Neth. 28/C5
Eltville am Rhein, Ger. 31/H3
Elūrū, India 62/D4
Elverum, Nor. 20/D3
Elwood, In, US 94/C3
Elyria, Oh, US 94/D3
Emāmshahr, Iran 51/H2
Embi, Kaz. 45/L2
Embu, Kenya 77/N8
Emden, Ger. 29/E2
Emeishan, China 60/D2
Emiliano Zapata, Mex. 102/D2
Emirdağ, Turk. 44/D5
Emmeloord, Neth. 28/C3
Emmen, Neth. 28/D3
Emmendingen, Ger. 36/D1
Emmerich, Ger. 28/D5
Empalme, Mex. 100/C3
Empangeni, SAfr. 81/E3
Emporia, Ks, US 93/H3
Emsdetten, Ger. 29/E4
Ena, Japan 57/E3
Encarnación, Par. 109/E2
Encarnación de Díaz, Mex. 100/E4
Encinitas, Ca, US 92/C4
Ende, Indo. 67/F5
Endicott, NY, US 94/E3
Engel's, Rus. 45/H2
Engelskirchen, Ger. 31/G2
Enger, Ger. 29/F4
England, UK 24/D2
English (chan.), UK, Fr. 32/B2
English Bāzār, India 62/E2
Enid, Ok, US 93/H3
Enkhuizen, Neth. 28/C3
Enköping, Swe. 42/C4
Enna, It. 38/D4
Ennepetal, Ger. 29/E6
Enningerloh, Ger. 29/F5
Ennis, Tx, US 93/H4
Enschede, Neth. 28/D4
Ensenada, Mex. 92/C5
Enshi, China 61/F2
Entebbe, Ugan. 77/M7
Enterprise, Al, US 97/G4
Enugu, Nga. 79/G5
Enzan, Japan 57/F3
Epe, Nga. 79/F5
Epe, Neth. 28/C4
Épernay, Fr. 30/C5
Épinal, Fr. 36/C1
Eppelborn, Ger. 31/F5
Epsom and Ewell, Eng, UK 25/F4
Equatorial Guinea (ctry.), EqG. 76/G7
Er Rachidia, Mor. 76/E1
Eravur, SrL. 62/D6
Erba, It. 33/H4
Erbaa, Turk. 44/F4
Erciş, Turk. 51/E2
Érd, Hun. 40/D2
Erdemli, Turk. 49/D1
Erdenet, Mong. 54/E2
Erding, Ger. 33/J2
Erechim, Braz. 108/A3
Ereğli, Turk. 41/K5
Ereğli, Turk. 50/C2
Erenler, Turk. 41/K5
Ereymentaū, Kaz. 46/H4
Erfoud, Mor. 76/E1
Erftstadt, Ger. 31/F2
Erfurt, Ger. 26/F3
Erie (lake), Can.,US 94/D3
Eritrea (ctry.) 77/N5
Erkelenz, Ger. 28/D6
Erkrath, Ger. 28/D6
Erlangen, Ger. 33/J2
Ermelo, SAfr. 80/Q13
Ermelo, Neth. 28/C4
Erode, India 62/C5
Eruwa, Nga. 79/F5
Erzincan, Turk. 44/F5
Erzurum, Turk. 45/G5
Esbjerg, Den. 26/E1
Esbo (Espoo), Fin. 42/E3
Esch-sur-Alzette, Lux. 31/E4
Eschwege, Ger. 29/H6
Eschweiler, Ger. 31/F2
Escondido, Ca, US 92/C4
Escuinapa de Hidalgo, Mex. 100/D4
Escuintla, Guat. 102/D3
Eséka, Camr. 76/H7
Eşfahān, Iran 51/G3
Esher, Eng, UK 25/F4
Esil, Kaz. 46/G4
Eskil, Turk. 50/C2
Eskilstuna, Swe. 42/C4
Eskimalatya, Turk. 50/D2
Eskişehir, Turk. 44/D5
Eslāmābād, Iran 51/F3
Esmeralda, Cuba 103/G1
Esmeraldas, Ecu. 106/C3
Espelkamp, Ger. 29/F4
Esperanza, Mex. 100/C3
Espinal, Col. 106/D3
Esplanada, Braz. 107/L6
Espluges, Sp. 35/L7
Esquel, Arg. 109/B5
Essaouira, Mor. 76/D1
Essen, Belg. 28/B6
Essen, Ger. 28/E6
Esslingen, Ger. 33/H2
Eşţahbān, Iran 51/H4
Estância, Braz. 107/L6
Este, It. 33/J4
Esteio, Braz. 108/B4
Estelí, Nic. 102/E3
Estepona, Sp. 34/C4
Eston and South Bank, Eng, UK 23/G2
Estonia (ctry.), Est. 20/H4
Estoril, Port. 35/P10
Esztergom, Hun. 40/D2
Eţ Taiyiba, Isr. 49/G7
Etāwah, India 62/C2
Ethiopia (ctry.) 77/N5
Etna (peak), It. 38/D4
Etten-Leur, Neth. 28/B5
Etterbeek, Belg. 31/D2
Ettlingen, Ger. 33/H2
Euclid, Oh, US 94/D3
Eufaula, Al, US 97/G4
Eugene, Or, US 90/C4
Eunice, La, US 93/J5
Eupen, Belg. 31/F2
Euphrates (riv.), Asia 51/F4
Eureka, Ca, US 90/B5
Eurodisney, Fr. 30/B6
Europe (cont.) 18/*
Euskirchen, Ger. 31/F2
Eustis, Fl, US 97/H4
Eutin, Ger. 26/F1
Eutini, Malw. 82/F3
Evans (mt.), Co, US 93/F3
Evanston, Wy, US 90/F5
Evanston, Il, US 99/Q15
Evansville, In, US 97/G2

117

Evato – Grača

Evaton, SAfr. 80/P13
Everest (peak), China, Nep 62/E2
Everett, Wa, US 99/B2
Evergem, Belg. 28/A6
Everglades National Park, Fl, US 97/H5
Evergreen Park, Il, US 99/Q16
Evesham, Eng, UK 25/E2
Évora, Port. 34/B3
Évreux, Fr. 30/A5
Évry, Fr. 30/B6
Évvoia (isl.), Gre. 39/H3
Ewa Beach, Hi, US 88/V13
Excelsior Springs, Mo, US 93/J3
Exeter, NH, US 95/G3
Eyre (lake), Austl. 70/F5
Ezhou, China 61/G2

F

Faaa, FrPol. 69/L6
Faaa, FrPol. 69/X15
Fabriano, It. 38/C1
Facatativá, Col. 106/D3
Faches-Thumesnil, Fr. 30/C2
Fada-N'Gourma, Burk. 79/F3
Faenza, It. 33/J4
Făgăraş, Rom. 41/G3
Failsworth, Eng, UK 23/F4
Fair Oaks, Ca, US 99/M9
Fairbanks, Ak, US 85/J3
Fairfield, Ca, US 99/K10
Fairmont, Mn, US 91/K5
Fairmont, WV, US 97/H2
Faisalābad, Pak. 53/K2
Faizābād, India 62/D2
Fajardo, PR 104/E3
Falconara Marittima, It. 40/A4
Falkenberg, Swe. 20/E4
Falkland (Malvinas) (isls.), UK 109/D7
Falköping, Swe. 20/E4
Fall River, Ma, US 95/G3
Falmouth, Eng, UK 24/A6
Fălticeni, Rom. 41/H2
Falun, Swe. 20/E3
Famagusta, Cyp. 49/C2
Fandriana, Madg. 81/H8
Fano, It. 33/K5
Fāqūs, Egypt 49/B4
Farafangana, Madg. 81/H8
Farāh, Afg. 46/G6
Fareham, Eng, UK 25/E5
Farghona, Uzb. 46/H5
Fargo, ND, US 91/J4
Farīdābād, India 62/C2
Farīdpur, Bang. 62/E3
Fāriskūr, Egypt 49/B4
Farmington, Mo, US 93/K3
Farmington, NM, US 92/E3
Farmington, Mi, US 99/F7
Farmington Hills, Mi, US 99/E6
Farnborough, Eng, UK 25/F4
Farnham, Eng, UK 25/F4
Farnworth, Eng, UK 23/F4
Faro, Port. 34/B4
Faroe (isls.), Den. 18/C2
Farroupilha, Braz. 108/B4
Fasā, Iran 51/H4
Fasano, It. 40/C5
Fastiv, Ukr. 44/D2
Fatehpur, India 62/D2
Fatehpur, India 62/B2
Fatick, Sen. 78/A3
Fatsa, Turk. 44/F4
Favara, It. 38/C4
Faversham, Eng, UK 25/G4
Faya-Largeau, Chad 77/J4
Fayetteville, NC, US 97/J3
Fdérik, Mrta. 76/C3
Fear (cape), NC, US 97/J3
Fécamp, Fr. 32/D2
Federal Way, Wa, US 99/C3
Feira de Santana, Braz. 107/L6
Feldkirch, Aus. 37/F3
Felixstowe, Eng, UK 25/H3
Felling, Eng, UK 23/G2
Fene, Sp. 34/A1
Fengcheng, China 58/C2
Fengyüan, Tai. 61/J3
Feodosiya, Ukr. 44/E3
Fergus Falls, Mn, US 91/J4
Ferkéssédougou, C.d'Iv. 78/D4
Fermo, It. 40/A4
Fernandópolis, Braz. 108/B2
Ferndale, Mi, US 99/F7
Ferrara, It. 33/J4
Fès, Mor. 76/E1
Feteşti, Rom. 41/H3
Fethiye, Turk. 50/B2
Feyzābād, Afg. 53/K1
Fianarantsoa, Madg. 81/H8
Fidenza, It. 33/J4
Fier, Alb. 40/D5
Figueres, Sp. 35/G1
Fiji (ctry.) 69/Y17
Filchner Ice Shelf, Ant. 83/Y
Filiaşi, Rom. 41/F3
Findlay, Oh, US 94/D3
Finger (lakes), NY, US 94/A1
Finland (ctry.) 20/H2
Finland (gulf), Fin. 42/E4
Finnentrop, Ger. 29/E6
Finspång, Swe. 20/E4
Firenze (Florence), It. 33/J5
Firminy, Fr. 32/F4
Firozābād, India 62/C2
Firozpur, India 53/K2
Fiumicino, It. 38/C2
Fjell, Nor. 20/C3
Flagstaff, Az, US 92/E4
Flamborough, On, Can. 95/T9
Fleet, Eng, UK 25/F4
Fleetwood, Eng, UK 23/E4
Flensburg, Ger. 26/E1
Fleron, Belg. 31/E2
Flers, Fr. 32/C2
Fleurus, Belg. 31/D3
Fleury-les-Aubrais, Fr. 32/D3
Flint, Mi, US 99/E5
Florence, SC, US 97/J3
Florence, Al, US 97/G3
Florence (Firenze), It. 33/J5
Florencia, Col. 106/C3
Flores, Guat. 102/D2
Floriano, Braz. 107/K5
Florianópolis, Braz. 108/B3
Florida, Cuba 103/G1
Florida, Uru. 109/E3
Florida (state), US 97/H4
Floridia, It. 38/D4
Florin, Ca, US 99/M10
Florissant, Mo, US 93/K3
Foča, Bosn. 40/D4
Focşani, Rom. 41/H3
Foggia, It. 40/B5
Foligno, It. 38/C1
Folkestone, Eng, UK 25/H4
Fond du Lac, Wi, US 91/L5
Fondi, It. 38/C2
Fonseca, Col. 103/H4
Fontaine, Fr. 32/F4
Fontaine-L'Evêque, Belg. 31/D3
Fontainebleau, Fr. 32/E2
Fontenay-le-Comte, Fr. 32/C3
Forbach, Fr. 31/F5
Forchheim, Ger. 33/J2
Forlì, It. 33/K4
Formby, Eng, UK 23/E4
Formia, It. 38/C2
Formiga, Braz. 108/C2
Formosa, Braz. 107/J7
Formosa, Arg. 109/E2
Fornacelle, It. 33/J5
Forrest City, Ar, US 93/K4
Forssa, Fin. 42/D3
Fort Abbās, Pak. 62/B2
Fort Collins, Co, US 93/F2
Fort Dodge, Ia, US 91/K5
Fort Erie, On, Can. 95/V10
Fort Lauderdale, Fl, US 97/H5
Fort Lewis, Wa, US 99/B3
Fort Lewis, Wa, US 99/B3
Fort Liberté, Haiti 103/J2
Fort Madison, Ia, US 91/L5
Fort McMurray, Ab, Can. 86/E3
Fort Morgan, Co, US 93/G2
Fort Myers, Fl, US 97/H5
Fort Payne, Al, US 97/G3
Fort Pierce, Fl, US 97/H5
Fort Portal, Ugan. 77/M7
Fort Saint John, BC, Can. 86/D3
Fort Smith, Ar, US 93/J4
Fort Walton Beach, Fl, US 97/G4
Fort Wayne, In, US 94/C3
Fort-de-France, Fr. 104/F4
Fortaleza, Braz. 107/L4
Fortín, Mex. 101/N8
Fortuna Ledge, Ak, US 85/F3
Foshan, China 61/G4
Fossano, It. 33/G4
Fostoria, Oh, US 94/D3
Fougères, Fr. 32/C2
Foumban, Camr. 79/H5
Fountain, Co, US 93/F3
Fourmies, Fr. 30/D4
Foz do Iguaçu, Braz. 109/F2
Fraiburgo, Braz. 108/B3
Frameries, Belg. 30/C3
Franca, Braz. 108/C2
Francavilla Fontana, It. 40/C5
France (ctry.) 32/D3
Franceville, Gabon 82/B1
Francisco Escárcega, Mex. 102/D2
Francisco I. Madero, Mex. 100/E3
Francistown, Bots. 82/E5
Franco da Rocha, Braz. 108/G8
Franconville, Fr. 30/B6
Franeker, Neth. 28/C2
Frankenberg-Eder, Ger. 29/F6
Frankenthal, Ger. 26/E4
Frankfort, In, US 97/G1
Frankfort (cap.), Ky, US 94/C4
Frankfurt, Ger. 27/H2
Frankfurt am Main, Ger. 33/H1
Franklin, La, US 93/K5
Franklin, In, US 97/G2
Franklin, Tn, US 97/G3
Franklin, Wi, US 99/Q14
Franklin Park, Il, US 99/Q16
Fransisco Beltrão, Braz. 109/F2
Fransisco Morato, Braz. 108/G8
Fraser (riv.), BC, Can. 90/C2
Fraser, Mi, US 99/G6
Frauenfeld, Swi. 37/E2
Frechen, Ger. 31/F2
Fredericia, Den. 26/E1
Frederick, Md, US 97/J2
Fredericksburg, Va, US 97/J2
Fredericton (cap.), NB, Can. 95/H2
Frederikshavn, Den. 20/D4
Fredonia, NY, US 94/E3
Fredrikstad, Nor. 20/D4
Freeport, Tx, US 93/J5
Freeport, Il, US 91/L5
Freetown (cap.), SLeo. 78/B4
Freiberg, Ger. 27/G3
Freiburg, Ger. 36/D2
Freising, Ger. 33/J2
Freital, Ger. 27/G3
Fréjus, Fr. 33/G5
Fremont, Ne, US 91/J5
Fremont, Oh, US 94/D3
Fremont, Ca, US 99/L11
French Guiana (dpcy.), Fr. 107/H3
Fresnillo, Mex. 100/E4
Fresno, Ca, US 92/C3
Freudenberg, Ger. 31/G2
Freudenstadt, Ger. 37/E1
Freyming-Merlebach, Fr. 31/F5
Frías, Arg. 109/C2
Fribourg, Swi. 36/D4
Friedberg, Ger. 37/G1
Friedberg, Ger. 33/H1
Friedrichsdorf, Ger. 33/H1
Friedrichshafen, Ger. 37/F2
Friesoythe, Ger. 29/E2
Frolovo, Rus. 45/G2
Frome, Eng, UK 24/D4
Front Royal, Va, US 97/J2
Frontera, Mex. 102/C2
Frontignan, Fr. 32/E5
Frosinone, It. 38/C2
Frutal, Braz. 108/B1
Fryazino, Rus. 43/X9
Frýdek-Místek, Czh. 27/K4
Fu'an, China 61/H3
Fuchū, Japan 56/C3
Fuengirola, Sp. 34/C4
Fuenlabrada, Sp. 35/N9
Fuerte Olimpo, Par. 106/G8
Fuji, Japan 57/F3
Fuji-san (peak), Japan 57/F3
Fujieda, Japan 57/F3
Fujioka, Japan 57/F2
Fujisawa, Japan 57/F3
Fujiyoshida, Japan 57/F3
Fukuchiyama, Japan 56/D3
Fukue, Japan 56/A4
Fukui, Japan 56/E2
Fukuoka, Japan 56/B4
Fukuroi, Japan 57/E3
Fukushima, Japan 57/G2
Fukuyama, Japan 56/C3
Fulda, Ger. 33/H1
Fuling, China 61/E2
Fulton, Mo, US 93/K3
Fulton, NY, US 94/E3
Funafuti (cap.), Tuv. 68/G5
Funchal, Madr. 35/V15
Fundación, Col. 103/H4
Fundy (bay), US,Can. 95/H2
Funhalouro, Moz. 82/F5
Furmanov, Rus. 42/J4
Fürstenfeldbruck, Ger. 37/H1
Fürstenwalde, Ger. 27/H2
Fürth, Ger. 33/J2
Furukawa, Japan 55/N4
Fushun, China 58/B2
Futog, Yugo. 40/D3
Futtsu, Japan 57/F3
Fuwah, Egypt 49/B4
Fuxin, China 58/A1
Fuyu, China 55/J2
Fuzhou, China 61/H3

G

Gaast, Neth. 28/C2
Gabon (ctry.), Gabon 76/H7
Gaborone (cap.), Bots. 80/D2
Gabriel Leyva Solano, Mex. 100/C3
Gabrovo, Bul. 41/G4
Gadsden, Al, US 97/G3
Găeşti, Rom. 41/G3
Gaeta, It. 38/C2
Gaffney, SC, US 97/H3
Gagarin, Rus. 42/G5
Gagnoa, C.d'Iv. 78/D5
Gagny, Fr. 30/B6
Gagra, Geo. 44/G4
Gainesville, Tx, US 93/H4
Gainesville, Ga, US 97/H3
Gainesville, Fl, US 97/H4
Gainsborough, Eng, UK 23/H5
Galaţi, Rom. 41/J3
Galatina, It. 39/F2
Galatone, It. 39/F2
Galdácano, Sp. 34/D1
Gáldar, Canl. 35/X16
Galesburg, Il, US 91/L5
Galich, Rus. 42/J4
Galion, Oh, US 94/D3
Gallatin, Tn, US 97/G2
Galle, SrL. 62/D6
Gallipoli, It. 39/E2
Gällivare, Swe. 42/D2
Gallup, NM, US 92/E4
Galveston, Tx, US 93/J5
Galveston (bay), Tx, US 93/J5
Galway, Ire. 21/A10
Gamagōri, Japan 57/E3
Gambat, Pak. 62/A2
Gambia (ctry.) 78/B3
Gäncä, Azer. 45/H4
Gandajika, D.R. Congo 82/D2
Ganderkesee, Ger. 29/F2
Gāndhīdhām, India 62/B3
Gandhinagar, India 62/B3
Gandía, Sp. 35/E3
Gangāpur, India 62/C2
Gangārāmpur, India 62/E2
Ganges (riv.), India 62/D2
Ganges, Mouths of the (delta), Bang.,Ind 62/E3
Gangtok, India 62/E2
Ganzhou, China 61/G3
Gao, Mali 79/E2
Gaocheng, China 59/C3
Gaoua, Burk. 78/E4
Gap, Fr. 33/G4
Garanhuns, Braz. 107/L5
Garbsen, Ger. 29/G4
Garça, Braz. 108/B2
Garden City, Ks, US 93/G3
Garden City, Mi, US 99/F7
Gardēz, Afg. 53/J2
Garforth, Eng, UK 23/G4
Garibaldi, Braz. 108/B4
Garissa, Kenya 82/G1
Garland, Tx, US 93/H4
Garmisch-Partenkirchen, Ger. 37/H3
Garoua, Camr. 76/H6
Garut, Indo. 66/C5
Garwolin, Pol. 27/L3
Gary, In, US 99/R16
Garza García, Mex. 101/E3
Garzón, Col. 106/C3
Gaspar, Braz. 108/B3
Gaspé, Qu, Can. 95/H1
Gaspé (pen.), Can. 95/H1
Gastonia, NC, US 97/H3
Gatchina, Rus. 42/F4
Gateshead, Eng, UK 23/G2
Gatesville, Tx, US 96/D4
Gatineau, Qu, Can. 94/F2
Gauripur, India 62/E2
Gauting, Ger. 37/H1
Gavà, Sp. 35/L7
Gävle, Swe. 42/C3
Gay, Rus. 45/L2
Gayā, India 62/E3
Gaya, Niger 79/F4
Gaza Strip (ctry.), Isr. 49/C4
Gaziantep, Turk. 50/D2
Gbadolite, D.R. Congo 77/K7
Gbarnga, Libr. 78/C5
Gbongan, Nga. 79/G5
Gdańsk, Pol. 27/K1
Gdynia, Pol. 27/K1
Gebze, Turk. 41/J5
Geel, Belg. 28/B6
Geelong, Austl. 73/C3
Geesthacht, Ger. 29/H2
Geilenkirchen, Ger. 31/F2
Geislingen an der Steige, Ger. 33/H2
Gejiu, China 60/D4
Gela, It. 38/D4
Geldermalsen, Neth. 28/C5
Geldern, Ger. 28/D5
Geldrop, Neth. 28/C6
Geleen, Neth. 31/E2
Gelendzhik, Rus. 44/F3
Gelibolu, Turk. 41/H5
Gelligaer, Wal, UK 24/C3
Gelsenkirchen, Ger. 28/E5
Gembloux, Belg. 31/D2
Gemena, D.R. Congo 77/J7
Gemert, Neth. 28/C5
Gemlik, Turk. 41/J5
Gendringen, Neth. 28/D5
General Alvear, Arg. 109/C3
General Juan José Rios, Mex. 100/C3
General Juan Madariaga, Arg. 109/E4
General Martín Miguel de Güemes, Arg. 109/C1
General Pico, Arg. 109/D4
General Roca, Arg. 109/C4
Geneva, NY, US 94/E3
Geneva (lake), Fr.,Swi 36/C5
Geneva, Il, US 99/P16
Geneva (Genève), Swi. 33/G3
Genève, Swi. 36/C5
Genk, Belg. 31/E2
Gennep, Neth. 28/C5
Genova (Genoa), It. 33/H4
Gent, Belg. 28/A6
Genteng, Indo. 66/D5
George, SAfr. 80/C4
George Town, Malay. 66/B2
George Town (cap.), UK 103/F2
Georgetown, Tx, US 93/H5
Georgetown, Ky, US 97/G2
Georgetown, SC, US 97/J3
Georgetown (cap.), Guy. 106/G2
Georgia (ctry.) 45/G4
Georgia (state), US 97/G3
Georgian (bay), Can. 94/D2
Georgsmarienhütte, Ger. 29/F4
Gera, Ger. 26/G3
Geraardsbergen, Belg. 30/C2
Geraldton, Austl. 68/A7
Gerede, Turk. 41/L5
Geretsried, Ger. 37/H2
Germantown, Tn, US 93/K4
Germany (ctry.) 26/E3
Germering, Ger. 37/H1
Germiston, SAfr. 80/Q13
Gersthofen, Ger. 37/G1
Gescher, Ger. 28/E5
Geseke, Ger. 29/F5
Getafe, Sp. 35/N9
Gevelsberg, Ger. 29/E6
Gevgelija, FYROM 40/F5
Ghana (ctry.) 79/E4
Ghanzi, Bots. 82/D5
Ghardaïa, Alg. 76/F1
Gharyān, Libya 76/H1
Ghaznī, Afg. 53/J2
Gheorghe Gheorghiu-Dej, Rom. 41/H2
Gheorgheni, Rom. 41/G2
Gherla, Rom. 41/F2
Ghinda (Gīnda), Erit. 52/C5
Ghotki, Pak. 62/A2
Giarre, It. 38/D4
Gibraltar (cap.), Gib. 34/C4
Gibraltar (str.), Eur.,Afr. 34/C5
Gien, Fr. 32/E3
Giengen an der Brenz, Ger. 33/J2
Giessen, Ger. 33/H1
Giessendam, Neth. 28/B5
Gif-sur-Yvette, Fr. 30/B6
Gifhorn, Ger. 29/H4
Gifu, Japan 57/E3
Gijón, Sp. 34/C1
Gillette, Wy, US 91/G4
Gillingham, Eng, UK 25/G4
Gilze, Neth. 28/B5
Gīmbī, Eth. 77/N6
Gingoog, Phil. 67/G2
Ginosa, It. 40/C5
Gioia del Colle, It. 40/C5
Gioia Tauro, It. 38/D3
Girardot, Col. 106/D3
Giresun, Turk. 44/F4
Girīdīh, India 62/E3
Girona, Sp. 35/G2
Gisborne, NZ 71/S10
Gitega, Buru. 82/E1
Giugliano in Campania, It. 40/B5
Giulianova, It. 40/A4
Giurgiu, Rom. 41/G4
Giv'atayim, Isr. 49/F7
Givors, Fr. 32/F4
Giyani, SAfr. 82/F5
Gizo, Sol. 68/E5
Giżycko, Pol. 27/L1
Gjirokastër, Alb. 39/G2
Gjøvik, Nor. 20/D3
Glace Bay, NS, Can. 95/K2
Glacier Bay National Park and Preserve, Ak, US 85/L4
Glacier National Park, BC, Can. 86/E3
Glacier National Park, Can. 90/D3
Gladbeck, Ger. 28/D5
Gladstone, Austl. 72/C3
Glan, Phil. 67/G2
Glarus, Swi. 37/F3
Glasgow, Ky, US 97/G2
Glazov, Rus. 43/M4
Glen Canyon Nat'l Rec. Area, US 92/E3
Glendale, Ca, US 92/C4
Glendale, Az, US 92/D4
Glendale Heights, Il, US 99/P16
Glenview, Il, US 99/Q15
Glifádha, Gre. 39/N9
Glinde, Ger. 29/H1
Gliwice, Pol. 27/K3
Głogów, Pol. 27/J3
Glossop, Eng, UK 23/G5
Gloucester, On, Can. 94/F2
Gloucester, Eng, UK 24/D3
Głowno, Pol. 27/K3
Głuchołazy, Pol. 27/J3
Gniezno, Pol. 27/J2
Gnjilane, Yugo. 40/E4
Go Cong, Viet. 65/D4
Goālpāra, India 62/F2
Goba, Eth. 77/N6
Gobi (des.), Mong. 47/L5
Gobō, Japan 56/D4
Goch, Ger. 28/D5
Godalming, Eng, UK 25/F4
Gödöllő, Hun. 27/K5
Godoy Cruz, Arg. 109/C3
Goes, Neth. 28/A5
Goiana, Braz. 107/M5
Goiânia, Braz. 107/J7
Goiás, Braz. 107/H7
Goiatuba, Braz. 108/B1
Goirle, Neth. 28/C5
Gojō, Japan 56/D3
Göksun, Turk. 50/D2
Gölbaşı, Turk. 50/D2
Gölbaşı, Turk. 44/E5
Golborne, Eng, UK 23/F5
Gölcük, Turk. 41/J5
Gold (coast), Gha. 79/E5
Gold Coast, Austl. 72/D5
Golden, Co, US 93/F3
Goldsboro, NC, US 97/J3
Goleniów, Pol. 27/H2
Gölköy, Turk. 44/F4
Golmud, China 54/C4
Golpāyegān, Iran 51/G3
Goma, D.R. Congo 82/E1
Gómez Palacio, Mex. 96/C5
Gonaïves, Haiti 103/H2
Gonbad-e Qābūs, Iran 51/H2
Gondā, India 62/D2
Gonder, Eth. 77/N5
Gondia, India 62/D3
Gondomar, Port. 34/A2
Gönen, Turk. 41/H5
Gonesse, Fr. 30/B6
Gongzhuling, China 59/F2
Good Hope, Cape of (cape), SAfr. 80/L11
Goodwood, SAfr. 80/L10
Goole, Eng, UK 23/H4
Göppingen, Ger. 33/H2
Gorakhpur, India 62/D2
Gorē, Eth. 77/N6
Görele, Turk. 44/F4
Gorgān, Iran 51/H2
Gori, Geo. 45/H4
Gorinchem, Neth. 28/B5
Gorizia, It. 40/A3
Gorki, Bela. 42/F5
Gorlice, Pol. 27/L4
Görlitz, Ger. 27/H3
Gorna Oryakhovitsa, Bul. 41/G4
Gornji Milanovac, Yugo. 40/E3
Gornji Vakuf, Bosn. 40/C4
Gorno-Altaysk, Rus. 46/J4
Gornyak, Rus. 46/J4
Gorodets, Rus. 43/J4
Goroka, PNG 68/D5
Gorontalo, Indo. 67/F3
Gorzów Wielkopolski, Pol. 27/H2
Gōse, Japan 56/D3
Gosen, Japan 57/F2
Gosford, Austl. 73/D2
Gosforth, Eng, UK 23/G2
Goshogawara, Japan 55/N3
Goslar, Ger. 29/H5
Gospić, Cro. 40/B3
Gosport, Eng, UK 25/E5
Gossau, Swi. 37/F3
Gossensass (Colle Isarco), It. 37/H4
Gostivar, FYROM 40/E5
Gostyń, Pol. 27/J3
Gostynin, Pol. 27/K2
Göteborg, Swe. 20/D4
Gotemba, Japan 57/F3
Gotha, Ger. 29/H7
Gotse Delchev, Bul. 41/F5
Gōtsu, Japan 56/C3
Göttingen, Ger. 29/G5
Gouda, Neth. 28/B4
Goulburn, Austl. 73/D2
Governador Valadares, Braz. 108/D1
Goya, Arg. 109/E2
Graaff-Reinet, SAfr. 80/D4
Gračanica, Bosn. 40/D3

Graci – Hrodn

H

119

Hrubi – Kakam

Hrubieszów, Pol. 27/M3
Hsinchu, Tai. 61/J3
Hua Hin, Thai. 65/B3
Huacho, Peru 106/C6
Huadian, China 55/K3
Huai'an, China 59/D4
Huaibei, China 54/H5
Huaihua, China 61/F3
Huainan, China 59/D4
Huaiyin, China 59/D4
Huajuapan de León, Mex. 102/B2
Hualien, Tai. 61/J4
Huamantla, Mex. 101/M7
Huambo, Ang. 82/C3
Huancavelica, Peru 106/C6
Huancayo, Peru 106/C6
Huanchaca (peak), Bol. 106/E8
Huang (Yellow) (riv.), China 55/H4
Huangshan, China 61/H2
Huangshi, China 61/G2
Huánuco, Peru 106/C5
Huaral, Peru 106/C6
Huaraz, Peru 106/C5
Huascarán (peak), Peru 106/C5
Huatabampo, Mex. 100/C3
Huatuxco, Mex. 101/N7
Huauchinango, Mex. 101/L6
Huaying, China 61/E2
Hubli-Dhārwār, India 62/C4
Hückelhoven, Ger. 28/D6
Hückeswagen, Ger. 29/E6
Hucknall, Eng, UK 23/G5
Huddersfield, Eng, UK 23/G4
Huddinge, Swe. 42/C4
Hudiksvall, Swe. 42/C3
Hudson (bay), Can. 87/H2
Hue, Viet. 65/D2
Huehuetenango, Guat. 102/D3
Huejotzingo, Mex. 101/L7
Huejutla de Reyes, Mex. 102/B1
Huelva, Sp. 34/B4
Huesca, Sp. 35/E1
Huetamo de Nuñez, Mex. 101/E5
Hui Xian, China 59/C4
Huimanguillo, Mex. 102/C2
Huissen, Neth. 28/C5
Huixtla, Mex. 102/C3
Huizen, Neth. 28/C4
Huizhou, China 61/G4
Hull, Qu, Can. 94/F2
Hulst, Neth. 28/B6
Hultsfred, Swe. 20/E4
Humaitá, Braz. 106/F5
Humble, Tx, US 93/J5
Humboldt, Tn, US 97/F3
Humenné, Slvk. 27/L4
Hunchun, China 55/L3
Hunedoara, Rom. 40/F3
Hungary (ctry.) 40/D2
Hunjiang, China 58/D2
Huntingdon, Eng, UK 25/F2
Huntington, WV, US 97/H2
Huntington, In, US 94/C3
Huntington Beach, Ca, US 92/C4
Huntsville, Tx, US 93/J5
Huntsville, On, Can. 94/E2
Huntsville, Al, US 97/G3
Hunucmá, Mex. 102/D1
Huolin Gol, China 55/H2
Huozhou, China 59/B3
Huron (lake), Can.,US 94/D2
Hürth, Ger. 31/F2
Huşi, Rom. 41/J2
Husum, Ger. 26/E1
Hutchinson, Mn, US 91/K4
Hutchinson, Ks, US 93/H3
Huy, Belg. 31/E2
Huyton-with-Roby, Eng, UK 23/F5
Huzhou, China 59/L9
Hwange, Zim. 82/E4
Hyde, Eng, UK 23/F5
Hyderābād, India 62/C4
Hyderābād, Pak. 62/A2
Hyères, Fr. 33/G5
Hythe, Eng, UK 25/H4
Hyūga, Japan 56/B4
Hyvinkää, Fin. 42/E3

I

I-n-Guezzâm, Alg. 79/G2
I-n-Salah, Alg. 76/F2
Iaşi, Rom. 41/H2
Ibadan, Nga. 79/F5
Ibagué, Col. 106/C3
Ibara, Japan 56/C3
Ibarra, Ecu. 106/C3
Ibb, Yem. 52/D6
Ibbenbüren, Ger. 29/E4
Ibi, Sp. 35/E3
Ibicaraí, Braz. 107/L6
Ibitinga, Braz. 108/B2
Ibiúna, Braz. 108/F8
Ibiza, Sp. 35/F3
Ibotirama, Braz. 107/K6
Ibshawāy, Egypt 49/B5
Ica, Peru 106/C6
Iceland (ctry.) 20/N6
Ichalkaranji, India 62/B4
Ichchāpuram, India 62/D4
Ichinomiya, Japan 57/E3
Ichinoseki, Japan 55/N4
Icó, Braz. 107/L5
Icod de los Vinos, Canl. 35/X16
Idaho (state), US 90/E3
Idar, India 62/B3
Idar-Oberstein, Ger. 31/G4
Idfū, Egypt 52/B4
Idlib, Syria 49/E2
Idstein, Ger. 31/H3
Ieper, Belg. 30/B2
Ifanadiana, Madg. 81/H8
Ife, Nga. 79/G5
Igarapava, Braz. 108/C2
Igarapé-Miri, Braz. 107/J4
Igarka, Rus. 46/J3
Igatpuri, India 62/B4
Iğdır, Turk. 45/H5
Iglesias, It. 38/A3
Ignacio, Ca, US 99/J10
Igra, Rus. 43/M4
Iguala, Mex. 101/K8
Igualada, Sp. 35/F2
Iguape, Braz. 108/C3
Iguatu, Braz. 107/L5
Iida, Japan 57/E3
Iisalmi, Fin. 42/E3
Iiyama, Japan 57/F2
Iizuka, Japan 56/B4
Ijebu Ode, Nga. 79/F5
IJsselstein, Neth. 28/C4
Ijuí, Braz. 109/F2
Ijūin, Japan 56/B5
Ikare, Nga. 79/G5
Ikeda, Japan 56/C3
Ikeja, Nga. 79/F5
Ikerre, Nga. 79/G5
Ikire, Nga. 79/G5
Ikirun, Nga. 79/G5
Ikorodu, Nga. 79/F5
Ila Orangun, Nga. 79/G4
Ilam, Nepal 62/E2
Ilan, Tai. 61/J3
Ilaro, Nga. 79/F5
Iława, Pol. 27/K2
Ilawe-Ekiti, Nga. 79/G5
Ilebo, D.R. Congo 82/D1
Ilesha, Nga. 79/G5
Ilgın, Turk. 50/B2
Ílhavo, Port. 34/A2
Ilhéus, Braz. 107/L6
Iligan, Phil. 67/F2
Ilium (Troy) (ruin), Turk. 39/K3
Ilkeston, Eng, UK 23/G6
Illapel, Chile 109/B3
Illingen, Ger. 31/G5
Illinois (state), US 94/B4
Illizi, Alg. 76/G2
Illkirch-Graffenstaden, Fr. 31/G6
Illzach, Fr. 36/D2
Ilmenau, Ger. 33/J1
Ilo, Peru 106/D7
Ilobu, Nga. 79/G5
Iloilo, Phil. 67/F1
Ilorin, Nga. 79/G4
Imabari, Japan 56/C3
Imaichi, Japan 57/F2
Imamoğlu, Turk. 50/C2
Imari, Japan 56/A4
Imatra, Fin. 42/F3
Imerimandroso, Madg. 81/J7
İmişli, Azer. 51/G2
Immokalee, Fl, US 97/H5
Imola, It. 33/J4
Imperatriz, Braz. 107/J5
Imperia, It. 33/H5
Imphāl, India 60/B3
Ina, Japan 57/E3
Inca, Sp. 35/G3
Inch'ŏn, SKor. 58/F7
İncirliova, Turk. 50/A2
Indaiatuba, Braz. 108/C2
Indanan, Phil. 67/F2
Independence, Mo, US 93/J3
Independence, Ks, US 93/J3
India (ctry.) 62/C3
Indian (ocean) 17/N6
Indiana, Pa, US 94/E3
Indiana (state), US 94/C3
Indianapolis (cap.), In, US 94/C4
Indianola, Ms, US 93/K4
Indija, Yugo. 40/E3
Indio, Ca, US 92/C4
Indochina (reg.), Laos 65/C1
Indonesia (ctry.) 67/E4
Indore, India 62/C3
İnegöl, Turk. 44/D4
Inezgane, Mor. 76/D1
Ingenio, Canl. 35/X17
Inglewood-Finn Hill, Wa, US 99/C2
Ingolstadt, Ger. 33/J2
Inhambane, Moz. 82/G5
Inhumas, Braz. 107/J7
Inkster, Mi, US 99/F7
Innichen (San Candido), It. 33/K3
Ino, Japan 56/C4
Inowrocław, Pol. 27/K2
Insein, Myan. 60/C5
Inta, Rus. 43/N2
Inuyama, Japan 57/E3
Invercargill, NZ 71/Q12
Inza, Rus. 45/H1
Ioánnina, Gre. 39/G3
Iowa (state), US 93/J2
Ipameri, Braz. 108/B1
Ipatinga, Braz. 108/D1
Ipiales, Col. 106/C3
Ipiaú, Braz. 107/L6
Ipoh, Malay. 66/B3
Iporá, Braz. 107/H7
Ipswich, Eng, UK 25/H2
Ipu, Braz. 107/K4
Iquique, Chile 106/D8
Iquitos, Peru 106/D4
Iráklion, Gre. 39/J5
Iran (ctry.) 48/E6
Irapuato, Mex. 101/E4
Iraq (ctry.) 50/E3
Irati, Braz. 108/B3
Irbid, Jor. 49/D3
Irbīl, Iraq 51/F2
Irecê, Braz. 107/K6
Ireland (ctry.), Ire. 21/A4
Iri, SKor. 58/D5
Iringa, Tanz. 82/G2
Irish (sea), Ire.,UK 22/C4
Irkutsk, Rus. 54/E1
Irlam, Eng, UK 23/F5
Ironton, Oh, US 97/H2
Irún, Sp. 34/E1
Irvine, Ca, US 92/C4
Irving, Tx, US 96/D3
Isahaya, Japan 56/B4
Ischia, It. 40/A5
Ise, Japan 57/E3
Isehara, Japan 57/F3
Iserlohn, Ger. 29/E6
Isernia, It. 40/B5
Isesaki, Japan 57/F2
Iseyin, Nga. 79/F5
Ishibashi, Japan 57/F2
Ishigaki, Japan 68/B2
Ishige, Japan 57/F2
Ishikawa, Japan 57/G2
Ishim, Rus. 43/R4
Ishimbay, Rus. 45/L1
Ishinomaki, Japan 57/G1
Ishioka, Japan 57/G1
Isil'kul', Rus. 46/H4
Isiro, D.R. Congo 77/L7
İskenderun, Turk. 49/E1
İskilip, Turk. 44/E4
Isla, Mex. 102/C2
Isla Cristina, Sp. 34/B4
Islâhiye, Turk. 49/E1
Islāmābād (cap.), Pak. 53/K2
Islāmpur, India 62/E2
Isle Royale National Park, Mi, US 94/B2
Ismail Samani (peak), Taj. 46/H6
Isnā, Egypt 52/B3
Isoanala, Madg. 81/H8
Isparta, Turk. 50/B2
Israel (ctry.) 49/C3
Issoire, Fr. 32/E4
Issy-les-Moulineaux, Fr. 30/B6
İstanbul, Turk. 51/M6
Istres, Fr. 32/F5
Isulan, Phil. 67/F2
Itabaiana, Braz. 107/L6
Itaberaba, Braz. 107/K6
Itabira, Braz. 108/D1
Itabirito, Braz. 108/D2
Itaboraí, Braz. 108/L7
Itabuna, Braz. 107/L6
Itacoatiara, Braz. 106/G4
Itaguaí, Braz. 108/K7
Itagüí, Col. 106/C2
Itaituba, Braz. 107/G4
Itajaí, Braz. 108/B3
Itajubá, Braz. 108/H7
Itako, Japan 57/G3
Italy (ctry.) 18/E4
Itamaraju, Braz. 107/L7
Itampolo, Madg. 81/G9
Itanhaém, Braz. 108/G9
Itaobim, Braz. 107/K7
Itapagé, Braz. 107/L4
Itapecuru-Mirim, Braz. 107/K4
Itapemirim, Braz. 108/D2
Itaperuna, Braz. 108/D2
Itapetinga, Braz. 107/K7
Itapetininga, Braz. 108/B2
Itapeva, Braz. 108/B2
Itapevi, Braz. 108/G8
Itapipoca, Braz. 107/L4
Itapira, Braz. 108/G7
Itaquaquecetuba, Braz. 108/G8
Itararé, Braz. 108/B3
Itārsi, India 62/C3
Itatiba, Braz. 108/G7
Itaúna, Braz. 108/C2
Itayanagi, Japan 55/N3
Ithaca, NY, US 94/E3
Itō, Japan 57/F3
Itoigawa, Japan 57/E2
Itu, Braz. 108/C2
Ituiutaba, Braz. 108/B1
Itumbiara, Braz. 108/B1
Iturama, Braz. 108/B1
Ituverava, Braz. 108/C2
Ityāy al Bārūd, Egypt 49/B4
Itzehoe, Ger. 26/E2
Ivaiporã, Braz. 108/B3
Ivangrad, Yugo. 40/D4
Ivanjica, Yugo. 40/E4
Ivano-Frankivs'k, Ukr. 44/C2
Ivanovo, Rus. 42/J4
Ivdel, Rus. 46/G3
Ivohibe, Madg. 81/H8
Ivory (coast), C.d'Iv. 78/D5
Ivrea, It. 33/G4
Iwai, Japan 57/F2
Iwaki, Japan 57/G2
Iwakuni, Japan 56/C3
Iwami, Japan 56/D3
Iwamizawa, Japan 55/N3
Iwanuma, Japan 57/G1
Iwata, Japan 57/E3
Iwo, Nga. 79/G5
Ixelles, Belg. 31/D2
Ixmiquilpan, Mex. 101/K6
Ixtapaluca, Mex. 101/L7
Ixtlán del Río, Mex. 100/D4
Iyo, Japan 56/C4
Izberbash, Rus. 45/H4
Izegem, Belg. 30/C2
Izhevsk, Rus. 43/M4
Izkī, Oman 53/G4
Izmayil, Ukr. 41/J3
İzmir, Turk. 44/C5
İzmit, Turk. 41/J5
İznik, Turk. 41/J5
Izúcar de Matamoros, Mex. 101/L8
Izuhara, Japan 56/A3
Izumi, Japan 56/D3
Izumi, Japan 56/B4
Izumi-Sano, Japan 56/D3
Izumo, Japan 56/C3
Izyum, Ukr. 44/F2

J

Jabalpur, India 62/C3
Jablah, Syria 49/D2
Jablonec nad Nisou, Czh. 27/H3
Jaboatão dos Guararapes, Braz. 107/L5
Jaboticabal, Braz. 108/B2
Jacareí, Braz. 108/H8
Jackson, Mo, US 93/K3
Jackson, Mi, US 94/C3
Jackson, Tn, US 97/F3
Jackson (cap.), Ms, US 93/K4
Jacksonville, Il, US 93/K3
Jacksonville, Ar, US 93/J4
Jacksonville, NC, US 97/J3
Jacksonville, Al, US 97/G3
Jacksonville, Fl, US 97/H4
Jacksonville Beach, Fl, US 97/H4
Jacmel, Haiti 103/H2
Jacobābād, Pak. 62/A2
Jacobina, Braz. 107/K6
Jacona de Plancarte, Mex. 100/E5
Jaén, Sp. 34/D4
Jaffna, SrL. 62/C6
Jagdalpur, India 62/D4
Jagtiāl, India 62/C4
Jaguaquara, Braz. 107/L6
Jaguarão, Braz. 109/F3
Jaguariaíva, Braz. 108/B3
Jaguariúna, Braz. 108/G7
Jahrom, Iran 51/H4
Jailolo, Indo. 67/G3
Jaisalmer, India 62/B2
Jājapur, India 62/E3
Jajce, Bosn. 40/C3
Jakarta (cap.), Indo. 66/C5
Jakobstad (Pietarsaari), Fin. 42/D3
Jalal-Abad, Kyr. 46/H5
Jalālābād, Afg. 53/K2
Jalapa, Guat. 102/D3
Jalapa, Mex. 101/N7
Jales, Braz. 108/B2
Jalīb ash Shuyūkh, Kuw. 51/F4
Jalisco, Mex. 100/D4
Jalostotitlán, Mex. 100/E4
Jalpaiguri, India 62/E2
Jáltipan de Morelos, Mex. 102/C2
Jamaica (chan.), NAm. 103/H2
Jamaica (ctry.), Jam. 103/G2
Jamālpur, India 62/E2
Jamālpur, Bang. 62/E3
Jambi, Indo. 66/B4
Jamestown, NY, US 94/E3
Jammāl, Tun. 38/B5
Jammu, India 53/K2
Jāmpur, Pak. 53/K3
Jamshedpur, India 62/E3
Jamūi, India 62/E3
Janakkala, Fin. 42/E3
Janaúba, Braz. 107/K7
Jandaia do Sul, Braz. 108/B2
Jangaon, India 62/C4
Jangipur, India 62/E3
Januária, Braz. 107/K7
Japan (sea), Asia 55/L3
Japan (ctry.) 55/M4
Jaramānah, Syria 49/E3
Jardín América, Arg. 109/E2
Jardinópolis, Braz. 108/C2
Jaridih, India 62/E3
Jarjīs, Tun. 76/H1
Jarocin, Pol. 27/J3
Jarosław, Pol. 27/M3
Jarrow, Eng, UK 23/G2
Järvenpää, Fin. 20/H3
Jasło, Pol. 27/L4
Jasper, In, US 97/G2
Jasper, Al, US 97/G3
Jaspur, India 62/C2
Jastrzębie Zdroj, Pol. 27/K4
Jászberény, Hun. 40/D2
Jataí, Braz. 108/B1
Jatibonico, Cuba 103/G1
Játiva, Sp. 35/E3
Jaú, Braz. 108/B2
Java (isl.), Indo. 66/C5
Java (sea), Indo. 66/D5
Jávea, Sp. 35/F3
Jawor, Pol. 27/J3
Jayapura, Indo. 67/K4
Jędrzejów, Pol. 27/L3
Jefferson City (cap.), Mo, US 93/J3
Jeffersonville, In, US 97/G2
Jēkabpils, Lat. 42/E4
Jelenia Góra, Pol. 27/H3
Jelgava, Lat. 42/D4
Jemappes, Belg. 30/C3
Jember, Indo. 66/D5
Jena, Ger. 26/F3
Jennings, La, US 93/J5
Jequié, Braz. 107/K6
Jequitinhonha, Braz. 107/K7
Jérémie, Haiti 103/H2
Jerez de García Salinas, Mex. 100/E4
Jerez de la Frontera, Sp. 34/B4
Jerusalem (cap.), Isr. 49/G8
Jesenice, Slov. 40/B2
Jesi, It. 33/K5
Jessheim, Nor. 20/D3
Jessore, Bang. 62/E3
Jesús María, Arg. 109/D3
Jesús Menéndez, Cuba 103/G1
Jetpur, India 62/B3
Jeypore, India 62/D4
Jhā Jhā, India 62/E3
Jhālawār, India 62/C3
Jhang Sadar, Pak. 53/K2
Jhanjhārpur, India 62/E2
Jhānsi, India 62/C2
Jhārsuguda, India 62/D3
Jhelum, Pak. 53/K2
Ji-Paraná, Braz. 106/F6
Jiamusi, China 55/L2
Ji'an, China 61/G3
Jiangmen, China 61/G4
Jiangyin, China 61/J2
Jiaohe, China 55/K3
Jiaojiang, China 61/J2
Jiaozuo, China 59/C4
Jiaxing, China 59/L9
Jiayuguan, China 54/D4
Jičín, Czh. 33/L1
Jiddah, SAr. 52/C4
Jieshou, China 59/C4
Jiguaní, Cuba 103/G1
Jihlava, Czh. 33/L2
Jijel, Alg. 76/G1
Jijiga, Eth. 77/P6
Jilin, China 55/K3
Jīma, Eth. 77/N6
Jimaní, DRep. 103/J2
Jiménez, Mex. 96/B5
Jimo, China 59/E3
Jinan, China 59/D3
Jinchang, China 54/E4
Jincheng, China 59/C4
Jīnd, India 62/C2
Jindřichuv Hradec, Czh. 33/L2
Jingdezhen, China 61/H2
Jingmen, China 61/G2
Jinhua, China 61/H2
Jining, China 59/D4
Jining, China 59/C2
Jinja, Ugan. 77/M7
Jinotega, Nic. 102/E3
Jinotepe, Nic. 102/E4
Jinshi, China 61/F2
Jintūr, India 62/C4
Jinxi, China 59/E2
Jinzhou, China 59/E2
Jipijapa, Ecu. 106/B4
Jiquilpan de Juárez, Mex. 100/E5
Jishou, China 61/F2
Jisr ash Shughūr, Syria 49/E2
Jitra, Malay. 65/C5
Jiujiang, China 61/G2
Jiutai, China 55/K3
Jiutepec, Mex. 101/K8
Jixi, China 55/L2
Jiyuan, China 59/C4
Jīzān, SAr. 52/D5
Jizzakh, Uzb. 46/G5
Joaçaba, Braz. 108/B3
João Monlevade, Braz. 108/D1
João Pessoa, Braz. 107/M5
João Pinheiro, Braz. 108/C1
Jobabo, Cuba 103/G1
Jodhpur, India 62/B2
Joensuu, Fin. 42/F3
Jōetsu, Japan 57/F2
Jogbani, India 62/E2
Johannesburg, SAfr. 80/Q13
Johnson City, Tn, US 97/H2
Johnstown, Pa, US 94/E3
Johor Baharu, Malay. 66/B3
Joinvile, Braz. 108/B3
Jojutla, Mex. 101/K8
Joliet, Il, US 99/P16
Joliette, Qu, Can. 94/F2
Jollyville, Tx, US 93/H5
Jolo, Phil. 67/F2
Jombang, Indo. 66/D5
Jona, Swi. 37/E3
Jönköping, Swe. 20/E4
Jonquière, Qu, Can. 95/G1
Joplin, Mo, US 93/J3
Jordan (ctry.) 49/D4
Jorhāt, India 60/B3
Jos, Nga. 79/H4
Jose Abad Santos, Phil. 67/G2
José Bonifácio, Braz. 108/B2
José Cardel, Mex. 101/N7
Joshua Tree National Park, Ca, US 92/D4
Joué-lès-Tours, Fr. 32/D3
Jovellanos, Cuba 103/F1
Jowai, India 60/B3
Juan de Fuca (str.), US,Can. 90/B3
Juazeiro, Braz. 107/K5
Juazeiro do Norte, Braz. 107/L5
Juba, Sudan 77/M7
Jüchen, Ger. 28/D6
Juchitán de Zaragoza, Mex. 102/C2
Juigalpa, Nic. 102/E3
Juiz de Fora, Braz. 108/K6
Juliaca, Peru 106/D7
Jülich, Ger. 31/F2
Julio A. Mella, Cuba 103/H1
Jullundur, India 53/L2
Jumilla, Sp. 34/E3
Jumla, Nepal 62/D2
Junāgadh, India 62/B3
Junction City, Ks, US 93/H3
Jundiaí, Braz. 108/G8
Juneau (cap.), Ak, US 85/M4
Junín, Arg. 109/D3
Jupiter, Fl, US 97/H5
Juquitiba, Braz. 108/F8
Jūrmala, Lat. 42/D4
Jutiapa, Guat. 102/D3
Juticalpa, Hon. 102/E3
Jyväskylä, Fin. 42/E3

K

Kaalualu, Hi, US 88/U11
Kaarina, Fin. 42/D3
Kaarst, Ger. 28/D6
Kabale, Ugan. 82/E1
Kabankalan, Phil. 67/F2
Kabul (cap.), Afg. 53/J2
Kabwe, Zam. 82/E3
Kadaianallur, India 62/C6
Kadaň, Czh. 33/K1
Kadınhanı, Turk. 50/C2
Kadiri, India 62/C5
Kadirli, Turk. 50/D2
Kadoma, Zim. 82/E4
Kaduna, Nga. 79/G4
Kāduqlī, Sudan 77/L5
Kaédi, Mrta. 78/B2
Kaélé, Camr. 76/H5
Kaesŏng, NKor. 58/D3
Kaffrine, Sen. 78/B3
Kafr ash Shaykh, Egypt 49/B4
Kafr az Zayyāt, Egypt 49/B4
Kafue, Zam. 82/E4
Kaga, Japan 56/E2
Kaga Bandoro, CAfr. 77/J6
Kagan, Uzb. 46/G6
Kağıthane, Turk. 51/M6
Kağızman, Turk. 45/G4
Kagoshima, Japan 56/B5
Kahramanmaraş, Turk. 50/D2
Kahror Pakka, Pak. 53/K3
Kâhta, Turk. 50/D2
Kahului, Hi, US 88/T10
Kaifeng, China 59/C4
Kaili, China 61/E3
Kailua, Hi, US 88/U11
Kailua, Hi, US 88/W13
Kainan, Japan 56/D3
Kaiserslautern, Ger. 31/G5
Kaiyuan, China 59/F2
Kaiyuan, China 60/D4
Kajaani, Fin. 20/H2
Kakamega, Kenya 77/M7
Kakamigahara, Japan 57/E3

Kakho – Kryvy

121

Krzyż – Lough

Krzyż, Pol. 27/J2
Kuala Belait, Bru. 66/D3
Kuala Dungun, Malay. 66/B3
Kuala Lumpur (cap.), Malay. 66/B3
Kuala Terengganu, Malay. 66/B2
Kuantan, Malay. 66/B3
Kubokawa, Japan 56/C4
Kuching, Malay. 66/D3
Kudamatsu, Japan 56/B3
Kudat, Malay. 67/E2
Kudus, Indo. 66/D5
Kudymkar, Rus. 43/M4
Kuji, Japan 55/N3
Kuki, Japan 57/F2
Kula, Yugo. 40/D3
Kula, Turk. 44/D5
Kulai, Malay. 66/B3
Kulebaki, Rus. 45/G1
Kullu, India 53/L2
Kulmbach, Ger. 33/J1
Külob, Taj. 53/J1
Kul'sary, Kaz. 45/K3
Kulu, Turk. 44/E5
Kulunda, Rus. 46/H4
Kumagaya, Japan 57/F2
Kumamoto, Japan 56/B4
Kumano, Japan 56/E4
Kumanovo, FYROM 40/E4
Kumasi, Gha. 79/E5
Kumba, Camr. 79/H5
Kumbo, Camr. 79/H5
Kumertau, Rus. 45/K1
Kumi, SKor. 56/A2
Kumla, Swe. 20/E4
Kumluca, Turk. 49/B1
Kumo, Nga. 79/H4
Kumta, India 62/B5
Künch, India 62/C2
Kundapura, India 62/B5
Kundiān, Pak. 53/K2
Kundiawa, PNG 68/D5
Kundla, India 62/B3
Kungälv, Swe. 20/D4
Kungsbacka, Swe. 20/E4
Kungur, Rus. 43/N4
Kuningan, Indo. 66/C5
Kunming, China 60/D3
Kunsan, SKor. 58/D5
Kunshan, China 59/L8
Kuopio, Fin. 42/E3
Kupang, Indo. 67/F6
Kupino, Rus. 46/H4
Kup'yans'k, Ukr. 44/F2
Kurashiki, Japan 56/C3
Kurayoshi, Japan 56/C3
Kŭrdzhali, Bul. 41/G5
Kure, Japan 56/C3
Kurgan, Rus. 43/Q5
Kuri, SKor. 58/G6
Kuril (isls.), Rus. 47/Q5
Kurnool, India 62/C4
Kuroiso, Japan 57/G2
Kurseong, India 62/E2
Kursk, Rus. 44/F2
Kurtalan, Turk. 50/E2
Kürten, Ger. 29/E6
Kurume, Japan 56/B4
Kurunegala, SrL. 62/D6
Kuşadası, Turk. 50/A2
Kushikino, Japan 56/B5
Kushima, Japan 56/B5
Kushimoto, Japan 56/D4
Kushiro, Japan 55/N3
Kūstī, Sudan 77/M5
Kütahya, Turk. 44/D5
K'ut'aisi, Geo. 45/G4
Kutná Hora, Czh. 33/L2
Kutno, Pol. 27/K2
Kuusamo, Fin. 20/J2
Kuusankoski, Fin. 42/E3
Kuvandyk, Rus. 45/L2
Kuwait (ctry.) 51/F4
Kuwait (cap.), Kuw. 51/F4
Kuwana, Japan 57/E3
Kuznetsk, Rus. 45/H1
Kwach'ŏn, SKor. 58/F7
Kwamashu, SAfr. 81/E3
Kwangju, SKor. 58/D5
Kwangju, SKor. 58/G7
Kwangmyŏng, SKor. 58/F7
Kwekwe, Zim. 82/E4
Kwidzyn, Pol. 27/K2
Kyakhta, Rus. 54/F1
Kymore, India 62/C3
Kyŏngju, SKor. 56/A3
Kyŏngsan, SKor. 56/A3
Kyōto, Japan 56/D3
Kyrenia, Cyp. 49/C2
Kyrgyzstan (ctry.) 46/H5
Kyustendil, Bul. 40/E4
Kyzyl, Rus. 54/C1

L

La Asunción, Ven. 104/F5
La Baie, Qu, Can. 95/G1
La Banda, Arg. 109/D2
La Baule-Escoublac, Fr. 32/B3
La Carolina, Sp. 34/D3
La Ceiba, Hon. 102/E3
La Chapelle-Saint-Luc, Fr. 32/F2
La Chaux-de-Bonds, Swi. 36/C3
La Chorrera, Pan. 103/G4
La Ciotat, Fr. 32/F5
La Concepción, Nic. 102/E4
La Coruña, Sp. 34/A1
La Crosse, Wi, US 91/L5
La Dorada, Col. 106/D2
La Esperanza, Hon. 102/D3
La Estrada, Sp. 34/A1
La Flèche, Fr. 32/C3
La Grande, Or, US 90/D4
La Grange, Ga, US 97/G3
La Laguna, Canl. 35/X16
La Libertad, Ecu. 106/B4
La Libertad, Guat. 102/D2
La Línea de la Concepción, Sp. 34/C4
La Louvière, Belg. 31/D3
La Madeleine, Fr. 30/C2
La Oroya, Peru 106/C6
La Paz, Arg. 109/E3
La Paz, Mex. 100/C3
La Paz, Hon. 102/E3
La Paz (cap.), Bol. 106/E7
La Piedad Cavadas, Mex. 100/E4
La Porte, In, US 94/C3
La Prairie, Qu, Can. 95/P7
La Rinconada, Sp. 34/C4
La Rioja, Arg. 109/C2
La Roche-sur-Yon, Fr. 32/C3
La Rochelle, Fr. 32/C3
La Salle, Il, US 91/L5
La Serena, Chile 109/B2
La Seyne-sur-Mer, Fr. 32/F5
La Solana, Sp. 34/D3
La Spezia, It. 33/H4
La Teste, Fr. 32/C4
La Trinidad, Phil. 61/J5
La Unión, ESal. 102/E3
La Unión, Chile 109/B5
La Victoria, Ven. 106/E1
Laas (Lasa), It. 37/G4
Laatzen, Ger. 29/G4
Labé, Gui. 78/B4
Labinsk, Rus. 45/G3
Laboulaye, Arg. 109/D3
Lábrea, Braz. 106/F5
Laces (Latsch), It. 37/G4
Lacey, Wa, US 99/B3
Lachenaie, Qu, Can. 95/N6
Lachine, Qu, Can. 95/N7
Lackawanna, NY, US 95/V10
Laconia, NH, US 95/G3
Ladysmith, SAfr. 81/E3
Lafayette, In, US 94/C3
Lafayette, La, US 93/J5
Lafayette, Ca, US 99/K11
Lafia, Nga. 79/H4
Lagarto, Braz. 107/L6
Lagawe, Phil. 61/J5
Lage, Ger. 29/F5
Lages, Braz. 108/B3
Laghouat, Alg. 76/F1
Lagny-sur-Marne, Fr. 30/B6
Lagoa da Prata, Braz. 108/C2
Lagoa Vermelha, Braz. 108/B4
Lagos, Nga. 79/F5
Lagos, Port. 34/A4
Lagos de Moreno, Mex. 100/E4
Laguna, Braz. 108/B4
Lahad Datu, Malay. 67/E2
Lahat, Indo. 66/B4
Lāhījān, Iran 51/G2
Lahnstein, Ger. 31/G3
Laholm, Swe. 20/E4
Lahore, Pak. 53/K2
Lahr, Ger. 36/D1
Lahti, Fin. 42/E3
Laï, Chad 76/J6
Lai Chau, Viet. 65/C1
Laiwu, China 59/D3
Lajatico, It. 33/J5
Lajeado, Braz. 108/B4
Lake Charles, La, US 93/J5
Lake City, Fl, US 97/H4
Lake Forest, Il, US 99/Q15
Lake Havasu City, Az, US 92/D4
Lake Jackson, Tx, US 93/J5
Lake of the Woods (lake), Can.,US 94/A1
Lake Station, In, US 99/R16
Lake Wales, Fl, US 97/H5
Lake Worth, Fl, US 97/H5
Lake Zurich, Il, US 99/P15
Lakeland, Fl, US 97/H4
Lakewood, Co, US 93/F3
Lakewood, Wa, US 99/B3
Lakhīmpur, India 62/D2
Lakki, Pak. 53/K2
Lakshadweep (isls.), India 62/B5
Lāla Mūsa, Pak. 53/K2
Lalín, Sp. 34/A1
Lalitpur, India 62/C3
Lambaré, Par. 109/E2
Lambaréné, Gabon 82/B1
Lambayeque, Peru 106/C5
Lamesa, Tx, US 93/G4
Lamía, Gre. 39/H3
Lamitan, Phil. 67/F2
Lamont, Ca, US 92/C4
Lampang, Thai. 65/B2
Lampertheim, Ger. 33/H2
Lanaken, Belg. 31/E2
Lancaster, Pa, US 94/E3
Lancaster, Ca, US 92/C4
Lancaster, NY, US 95/V10
Lancaster, Eng, UK 23/F3
Lanciano, It. 40/B4
L'Ancienne-Lorette, Qu, Can. 95/G2
Łańcut, Pol. 27/M3
Lancy, Swi. 36/C5
Land's End (pt.), Eng, UK 24/A6
Landau in der Pfalz, Ger. 31/H5
Landerneau, Fr. 32/A2
Landsberg, Ger. 37/G1
Landshut, Ger. 33/K2
Lanester, Fr. 32/B3
Lang Son, Viet. 65/D1
Langen, Ger. 29/F1
Langenfeld, Ger. 28/D6
Langenhagen, Ger. 29/G4
Langenthal, Swi. 36/D3
Langfang, China 59/H7
Langsa, Indo. 66/A3
Länkärän, Azer. 51/G2
Lannion, Fr. 32/B2
Lansing (cap.), Mi, US 94/C3
Lansing, Il, US 99/Q16
Lanxi, China 61/H2
Lanzhou, China 54/E4
Lanzo d'Intelvi, It. 37/F6
Lao Cai, Viet. 65/C1
Laohekou, China 61/F1
Laon, Fr. 30/C4
Laos (ctry.) 65/C2
Lapa, Braz. 108/B3
Lapland (reg.), Swe. 20/F1
Lappeenranta, Fin. 42/F3
Lapua, Fin. 42/D3
Łapy, Pol. 27/M2
L'Aquila, It. 38/C1
Lār, Iran 51/H5
Larache, Mor. 76/D1
Laramie, Wy, US 93/F2
Laranjeiras do Sul, Braz. 108/A3
Laredo, Tx, US 96/D5
Largo, Fl, US 97/H5
Lárisa, Gre. 39/H3
Lārkāna, Pak. 62/A2
Larkspur, Ca, US 99/J11
Larnaca, Cyp. 49/C2
Larne, NI, UK 22/C2
Larreynaga, Nic. 102/E3
Larsen Ice Shelf, Ant. 83/V
Las Cabezas de San Juan, Sp. 34/C4
Las Choapas, Mex. 101/G5
Las Cruces, NM, US 92/F4
Las Flores, Arg. 109/E4
Las Guacamayas, Mex. 100/E5
Las Matas de Farfán, DRep. 103/J2
Las Palmas, Pan. 103/F4
Las Palmas de Gran Canaria, Canl. 35/X16
Las Rozas de Madrid, Sp. 35/N9
Las Tablas, Pan. 103/F5
Las Vegas, NM, US 93/F4
Las Vegas, Nv, US 92/D3
Lasa (Laas), It. 37/G4
Lasalle, Qu, Can. 95/N7
Lashio, Myan. 60/C4
Lashkar Gāh, Afg. 53/H2
Latacunga, Ecu. 106/C4
Latina, It. 38/C2
Latsch (Laces), It. 37/G4
Lātūr, India 62/C4
Latvia (ctry.) 20/H4
Lauf, Ger. 33/J2
Laukaa, Fin. 42/E3
Launceston, Austl. 73/C4
Laupheim, Ger. 37/F1
Laurel, Ms, US 97/F4
Laurens, SC, US 97/H3
Laurinburg, NC, US 97/J3
Lausanne, Swi. 36/C4
Lauterbach, Ger. 33/H1
Lautoka, Fiji 69/Y18
Laval, Qu, Can. 95/N6
Laval, Fr. 32/C2
Lavras, Braz. 108/C2
Lawrence, Ma, US 95/G3
Lawrence, Ks, US 93/J3
Lawrenceburg, Tn, US 97/G3
Lawrenceville, Ga, US 97/H3
Laxou, Fr. 31/F6
Lázaro Cárdenas, Mex. 100/E5
Le Blanc-Mesnil, Fr. 30/B6
Le Cannet, Fr. 33/G5
Le Creusot, Fr. 32/F3
Le Havre, Fr. 32/D2
Le Mans, Fr. 32/D2
Le Port, Reun. 81/S15
Le Puy-en-Velay, Fr. 32/E4
Le Tampon, Reun. 81/S15
League City, Tx, US 93/J5
Leamington, On, Can. 99/G7
Leatherhead, Eng, UK 25/F4
Leavenworth, Ks, US 93/J3
Lebach, Ger. 31/F5
Lebanon, Or, US 90/C4
Lebanon, Tn, US 97/G2
Lebanon, Mo, US 93/J3
Lebanon, NH, US 95/F3
Lebanon, Pa, US 94/E3
Lebanon, In, US 97/G1
Lebanon (ctry.) 49/D3
Lebbeke, Belg. 28/B6
Lebedyn, Ukr. 44/E2
Lębork, Pol. 27/J1
Lebowakgomo, SAfr. 81/E2
Lebrija, Sp. 34/B4
Lebu, Chile 109/B4
Lecce, It. 39/F2
Lecco, It. 33/H4
Łęczna, Pol. 27/M3
Lede, Belg. 28/A7
Leeds, Eng, UK 23/G4
Leek, Eng, UK 23/F5
Leek, Neth. 28/D2
Leer, Ger. 29/E2
Leerdam, Neth. 28/C5
Leesburg, Fl, US 97/H4
Leeuwarden, Neth. 28/C2
Leganés, Sp. 35/N9
Legaspi, Phil. 68/B3
Legionowo, Pol. 27/L2
Legnago, It. 33/J4
Legnano, It. 33/H4
Legnica, Pol. 27/J3
Lehigh Acres, Fl, US 97/H5
Lehrte, Ger. 29/G4
Leiah, Pak. 53/K2
Leicester, Eng, UK 25/E1
Leichlingen, Ger. 28/E6
Leiden, Neth. 28/B4
Leiderdorp, Neth. 28/B4
Leidschendam, Neth. 28/B4
Leifers (Laives), It. 37/H5
Leigh, Eng, UK 23/F5
Leinefelde, Ger. 29/H6
Leipzig, Ger. 26/G3
Leiria, Port. 34/A3
Leksands-Noret, Swe. 20/E3
Lelystad, Neth. 28/C3
Leme, Braz. 108/C2
Lemgo, Ger. 29/F4
Lempäälä, Fin. 20/G3
Lençóis Paulista, Braz. 108/B2
Lengerich, Ger. 29/E4
Lengshuitan, China 61/F3
Leninogor, Kaz. 46/J4
Leninogorsk, Rus. 43/M5
Leninsk-Kuznetskiy, Rus. 46/J4
Leninváros, Hun. 27/L5
Lennestadt, Ger. 29/F6
Lenoir, NC, US 97/H3
Lens, Fr. 30/B3
Lensk, Rus. 47/M3
Lentini, It. 38/D4
Léo, Burk. 79/E4
Leoben, Aus. 40/B2
León, Mex. 101/E4
León, Nic. 102/E3
León, Sp. 34/C1
Leon Valley, Tx, US 93/H5
Leonberg, Ger. 26/E4
Leonding, Aus. 33/L2
Leonforte, It. 38/D4
Leopoldina, Braz. 108/L6
Lepe, Sp. 34/B4
Lerdo de Tejada, Mex. 101/P8
Les Cayes, Haiti 103/H2
Les Mureaux, Fr. 30/A6
Les Sables-d'Olonne, Fr. 32/C3
Les Ulis, Fr. 30/B6
Leshan, China 60/D2
Leskovac, Yugo. 40/E4
Lesotho (ctry.) 80/D3
Lesozavodsk, Rus. 55/L2
Lesser Antilles (isls.), Neth. 104/E3
Lessines, Belg. 30/C2
Leszno, Pol. 27/J3
Letchworth, Eng, UK 25/F3
Lethbridge, Ab, Can. 90/E3
Leticia, Col. 106/E4
Letpadan, Myan. 60/B5
Leuca, It. 39/F3
Leusden-Zuid, Neth. 28/C4
Leutkirch im Allgäu, Ger. 37/G2
Levádhia, Gre. 39/H3
Levanger, Nor. 20/D3
Levelland, Tx, US 93/G4
Leventina (Prato), Swi. 37/E5
Leverkusen, Ger. 28/D6
Levice, Slvk. 40/D1
Levin, NZ 71/S11
Lévis, Qu, Can. 95/G2
Levittown, Pa, US 94/F3
Lewes, Eng, UK 25/G5
Lewisburg, Tn, US 97/G3
Lewiston, Id, US 90/D4
Lewiston, Me, US 95/G2
Lewistown, Pa, US 94/E3
Lexington, NC, US 97/H3
Lexington, Ky, US 97/G2
Lexington Park, Md, US 97/J2
Leyland, Eng, UK 23/F4
Lezhë, Alb. 40/D5
L'gov, Rus. 44/E2
Lhasa, China 60/A2
L'Hospitalet de Llobregat, Sp. 35/L7
Lianyungang, China 59/D4
Liaocheng, China 59/C3
Liaoyang, China 58/B2
Liaoyuan, China 59/F2
Liāquatpur, Pak. 53/K3
Liberal, Ks, US 93/G3
Liberec, Czh. 27/H3
Liberia, CR 102/E4
Liberia (ctry.) 78/C5
Libertador General San Martín, Arg. 109/D1
Liberty, Mo, US 93/J3
Libertyville, Il, US 99/P15
Libreville (cap.), Gabon 76/G7
Libya (ctry.) 77/J2
Libyan (des.), Afr. 77/K2
Libyan (plat.), Libya 77/K1
Licata, It. 38/C4
Lichfield, Eng, UK 25/E1
Lichinga, Moz. 82/G3
Lichtenfels, Ger. 33/J1
Lichtenvoorde, Neth. 28/D5
Lichuan, China 61/F2
Lida, Bela. 42/E5
Lidköping, Swe. 20/E4
Lido, It. 33/K4
Lido di Ostia, It. 38/C2
Lidzbark Warmiński, Pol. 27/L1
Liechtenstein (ctry.) 37/F3
Liège, Belg. 31/E2
Lieksa, Fin. 42/F3
Liepāja, Lat. 42/D4
Lier, Belg. 28/B6
Liestal, Swi. 36/D3
Liévin, Fr. 30/B3
Ligao, Phil. 67/F1
Likasi, D.R. Congo 82/E3
Lilienthal, Ger. 29/F2
Liling, China 63/K2
Lille, Fr. 30/C2
Lillehammer, Nor. 20/D3
Lillestrøm, Nor. 20/D4
Lilongwe (cap.), Malw. 82/F3
Lima, Oh, US 94/C3
Lima (cap.), Peru 106/C6
Limassol, Cyp. 49/C2
Limbdi, India 62/B3
Limburg an der Lahn, Ger. 31/H3
Limeira, Braz. 108/C2
Limerick, Ire. 21/A10
Limoges, Fr. 32/D4
Limón, CR 103/F4
Linares, Chile 109/B4
Linares, Mex. 96/D5
Linares, Sp. 34/D3
Linchuan, China 61/H3
Lincoln, Il, US 93/K2
Lincoln, Eng, UK 23/H5
Lincoln, On, Can. 95/U9
Lincoln (cap.), Ne, US 91/J5
Lincoln Park, Mi, US 99/F7
Lindau, Ger. 37/F2
Linden, Guy. 106/G2
Lindesberg, Swe. 20/E4
Lindi, Tanz. 82/G3
Lindlar, Ger. 29/E6
Lindsay, On, Can. 94/E2
Linfen, China 59/B3
Lingen, Ger. 29/E3
Lingolsheim, Fr. 31/G6
Linhai, China 61/J2
Linhai, China 55/J1
Linhares, Braz. 108/D1
Linhe, China 59/A2
Linköping, Swe. 20/E4
Linosa, It. 38/C5
Linqing, China 59/C3
Lins, Braz. 108/B2
Linyi, China 59/D4
Linz, Aus. 40/B1
Lion (gulf), Fr.,Sp. 32/D5
Lipetsk, Rus. 44/F1
Lippstadt, Ger. 29/F5
Liptovský Svätý Mikuláš, Slvk. 27/K4
Lira, Ugan. 77/M7
Liria, Sp. 35/E3
Lisbon, Me, US 95/G2
Lisbon (cap.), Port. 35/P10
Lisburn, NI, UK 22/B2
Lishui, China 61/H2
Lisieux, Fr. 32/D2
Liski, Rus. 44/F2
Lisle, Il, US 99/P16
L'Isle-sur-la-Sorgue, Fr. 32/F5
Lismore, Austl. 73/E1
Lisse, Neth. 28/B4
Litherland, Eng, UK 23/F5
Lithuania (ctry.) 42/D5
Littau, Swi. 37/E3
Little Rock (cap.), Ar, US 93/J4
Littlehampton, Eng, UK 25/F5
Liuzhou, China 61/F3
Livermore, Ca, US 99/L11
Liverpool, Eng, UK 23/F5
Livingston, Guat. 102/D3
Livingstone, Zam. 82/E4
Livingstone (falls), Congo 82/B2
Livno, Bosn. 40/C4
Livny, Rus. 44/F1
Livonia, Mi, US 99/F7
Livorno, It. 33/J5
Livry-Gargan, Fr. 30/B6
Ljubljana (cap.), Slov. 40/B2
Ljubuški, Bosn. 40/C4
Ljungby, Swe. 20/E4
Ljusdal, Swe. 42/C3
Llallagua, Bol. 106/E7
Llandudno, Wal, UK 22/E5
Llanes, Sp. 34/C1
Lleida, Sp. 35/F2
Llodio, Sp. 34/D1
Lloret de Mar, Sp. 35/G2
Lloydminster, Sk, Can. 90/F2
Lluchmayor, Sp. 35/G3
Llullaillaco (vol.), Arg.,Chile 109/C1
Lobatse, Bots. 80/N12
Lobito, Ang. 82/B3
Lobos, Arg. 109/E4
Locarno, Swi. 37/E5
Lochem, Neth. 28/D4
Lochristi, Belg. 28/A6
Lock Haven, Pa, US 94/E3
Lockport, NY, US 95/V9
Lockport, Il, US 99/P16
Lod, Isr. 49/F8
Lodeynoye Pole, Rus. 42/G3
Lodi, Ca, US 99/M10
Lodi, It. 33/H4
Łódź, Pol. 27/K3
Logan, Ut, US 92/E2
Logan (mt.), Can. 85/K3
Logansport, In, US 94/C3
Logroño, Sp. 34/D1
Lohja, Fin. 42/E3
Lohmar, Ger. 31/G2
Lohne, Ger. 29/F3
Löhne, Ger. 29/F4
Lohr, Ger. 26/E4
Loja, Ecu. 106/C4
Loja, Sp. 34/C4
Lokeren, Belg. 28/A6
Lokossa, Ben. 79/F5
Lom, Nor. 20/D3
Loma Bonita, Mex. 102/C2
Lomas de Zamora, Arg. 109/E3
Lombard, Il, US 99/P16
Lomé (cap.), Togo 79/F5
Lomme, Fr. 30/B2
Lommel, Belg. 28/C6
Lomonosov, Rus. 43/S7
Lompoc, Ca, US 92/B4
Łomża, Pol. 27/M2
Lonāvale, India 62/B4
Londerzeel, Belg. 28/B6
London, On, Can. 94/D3
London (cap.), Eng, UK 25/F3
Londonderry, NI, UK 22/A2
Londrina, Braz. 108/B2
Long (isl.), NY, US 95/F3
Long Beach, Ca, US 92/C4
Long Branch, NJ, US 94/F3
Long Eaton, Eng, UK 23/G6
Long Xuyen, Viet. 65/D4
Longjumeau, Fr. 30/B6
Longkou, China 59/E3
Longmont, Co, US 93/F2
Longueuil, Qu, Can. 95/P6
Longview, Wa, US 90/C4
Longview, Tx, US 93/J4
Longwy, Fr. 31/E4
Longyan, China 61/H3
Lons-le-Saunier, Fr. 36/B4
Loon op Zand, Neth. 28/C5
Loos, Fr. 30/C2
Lop Buri, Thai. 65/C3
López Mateos, Mex. 101/Q9
Lora del Río, Sp. 34/C4
Lorain, Oh, US 94/D3
Lorca, Sp. 34/E4
Lorena, Braz. 108/H7
Lorengau, PNG 68/D5
Loreto, Mex. 100/E4
Lorica, Col. 103/H4
Lorient, Fr. 32/B3
Lörrach, Ger. 36/D2
Los Alamos, NM, US 93/F4
Los Altos, Ca, US 99/K12
Los Amates, Guat. 102/D3
Los Andes, Chile 109/B3
Los Angeles, Chile 109/B4
Los Angeles, Ca, US 92/C4
Los Banos, Ca, US 92/B3
Los Barrios, Sp. 34/C4
Los Llanos de Aridane, Canl. 35/X16
Los Mochis, Mex. 100/C3
Los Palacios y Villafranca, Sp. 34/C4
Los Reyes, Mex. 101/R10
Los Reyes de Salgado, Mex. 100/E5
Los Teques, Ven. 106/E1
Losheim, Ger. 31/F4
Losser, Neth. 28/E4
Lota, Chile 109/B4
Louangphrabang, Laos 65/C2
Loubomo, Congo 82/B1
Loudi, China 61/F3
Louga, Sen. 78/A3
Loughborough, Eng, UK 23/G6

Louis – Meppe

Louisiana (state), US 96/E4
Louisville, Ky, US 97/G2
Loulé, Port. 34/A4
Louny, Czh. 33/K1
Lourdes, Fr. 32/C5
Loures, Port. 35/P10
Louvain (Leuven), Belg. 31/D2
Louviers, Fr. 30/A5
Loveland, Co, US 93/F2
Lovington, NM, US 93/G4
Lowell, Ma, US 95/G3
Lower Hutt, NZ 71/R11
Lowestoft, Eng, UK 25/H2
Łowicz, Pol. 27/K2
Loxstedt, Ger. 29/F2
Loznica, Yugo. 40/D3
Lozova, Ukr. 44/F2
Lu'an, China 61/H2
Luanda (cap.), Ang. 82/B2
Luanshya, Zam. 82/E3
Luarca, Sp. 34/B1
Lubań, Pol. 27/H3
Lubango, Ang. 82/B3
Lubartów, Pol. 27/M3
Lübbecke, Ger. 29/F4
Lubbock, Tx, US 93/G4
Lübeck, Ger. 26/F2
Lubin, Pol. 27/J3
Lublin, Pol. 27/M3
Lubliniec, Pol. 27/K3
Lubny, Ukr. 44/E2
Luboń, Pol. 27/J2
Lubsko, Pol. 27/H3
Lubuklinggau, Indo. 66/B4
Lubuksikaping, Indo. 66/B3
Lubumbashi, D.R. Congo 82/E3
Lucca, It. 33/J5
Lucélia, Braz. 108/B2
Lucena, Phil. 68/B3
Lucena, Sp. 34/C4
Lučenec, Slvk. 40/D1
Luckenwalde, Ger. 27/G2
Lucknow, India 62/D2
Lüdenscheid, Ger. 29/E6
Ludhiāna, India 53/L2
Ludinghausen, Ger. 29/E5
Ludvika, Swe. 20/E3
Ludwigsburg, Ger. 33/H2
Ludwigsfelde, Ger. 27/G2
Ludwigshafen, Ger. 33/H2
Luena, Ang. 82/C3
Lufkin, Tx, US 93/J5
Luga, Rus. 42/F4
Lugano, Swi. 37/E6
Lugo, Sp. 34/B1
Lugoj, Rom. 40/E3
Luhans'k, Ukr. 44/F2
Łuków, Pol. 27/M3
Luleå, Swe. 42/D2
Lüleburgaz, Turk. 41/H5
Lumberton, NC, US 97/J3
Lumding, India 60/B3
Lund, Swe. 27/G1
Lüneburg, Ger. 29/H2
Lunel, Fr. 32/F5
Lünen, Ger. 29/E5
Lunéville, Fr. 33/G2
Lunglei, India 60/B4
Luohe, China 59/C4
Luoyang, China 59/C4
Lupanshui, China 60/E3
Lurgan, NI, UK 22/B3
Lusaka (cap.), Zam. 82/E4
Lushnjë, Alb. 40/D5
Lustenau, Aus. 37/F3
Luton, Eng, UK 25/F3
Luts'k, Ukr. 44/C2
Luxembourg (ctry.) 31/E4
Luxembourg (cap.), Lux. 31/F4
Luzern, Swi. 37/E3
Luzhou, China 60/E2
Luziânia, Braz. 107/J7
Luzon (isl.), Phil. 68/B3
L'viv, Ukr. 27/N4
Lynchburg, Va, US 97/J2
Lynn, Ma, US 95/G3
Lynn Haven, Fl, US 97/G4
Lynnwood, Wa, US 99/C2
Lyon, Fr. 36/A6
Lys'va, Rus. 43/N4
Lysychans'k, Ukr. 44/F2
Lytham Saint Anne's, Eng, UK 23/E4
Lyubertsy, Rus. 43/W9
Lyubotyn, Ukr. 44/E2
Lyudinovo, Rus. 44/E1

M

Ma-ubin, Myan. 60/B5
Ma'alot-Tarshiha, Isr. 49/D3
Ma'ān, Jor. 49/D4
Ma'anshan, China 61/H2
Maarianhamina, Fin. 42/C3
Ma'arrat an Nu'mān, Syria 49/E2
Maarssen, Neth. 28/C4
Maaseik, Belg. 28/C6
Maasin, Phil. 67/F1
Maassluis, Neth. 28/B5
Maastricht, Neth. 31/E2
Mabopane, SAfr. 80/Q12
Mabote, Moz. 82/F5
Macaé, Braz. 108/D2
Macaíba, Braz. 107/L5
Macapá, Braz. 107/H3
Macau, Braz. 107/L5
Macau 61/G4
Macau (cap.), Macau 61/G4
Macclesfield, Eng, UK 23/F5
Macedonia, Former Yugoslavia Rep. of (ctry.) 40/E5
Maceió, Braz. 107/L5
Macerata, It. 40/A4
Machado, Braz. 108/H6
Machakos, Kenya 77/N8
Machala, Ecu. 106/C4
Machanga, Moz. 82/F5
Machaze, Moz. 82/F5
Macheng, China 61/G2
Machilipatnam, India 62/D4
Machiques, Ven. 103/H4
Machu Picchu (ruin), Peru 106/D6
Mackay, Austl. 72/C3
Mackenzie (bay), NW,Yk, Can. 86/C2
Mackenzie (riv.), NW, Can. 86/D2
Macomb, Il, US 93/K2
Macon, Ga, US 97/H3
Mâcon, Fr. 36/A5
Macuspana, Mex. 102/C2
Mādabā, Jor. 49/D4
Madagascar (ctry.) 81/H8
Madanapalle, India 62/C5
Madanīyīn, Tun. 76/H1
Mādārīpur, Bang. 62/F3
Madgaon (Margao), India 62/B4
Madhipura, India 62/E2
Madīnat ath Thawrah, Syria 50/D3
Madison, Al, US 97/G3
Madison, In, US 97/G2
Madison (cap.), Wi, US 94/B3
Madison Heights, Mi, US 99/F6
Madisonville, Ky, US 97/G2
Madiun, Indo. 66/D5
Madrid (cap.), Sp. 35/N9
Madurai, India 62/C6
Maebashi, Japan 57/F2
Mafra, Braz. 108/B3
Magadan, Rus. 47/R4
Magangué, Col. 103/H4
Maganoy, Phil. 67/F2
Magdagachi, Rus. 55/K1
Magdalena de Kino, Mex. 92/E5
Magdeburg, Ger. 26/F2
Magé, Braz. 108/K7
Magelang, Indo. 66/D5
Magellan (str.), Chile 109/A7
Maghāghah, Egypt 50/B4
Maglaj, Bosn. 40/D3
Maglie, It. 39/F2
Magnitogorsk, Rus. 43/N5
Magnolia, Ar, US 93/J4
Magway (Magwe), Myan. 60/B4
Maha Sarakham, Thai. 65/C2
Mahābād, Iran 51/F2
Mahabe, Madg. 81/H8
Mahād, India 62/B4
Mahajanga, Madg. 81/H6
Mahalapye, Bots. 82/E5
Mahanoro, Madg. 81/J7
Mahārajpur, India 62/C2
Mahasoabe, Madg. 81/H8
Mahbubnagar, India 62/C4
Mahébourg, Mrts. 81/T15
Mahesāna, India 62/B3
Mahilyow, Bela. 42/F5
Mahitsy, Madg. 81/H7
Mahoba, India 62/C2
Mahón, Sp. 35/H3
Mahuva, India 62/B3
Maicao, Col. 103/H4
Maidenhead, Eng, UK 25/F3
Maidstone, Eng, UK 25/G4
Maiduguri, Nga. 76/H5
Maihar, India 62/D3
Mailsi, Pak. 53/K3
Maine (state), US 95/G2
Mainz, Ger. 31/H4
Maitland, Austl. 73/D2
Maizuru, Japan 56/D3
Majadahonda, Sp. 35/N9
Majāz Al Bāb, Tun. 38/A4
Majene, Indo. 67/E4
Majuro (cap.), Mrsh. 68/G4
Makakilo City, Hi, US 88/V13
Makarska, Cro. 40/C4
Makeni, SLeo. 78/B4
Makhachkala, Rus. 45/H4
Makinsk, Kaz. 46/H4
Makiyivka, Ukr. 44/F2
Makkah, SAr. 52/C4
Makó, Hun. 40/E2
Makurazaki, Japan 56/B5
Makurdi, Nga. 79/H5
Malabar (coast), India 62/B5
Malabo (cap.), EqG. 76/G7
Malacky, Slvk. 27/J4
Maladzyechna, Bela. 42/E5
Málaga, Sp. 34/C4
Malakāl, Sudan 77/M6
Malambo, Col. 103/H4
Malang, Indo. 66/D5
Malanje, Ang. 82/C2
Malanville, Ben. 79/F4
Malargüe, Arg. 109/C4
Malatya, Turk. 50/D2
Malay (pen.), Malay.,Tha 66/B2
Malaya Vishera, Rus. 42/G4
Malāyer, Iran 51/G3
Malaysia (ctry.) 66/C2
Malazgirt, Turk. 50/E2
Malbork, Pol. 27/K1
Maldegem, Belg. 28/A6
Maldive (isls.), Mald. 62/B6
Maldives (ctry.) 62/B6
Maldon, Eng, UK 25/G3
Maldonado, Uru. 109/F3
Male (cap.), Mald. 48/G9
Māler Kotla, India 53/L2
Malgobek, Rus. 45/H4
Mali (ctry.) 76/E4
Malīr Cantonment, Pak. 62/A3
Malita, Phil. 67/G2
Malkara, Turk. 41/H5
Mallawī, Egypt 50/B5
Malmesbury, SAfr. 80/L10
Malmö, Swe. 26/G1
Mals (Malles), It. 37/G4
Malta (ctry.), Malta 38/C5
Maltby, Eng, UK 23/G5
Malyn, Ukr. 44/D2
Mamanguape, Braz. 107/L5
Mambij, Syria 50/D2
Mamburao, Phil. 67/F1
Mamelodi, SAfr. 80/Q12
Mamoutzou, May. 81/H6
Mampikony, Madg. 81/H7
Mampong, Gha. 79/E5
Mamuju, Indo. 67/E4
Man, C.d'Iv. 78/D5
Man, Isle of (isl.), IM, UK 22/D3
Manacapuru, Braz. 106/F4
Manacor, Sp. 35/G3
Manado, Indo. 67/F3
Manage, Belg. 31/D3
Managua (cap.), Nic. 102/E3
Manakambahiny, Madg. 81/J7
Manakara, Madg. 81/J8
Manama (cap.), Bahr. 52/F3
Mananara, Madg. 81/J7
Mananjary, Madg. 81/J8
Manaratsandry, Madg. 81/H7
Manassas, Va, US 97/J2
Manaus, Braz. 106/F4
Manavgat, Turk. 49/B1
Mancherāl, India 62/C4
Manchester, NH, US 95/G3
Manchester, Eng, UK 23/F5
Mandaguari, Braz. 108/B2
Mandalay, Myan. 65/B1
Mandalgovĭ, Mong. 54/F2
Mandan, ND, US 91/H4
Mandeville, Jam. 103/G2
Māndi, India 53/L2
Mandié, Moz. 82/F4
Mandla, India 62/D3
Mandoto, Madg. 81/H7
Manduria, It. 40/C5
Mandya, India 62/C5
Manendragarh, India 62/D3
Manfalūt, Egypt 50/B5
Manfredonia, It. 40/B5
Mangaldai, India 60/B3
Mangalia, Rom. 41/J4
Mangalore, India 62/B5
Mangghystau, Kaz. 46/F5
Mangoche, Malw. 82/G3
Mangotsfield, Eng, UK 24/D4
Manhattan, Ks, US 93/H3
Manhuaçu, Braz. 108/D2
Manila (cap.), Phil. 68/A3
Manisa, Turk. 44/C5
Manitoba (prov.), Can. 86/G3
Manitoba (lake), Mb, Can. 86/G3
Manitowoc, Wi, US 91/M4
Manizales, Col. 106/C2
Manjakandriana, Madg. 81/J7
Manlleu, Sp. 34/D1
Mannheim, Ger. 33/H2
Manosque, Fr. 32/F5
Manresa, Sp. 35/K6
Mansa, Zam. 82/E3
Mansa Konko, Gam. 78/B3
Mansalay, Phil. 67/F1
Mansfield, Oh, US 94/D3
Mansfield, Eng, UK 23/G5
Mansfield Woodhouse, Eng, UK 23/G5
Manta, Ecu. 106/B4
Manteca, Ca, US 92/B3
Mantena, Braz. 108/D1
Mantes-la-Jolie, Fr. 30/A6
Mantes-la-Ville, Fr. 30/A6
Manthani, India 62/C4
Mantova, It. 33/J4
Manturovo, Rus. 43/K4
Manukau, NZ 71/R10
Manzanares, Sp. 34/D3
Manzanillo, Cuba 103/G1
Manzanillo, Mex. 100/D5
Manzhouli, China 55/H2
Manzil Tamīn, Tun. 38/B4
Manzini, Swaz. 81/E2
Mao, DRep. 103/J2
Mao, Chad 76/J5
Maoming, China 61/F4
Maputo (cap.), Moz. 81/F2
Mar del Plata, Arg. 109/E4
Marabá, Braz. 107/J5
Maracaibo, Ven. 106/D1
Maracay, Ven. 106/E1
Maradi, Niger 79/G3
Marāgheh, Iran 51/F2
Marand, Iran 45/H5
Maranguape, Braz. 107/L4
Marau, Braz. 108/A4
Maravatío de Ocampo, Mex. 101/E5
Marawi, Phil. 67/F2
Marbella, Sp. 34/C4
Marburg, Ger. 33/H1
March, Eng, UK 25/G1
Marche-en-Famenne, Belg. 31/E3
Marchena, Sp. 34/C4
Marco, Fl, US 97/H5
Marcona, Peru 106/C7
Marcos Juárez, Arg. 109/D3
Marcq-en-Barœul, Fr. 30/C2
Mardān, Pak. 53/K2
Mardin, Turk. 50/E2
Marganets', Ukr. 44/E3
Margao (Madgaon), India 53/K5
Margate, Eng, UK 25/H4
Margherita (peak), Ugan. 77/L7
Marghita, Rom. 27/M5
Margosatubig, Phil. 67/F2
Marianao, Cuba 103/F1
Mariánské Lázně, Czh. 33/K2
Maribor, Slov. 40/B2
Maricá, Braz. 108/L7
Mariel, Cuba 103/F1
Mariestad, Swe. 20/E4
Marietta, Oh, US 97/H2
Marietta, Ga, US 97/G3
Marignane, Fr. 32/F5
Marijampolė, Lith. 27/M1
Marília, Braz. 108/B2
Marín, Sp. 34/A1
Marinette, Wi, US 91/M4
Maringá, Braz. 108/B2
Marinha Grande, Port. 34/A3
Marion, Oh, US 94/D3
Marion, In, US 94/C3
Mariupol', Ukr. 44/F3
Marka (Merca), Som. 77/P7
Market Harborough, Eng, UK 25/F2
Marki, Pol. 27/L2
Marks, Rus. 45/H2
Marktoberdorf, Ger. 37/G2
Marktredwitz, Ger. 33/K2
Marl, Ger. 29/E5
Marling (Marlengo), It. 37/H4
Marlow, Eng, UK 25/F3
Marly-le-Roi, Fr. 30/B6
Marmagão, India 62/B4
Marmande, Fr. 32/D4
Marmaris, Turk. 50/B2
Maroantsetra, Madg. 81/J6
Marondera, Zim. 82/F4
Maroochydore-Mooloolaba, Austl. 72/D4
Maroua, Camr. 76/H5
Marovoay, Madg. 81/H7
Marovoay, Madg. 82/K10
Marple, Eng, UK 23/F5
Marrakech, Mor. 76/D1
Marsá Matrūh, Egypt 50/A4
Marsala, It. 38/C4
Marsberg, Ger. 29/F6
Marseille, Fr. 32/F5
Marshall, Mn, US 91/K4
Marshall, Tx, US 93/J4
Marshall, Mo, US 93/J3
Marshall Islands (ctry.) 68/G3
Marshalltown, Ia, US 93/J2
Martapura, Indo. 66/D4
Martigues, Fr. 32/F5
Martina Franca, It. 40/C5
Martinez, Ga, US 97/H3
Martinez, Ca, US 99/K10
Martínez de la Torre, Mex. 101/M6
Martinique (dpcy.), Fr. 104/F4
Martinique Passage (chan.), NAm. 104/F4
Martinsburg, WV, US 97/J2
Martinsville, Va, US 97/J2
Martorell, Sp. 35/K7
Martos, Sp. 34/D4
Marugame, Japan 56/C3
Maruko, Japan 57/F2
Maruoka, Japan 56/E2
Marv Dasht, Iran 51/H4
Mary, Trkm. 53/H1
Maryborough, Austl. 72/D4
Maryland (state), US 94/E4
Marysville, Wa, US 99/C1
Maryville, Tn, US 97/H3
Maryville, Mo, US 93/J2
Marzūq, Libya 76/H2
Masaka, Ugan. 82/F1
Masākin, Tun. 38/B5
Masamba, Indo. 67/F4
Masan, SKor. 56/A3
Masaya, Nic. 102/E4
Masbate, Phil. 67/F1
Mascara, Alg. 76/F1
Mascouche, Qu, Can. 95/N6
Maseru (cap.), Les. 80/D3
Mashhad, Iran 53/G1
Mashtūl as Sūq, Egypt 49/B4
Masjed-e Soleymān, Iran 51/G4
Masnou, Sp. 35/L7
Mason City, Ia, US 93/J2
Massa, It. 33/J4
Massachusetts (state), US 95/F3
Massafra, It. 40/C5
Massena, NY, US 94/F2
Massillon, Oh, US 94/D3
Massy, Fr. 30/B6
Masterton, NZ 71/S11
Mastung, Pak. 53/J3
Masuda, Japan 56/B3
Masvingo, Zim. 82/F5
Mata Utu, Fr. 69/H6
Matadi, D.R. Congo 82/B2
Matagalpa, Nic. 102/E3
Matale, SrL. 62/D6
Matamoros, Mex. 96/C5
Matanzas, Cuba 103/F1
Matão, Braz. 108/B2
Matara, SrL. 62/D6
Mataram, Indo. 67/E5
Mataró, Sp. 35/L6
Matehuala, Mex. 101/E4
Mátészalka, Hun. 27/M5
Mathurā, India 62/C2
Mati, Phil. 67/G2
Matías Romero, Mex. 102/C2
Matiguas, Nic. 102/E3
Mātir, Tun. 38/A4
Matlock, Eng, UK 23/G5
Matopos, Zim. 82/E5
Matosinhos, Port. 34/A2
Maţraḩ, Oman 53/G4
Matsoandakana, Madg. 81/J6
Matsue, Japan 56/C3
Matsumae, Japan 55/N3
Matsumoto, Japan 57/E2
Matsusaka, Japan 56/E3
Matsushima, Japan 57/G1
Matsutō, Japan 56/E2
Matsuyama, Japan 56/C4
Matteson, Il, US 99/Q17
Mattō, Japan 56/E2
Mattoon, Il, US 93/K3
Maturín, Ven. 106/F2
Mau Rānīpur, India 62/C2
Mauá, Braz. 108/C2
Maubeuge, Fr. 30/C3
Maudaha, India 62/D2
Maués, Braz. 106/G4
Maui (isl.), US 88/S10
Maun, Bots. 82/D4
Mauna Kea (peak), Hi, US 88/U11
Mauna Loa (peak), Hi, US 88/U11
Maunath Bhanjan, India 62/D2
Maurepas, Fr. 30/A6
Mauritania (ctry.) 76/C4
Mauritius (ctry.) 81/S15
Mawāna, India 53/L3
Mawlamyine (Moulmein), Myan. 65/B2
May Pen, Jam. 103/G2
Mayagüez, PR 104/E3
Mayāng Imphāl, India 60/B3
Mayaoyao, Phil. 61/J5
Mayarí, Cuba 103/H1
Mayen, Ger. 31/G3
Mayenne, Fr. 32/C2
Mayfield, Ky, US 97/F2
Maykop, Rus. 44/G3
Maymyo, Myan. 60/C4
Mayotte (dpcy.), Fr. 81/H6
Maywood, Il, US 99/Q16
Mazabuka, Zam. 82/E4
Mazār-e Sharīf, Afg. 53/J1
Mazara del Vallo, It. 38/C4
Mazarrón, Sp. 34/E4
Mazatenango, Guat. 102/D3
Mazatlán, Mex. 100/D4
Mazyr, Bela. 44/D1
Mbabane (cap.), Swaz. 81/E2
Mbacké, Sen. 78/B3
Mbaïki, CAfr. 76/J7
Mbale, Ugan. 77/M7
Mbalmayo, Camr. 76/H7
Mbandaka, D.R. Congo 77/J7
Mbarara, Ugan. 82/F1
Mbeya, Tanz. 82/F2
M'bour, Sen. 78/A3
Mbuji-Mayi, D.R. Congo 82/D2
McAlester, Ok, US 93/J4
McAllen, Tx, US 96/D5
McComb, Ms, US 93/K5
McHenry, Il, US 99/P15
McKeesport, Pa, US 94/E3
McKinley (mt.), Ak, US 85/H3
McKinleyville, Ca, US 92/A2
McMinnville, Or, US 90/C4
McMinnville, Tn, US 97/G3
McPherson, Ks, US 93/H3
Mdantsane, SAfr. 80/D4
Meadville, Pa, US 94/D3
Meaux, Fr. 30/B6
Mechelen, Belg. 28/B6
Meckenheim, Ger. 31/G2
Medak, India 62/C4
Medan, Indo. 66/A3
Medellín, Col. 106/C2
Medford, Or, US 92/B2
Medgidia, Rom. 41/J3
Mediaş, Rom. 41/G2
Medicine Hat, Ab, Can. 90/F3
Medina, Oh, US 94/D3
Medina del Campo, Sp. 34/C2
Mediterranean (sea) 18/D5
Mednogorsk, Rus. 45/L2
Medvezh'yegorsk, Rus. 42/G3
Meerbusch, Ger. 28/D6
Meerssen, Neth. 31/E2
Meerut, India 62/C2
Mégara, Gre. 39/H3
Meiganga, Camr. 76/H6
Meihekou, China 55/K3
Meiktila, Myan. 65/A1
Meinerzhagen, Ger. 29/E6
Meiningen, Ger. 33/J1
Meissen, Ger. 27/G3
Meizhou, China 61/H3
Mejorada del Campo, Sp. 35/N9
Mek'elē, Eth. 77/N5
Meknès, Mor. 76/D1
Mekong (riv.), Asia 65/D4
Melaka, Malay. 66/B3
Melappālaiyam, India 62/C6
Melbourne, Fl, US 97/H4
Melbourne, Austl. 73/F5
Melbu, Nor. 20/E1
Melchor Múzquiz, Mex. 96/C5
Melchor Ocampo, Mex. 101/Q9
Melenki, Rus. 45/G1
Meleuz, Rus. 45/K1
Melitopol', Ukr. 44/E3
Melle, Ger. 29/F4
Mělník, Czh. 33/L1
Melo, Uru. 109/F3
Melrose Park, Il, US 99/Q16
Melton, Austl. 73/C3
Melton Mowbray, Eng, UK 25/F1
Melun, Fr. 32/E2
Melvindale, Mi, US 99/F7
Memmingen, Ger. 37/G2
Memphis, Tn, US 93/K4
Memphis (ruin), Egypt 49/B5
Menden, Ger. 29/E6
Mendes, Braz. 108/K7
Mendoza, Arg. 109/C3
Menemen, Turk. 44/C5
Menen, Belg. 30/C2
Menggala, Indo. 66/C4
Menlo Park, Ca, US 99/K12
Menomonee Falls, Wi, US 94/B3
Menomonie, Wi, US 91/L4
Menongue, Ang. 82/C3
Mentor, Oh, US 94/D3
Menzel Bourquiba, Tun. 38/A4
Meoqui, Mex. 96/B4
Meppel, Neth. 28/D3
Meppen, Ger. 29/E3

123

Meran – Narra

Merano, It. 37/H4
Merauke, Indo. 67/K5
Merced, Ca, US 92/B3
Mercedes, Arg. 109/C3
Mercedes, Uru. 109/E3
Mercedes, Arg. 109/E2
Mercer Island, Wa, US 99/C2
Merefa, Ukr. 44/F2
Merelbeke, Belg. 28/A6
Mergui (Myeik), Myan. 65/B3
Mérida, Ven. 106/D2
Mérida, Mex. 102/D1
Mérida, Sp. 34/B3
Meridian, Ms, US 97/F3
Mérignac, Fr. 32/C4
Merksem, Belg. 28/B6
Merlo, Arg. 109/E3
Merrimack, NH, US 95/G3
Merritt Island, Fl, US 97/H4
Mersin, Turk. 49/D1
Merthyr Tydfil, Wal, UK 24/C3
Meru, Kenya 77/N7
Merzifon, Turk. 44/E4
Merzig, Ger. 31/F5
Mesa, Az, US 92/E4
Mesa Verde National Park, Co, US 92/E3
Mesagne, It. 40/C5
Meschede, Ger. 29/F6
Mesomeloka, Madg. 81/J8
Mesquite, Tx, US 93/H4
Messaad, Alg. 76/F1
Messina, It. 38/D3
Mestre, It. 33/K4
Metairie, La, US 97/F4
Metán, Arg. 109/D2
Metepec, Mex. 101/Q10
Mettmann, Ger. 28/D6
Metz, Fr. 31/F5
Metzingen, Ger. 37/F1
Mevasseret Ẕiyyon, Isr. 49/G8
Mexborough, Eng, UK 23/G5
Mexicali, Mex. 92/D4
Mexico, Mo, US 93/K3
Mexico (gulf), NAm. 89/H6
Mexico (ctry.), Mex. 84/G7
Mexico (cap.), Mex. 101/Q10
Meybod, Iran 51/H3
Meyerton, SAfr. 80/Q13
Meyrin, Swi. 36/C5
Meyzieu, Fr. 36/A6
Mezhdurechensk, Rus. 46/J4
Mezőkövesd, Hun. 27/L5
Mezőtúr, Hun. 40/E2
Mhamdia Fūshānah, Tun. 38/B4
Mhow, India 62/C3
Miami, Ok, US 93/J3
Miami, Fl, US 97/H5
Miami Beach, Fl, US 97/H5
Mīāndoāb, Iran 51/F2
Miandrivazo, Madg. 81/H7
Mīāneh, Iran 51/F2
Miānwāli, Pak. 53/K2
Mianyang, China 60/E2
Miass, Rus. 43/P5
Michalovce, Slvk. 27/L4
Michigan (lake), US 94/C2
Michigan (state), US 94/C2
Michigan City, In, US 94/C3
Michurinsk, Rus. 45/G1
Micronesia, Federated States of (ctry.) 68/D4
Middelburg, SAfr. 80/Q12
Middelburg, Neth. 28/A5
Middelharnis, Neth. 28/B5
Middelkerke, Belg. 30/B1
Middlesboro, Ky, US 97/H2
Middlesbrough, Eng, UK 23/G2
Middleton, Eng, UK 23/F4
Midland, On, Can. 94/E2
Midland, Mi, US 94/C3
Midland, Tx, US 93/G5
Midlothian, Il, US 99/Q16
Midyat, Turk. 50/E2
Mie, Japan 56/B4
Międzyrzec Podlaski, Pol. 27/M3
Międzyrzecz, Pol. 27/H2
Mielec, Pol. 27/L3
Miercurea Ciuc, Rom. 41/G2
Mieres, Sp. 34/C1
Migdal Ha'emeq, Isr. 49/G6
Miguelópolis, Braz. 108/B2
Mihara, Japan 56/C3
Miharu, Japan 57/G2
Mihrābpur, Pak. 53/J3
Mijas, Sp. 34/C4
Mikhaylovka, Rus. 45/G2
Mikkeli, Fin. 42/E3
Mikuni, Japan 56/E2
Milagro, Ecu. 106/C4
Milan (Milano), It. 33/H4
Milano (Milan), It. 33/H4
Milas, Turk. 50/A2
Milazzo, It. 38/D3
Mildura, Austl. 73/B2
Mililani Town, Hi, US 88/V13
Mill Valley, Ca, US 99/J11
Millau, Fr. 32/E4
Millbrae, Ca, US 99/K11
Milledgeville, Ga, US 97/H3
Millerovo, Rus. 45/G2
Milpitas, Ca, US 99/L12
Milton, On, Can. 95/T8
Milton Keynes, Eng, UK 25/F2
Milwaukee, Wi, US 99/Q13
Mīnā' Su'ūd, Kuw. 51/G4
Minamata, Japan 56/B4
Minas, Cuba 103/G1
Minas, Uru. 109/E3
Minas de Matahambre, Cuba 103/F1
Minatitlán, Mex. 102/C2
Minden, La, US 93/J4
Minden, Ger. 29/F4
Mineiros, Braz. 107/H7
Mineral Wells, Tx, US 93/H4
Mineral'nye Vody, Rus. 45/G3
Mingäçevir, Azer. 45/H4
Mingāora, Pak. 53/K2
Minna, Nga. 79/G4
Minnesota (state), US 91/K4
Mino, Japan 57/E3
Minorca (isl.), Sp. 35/H2
Minsk (cap.), Bela. 42/E5
Mińsk Mazowiecki, Pol. 27/L2
Minturno, It. 40/A5
Minūf, Egypt 49/B4
Minusinsk, Rus. 46/K4
Minyā al Qamḩ, Egypt 49/B4
Mirabel, Qu, Can. 95/M6
Miracema, Braz. 108/D2
Miracema do Norte, Braz. 107/J5
Miraj, India 62/B4
Miramar, Arg. 109/E4
Miranda de Ebro, Sp. 34/D1
Mirandola, It. 33/J4
Mirandópolis, Braz. 108/B2
Mirassol, Braz. 108/B2
Mirfield, Eng, UK 23/G4
Miri, Malay. 66/D3
Mirnyy, Rus. 47/M3
Miryang, SKor. 56/A3
Misaki, Japan 56/D3
Misantla, Mex. 101/N7
Mishawaka, In, US 94/C3
Mishima, Japan 57/F3
Misilmeri, It. 38/C3
Miskolc, Hun. 27/L4
Mişrātah, Libya 76/J1
Mission, Tx, US 96/D5
Mission Viejo, Ca, US 92/C4
Mississauga, On, Can. 95/T8
Mississippi (riv.), US 89/H5
Mississippi (state), US 97/F3
Missouri (state), US 93/J3
Missouri (riv.), US 88/G3
Missouri City, Tx, US 93/J5
Mitchell, SD, US 93/H2
Mitilíni, Gre. 39/K3
Mito, Japan 57/G2
Mitry-Mory, Fr. 30/B6
Mitsinjo, Madg. 81/H7
Mits'iwa, Erit. 77/N4
Mitsukaidō, Japan 57/F2
Mitsuke, Japan 57/F2
Mittweida, Ger. 26/G3
Mitú, Col. 106/D3
Mixquiahuala, Mex. 101/K6
Miyako, Japan 55/N4
Miyakonojō, Japan 56/B5
Miyanojō, Japan 56/B5
Miyazaki, Japan 56/B5
Miyazu, Japan 56/D3
Miyoshi, Japan 56/C3
Mizunami, Japan 57/E3
Mjölby, Swe. 20/E4
Mkokotoni, Tanz. 82/G2
Mladá Boleslav, Czh. 33/L1
Mladenovac, Yugo. 40/E3
Mława, Pol. 27/L2
Moa, Cuba 103/H1
Moaña, Sp. 34/A1
Moanda, Gabon 82/B1
Mobaye, CAfr. 77/K7
Moberly, Mo, US 93/J3
Mobile, Al, US 97/F4
Mochudi, Bots. 80/D2
Mocoa, Col. 106/C3
Mococa, Braz. 108/F6
Modāsa, India 62/B3
Modena, It. 33/J4
Modesto, Ca, US 92/B3
Modica, It. 38/D4
Mödling, Aus. 40/C1
Modriča, Bosn. 40/D3
Modugno, It. 40/C5
Moe, Austl. 73/C3
Moers, Ger. 28/D6
Moga, India 53/L2
Mogadishu (cap.), Som. 77/Q7
Mogi das Cruzes, Braz. 108/G8
Mogi-Guaçu, Braz. 108/G7
Mogi-Mirim, Braz. 108/G7
Mogocha, Rus. 55/H1
Mohács, Hun. 40/D3
Mohammedia, Mor. 76/D1
Mohyliv-Podil's'kyy, Ukr. 41/H1
Moineşti, Rom. 41/H2
Moita, Port. 35/Q10
Mojave (des.), Ca, US 88/C5
Mōka, Japan 57/F2
Mokokchūng, India 60/B3
Mokp'o, SKor. 58/D5
Mol, Belg. 28/C6
Mola di Bari, It. 40/C5
Molde, Nor. 20/C3
Moldova (ctry.) 41/H2
Moldova Nouă, Rom. 40/E3
Molepolole, Bots. 80/D2
Molfetta, It. 40/C5
Molina de Segura, Sp. 34/E3
Moline, Il, US 93/K2
Molins de Rei, Sp. 35/L7
Mollendo, Peru 106/D7
Mollet del Vallès, Sp. 35/L6
Mölln, Ger. 26/F2
Moluccas (arch.), Indo. 67/G3
Mombasa, Kenya 82/G1
Mombetsu, Japan 55/N3
Mona Passage (chan.), NAm. 104/D3
Monaco (cap.), Mona. 33/G5
Monaco (ctry.) 33/G5
Moncada, Sp. 35/E3
Moncalieri, It. 33/G4
Monchegorsk, Rus. 42/G2
Mönchengladbach, Ger. 28/D6
Monclova, Mex. 96/C5
Moncton, NB, Can. 95/H2
Mondovi, It. 33/G4
Mondragón, Sp. 34/D1
Mondragone, It. 40/A5
Monfalcone, It. 40/A3
Monforte, Sp. 34/B1
Mongaguá, Braz. 108/G9
Mongo, Chad 77/J5
Mongolia (ctry.) 54/D2
Mongu, Zam. 82/D4
Monheim, Ger. 28/D6
Monmouth, Il, US 93/K2
Monopoli, It. 40/C5
Monor, Hun. 40/D2
Monreale, It. 38/C3
Monroe, Ga, US 97/H3
Monroe, La, US 93/J4
Monroe, NC, US 97/H3
Monroe, Wi, US 93/K2
Monroe, Mi, US 94/D3
Monrovia (cap.), Libr. 78/C5
Mons, Belg. 30/C3
Monster, Neth. 28/B4
Mont-de-Marsan, Fr. 32/C5
Mont-Royal, Qu, Can. 95/N6
Montana (state), US 90/F4
Montana, Bul. 41/F4
Montargis, Fr. 32/E2
Montauban, Fr. 32/D4
Montbéliard, Fr. 36/C2
Montcada i Reixac, Sp. 35/L7
Montceau-les-Mines, Fr. 32/F3
Monte Alegre, Braz. 107/H4
Monte Alto, Braz. 108/B2
Monte Carmelo, Braz. 108/C1
Monte Caseros, Arg. 109/E3
Monte Sant'Angelo, It. 40/B5
Montego Bay, Jam. 103/G2
Montélimar, Fr. 32/F4
Montemorelos, Mex. 96/D5
Montenegro, Braz. 108/B4
Montereau-Faut-Yonne, Fr. 32/E2
Monterey, Ca, US 92/B3
Montería, Col. 103/H4
Montero, Bol. 106/F7
Monteros, Arg. 109/C2
Monterotondo, It. 38/C1
Monterrey, Mex. 96/C5
Montes Claros, Braz. 107/K7
Montesilvano Marina, It. 40/B4
Montevideo (cap.), Uru. 109/E3
Montgeron, Fr. 30/B6
Montgomery (cap.), Al, US 97/G3
Montigny-le-Bretonneux, Fr. 30/B6
Montigny-lès-Metz, Fr. 31/F5
Montijo, Port. 35/Q10
Montijo, Sp. 34/B3
Montilla, Sp. 34/C4
Montivilliers, Fr. 32/D2
Montluçon, Fr. 32/E3
Montpelier (cap.), Vt, US 95/F2
Montpellier, Fr. 32/E5
Montréal, Qu, Can. 95/N6
Montréal-Nord, Qu, Can. 95/N6
Montreux, Swi. 36/C5
Montserrat (dpcy.), Fr. 104/F3
Monywa, Myan. 60/B4
Monza, It. 33/H4
Monzón, Sp. 35/F2
Moore, Ok, US 93/H4
Mooresville, NC, US 97/H3
Moosburg, Ger. 33/J2
Moose Jaw, Sk, Can. 91/G3
Mopti, Mali 78/D3
Moquegua, Peru 106/D7
Mór, Hun. 40/D2
Mora, NM, US 93/F4
Mora, Swe. 20/E3
Morada Nova, Braz. 107/L5
Morādābād, India 62/C2
Morafenobe, Madg. 81/H7
Moraga, Ca, US 99/K11
Morales, Guat. 102/D3
Moramanga, Madg. 81/J7
Morarano Chrome, Madg. 81/J7
Moratuwa, SrL. 62/C6
Morelia, Mex. 101/E5
Morena, India 62/C2
Moreni, Rom. 41/G3
Moreno Valley, Ca, US 92/C4
Morgan City, La, US 93/K5
Morganton, NC, US 97/H3
Morioka, Japan 55/N4
Moriyama, Japan 56/D3
Morlaix, Fr. 32/B2
Morlanwelz, Belg. 31/D3
Morley, Eng, UK 23/G4
Moro, Pak. 62/A2
Morocco (ctry.) 76/C1
Morogoro, Tanz. 82/G2
Morombe, Madg. 81/G8
Morón, Cuba 103/G1
Morón, Arg. 109/E3
Mörön, Mong. 54/E2
Morón de la Frontera, Sp. 34/C4
Morondava, Madg. 81/H8
Moroni (cap.), Com. 81/G5
Moroto, Ugan. 77/M7
Morrinhos, Braz. 108/B1
Morris, Il, US 93/K2
Morristown, Tn, US 97/H2
Morro Bay, Ca, US 92/B4
Morshansk, Rus. 45/G1
Morton, Il, US 93/K2
Morton Grove, Il, US 99/Q15
Mortsel, Belg. 28/B6
Morvi, India 62/B3
Morwell, Austl. 73/C3
Mosbach, Ger. 33/H2
Moscow (cap.), Rus. 43/W9
Moscow Univ. Ice Shelf, Ant. 83/J
Moses Lake, Wa, US 90/D4
Moshi, Tanz. 82/G1
Mosonmagyaróvár, Hun. 40/C2
Moss, Nor. 20/D4
Moss Point, Ms, US 97/F4
Mosselbaai, SAfr. 80/C4
Mössingen, Ger. 37/F1
Mossoró, Braz. 107/L5
Most, Czh. 33/K1
Mostaganem, Alg. 76/F1
Mostar, Bosn. 40/C4
Móstoles, Sp. 35/N9
Mosul (Al Mawşil), Syria 51/E2
Motala, Swe. 20/E4
Motīhāri, India 62/D2
Motomiya, Japan 57/G2
Motril, Sp. 34/D4
Motul de Carrillo Puerto, Mex. 102/D1
Mouila, Gabon 82/B1
Moulins, Fr. 32/E3
Moultrie, Ga, US 97/H4
Moundou, Chad 76/J6
Moundsville, WV, US 97/H2
Mount Abu, India 62/B3
Mount Baker-Snoqualmie, Wa, US 99/D1
Mount Clemens, Mi, US 99/G6
Mount Gambier, Austl. 73/B3
Mount Hagen, PNG 68/D5
Mount Pearl, Nf, Can. 95/L2
Mount Pleasant, Tx, US 93/J4
Mount Pleasant, Mi, US 94/C3
Mount Prospect, Il, US 99/P15
Mount Rainier National Park, Wa, US 90/C4
Mount Vernon, Wa, US 90/C3
Mount Vernon, Il, US 93/K3
Mount Vernon, Oh, US 94/D3
Mountain Ash, Wal, UK 24/C3
Mountain View, Ca, US 99/K12
Mountlake Terrace, Wa, US 99/C2
Mouscron, Belg. 30/C2
Mouths of the Niger, Nga. 76/G6
Moyuta, Guat. 102/D3
Mozambique (ctry.) 82/G4
Mozambique (chan.), Afr. 82/J10
Mozhaysk, Rus. 42/H5
Mozhga, Rus. 43/M4
Mpika, Zam. 82/F3
Mrągowo, Pol. 27/L2
Mtsensk, Rus. 44/F1
Mualama, Moz. 82/G4
Muar, Malay. 66/B3
Muarabungo, Indo. 66/B4
Mucojo, Moz. 82/H3
Mudanjiang, China 55/K3
Mudanya, Turk. 41/J5
Mudon, Myan. 65/B2
Mufulira, Zam. 82/E3
Muğla, Turk. 50/B2
Mühldorf, Ger. 33/K2
Muju, SKor. 58/D4
Mukacheve, Ukr. 27/M4
Mukhayyam al Yarmūk, Syria 49/E3
Muktsar, India 53/K2
Mülhausen, Ger. 29/H6
Mülheim an der Ruhr, Ger. 28/D6
Mulhouse, Fr. 36/D2
Müllheim, Ger. 36/D2
Multān, Pak. 53/K2
Mumbai (Bombay), India 62/B4
Muncar, Indo. 66/D5
München, Ger. 37/H1
Muncie, In, US 97/G1
Mundelein, Il, US 99/Q15
Münden, Ger. 29/G6
Mundo Novo, Braz. 109/F1
Mungaolī, India 62/C3
Munger, India 62/E2
Münster, Ger. 29/E5
Munster, Ger. 29/H3
Munster, In, US 99/R16
Münstereifel, Ger. 31/F2
Muntok, Indo. 66/C4
Murakami, Japan 57/F1
Murcia, Sp. 35/E4
Muret, Fr. 32/D5
Murfreesboro, Tn, US 97/G3
Muriaé, Braz. 108/D2
Murmansk, Rus. 42/G1
Murom, Rus. 42/J5
Muroran, Japan 55/N3
Muroto, Japan 56/D4
Murphysboro, Il, US 93/K3
Murray, Ky, US 97/F2
Murray (riv.), Austl. 73/A2
Murwāra, India 62/D3
Muş, Turk. 50/E2
Muscat (cap.), Oman 53/G4
Mushābani, India 62/E3
Mushin, Nga. 79/F5
Muskego, Wi, US 99/P14
Musoma, Tanz. 82/F1
Mustafakemalpaşa, Turk. 44/D4
Mustang, Ok, US 93/H4
Mut, Turk. 49/C1
Mutare, Zim. 82/F4
Mutsamudu, Com. 81/H6
Mutsu, Japan 55/N3
Muttenz, Swi. 36/D2
Muzaffargarh, Pak. 53/K2
Muzaffarnagar, India 62/C2
Muzaffarpur, India 62/E2
Mwanza, Tanz. 82/F1
Mwene-Ditu, D.R. Congo 82/D2
My Tho, Viet. 65/D4
Myanmar (Burma) (ctry.) 63/G3
Myaungmya, Myan. 60/B5
Myingyan, Myan. 60/B4
Myitkyinā, Myan. 60/C3
Mykolayiv, Ukr. 41/L2
Myrhorod, Ukr. 44/E2
Myrtle Beach, SC, US 97/J3
Myślenice, Pol. 27/K4
Mysore, India 62/C5
Myszków, Pol. 27/K3
Mytishchi, Rus. 43/W9
Mzuzu, Malw. 82/F3

N

N'Djamena (cap.), Chad 76/J5
Naaldwijk, Neth. 28/B4
Naarden, Neth. 28/C4
Nabadwīp, India 62/E3
Nabari, Japan 56/E3
Naberezhnye Chelny, Rus. 43/M5
Nābul, Tun. 38/B4
Nacaome, Hon. 102/E3
Nachi-Katsuura, Japan 56/D4
Náchod, Czh. 33/M1
Nacogdoches, Tx, US 93/J5
Nadiād, India 62/B3
Nador, Mor. 76/E1
Naga, Phil. 68/B3
Nagahama, Japan 56/E3
Nagai, Japan 57/G1
Nagano, Japan 57/F2
Nagaoka, Japan 57/F2
Nagaokakyō, Japan 56/D3
Nagaon (Nowgong), India 60/B3
Nagasaki, Japan 56/A4
Nagato, Japan 56/B3
Nāgaur, India 62/B2
Nāgda, India 62/C3
Nāgercoil, India 62/C6
Nagold, Ger. 37/E1
Nagoya, Japan 57/E3
Nāgpur, India 62/C3
Nagykanizsa, Hun. 40/C2
Nagykőrös, Hun. 40/D2
Naha, Japan 68/B2
Nahariyya, Isr. 49/D3
Nahāvand, Iran 51/G3
Nainpur, India 62/D3
Nairobi (cap.), Kenya 77/N8
Najafābād, Iran 51/G3
Najībābād, India 62/C2
Naju, SKor. 58/D5
Nakajō, Japan 57/F1
Nakaminato, Japan 57/G2
Nakamura, Japan 56/C4
Nakano, Japan 57/F2
Nakatsu, Japan 56/B4
Nakatsugawa, Japan 57/E3
Nakhodka, Rus. 55/L3
Nakhon Pathom, Thai. 65/C3
Nakhon Phanom, Thai. 65/D2
Nakhon Ratchasima, Thai. 65/C3
Nakhon Sawan, Thai. 65/C3
Nakhon Si Thammarat, Thai. 65/B4
Nakło nad Notecią, Pol. 27/J2
Nakskov, Den. 26/F1
Nakuru, Kenya 82/G1
Nal'chik, Rus. 45/G4
Nalgonda, India 62/C4
Nālūt, Libya 76/H1
Nam Dinh, Viet. 65/D1
Namangan, Uzb. 46/H5
Namerikawa, Japan 57/E2
Namibe, Ang. 82/B4
Namibia (ctry.) 82/C5
Namie, Japan 57/G2
Namp'o, NKor. 58/C3
Nampula, Moz. 82/G4
Nāmrup, India 60/B3
Namur, Belg. 31/D3
Namwŏn, SKor. 58/D5
Namysłów, Pol. 27/J3
Nan, Thai. 65/C2
Nanaimo, BC, Can. 90/C3
Nanakuli, Hi, US 88/V13
Nanao, Japan 57/E2
Nanchang, China 61/G2
Nanchong, China 60/E2
Nancy, Fr. 31/F6
Nānded, India 62/C4
Nandurbār, India 62/B3
Nandyāl, India 62/C4
Nangapinoh, Indo. 66/D4
Nangong, China 59/C3
Nanjing, China 61/H1
Nankoku, Japan 56/C4
Nanning, China 65/E1
Nānpāra, India 62/D2
Nanping, China 61/H3
Nanterre, Fr. 30/B6
Nantes, Fr. 32/C3
Nanticoke, Pa, US 94/E3
Nanticoke, On, Can. 95/R10
Nantong, China 61/J1
Nanuque, Braz. 108/D1
Nanyang, China 59/C4
Náousa, Gre. 40/F5
Napa, Ca, US 99/K10
Naperville, Il, US 99/P16
Napier, NZ 71/S10
Naples, Fl, US 97/H5
Napoli, It. 40/B5
Nara, Japan 56/D3
Naranjos, Mex. 102/B1
Narasannapeta, India 62/D4
Narathiwat, Thai. 65/C5
Nārāyanganj, Bang. 62/F3
Nārāyanpet, India 62/C4
Narbonne, Fr. 32/E5
Nardò, It. 39/F2
Narkatiāganj, India 62/D2
Narón, Sp. 34/A1
Nārowāl, Pak. 53/K2
Närpiö (Närpes), Fin. 42/D3
Narra, Phil. 67/E2

Opoczno, Pol. 27/L3
Opole, Pol. 27/J3
Opportunity, Wa, US 90/D4
Or 'Aqiva, Isr. 49/F6
Or Yehuda, Isr. 49/F7
Orai, India 62/C2
Oral, Kaz. 45/J2
Oran, Alg. 76/E1
Orange, Austl. 73/D2
Orange, Tx, US 93/J5
Orange (riv.), Nam,SAfr. 80/B3
Orange, Fr. 32/F4
Orange Park, Fl, US 97/H4
Orange Walk, Belz. 102/D2
Orangeburg, SC, US 97/H3
Orangeville, On, Can. 95/S8
Oranienburg, Ger. 27/G2
Oranjestad, Aru.. 106/D1
Orăştie, Rom. 41/F3
Oraviţa, Rom. 40/E3
Orchard Homes, Mt, US 90/E4
Ordu, Turk. 44/F4
Örebro, Swe. 20/E4
Oregon (state), US 90/C4
Oregon City, Or, US 90/C4
Orekhovo-Zuyevo, Rus. 42/H5
Orël, Rus. 44/F1
Orenburg, Rus. 45/K2
Orense, Sp. 34/B1
Orhangazi, Turk. 41/J5
Orhei, Mol. 41/J2
Oria, Sp. 34/D4
Oriental, Cordillera (mts.), Col.,Ecu. 106/C5
Orihuela, Sp. 35/E3
Orillia, On, Can. 94/E2
Orinda, Ca, US 99/J11
Oristano, It. 38/A3
Oriximiná, Braz. 107/G4
Orizaba, Mex. 101/M8
Orkney, SAfr. 80/P13
Orland Park, Il, US 99/Q16
Orlândia, Braz. 108/C2
Orlando, Fl, US 97/H4
Orléans, Fr. 32/D3
Orlová, Czh. 27/K4
Ormoc, Phil. 67/F1
Ormond Beach, Fl, US 97/H4
Ormskirk, Eng, UK 23/F4
Örnsköldsvik, Swe. 42/C3
Orodara, Burk. 78/D4
Orono, Me, US 95/G2
Oroquieta, Phil. 67/F2
Orosháza, Hun. 40/E2
Oroszlány, Hun. 40/D2
Oroville, Ca, US 92/B3
Orsay, Fr. 30/B6
Orsha, Bela. 42/F5
Orsk, Rus. 45/L2
Orşova, Rom. 40/F3
Ortaköy, Turk. 50/C2
Ortaköy, Turk. 44/E4
Orūmīyeh, Iran 51/F2
Oruro, Bol. 106/E7
Osa, Rus. 43/M4
Ōsaka, Japan 56/D3
Osan, SKor. 58/D4
Osasco, Braz. 108/G8
Oschersleben, Ger. 26/F2
Osh, Kyr. 46/H5
Oshawa, On, Can. 95/V8
Oshogbo, Nga. 79/G5
Osijek, Cro. 40/D3
Osipovichi, Bela. 44/D1
Oskarshamn, Swe. 20/F4
Öskemen, Kaz. 46/J5
Oslo (cap.), Nor. 20/D4
Osmānābād, India 62/C4
Osmancık, Turk. 44/E4
Osmaniye, Turk. 49/E1
Osnabrück, Ger. 29/F4
Osório, Braz. 108/B4
Osorno, Chile 109/B5
Oss, Neth. 28/C5
Ossett, Eng, UK 23/G4
Ostashkov, Rus. 42/G4
Osten (Oostende), Belg. 30/B1
Osterholz-Scharmbeck, Ger. 29/F2
Osterode am Harz, Ger. 29/H5
Östersund, Swe. 20/E3
Östhammar, Swe. 42/C3
Ostrava, Czh. 27/K4
Ostróda, Pol. 27/K2
Ostrogozhsk, Rus. 44/F2
Ostrołęka, Pol. 27/L2
Ostrov, Rus. 42/F4
Ostrov, Czh. 33/K1
Ostrów Mazowiecka, Pol. 27/L2
Ostrów Wielkopolski, Pol. 27/J3
Ostrowiec Świętokrzyski, Pol. 27/L3
Ostuni, It. 40/C5
Osuna, Sp. 34/C4
Osvaldo Cruz, Braz. 108/B2
Oswego, NY, US 94/E3
Oswestry, Eng, UK 23/E6
Oświęcim (Auschwitz), Pol. 27/K3
Ōta, Japan 57/F2
Ōtake, Japan 56/C3
Otaru, Japan 47/Q5
Ōtawara, Japan 57/G2
Otradnyy, Rus. 45/J1
Otrokovice, Czh. 27/J4
Ōtsu, Japan 56/D3
Ottawa, Ks, US 93/J3
Ottawa (riv.), Can. 94/E2
Ottawa (cap.), On, Can. 94/F2
Ottignies-Louvain-la-Neuve, Belg. 31/D2
Ottobrunn, Ger. 33/J2
Ottumwa, Ia, US 93/J2
Ottweiler, Ger. 31/G5
Otwock, Pol. 27/L2
Ouagadougou (cap.), Burk. 79/E3
Ouargla, Alg. 76/G1
Ouarzazate, Mor. 76/D1
Oud-Beijerland, Neth. 28/B5
Oudenaarde, Belg. 30/C2
Oudtshoorn, SAfr. 80/C4
Oued Zem, Mor. 76/D1
Ouesso, Congo 76/J7
Ouezzane, Mor. 76/D1
Ouidah, Ben. 79/F5
Oujda, Mor. 76/E1
Oullins, Fr. 36/A6
Oulu, Fin. 42/E2
Oupeye, Belg. 31/E2
Ouricuri, Braz. 107/K5
Ourinhos, Braz. 108/B2
Ouro Fino, Braz. 108/G7
Ouro Preto, Braz. 108/D2
Outreau, Fr. 25/H5
Outremont, Qu, Can. 95/N6
Ovalle, Chile 109/B3
Overath, Ger. 31/G2
Overijse, Belg. 31/D2
Overland Park, Ks, US 93/J3
Oviedo, Sp. 34/C1
Owase, Japan 56/E3
Owasso, Ok, US 93/J3
Owen Sound, On, Can. 94/D2
Owensboro, Ky, US 97/G2
Owo, Nga. 79/G5
Owosso, Mi, US 94/C3
Oxford, Ms, US 97/F3
Oxford, Eng, UK 25/E3
Oxkutzcab, Mex. 102/D1
Oxnard, Ca, US 92/C4
Oyabe, Japan 57/E2
Oyama, Japan 57/F2
Oyem, Gabon 76/H7
Oyo, Nga. 79/F5
Oyonnax, Fr. 36/B5
Ozark, Al, US 97/G4
Ozark (mts.), Ar,Mo, US 96/E3
Ózd, Hun. 40/E1
Ozoir-la-Ferrière, Fr. 30/B6
Ozorków, Pol. 27/K3
Ōzu, Japan 56/C4

P

P'yŏngyang (cap.), NKor. 58/C3
Pa-an, Myan. 65/B2
Paarl, SAfr. 80/L10
Pabellón de Arteaga, Mex. 100/E4
Pabianice, Pol. 27/K3
Pābna, Bang. 62/E3
Pacasmayo, Peru 106/C5
Pachino, It. 38/D4
Pachuca, Mex. 101/L6
Pacific (ocean) 16/B4
Pacific Palisades, Hi, US 88/W13
Pacifica, Ca, US 99/K11
Pacitan, Indo. 66/D5
Paço de Arcos, Port. 35/P10
Padang, Indo. 66/B4
Padangpanjang, Indo. 66/B4
Padangsidempuan, Indo. 66/A3
Paderborn, Ger. 29/F5
Padova, It. 33/J4
Paducah, Ky, US 97/F2
Pagadian, Phil. 67/F2
Pago Pago (cap.), ASam. 69/T10
Paignton, Eng, UK 24/C6
Painesville, Oh, US 94/D3
Paithan, India 62/C4
Pakanbaru, Indo. 66/B3
Pakistan (ctry.) 53/H3
Pakokku, Myan. 60/B4
Pākpattan, Pak. 53/K2
Paks, Hun. 40/D2
Pakxe, Laos 65/D3
Palafrugell, Sp. 35/G2
Palagonia, It. 38/D4
Pālakollu, India 62/D4
Palangkaraya, Indo. 66/D4
Pālanpur, India 62/B3
Palapye, Bots. 82/E5
Palatine, Il, US 99/P15
Palatka, Fl, US 97/H4
Palau, Mex. 101/E3
Palau (ctry.) 68/C4
Pālayankottai, India 62/C6
Palembang, Indo. 66/B4
Palencia, Sp. 34/C1
Palenque, Mex. 102/D2
Palermo, It. 38/C3
Pālghar, India 53/K5
Palhoça, Braz. 108/B3
Pāli, India 62/B2
Pālitāna, India 62/B3
Palm Bay, Fl, US 97/H4
Palm Harbor, Fl, US 97/H4
Palm Springs, Ca, US 92/C4
Palma, Sp. 35/G3
Palma del Río, Sp. 34/C4
Palma di Montechiaro, It. 38/C4
Palma Soriano, Cuba 103/H1
Palmares, Braz. 107/L5
Palmas, Braz. 108/A3
Palmdale, Ca, US 92/C4
Palmeira, Braz. 108/B3
Palmeira dos Índios, Braz. 107/L5
Palmerston North, NZ 71/S11
Palmetto, Fl, US 97/H5
Palmi, It. 38/D3
Palmira, Col. 106/C3
Palni, India 62/C5
Palo Alto, Ca, US 99/K12
Palo Verde, CR 102/E4
Palos Hills, Il, US 99/Q16
Palpalá, Arg. 109/C1
Palu, Indo. 67/E4
Pamangkat, Indo. 66/C3
Pamiers, Fr. 32/D5
Pampa, Tx, US 93/G4
Pampas (plain), Arg. 109/D4
Pamplona, Col. 103/H5
Pamplona, Sp. 34/E1
Panagyurishte, Bul. 41/G4
Panaji, India 62/B4
Panama (canal), Pan. 106/B2
Panamá (cap.), Pan. 103/G4
Panama (ctry.), Pan. 103/F2
Panama City, Fl, US 97/G4
Panama, Golfo de (gulf), Pan. 103/G4
Panama, Isthmus of (isth.), Pan. 103/F4
Pančevo, Yugo. 40/E3
Pandharpur, India 62/C4
Panevėžys, Lith. 42/E5
Panfilov, Kaz. 46/J5
Pangkalanberandan, Indo. 66/A3
Pangkalpinang, Indo. 66/C4
Pangutaran, Phil. 67/F2
Pānīpat, India 62/C2
Panna, India 62/D3
Pánuco, Mex. 102/B1
Panzhihua, China 60/D3
Panzós, Guat. 102/D3
Pápa, Hun. 40/C2
Papantla, Mex. 101/M6
Papeete (cap.), FrPol. 69/X15
Papeete, FrPol. 69/X15
Papenburg, Ger. 29/E2
Papendrecht, Neth. 28/B5
Papillion, Ne, US 93/H2
Papua New Guinea (ctry.) 68/D5
Pará de Minas, Braz. 108/C1
Paracambi, Braz. 108/K7
Paracatu, Braz. 107/J7
Paraćin, Yugo. 40/E4
Paradip, India 62/E3
Paragominas, Braz. 107/J4
Paraguaçu Paulista, Braz. 108/B2
Paraguarí, Par. 109/E2
Paraguay (riv.), Par. 109/E1
Paraguay (ctry.) 105/C5
Paraíba do Sul, Braz. 108/K7
Paraíso, Mex. 102/C2
Paraíso do Norte de Goiás, Braz. 107/J6
Parakou, Ben. 79/F4
Paramaribo (cap.), Sur. 107/G2
Paraná, Arg. 109/D3
Paraná (riv.), Arg.,Braz. 109/E3
Paranaguá, Braz. 108/B3
Paranaíba, Braz. 108/B1
Paranavaí, Braz. 109/F1
Parang, Phil. 67/F2
Parbhani, India 62/C4
Parchim, Ger. 26/F2
Pardes Ḥanna-Karkur, Isr. 49/F7
Pardubice, Czh. 33/L1
Pare, Indo. 66/D5
Parede, Port. 35/P10
Parepare, Indo. 67/E4
Pariaman, Indo. 66/B4
Parintins, Braz. 107/G4
Paris, Tx, US 93/J4
Paris (cap.), Fr. 30/B6
Park Ridge, Il, US 99/Q16
Parkersburg, WV, US 97/H2
Parkland, Wa, US 99/C3
Parkway-Sacramento, Ca, US 99/L9
Parla, Sp. 35/N9
Parlakhemundi, India 62/D4
Parli, India 62/C4
Parma, Oh, US 94/D3
Parma, It. 33/J4
Parnaíba, Braz. 107/K4
Parnamirim, Braz. 107/L5
Pärnu, Est. 42/E4
Parow, SAfr. 80/L10
Parral, Chile 109/B4
Parras de la Fuente, Mex. 96/C5
Parsons, Ks, US 93/J3
Partinico, It. 38/C3
Partizansk, Rus. 55/L3
Partizánske, Slvk. 27/K4
Partūr, India 62/C4
Pārvathīpuram, India 62/D4
Pasadena, Ca, US 92/C4
Pasadena, Tx, US 93/J5
Pasaje, Ecu. 106/C4
Pasān, India 62/D3
Pascagoula, Ms, US 97/F4
Paşcani, Rom. 41/H2
Pasco, Wa, US 90/D4
Pāsighāt, India 60/B2
Pasinler, Turk. 45/G5
Pasni, Pak. 53/H3
Paso de los Libres, Arg. 109/E2
Paso Robles (El Paso de Robles), Ca, US 92/B4
Passau, Ger. 33/K2
Passo Fundo, Braz. 108/A4
Passos, Braz. 108/C2
Pastavy, Bela. 42/E5
Pasto, Col. 106/C3
Pasuruan, Indo. 66/D5
Patagonia (phys. reg.), Arg. 109/B6
Pātan, India 62/B3
Paterna, Sp. 35/E3
Paternò, It. 38/D4
Paterson, NJ, US 94/F3
Pathānkot, India 53/L2
Pathein (Bassein), Myan. 60/B5
Pati, Indo. 66/D5
Patía, Col. 106/C3
Patiāla, India 53/L2
Patikul, Phil. 67/F2
Patna, India 62/E2
Patnongon, Phil. 67/F1
Patnos, Turk. 51/E2
Pato Branco, Braz. 108/A3
Patos, Braz. 107/L5
Patos de Minas, Braz. 108/C1
Pátrai, Gre. 39/G3
Patrocínio, Braz. 108/C1
Pattani, Thai. 65/C5
Pattukkottai, India 62/C5
Patuākhāli, Bang. 62/F3
Pátzcuaro, Mex. 101/E5
Pau, Fr. 32/C5
Paulínia, Braz. 108/F7
Paulo Afonso, Braz. 107/L5
Paungde, Myan. 60/B5
Pavia, It. 33/H4
Pavlodar, Kaz. 46/H4
Pavlohrad, Ukr. 44/E2
Pavlovo, Rus. 42/J5
Pawtucket, RI, US 95/G3
Payakumbuh, Indo. 66/B4
Paysandú, Uru. 109/E3
Payson, Ut, US 92/E2
Pazarcık, Turk. 50/D2
Pazardzhik, Bul. 41/G4
Peace (riv.), BC, Can. 86/D3
Peachtree City, Ga, US 97/G3
Pearl, Ms, US 97/F3
Pearl (har.), Hi, US 88/W13
Pearl City, Hi, US 88/W13
Pechora, Rus. 43/N2
Pecos, Tx, US 96/C4
Pecos (riv.), NM,Tx, US 93/G5
Pécs, Hun. 40/D2
Pedernales, DRep. 103/J2
Pederneiras, Braz. 108/B2
Pedra Azul, Braz. 107/K7
Pedreira, Braz. 108/G7
Pedreiras, Braz. 107/K4
Pedro Betancourt, Cuba 103/F1
Pedro Juan Caballero, Par. 109/E1
Pedro Leopoldo, Braz. 108/C1
Pehuajó, Arg. 109/D4
Peine, Ger. 29/H4
Pekalongan, Indo. 66/C5
Pekin, Il, US 93/K2
Pelham, Al, US 97/G3
Pelhřimov, Czh. 33/L2
Pelotas, Braz. 108/A4
Pematangsiantar, Indo. 66/A3
Pemba, Moz. 82/H3
Penápolis, Braz. 108/B2
Penarth, Wal, UK 24/C4
Pendleton, Or, US 90/D4
Penedo, Braz. 107/L6
Peniche, Port. 34/A3
Penn Hills, Pa, US 94/E3
Pennsylvania (state), US 94/E3
Penonomé, Pan. 103/F4
Pensacola, Fl, US 97/G4
Penticton, BC, Can. 90/D3
Penza, Rus. 45/H1
Penzance, Eng, UK 24/A6
Perabumulih, Indo. 66/B4
Pérama, Gre. 39/N9
Pereira, Col. 106/C3
Pereira Barreto, Braz. 108/B2
Pergamino, Arg. 109/D3
Perico, Cuba 103/F1
Périgueux, Fr. 32/D4
Peringat, Malay. 65/C5
Peristéri, Gre. 39/N8
Perm', Rus. 43/N4
Pernik, Bul. 40/F4
Perote, Mex. 101/M7
Perpignan, Fr. 32/E5
Perry, Ga, US 97/H3
Persian (gulf), Asia 52/E3
Perth, Austl. 68/A8
Pertuis, Fr. 32/F5
Peru, In, US 94/C3
Peru, Il, US 93/K2
Peru (ctry.), Peru 106/C5
Perugia, It. 38/C1
Peruíbe, Braz. 108/G9
Péruwelz, Belg. 30/C2
Pervomaysk, Rus. 45/G1
Pervomays'k, Ukr. 41/K1
Pervoural'sk, Rus. 43/N4
Pesaro, It. 33/K5
Pescara, It. 40/B4
Peshāwar, Pak. 53/K2
Peshtera, Bul. 41/G4
Pessac, Fr. 32/C4
Pestovo, Rus. 42/G4
Petaḥ Tiqwa, Isr. 49/F7
Petaluma, Ca, US 99/J10
Petare, Ven. 106/E1
Petatlán, Mex. 101/E5
Peterborough, On, Can. 94/E2
Peterborough, Eng, UK 25/F1
Peterlee, Eng, UK 23/G2
Petersburg, Va, US 97/J2
Petershagen, Ger. 29/F4
Pétionville, Haiti 103/H2
Petlād, India 62/B3
Petrel, Sp. 35/E3
Petrich, Bul. 41/F5
Petrila, Rom. 41/F3
Petrodvorets, Rus. 43/S7
Petrolina, Braz. 107/K5
Petropavl, Kaz. 46/G4
Petropavlovsk-Kamchatskiy, Rus. 47/R4
Petrópolis, Braz. 108/K7
Petrovsk, Rus. 45/H1
Petrovsk-Zabaykal'skiy, Rus. 54/F1
Petrozavodsk, Rus. 42/G3
Pfaffenhofen an der Ilm, Ger. 33/J2
Pforzheim, Ger. 33/H2
Pfungstadt, Ger. 33/H2
Phalodi, India 62/B2
Phan Rang-Thap Cham, Viet. 65/E4
Phan Thiet, Viet. 65/E4
Pharr, Tx, US 96/D5
Phayao, Thai. 65/B2
Phenix City, Al, US 97/G3
Phet Buri, Thai. 65/B3
Philadelphia, Pa, US 94/F4
Philippine (sea), Asia 68/B3
Philippines (ctry.) 68/B3
Phitsanulok, Thai. 65/C2
Phnom Penh (cap.), Camb. 65/D4
Phoenix (cap.), Az, US 92/D4
Phra Nakhon Si Ayutthaya, Thai. 65/C3
Phrae, Thai. 65/C2
Phu Tho, Viet. 65/D1
Phuket, Thai. 65/B5
Piacenza, It. 33/H4
Piaseczno, Pol. 27/L2
Piazza Armerina, It. 38/D4
Picayune, Ms, US 97/F4
Pickering, On, Can. 95/U8
Picos, Braz. 107/K5
Piedade, Port. 35/P10
Piedmont, Ca, US 99/K11
Piedras Negras, Mex. 96/C4
Piekary Śląskie, Pol. 27/K3
Pierre (cap.), SD, US 91/H4
Pierrefonds, Qu, Can. 95/N7
Piešťany, Slvk. 27/J4
Pietarsdart (Jakobstad), Fin. 42/D3
Pietermaritzburg, SAfr. 81/E3
Pietersburg, SAfr. 82/E5
Pijnacker, Neth. 28/B4
Piła, Pol. 27/J2
Pilar, Par. 109/E2
Pilar, Phil. 67/F1
Pilcomayo (riv.), SAm. 109/D1
Pilkhua, India 62/C2
Pimpri-Chinchwad, India 53/K5
Pinamalayan, Phil. 67/F1
Pinar del Río, Cuba 103/F1
Pinatubo (mt.), Phil. 68/B3
Pindamonhangaba, Braz. 108/H7
Pindaré-Mirim, Braz. 107/J4
Pindi Gheb, Pak. 53/K2
Pindwāra, India 62/B3
Pine Bluff, Ar, US 93/J4
Pinerolo, It. 33/G4
Pinetown, SAfr. 81/E3
Pineville, La, US 93/J5
Pingdingshan, China 59/C4
Pingdu, China 59/D3
P'ingtung, Tai. 61/J4
Pingxiang, China 61/G3
Pingxiang, China 65/D1
Pinhal, Braz. 108/G7
Pinhal Novo, Port. 35/Q10
Pinheiro, Braz. 107/J4
Pinneberg, Ger. 29/G1
Pinole, Ca, US 99/K10
Pinsk, Bela. 44/C1
Pinto, Sp. 35/N9
Piombino, It. 38/B1
Pionki, Pol. 27/L3
Piotrków Trybunalski, Pol. 27/K3
Piplān, Pak. 53/K2
Piqua, Oh, US 94/C3
Piracicaba, Braz. 108/C2
Piraiévs, Gre. 39/N9
Piraju, Braz. 108/B2
Pirapora, Braz. 108/C1
Pirapòzinho, Braz. 108/B2
Piràssununga, Braz. 108/C2
Pires do Rio, Braz. 108/B1
Pírgos, Gre. 39/G4
Piripiri, Braz. 107/K4
Pirmasens, Ger. 31/G5
Pirna, Ger. 27/G3
Pirot, Yugo. 40/F4
Pisa, It. 33/J5
Pisco, Peru 106/C6
Písek, Czh. 33/L2
Pishīn, Pak. 53/J2
Pistoia, It. 33/J5
Pisz, Pol. 27/L2
Pitalito, Col. 106/C3
Pitcairn Islands (dpcy.), UK 69/N7
Piteå, Swe. 42/D2
Piteşti, Rom. 41/G3
Pittsburg, Ks, US 93/J3
Pittsburg, Ca, US 99/L10
Pittsburgh, Pa, US 94/E3
Pittsfield, Ma, US 94/F3
Pittston, Pa, US 94/F3
Piuí, Braz. 108/C2
Piura, Peru 106/B5
Pivdennyy Buh (riv.), Ukr. 44/D2
Pivijay, Col. 103/H4
Placetas, Cuba 103/G1
Plainview, Tx, US 93/G4
Plaisir, Fr. 30/A6
Planeta Rica, Col. 103/H4
Plant City, Fl, US 97/H4
Plantation, Fl, US 97/H5
Plasencia, Sp. 34/B2
Plata, Río de la (estu.), SAm. 109/E4
Plato, Col. 103/H4
Platte (riv.), Ne, US 93/H2
Plattsburgh, NY, US 94/F2
Plauen, Ger. 33/K1
Plav, Yugo. 40/D4
Playas, Ecu. 106/B4
Pleasant Hill, Ca, US 99/K11
Pleasant Prairie, Wi, US 99/Q14
Pleasanton, Ca, US 99/L11
Pleiku, Viet. 65/D3
Pleszew, Pol. 27/J3
Plettenberg, Ger. 29/E6
Pljevlja, Yugo. 40/D4
Płock, Pol. 27/K2
Ploemeur, Fr. 32/B3
Ploieşti, Rom. 41/H3
Płońsk, Pol. 27/L2
Plymouth, Eng, UK 24/B6
Plymouth (cap.), Monts. 104/F3
Plzeň, Czh. 33/K2
Pô, Burk. 79/E4
Po (riv.), It. 33/G4
Poá, Braz. 108/G8
Pobé, Ben. 79/F5
Pocatello, Id, US 92/D2
Pochep, Rus. 44/E1
Poconé, Braz. 107/G7
Poços de Caldas, Braz. 108/G6
Podgorica, Yugo. 40/D4
Podol'sk, Rus. 43/W9
Podporozh'ye, Rus. 42/G3
Podujevo, Yugo. 40/E4
Poggibonsi, It. 33/J5
Pogradec, Alb. 40/E5
P'ohang, SKor. 56/A2
Pohoiki, Hi, US 88/U11
Pointe-à-Pitre, Fr. 104/F3
Pointe-Claire, Qu, Can. 95/N7
Pointe-Noire, Congo 82/B1
Poitiers, Fr. 32/D3
Pokaran, India 53/K3
Pokharā, Nepal 62/D2
Pokhvistnevo, Rus. 45/K1
Pol-e Khomrī, Afg. 53/J1
Pola de Laviana, Sp. 34/C1
Pola de Lena, Sp. 34/C1
Pola de Siero, Sp. 34/C1

Polan – Rio d

Rio do Sul, Braz. 108/B3
Río Gallegos, Arg. 109/C7
Río Grande, Arg. 109/C7
Rio Grande, Braz. 108/A5
Rio Grande (riv.), Mex.,US 96/C4
Rio Grande City, Tx, US 96/D5
Rio Grande da Serra, Braz. 108/G8
Rio Largo, Braz. 107/L5
Rio Negrinho, Braz. 108/B3
Rio Negro, Braz. 108/B3
Rio Pardo, Braz. 108/A4
Rio Rancho, NM, US 92/F4
Río Tercero, Arg. 109/D3
Rio Verde, Braz. 108/B1
Río Verde, Mex. 102/B1
Riobamba, Ecu. 106/C4
Ríohacha, Col. 103/H4
Riom, Fr. 32/E4
Ripley, Eng, UK 23/G5
Ripollet, Sp. 35/L6
Rishon Leẕiyyon, Isr. 49/F8
Rîşnov, Rom. 41/G3
Rivadavia, Arg. 109/C3
Rivas, Nic. 102/E4
Rive-de-Gier, Fr. 32/F4
River Rouge, Mi, US 99/F7
Rivera, Uru. 109/E3
Riverside, Ca, US 92/C4
Riverton, Wy, US 92/E2
Riverview, NB, Can. 95/H2
Riverview, Mi, US 99/F7
Riviera Beach, Fl, US 97/H5
Rivière-du-Loup, Qu, Can. 95/G2
Rivne, Ukr. 44/C2
Rivoli, It. 33/G4
Rixensart, Belg. 31/D2
Riyadh (cap.), SAr. 52/E4
Rize, Turk. 45/G4
Road Town (cap.), BVI, UK 104/E3
Roanne, Fr. 32/F3
Robertsganj, India 62/D3
Robertsport, Libr. 78/C5
Robstown, Tx, US 96/D5
Rocha, Uru. 109/F3
Rochdale, Eng, UK 23/F4
Rochefort, Fr. 32/C4
Rochester, Mn, US 93/J1
Rochester, NY, US 94/E3
Rochester, NH, US 95/G3
Rochester, Eng, UK 25/G4
Rochester Hills, Mi, US 99/F6
Rock Forest, Qu, Can. 95/G2
Rock Hill, SC, US 97/H3
Rock Island, Il, US 93/K2
Rock Springs, Wy, US 92/E2
Rockford, Il, US 93/K2
Rockhampton, Austl. 72/C3
Rockingham, NC, US 97/J3
Rockledge, Fl, US 97/H4
Rockville, Md, US 97/J2
Rockwall, Tx, US 93/H4
Rocky (mts.), Can.,US 88/C1
Rocky Mount, NC, US 97/J3
Rocky Mountain National Park, Co, US 92/F2
Rodez, Fr. 32/E4
Ródhos (Rhodes), Gre. 50/B2
Roermond, Neth. 28/C6
Roeselare, Belg. 30/C2
Rogachev, Bela. 44/D1
Rogatica, Bosn. 40/D4
Rogers, Ar, US 93/J3
Rohri, Pak. 62/A2
Roi Et, Thai. 65/C2
Rolândia, Braz. 108/B2
Rolla, Mo, US 93/K3
Rolling Meadows, Il, US 99/P15
Roman, Rom. 41/H2
Romania (ctry.) 41/F3
Romans-sur-Isère, Fr. 32/F4
Romblon, Phil. 67/F1
Rome, NY, US 94/F3
Rome, Ga, US 97/G3
Rome (cap.), It. 38/C2
Romeoville, Il, US 99/P16
Romilly-sur-Seine, Fr. 32/E2
Romny, Ukr. 44/E2
Romorantin-Lanthenay, Fr. 32/D3
Romsey, Eng, UK 25/E5
Romulus, Mi, US 99/F7
Ronda, Sp. 34/C4
Rondonópolis, Braz. 107/H7
Rongcheng, China 58/B4
Rønne, Den. 27/H1
Ronne Ice Shelf, Ant. 83/W
Ronneby, Swe. 27/H1
Ronnenberg, Ger. 29/G4
Ronse, Belg. 30/C2
Roodepoort, SAfr. 80/P13
Roorkee, India 62/C2
Roosendaal, Neth. 28/B5
Roquetas de Mar, Sp. 34/D4
Rosa Zárate, Ecu. 106/C3
Rosario, Arg. 109/D3
Rosário, Braz. 107/K4
Rosario de la Frontera, Arg. 109/D2
Rosário do Sul, Braz. 109/F3
Rosarito, Mex. 92/C4
Roseau (cap.), Dom. 104/F4
Roseburg, Or, US 92/B2
Roselle, Il, US 99/P16
Rosenberg, Tx, US 93/J5
Rosenheim, Ger. 33/K3
Roseville, Ca, US 99/M9
Roseville, Mi, US 99/G6
Rosh Ha'ayin, Isr. 49/F7
Roşiori de Vede, Rom. 41/G3
Roskilde, Den. 26/G1
Roslavl', Rus. 44/E1
Rosmalen, Neth. 28/C5
Rosolini, It. 38/D4
Rösrath, Ger. 31/G2
Ross Ice Shelf, Ant. 83/N
Rossano Stazione, It. 38/E3
Rosso, Mrta. 78/B2
Rossosh', Rus. 44/F2
Rostock, Ger. 26/G1
Rostov, Rus. 42/H4
Rostov, Rus. 44/F3
Roswell, NM, US 93/F4
Rota, Sp. 34/B4
Rotenburg, Ger. 29/G2
Rotherham, Eng, UK 23/G5
Rothwell, Eng, UK 23/G4
Rothwell, Eng, UK 25/F2
Rotorua, NZ 71/S10
Rottenburg am Neckar, Ger. 37/E1
Rotterdam, Neth. 28/B5
Rottweil, Ger. 37/E1
Roubaix, Fr. 30/C2
Rouen, Fr. 32/D2
Round Lake Beach, Il, US 99/P15
Round Rock, Tx, US 93/H5
Rouyn-Noranda, Qu, Can. 94/E1
Rovaniemi, Fin. 42/E2
Rovereto, It. 37/H6
Rovigo, It. 33/J4
Rovinj, Cro. 40/A3
Roxas, Phil. 67/E1
Roxas, Phil. 67/F1
Roxas, Phil. 61/J5
Roy, Ut, US 92/D2
Royal Oak, Mi, US 99/F7
Royal Tunbridge Wells, Eng, UK 25/G4
Royan, Fr. 32/C4
Royston, Eng, UK 25/F2
Royton, Eng, UK 23/F4
Rožňava, Slvk. 27/L4
Rtishchevo, Rus. 45/G1
Rubí, Sp. 35/L7
Rubizhne, Ukr. 44/F2
Rubtsovsk, Rus. 46/J4
Rucphen, Neth. 28/B5
Rüdnyy, Kaz. 43/P5
Rudolstadt, Ger. 33/J1
Rufino, Arg. 109/D3
Rufisque, Sen. 78/A3
Rugby, Eng, UK 25/E2
Rugeley, Eng, UK 23/G6
Ruma, Yugo. 40/D3
Rumbek, Sudan 77/L6
Rumia, Pol. 27/K1
Rumoi, Japan 55/N3
Runcorn, Eng, UK 23/F5
Rundu, Namb. 82/C4
Ruse, Bul. 41/G4
Rushden, Eng, UK 25/F2
Russas, Braz. 107/L4
Russellville, Ar, US 93/J4
Russellville, Ar, US 97/G3
Rüsselsheim, Ger. 26/E4
Russia (ctry.) 46/H3
Rust'avi, Geo. 45/H4
Rustenburg, SAfr. 80/P12
Ruston, La, US 93/J4
Ruvo di Puglia, It. 38/E2
Ruzayevka, Rus. 45/H1
Ružomberok, Slvk. 27/K4
Rwanda (ctry.) 82/E1
Ryazan', Rus. 44/F1
Ryazhsk, Rus. 44/G1
Rybinsk, Rus. 42/H4
Rybnik, Pol. 27/K3
Ryde, Eng, UK 25/E5
Ryōtsu, Japan 57/F1
Rypin, Pol. 27/K2
Ryton, Eng, UK 23/G2
Ryūgasaki, Japan 57/G3
Ryukyu (isls.), Japan 68/B2
Rzeszów, Pol. 27/M3
Rzhev, Rus. 42/G4

S

's Heerenberg, Neth. 28/D5
's Hertogenbosch, Neth. 28/C5
Sa Dec, Viet. 65/D4
Saalfeld, Ger. 33/J1
Saarbrücken, Ger. 31/F5
Saarlouis, Ger. 31/F5
Šabac, Yugo. 40/D3
Sabadell, Sp. 35/L6
Sabae, Japan 56/E3
Sabanalarga, Col. 103/H4
Sabhā, Libya 76/H2
Sabinas, Mex. 96/C5
Sabinas Hidalgo, Mex. 96/C5
Sablayan, Phil. 67/F1
Sabzevār, Iran 51/J2
Sacavém, Port. 35/P10
Săcele, Rom. 41/G3
Saco, Me, US 95/G3
Sacramento (cap.), Ca, US 99/M9
Sādiqābād, Pak. 62/B2
Sadowara, Japan 56/B4
Sādri, India 62/B2
Safāqis, Tun. 76/H1
Säffle, Swe. 20/E4
Safford, Az, US 92/E4
Safi, Mor. 76/D1
Safonovo, Rus. 42/G5
Safranbolu, Turk. 44/E4
Saga, Japan 56/B4
Sagae, Japan 57/G1
Sagaing, Myan. 60/B4
Sagamihara, Japan 57/F3
Sāgar, India 62/C3
Sagay, Phil. 67/F1
Sagua de Tánamo, Cuba 103/H1
Sagua la Grande, Cuba 103/F1
Sagunto, Sp. 35/E3
Sahagún, Col. 103/H4
Sahagún, Mex. 101/L7
Sahara (des.), Afr. 76/G3
Sahāranpur, India 53/L3
Saharsa, India 62/E2
Sahavato, Madg. 81/J8
Sāhibganj, India 62/E2
Sāhīwāl, Pak. 53/K2
Sahuayo de Morelos, Mex. 100/E4
Saïda, Alg. 76/F1
Saidpur, India 62/D2
Saigō, Japan 56/C2
Saigon, Viet. 65/D4
Saijō, Japan 56/C4
Saiki, Japan 56/B4
Sailu, India 62/C4
Saint Albans, WV, US 97/H2
Saint Albans, Eng, UK 25/F3
Saint Albert, Ab, Can. 90/E2
Saint Augustine, Fl, US 97/H4
Saint Austell, Eng, UK 24/B6
Saint Catharines, On, Can. 95/U9
Saint Charles, Md, US 97/J2
Saint Charles, Mo, US 93/K3
Saint Charles, Il, US 99/P16
Saint Clair Shores, Mi, US 99/G6
Saint Francis, Wi, US 99/Q14
Saint George, Ut, US 92/D3
Saint George's (cap.), Gren. 104/F4
Saint Helens (mt.), Wa, US 90/C4
Saint Helens, Eng, UK 23/F5
Saint Helier (cap.), Chl, UK 32/B2
Saint Ives, Eng, UK 25/F2
Saint John, NB, Can. 95/H2
Saint John's (cap.), Anti. 104/F3
Saint John's (cap.), Nf, Can. 95/L2
Saint Johnsbury, Vt, US 95/F2
Saint Joseph, Mo, US 93/J3
Saint Kitts and Nevis (ctry.), StK. 104/F3
Saint Lawrence (gulf), Can. 95/J1
Saint Lawrence (riv.), Can.,US 94/F2
Saint Louis, Mo, US 93/K3
Saint Lucia (ctry.), StL. 104/F4
Saint Paul (cap.), Mn, US 94/A2
Saint Peter, Mn, US 91/K4
Saint Peter Port (cap.), Chl, UK 32/B2
Saint Petersburg, Fl, US 97/H5
Saint Petersburg, Rus. 43/T7
Saint Pierre and Miquelon (dpcy.), Can. 95/K2
Saint Simons Island, Ga, US 97/H4
Saint Thomas, On, Can. 94/D3
Saint Vincent and the Grenadines (ctry.), StV. 104/F4
Saint-Amand-les-Eaux, Fr. 30/C3
Saint-André, Reun. 81/S15
Saint-Avold, Fr. 31/F5
Saint-Benoît, Reun. 81/S15
Saint-Brieuc, Fr. 32/B2
Saint-Bruno-de-Montarville, Qu, Can. 95/P6
Saint-Chamond, Fr. 32/F4
Saint-Constant, Qu, Can. 95/N7
Saint-Cyr-l'École, Fr. 30/B6
Saint-Denis, Fr. 30/B6
Saint-Denis, Reun. 81/S15
Saint-Dié, Fr. 36/C1
Saint-Dizier, Fr. 31/D6
Saint-Étienne, Fr. 32/F4
Saint-Étienne-du-Rouvray, Fr. 32/D2
Saint-Eustache, Qu, Can. 95/N6
Saint-Georges, Qu, Can. 95/G2
Saint-Germain-en-Laye, Fr. 30/B6
Saint-Ghislain, Belg. 30/C3
Saint-Herblain, Fr. 32/C3
Saint-Hubert, Qu, Can. 95/P6
Saint-Hyacinthe, Qu, Can. 94/F2
Saint-Jean-de-la-Ruelle, Fr. 32/D3
Saint-Jean-sur-Richelieu, Qu, Can. 94/F2
Saint-Jérôme, Qu, Can. 95/N6
Saint-Joseph, Reun. 81/S15
Saint-Lambert, Qu, Can. 95/P6
Saint-Laurent, Qu, Can. 95/N6
Saint-Léonard, Qu, Can. 95/N6
Saint-Leu, Reun. 81/S15
Saint-Lô, Fr. 32/C2
Saint-Louis, Sen. 78/A2
Saint-Louis, Reun. 81/S15
Saint-Louis, Fr. 36/D2
Saint-Luc, Qu, Can. 95/P7
Saint-Malo, Fr. 32/B2
Saint-Marc, Haiti 103/H2
Saint-Martin-d'Hères, Fr. 32/F4
Saint-Maur-des-Fossés, Fr. 30/B6
Saint-Michel-sur-Orge, Fr. 30/B6
Saint-Nazaire, Fr. 32/B3
Saint-Nicolas, Belg. 31/E2
Saint-Omer, Fr. 30/B2
Saint-Paul, Reun. 81/S15
Saint-Pierre, Reun. 81/S15
Saint Pierre-des-Corps, Fr. 32/D3
Saint-Pol-sur-Mer, Fr. 30/B1
Saint-Quentin, Fr. 30/C4
Saint-Raphaël, Fr. 33/G5
Sainte-Foy, Qu, Can. 95/G2
Sainte-Foy-lès-Lyon, Fr. 36/A6
Sainte-Geneviève-des-Bois, Fr. 30/B6
Sainte-Julie, Qu, Can. 95/P6
Sainte-Marie, Fr. 104/F4
Sainte-Thérèse, Qu, Can. 95/N6
Saintes, Fr. 32/C4
Sainthia, India 62/E3
Saito, Japan 56/B4
Sakai, Japan 57/F2
Sakaide, Japan 56/C3
Sakaiminato, Japan 56/C3
Sakata, Japan 55/M4
Sakawa, Japan 56/C4
Sakété, Ben. 79/F5
Sakhalin (isl.), Rus. 47/Q4
Sakhnīn, Isr. 49/G6
Şäki, Azer. 45/H4
Sakon Nakhon, Thai. 65/D2
Sakrand, Pak. 53/J3
Saku, Japan 57/F2
Saky, Ukr. 44/E3
Sala, Swe. 42/C4
Šal'a, Slvk. 40/C1
Salado (riv.), Arg. 109/E4
Salamá, Guat. 102/D3
Salamanca, Mex. 101/E4
Salamanca, Sp. 34/C2
Salamís, Gre. 39/N9
Salamīyah, Syria 49/E2
Salavat, Rus. 45/K1
Salé, Mor. 76/D1
Sale, Eng, UK 23/F5
Salekhard, Rus. 46/G3
Salem, India 62/C5
Salem, NH, US 95/G3
Salem (cap.), Or, US 90/C4
Salerno, It. 40/B5
Salford, Eng, UK 23/F5
Salgótarján, Hun. 40/D1
Salgueiro, Braz. 107/L5
Salihli, Turk. 50/B2
Salina, Ks, US 93/H3
Salina Cruz, Mex. 102/C2
Salinas, Braz. 107/K7
Salinas, Ca, US 92/B3
Salinópolis, Braz. 107/J4
Salisbury, Md, US 97/K2
Salisbury, NC, US 97/H3
Salisbury, Eng, UK 25/E4
Salmās, Iran 51/F2
Salmon Arm, BC, Can. 90/D3
Salo, Fin. 42/D3
Salon-de-Provence, Fr. 32/F5
Salonta, Rom. 40/E2
Sal'sk, Rus. 45/G3
Salt Lake City (cap.), Ut, US 90/F5
Salta, Arg. 109/C1
Saltillo, Mex. 96/C5
Salto, Braz. 108/C2
Salto, Uru. 109/E3
Salto del Guairá, Par. 109/F1
Sālūr, India 62/D4
Salurn (Salorno), It. 37/H5
Salvador, Braz. 107/L6
Salvatierra, Mex. 101/E4
Salyan, Azer. 51/G2
Salzburg, Aus. 40/A2
Salzgitter, Ger. 29/H4
Salzkotten, Ger. 29/F5
Salzwedel, Ger. 26/F2
Sam Son, Viet. 65/D2
Sama, Sp. 34/C1
Sāmalkot, India 62/D4
Samālūt, Egypt 50/B4
Samandağı, Turk. 49/D1
Samandira, Turk. 51/N7
Samannūd, Egypt 49/B4
Samara, Rus. 45/J1
Samarinda, Indo. 67/E4
Samarqand, Uzb. 46/G6
Sāmarrā', Iraq 51/E3
Samasata, Pak. 53/K3
Şamaxi, Azer. 45/J4
Sambalpur, India 62/D3
Sambas, Indo. 66/C3
Sambava, Madg. 81/J6
Sambir, Ukr. 27/M4
Samch'ŏk, SKor. 56/A2
Samch'ŏnp'o, SKor. 58/E5
Samnangjin, SKor. 56/A3
Samoa (ctry.) 69/R9
Samobor, Cro. 40/B3
Samokov, Bul. 41/F4
Samsun, Turk. 44/F4
Samut Prakan, Thai. 65/C3
Samut Sakhon, Thai. 65/C3
Samut Songkhram, Thai. 65/B3
San, Mali 78/D3
San Andrés, Col. 103/F3
San Andrés del Rabanedo, Sp. 34/C1
San Andrés Tuxtla, Mex. 102/C2
San Angelo, Tx, US 96/C4
San Anselmo, Ca, US 99/J11
San Antonio, Chile 109/B3
San Antonio Abad, Sp. 35/F3
San Antonio del Táchira, Ven. 103/H5
San Benedetto del Tronto, It. 40/A4
San Bernardino, Ca, US 92/C4
San Bernardo, Chile 109/B3
San Bruno, Ca, US 99/K11
San Buenaventura, Mex. 96/C5
San Carlos, Nic. 103/E4
San Carlos, Ven. 106/E2
San Carlos, Chile 109/B4
San Carlos, Uru. 109/F3
San Carlos, Ca, US 99/K11
San Carlos de Bariloche, Arg. 109/B5
San Carlos del Zulia, Ven. 103/J4
San Cataldo, It. 40/D5
San Cristóbal, Ven. 103/H5
San Cristóbal, Cuba 103/F1
San Cristóbal de las Casas, Mex. 102/C2
San Diego, Ca, US 92/C4
San Felipe, Ven. 106/E1
San Felipe, Chile 109/B3
San Felipe Torres Mochas, Mex. 101/E4
San Fernando, Chile 109/B3
San Fernando, Trin. 104/F5
San Fernando, Phil. 61/J5
San Fernando, Sp. 34/B4
San Fernando de Apure, Ven. 106/E2
San Fernando de Henares, Sp. 35/N9
San Fernando de Monte Cristi, DRep. 103/J2
San Fernando de Presas, Mex. 101/F3
San Francisco, Arg. 109/D3
San Francisco, ESal. 102/D3
San Francisco, Ca, US 99/J11
San Francisco del Rincón, Mex. 101/E4
San Gil, Col. 106/D2
San Giovanni in Fiore, It. 38/E3
San Giovanni Rotondo, It. 40/B5
San Ignacio, Belz. 102/D2
San Isidro, CR 103/F4
San Jacinto, Col. 103/H4
San Javier, Sp. 35/E4
San Jose, Phil. 67/F1
San Jose, Ca, US 99/L12
San José (cap.), CR 103/E4
San José de los Remates, Nic. 102/E3
San José de Mayo, Uru. 109/E3
San José del Cabo, Mex. 100/C4
San José del Guaviare, Col. 106/D3
San Juan, Arg. 109/C3
San Juan, PR 104/E3
San Juan Bautista, Par. 109/E2
San Juan Bautista Tuxtepec, Mex. 102/B2
San Juan de Alicante, Sp. 35/E3
San Juan de Aznalfarache, Sp. 34/B4
San Juan de La Maguana, DRep. 103/J2
San Juan de los Lagos, Mex. 100/E4
San Juan de los Morros, Ven. 106/E2
San Juan del Río, Mex. 102/B1
San Juan Nepomuceno, Col. 103/H4
San Justo, Arg. 109/D3
San Leandro, Ca, US 99/K11
San Lorenzo, Hon. 102/E3
San Lorenzo, Nic. 102/E3
San Lorenzo, Ca, US 99/K11
San Luis, Cuba 103/H1
San Luis, Arg. 109/C3
San Luis, Guat. 102/D2
San Luis de la Paz, Mex. 102/A1
San Luis Obispo, Ca, US 92/B4
San Luis Potosí, Mex. 101/E4
San Luis Río Colorado, Mex. 92/D4
San Marcos, Col. 103/H4
San Marcos, Guat. 102/D3
San Marcos, Tx, US 93/H5
San Marino (cap.), SMar. 33/K5
San Marino (ctry.) 33/K5
San Martín, Arg. 109/C3
San Martín de los Andes, Arg. 109/B5
San Mateo, Ca, US 99/K11
San Miguel, ESal. 102/D3
San Miguel de Allende, Mex. 101/E4
San Miguel de Tucumán, Arg. 109/C2
San Nicolás de los Arroyos, Arg. 109/D3
San Nicolás de los Garza, Mex. 101/E3
San Onofre, Col. 103/H4
San Pablo, Ca, US 99/K11
San Pablo de las Salinas, Mex. 101/Q9
San Pédro, C.d'Iv. 78/D5
San Pedro, Arg. 109/E3
San Pedro, Arg. 109/D1
San Pedro, Par. 109/E1
San Pedro Carchá, Guat. 102/D3
San Pedro de las Colonias, Mex. 96/C5
San Pedro Sula, Hon. 102/D3
San Rafael, Arg. 109/C3
San Rafael, Ca, US 99/J11
San Ramon, Ca, US 99/L11
San Ramón de la Nueva Orán, Arg. 109/D1
San Remo, It. 33/G5
San Roque, Sp. 34/C4
San Salvador (cap.), ESal. 102/D3
San Salvador de Jujuy, Arg. 109/C1
San Sebastián, Sp. 34/E1
San Sebastián de los Reyes, Sp. 35/N8
San Sebastián de Yalí, Nic. 102/E3
San Sebastiano, It. 33/J4
San Severo, It. 40/B5
San Vicente, ESal. 102/D3
San Vicente de Cañete, Peru 106/C6
San Vicente del Raspeig, Sp. 35/E3
Sanaa (cap.), Yem. 52/D5
Sanandaj, Iran 51/F3
Sānāwad, India 62/C3
Sancti Spíritus, Cuba 103/G1
Sanda, Japan 56/D3
Sandakan, Malay. 67/E2
Sandanski, Bul. 41/F5
Sandbach, Eng, UK 23/F5
Sandefjord, Nor. 20/D4
Sandhurst, Eng, UK 25/F4
Sandıklı, Turk. 50/B2

128

Sandn – Siófo

Sandnes, Nor. 20/C4
Sandomierz, Pol. 27/L3
Sandusky, Oh, US 94/D3
Sandvika, Nor. 20/D4
Sandviken, Swe. 42/C3
Sandy, Ut, US 92/E2
Sandy Springs, Ga, US 97/G3
Sanford, NC, US 97/J3
Sanford, Fl, US 97/H4
Sanford, Me, US 95/G3
Sangamner, India 62/B4
Sangenjo, Sp. 34/A1
Sangju, SKor. 56/A2
Sāngli, India 62/B4
Sangmélima, Camr. 76/H7
Sanjō, Japan 57/F2
Sankt Augustin, Ger. 31/G2
Sankt Gallen, Swi. 37/F3
Sankt Ingbert, Ger. 31/G5
Sankt Jakob (San Giacomo), It. 37/H4
Sankt Leonhard in Passeier (San Leonardo in Passiria), It. 37/H4
Sankt Martin in Passeier (San Martino in Passiria), It. 37/H4
Sankt Pölten, Aus. 40/B1
Sankt Wendel, Ger. 31/G5
Sanlúcar de Barrameda, Sp. 34/B4
Sanmenxia, China 59/B4
Sanming, China 61/H3
Sannicandro Garganico, It. 40/B5
Sano, Japan 57/F2
Sanok, Pol. 27/M4
Sant Adrià de Besòs, Sp. 35/L7
Sant Boi de Llobregat, Sp. 35/L7
Sant Cugat del Vallès, Sp. 35/L7
Sant Feliu de Guíxols, Sp. 35/G2
Sant Feliu de Llobregat, Sp. 35/L7
Sant Pere de Ribes, Sp. 35/K7
Sant Vicenç dels Horts, Sp. 35/L7
Santa Ana, Bol. 106/E6
Santa Ana, Hon. 102/E3
Santa Ana, ESal. 102/D3
Santa Ana, Ca, US 92/C4
Santa Bárbara, Hon. 102/D3
Santa Bárbara, Braz. 108/D1
Santa Barbara, Ca, US 92/C4
Santa Bárbara d'oeste, Braz. 108/C2
Santa Catarina, Mex. 101/E3
Santa Clara, Cuba 103/G1
Santa Clara, Ca, US 99/L12
Santa Coloma de Gramanet, Sp. 35/L7
Santa Cruz, Phil. 61/J5
Santa Cruz, Ca, US 92/B3
Santa Cruz de Barahona, DRep. 103/J2
Santa Cruz de la Palma, Canl. 35/X16
Santa Cruz de la Sierra, Bol. 106/F7
Santa Cruz de Tenerife, Canl. 35/X16
Santa Cruz del Quiché, Guat. 102/D3
Santa Cruz do Rio Pardo, Braz. 108/B2
Santa Cruz do Sul, Braz. 108/A4
Santa Eugenia de Ribeira, Sp. 34/A1
Santa Eulalia del Río, Sp. 35/F3
Santa Fe, Arg. 109/D3
Santa Fe (cap.), NM, US 93/F4
Santa Fé do Sul, Braz. 108/B2
Santa Helena de Goiás, Braz. 108/B1
Santa Inês, Braz. 107/J4
Santa Isabel, Braz. 108/G8
Santa Luzia, Braz. 107/J4
Santa Luzia, Braz. 108/D1
Santa Maria, Braz. 109/F2
Santa Maria, Ca, US 92/B4
Santa Maria Capua Vetere, It. 40/B5
Santa Maria da Vitória, Braz. 107/K6
Santa Marta, Col. 103/H4
Santa Pola, Sp. 35/E3
Santa Rita, Braz. 107/M5
Santa Rita do Sapucaí, Braz. 108/H7
Santa Rosa, Arg. 109/D4
Santa Rosa, Braz. 109/F2
Santa Rosa, Ca, US 92/B3
Santa Rosa, CR 102/E4
Santa Rosa, Ecu. 106/C4
Santa Rosa de Copán, Hon. 102/D3
Santa Rosa de Viterbo, Braz. 108/C2
Santa Vitória do Palmar, Braz. 109/F3
Santana do Livramento, Braz. 109/E3
Santander, Sp. 34/D1
Santander de Quilichao, Col. 106/C3
Santarém, Braz. 107/H4
Santarém, Port. 34/A3
Santiago, Pan. 103/F4
Santiago, Phil. 61/J5
Santiago, Braz. 109/F2
Santiago (cap.), Chile 109/B3
Santiago de Compostela, Sp. 34/A1
Santiago de Cuba, Cuba 103/H1
Santiago del Estero, Arg. 109/D2
Santiago Ixcuintla, Mex. 100/D4
Santiago Papasquiaro, Mex. 100/D3
Santiago Pinotepa Nacional, Mex. 102/B2
Santo Anastácio, Braz. 108/B2
Santo André, Braz. 108/G8
Santo Ângelo, Braz. 109/F2
Santo António, SaoT. 76/G7
Santo Antônio de Pádua, Braz. 108/D2
Santo Domingo, Cuba 103/F1
Santo Domingo (cap.), DRep. 104/D3
Santo Domingo de los Colorados, Ecu. 106/C4
Santo Domingo Tehuantepec, Mex. 102/C2
Santo Tomé, Arg. 109/E2
Santo Tomé, Arg. 109/D3
Santos, Braz. 108/G8
Santos Dumont, Braz. 108/K6
Sanya, China 65/E2
São Bento do Sul, Braz. 108/B3
São Bernardo do Campo, Braz. 108/G8
São Borja, Braz. 109/E2
São Carlos, Braz. 108/C2
São Fidélis, Braz. 108/D2
São Francisco do Sul, Braz. 108/B3
São Gabriel, Braz. 109/F3
São Gonçalo, Braz. 108/K7
São Gonçalo do Sapucaí, Braz. 108/H6
São Gotardo, Braz. 108/C1
São Joachim da Barra, Braz. 108/C2
São João da Boa Vista, Braz. 108/G6
São João da Madeira, Port. 34/A2
São João de Meriti, Braz. 108/K7
São João del Rei, Braz. 108/C2
São João Nepomuceno, Braz. 108/K6
São José, Braz. 108/B3
São José do Rio Pardo, Braz. 108/G6
São José do Rio Prêto, Braz. 108/B2
São José dos Campos, Braz. 108/H8
São José dos Pinhais, Braz. 108/B3
São Leopoldo, Braz. 108/B4
São Lourenço, Braz. 108/H7
São Lourenço do Sul, Braz. 108/B4
São Luís, Braz. 107/K4
São Manoel, Braz. 108/B2
São Mateus, Braz. 108/E1
São Mateus do Sul, Braz. 108/B3
São Paulo, Braz. 108/G8
São Pedro da Aldeia, Braz. 108/D2
São Sebastião, Braz. 108/H8
São Sebastião do Paraíso, Braz. 108/C2
São Tomé (cap.), SaoT. 76/G7
São Tomé And Príncipe (ctry.) 76/F7
São Vicente, Braz. 108/G8
São Vicente (cape), Port. 34/A4
Sapele, Nga. 79/G5
Sappemeer, Neth. 28/D2
Sapporo, Japan 55/N3
Saqqez, Iran 51/F2
Sara Buri, Thai. 65/C3
Sarāb, Iran 51/F2
Sarajevo (cap.), Bosn. 40/D4
Saraland, Al, US 97/F4
Saran', Kaz. 46/H5
Sarandë, Alb. 39/G3
Sārangpur, India 62/C3
Saransk, Rus. 45/H1
Sarapul, Rus. 43/M4
Sarasota, Fl, US 97/H5
Saratoga, Ca, US 99/K12
Saratoga Springs, NY, US 94/F3
Saratov, Rus. 45/H2
Sarayköy, Turk. 50/B2
Sarcelles, Fr. 30/B6
Sardārshahar, India 62/B2
Sardinia (isl.) 38/A2
Sargodha, Pak. 53/K2
Sarh, Chad 76/J6
Sārī, Iran 51/H2
Sarıkamış, Turk. 45/G4
Sarikei, Malay. 66/D3
Sariwŏn, NKor. 58/C3
Sarkant, Kaz. 46/H5
Şarkışla, Turk. 44/F5
Sarnen, Swi. 37/E4
Sarnia, On, Can. 99/H6
Sarny, Ukr. 44/C2
Sárospatak, Hun. 27/L4
Sarrebourg, Fr. 31/G6
Sarreguemines, Fr. 31/G5
Sarstedt, Ger. 29/G4
Sartrouville, Fr. 30/B6
Sárvár, Hun. 40/C2
Sarzana, It. 33/H4
Sasarām, India 62/D3
Sasebo, Japan 56/A4
Saskatchewan (riv.), Sk, Can. 86/F3
Saskatchewan (prov.), Can. 86/F3
Saskatoon, Sk, Can. 90/G2
Sasolburg, SAfr. 80/P13
Sasovo, Rus. 45/G1
Sassari, It. 38/A2
Sassenheim, Neth. 28/B4
Sātāra, India 62/B4
Satna, India 62/D3
Sátoraljaújhely, Hun. 27/L4
Satpayev, Kaz. 46/G5
Satu Mare, Rom. 27/M5
Saudi Arabia (ctry.) 52/D4
Sauk Rapids, MN, US 91/K4
Saulgau, Ger. 37/F1
Sault Sainte Marie, On, Can. 94/C2
Saumur, Fr. 32/C3
Saurimo, Ang. 82/D2
Sava, It. 40/C5
Savalou, Ben. 79/F5
Savanna-la-Mar, Jam. 103/G2
Savannah, Ga, US 97/H3
Savannakhet, Laos 65/D2
Sāvantvādi, India 62/B4
Sāveh, Iran 51/G3
Savigny-sur-Orge, Fr. 30/B6
Savona, It. 33/H4
Savonlinna, Fin. 42/F3
Sawahlunto, Indo. 66/B4
Sawara, Japan 57/G3
Sayama, Japan 57/F3
Şaydā, Leb. 49/D3
Sayula, Mex. 100/E5
Saywūn, Yem. 52/E5
Scarborough, Eng, UK 23/H3
Schaerbeek, Belg. 31/D2
Schaffhausen, Swi. 37/E2
Schagen, Neth. 28/B3
Schaumburg, Il, US 99/P15
Schenefeld, Ger. 29/G1
Schererville, In, US 99/R17
Schertz, Tx, US 93/H5
Schiedam, Neth. 28/B5
Schiffweiler, Ger. 31/G5
Schijndel, Neth. 28/C5
Schilde, Belg. 28/B6
Schiltigheim, Fr. 31/H6
Schlanders (Silandro), It. 37/G4
Schleswig, Ger. 26/E1
Schloss Holte-Stukenbrock, Ger. 29/F5
Schlüchtern, Ger. 33/H1
Schluderns (Sluderno), It. 37/G4
Schmalkalden, Ger. 33/J1
Schmallenberg, Ger. 29/F6
Schmelz, Ger. 31/F5
Schneverdingen, Ger. 29/G2
Schofield Barracks, Hi, US 88/V12
Schönebeck, Ger. 26/F2
Schöningen, Ger. 26/F2
Schopfheim, Ger. 31/G4
Schortens, Ger. 29/E1
Schoten, Belg. 28/B6
Schramberg, Ger. 37/E1
Schrobenhausen, Ger. 26/F4
Schwabach, Ger. 33/J2
Schwäbisch Gmünd, Ger. 26/E4
Schwäbisch Hall, Ger. 33/H2
Schwalbach, Ger. 31/F5
Schwalmtal, Ger. 28/D6
Schwandorf im Bayern, Ger. 33/K2
Schwanewede, Ger. 29/F2
Schwechat, Aus. 40/C1
Schwedt, Ger. 27/H2
Schweinfurt, Ger. 33/J1
Schwelm, Ger. 29/E6
Schwerin, Ger. 26/F2
Schwerte, Ger. 29/E6
Schwyz, Swi. 37/E3
Sciacca, It. 38/C4
Scicli, It. 38/D4
Scordia, It. 38/D4
Scotland, UK 21/C2
Scottsbluff, Ne, US 93/G2
Scottsboro, Al, US 97/G3
Scottsdale, Az, US 92/E4
Scranton, Pa, US 94/F3
Scunthorpe, Eng, UK 23/H4
Sea-Tac, Wa, US 99/C3
Seaford, Eng, UK 25/G5
Seaham, Eng, UK 23/G2
Seahurst, Wa, US 99/C3
Searcy, Ar, US 93/K4
Seattle, Wa, US 99/C2
Sébaco, Nic. 102/E3
Sebastian, Fl, US 97/H5
Sebeş, Rom. 41/F3
Şebinkarahisar, Turk. 44/F4
Secunda, SAfr. 80/Q13
Secunderābād, India 62/C4
Sedalia, Mo, US 93/J3
Sedan, Fr. 31/D4
Sederot, Isr. 49/D4
Sedona, Az, US 92/E4
Seesen, Ger. 29/H5
Segamat, Malay. 66/B3
Segezha, Rus. 42/G3
Ségou, Mali 78/D3
Segovia, Sp. 34/C2
Seguin, Tx, US 93/H5
Sehnde, Ger. 29/G4
Sehore, India 62/C3
Seinäjoki, Fin. 42/D3
Seine (riv.), Fr. 32/F3
Seki, Japan 57/E3
Sekondi, Gha. 79/E5
Selb, Ger. 33/K1
Selby, Eng, UK 23/G4
Selçuk, Turk. 50/A2
Selebi-Phikwe, Bots. 82/E5
Sélestat, Fr. 36/D1
Sélibabi, Mrta. 78/B3
Selm, Ger. 29/E5
Selma, Al, US 97/G3
Semarang, Indo. 66/D5
Semenov, Rus. 43/K4
Semey, Kaz. 46/J4
Semiluki, Rus. 44/F2
Semnān, Iran 51/H3
Semporna, Malay. 67/E3
Sena, Thai. 65/C3
Sendai, Japan 57/G1
Sendai, Japan 56/B5
Senden, Ger. 29/E5
Senden, Ger. 37/G1
Senegal (ctry.) 78/B3
Senftenberg, Ger. 27/H3
Senhor do Bonfim, Braz. 107/K6
Senica, Slvk. 27/J4
Senigallia, It. 33/K5
Senlis, Fr. 30/B5
Sens, Fr. 32/E2
Sensuntepeque, ESal. 102/D3
Senta, Yugo. 40/E3
Seoni, India 62/C3
Seonī Mālwā, India 62/C3
Seoul (cap.), SKor. 58/F6
Seoul (cap.), SKor. 58/F6
Sept-Îles, Qu, Can. 95/H1
Sequoia National Park, Ca, US 92/C3
Seraing, Belg. 31/E2
Serang, Indo. 66/C5
Serdobsk, Rus. 45/H1
Seremban, Malay. 66/B3
Sergach, Rus. 43/K5
Sergiyev Posad, Rus. 42/H4
Seria, Bru. 66/D3
Seriate, It. 33/H4
Serik, Turk. 49/B1
Serov, Rus. 46/G4
Serowe, Bots. 82/E5
Serpukhov, Rus. 44/F1
Serra, Braz. 108/D2
Serra Talhada, Braz. 107/L5
Sérrai, Gre. 41/F5
Serrinha, Braz. 107/L6
Sertãozinho, Braz. 108/C2
Sesimbra, Port. 34/A3
Sestroretsk, Rus. 43/S6
Sesvete, Cro. 40/C3
Sète, Fr. 32/E5
Sete Lagoas, Braz. 108/C1
Sethārja, Pak. 62/A2
Sétif, Alg. 76/G1
Seto, Japan 57/E3
Settimo Torinese, It. 33/G4
Setúbal, Port. 35/Q10
Setúbal (bay), Port. 34/A3
Sevastopol', Ukr. 44/E3
Sevenoaks, Eng, UK 25/G4
Severnyy, Rus. 43/P2
Severodvinsk, Rus. 42/H2
Severomorsk, Rus. 42/G1
Severoural'sk, Rus. 43/N3
Seville, Sp. 34/C4
Sevlievo, Bul. 41/G4
Seward (pen.), US 85/E2
Seychelles (ctry.) 75/H5
Seydişehir, Turk. 50/B2
Seynod, Fr. 36/C6
Sfîntu Gheorghe, Rom. 41/G3
Shadrinsk, Rus. 43/P4
Shagamu, Nga. 79/F5
Shah Alam, Malay. 66/B3
Shāhdādkot, Pak. 62/A2
Shahdol, India 62/D3
Shaḥḥāt, Libya 77/K1
Shāhjahānpur, India 62/C2
Shahr-e Kord, Iran 51/G3
Shājāpur, India 62/C3
Shakargarh, Pak. 53/L2
Shakhtinsk, Kaz. 46/H5
Shakhty, Rus. 44/G3
Shakhun'ya, Rus. 43/K4
Shaki, Nga. 79/F4
Shalqar, Kaz. 45/L3
Shāmgarh, India 62/C3
Shāmli, India 53/L3
Shamokin, Pa, US 94/E3
Shanghai, China 59/L8
Shangqiu, China 59/C4
Shangrao, China 61/H2
Shantou, China 61/H4
Shaoguan, China 61/G3
Shaoxing, China 61/J2
Shaoyang, China 61/F3
Sharon, Pa, US 94/D3
Shar'ya, Rus. 43/K4
Shashi, China 61/G2
Shaw, Eng, UK 25/E4
Shawinigan, Qu, Can. 95/F2
Shawnee, Ok, US 93/H4
Shchekino, Rus. 44/F1
Shchelkovo, Rus. 43/W9
Shchigry, Rus. 44/F2
Shchūchīnsk, Kaz. 46/H4
Sheberghān, Afg. 53/J1
Sheboygan, Wi, US 91/M5
Shefar'am, Isr. 49/G6
Sheffield, Al, US 97/G3
Sheffield, Eng, UK 23/G5
Shekhūpura, Pak. 53/K2
Shelby, NC, US 97/H3
Shelbyville, Tn, US 97/G3
Shelbyville, In, US 97/G2
Shenandoah National Park, Va, US 97/J2
Shenyang, China 58/B2
Shenzhen, China 61/G4
Shepetivka, Ukr. 44/C2
Sherbrooke, Qu, Can. 95/G2
Sherghāti, India 62/D3
Sheridan, Wy, US 92/F1
Sherman, Tx, US 93/H4
Shetland (isls.), UK 18/C2
Shibata, Japan 57/F2
Shibīn al Kawm, Egypt 49/B4
Shibīn al Qanāţir, Egypt 49/B4
Shido, Japan 56/D3
Shijiazhuang, China 59/C3
Shikārpur, Pak. 62/A2
Shilka, Rus. 54/H1
Shillong, India 60/A3
Shimabara, Japan 56/B4
Shimamoto, Japan 56/D3
Shimanovsk, Rus. 55/K1
Shimizu, Japan 57/F3
Shimoda, Japan 57/F3
Shimodate, Japan 57/F2
Shimonoseki, Japan 56/B4
Shingū, Japan 56/D4
Shinjō, Japan 55/N4
Shinminato, Japan 57/E2
Shinyanga, Tanz. 82/F1
Shiogama, Japan 57/G1
Shipley, Eng, UK 23/G4
Shirakawa, Japan 57/G2
Shīrāz, Iran 51/H4
Shirbīn, Egypt 49/B4
Shiroishi, Japan 57/G1
Shirone, Japan 57/F2
Shīrvān, Iran 51/J2
Shishou, China 61/G2
Shivpurī, India 62/C2
Shiyan, China 61/F1
Shizuishan, China 54/F4
Shizunai, Japan 55/N3
Shizuoka, Japan 57/F3
Shkodër, Alb. 40/D4
Shōbara, Japan 56/C3
Sholāpur, India 62/C4
Shorāpur, India 62/C4
Shoreham-by-Sea, Eng, UK 25/F5
Shorewood, Wi, US 99/Q13
Shorkot, Pak. 53/K2
Shostka, Ukr. 44/E2
Shpola, Ukr. 44/D2
Shreveport, La, US 93/J4
Shrewsbury, Eng, UK 24/D1
Shuangcheng, China 47/N5
Shuangyashan, China 55/L2
Shubrā al Khaymah, Egypt 49/B4
Shubrā Khīt, Egypt 49/B4
Shujāābād, Pak. 53/K3
Shumen, Bul. 41/H4
Shumerlya, Rus. 43/K5
Shurugwi, Zim. 82/E4
Shūshtar, Iran 51/G3
Shuya, Rus. 42/J4
Shwebo, Myan. 65/A1
Shymkent, Kaz. 46/G5
Siālkot, Pak. 53/K2
Siasi, Phil. 67/F2
Šiauliai, Lith. 42/D5
Sibay, Rus. 45/L1
Šibenik, Cro. 40/B4
Siberia (reg.), Rus. 46/K3
Sibi, Pak. 53/J3
Sibiu, Rom. 41/G3
Sibolga, Indo. 66/A3
Sibsāgar, India 60/B3
Sibu, Malay. 66/D3
Sibuco, Phil. 67/F2
Sibut, CAfr. 77/J6
Sicily (isl.), It. 38/C3
Sicuani, Peru 106/D6
Šid, Yugo. 40/D3
Siddipet, India 62/C4
Sidhi, India 62/D3
Sidhpur, India 62/B3
Sidi Bel-Abbes, Alg. 76/E1
Sīdī Bū Zayd, Tun. 76/G1
Sidi Ifni, Mor. 76/C2
Sīdī Sālim, Egypt 49/B4
Sidney, Oh, US 94/C3
Siedlce, Pol. 27/M2
Siegburg, Ger. 31/G2
Siegen, Ger. 31/H2
Siemreab, Camb. 65/C3
Siena, It. 33/J5
Sieradz, Pol. 27/K3
Sierpc, Pol. 27/K2
Sierra Leone (ctry.) 78/B4
Sierra Madre Occidental (mts.), Mex. 100/C2
Sierra Madre Oriental (mts.), Mex. 100/E3
Sierra Nevada (mts.), Ca, US 92/B3
Sierra Vista, Az, US 100/C2
Sighetu Marmaţiei, Rom. 41/F2
Sighişoara, Rom. 41/G2
Sigmaringen, Ger. 37/F1
Sigtuna, Swe. 42/C4
Siguatepeque, Hon. 102/E3
Sihorā, India 62/D3
Siilinjärvi, Fin. 42/E3
Siirt, Turk. 50/E2
Sīkar, India 62/C
Sikasso, Mali 78/D4
Sikeston, Mo, US 93/K3
Silao, Mex. 101/E
Silay, Phil. 67/F
Silchar, India 60/B
Silifke, Turk. 49/C
Silīguri, India 62/E
Silistra, Bul. 41/H
Silivri, Turk. 41/J
Silkeborg, Den. 20/D
Silla, Sp. 35/E
Silopi, Turk. 50/E
Silvassa, India 62/B
Silver City, NM, US 92/E
Silver Lake-Fircrest, Wa, US 99/C
Silyānah, Tun. 38/A
Simav, Turk. 50/B
Simcoe, On, Can. 95/S1
Simeria, Rom. 40/F
Simferopol', Ukr. 44/E
Şimleu Silvaniei, Rom. 40/F
Simrishamn, Swe. 27/H
Simunul, Phil. 67/E
Sin-le-Noble, Fr. 30/C
Sinai (pen.), Egypt 50/C
Sinaia, Rom. 41/G
Sincé, Col. 103/H
Sincelejo, Col. 103/H
Sindangbarang, Indo. 66/C
Sindelfingen, Ger. 33/H
Sinendé, Ben. 79/F
Sinfra, C.d'Iv. 78/D
Singapore (ctry.) 66/B
Singapore (cap.), Sing. 66/B
Singen, Ger. 37/E
Singida, Tanz. 82/F
Singkawang, Indo. 66/C
Sinop, Braz. 107/G
Sinop, Turk. 44/E
Sint-Genesius-Rode, Belg. 31/D
Sint-Gillis-Waas, Belg. 28/E
Sint-Katelijne-Waver, Belg. 28/E
Sint-Niklaas, Belg. 28/E
Sint-Oedenrode, Neth. 28/
Sint-Pieters-Leeuw, Belg. 31/D
Sint-Truiden, Belg. 31/
Sintang, Indo. 66/D
Sintra, Port. 35/P
Sinŭiju, NKor. 58/
Sinzig, Ger. 31/
Siocon, Phil. 67/
Siófok, Hun. 40/

Sion, Swi. 36/D5
Sioux City, Ia, US 93/H2
Siping, China 59/F2
Siracusa (Syracuse), It. 38/D4
Sirājganj, Bang. 62/E3
Sīrjān, Iran 51/H4
Şırnak, Turk. 50/E2
Sironj, India 62/C3
Sirsa, India 62/C2
Sirsi, India 62/B5
Sisak, Cro. 40/C3
Sisimiut, Grld. 87/L2
Sītākunda, Bang. 63/F3
Sitges, Sp. 35/K7
Sitka, Ak, US 85/L4
Sittard, Neth. 28/C7
Sittingbourne, Eng, UK 25/G4
Sittwe (Akyab), Myan. 60/B4
Sivakāsi, India 62/C6
Sivas, Turk. 44/F5
Siverek, Turk. 50/D2
Siwān, India 62/D2
Siyabuswa, SAfr. 80/Q12
Sjenica, Yugo. 40/D4
Skalica, Slvk. 27/J4
Skara, Swe. 20/E4
Skarżysko-Kamienna, Pol. 27/L3
Skawina, Pol. 27/K4
Skegness, Eng, UK 23/J5
Skellefteå, Swe. 42/D2
Skelmersdale, Eng, UK 23/F4
Ski, Nor. 20/D4
Skien, Nor. 20/D4
Skierniewice, Pol. 27/L3
Skikda, Alg. 76/G1
Skive, Den. 20/D4
Skokie, Il, US 99/Q15
Skopin, Rus. 44/F1
Skopje (cap.), FYROM 40/E4
Skövde, Swe. 20/E4
Slagelse, Den. 20/D5
Slantsy, Rus. 42/F4
Slatina, Rom. 41/G3
Slave (coast), Afr. 79/F5
Slavgorod, Rus. 46/H4
Slavonska Požega, Cro. 40/C3
Slavonski Brod, Cro. 40/D3
Slavuta, Ukr. 44/C2
Slavyansk-na-Kubani, Rus. 44/F3
Slidell, La, US 97/F4
Sliedrecht, Neth. 28/B5
Sliema, Malta 38/D5
Sliven, Bul. 41/H4
Slobodskoy, Rus. 43/L4
Slobozia, Rom. 41/H3
Slonim, Bela. 42/E5
Slough, Eng, UK 25/F4
Slovakia (ctry.) 27/K4
Slovenia (ctry.) 40/B3
Slov'yans'k, Ukr. 44/F2
Słubice, Pol. 27/H2
Słupsk, Pol. 27/J1
Slutsk, Bela. 44/C1
Slyudyanka, Rus. 54/E1
Smederevo, Yugo. 40/E3
Smederevska Palanka, Yugo. 40/E3
Smila, Ukr. 44/D2
Smolensk, Rus. 42/G5
Smolyan, Bul. 41/G5
Smyrna, Ga, US 97/G3
Snake (riv.), US 90/D4
Sneek, Neth. 28/C2
Soanierana-Ivongo, Madg. 81/J7
Soanindrariny, Madg. 81/H7
Soavina, Madg. 81/J8
Sobral, Braz. 107/K4
Soc Trang, Viet. 65/D4
Sochaczew, Pol. 27/L2
Sochi, Rus. 44/F4
Socorro, Tx, US 93/F5
Socorro, Braz. 108/G7
Söderhamn, Swe. 42/C3
Södertälje, Swe. 42/C4
Soest, Ger. 29/F5
Soest, Neth. 28/C4
Sofia (cap.), Bul. 41/F5
Sogamoso, Col. 106/D2
Sögwip'o, SKor. 55/K5
Soignies, Belg. 31/D2
Soissons, Fr. 30/C5
Sōja, Japan 56/C3
Sojat, India 62/B2
Sokch'o, SKor. 58/E3
Söke, Turk. 50/A2
Sokhumi, Geo. 45/G4
Sokodé, Togo 79/F4
Sokol, Rus. 42/J4
Sokółka, Pol. 27/M2
Sokolov, Czh. 33/K1
Sokołów Podlaski, Pol. 27/M2
Sokoto, Nga. 79/G3
Sol, Costa del (coast), Sp. 34/C4
Sol'-Iletsk, Rus. 45/K2
Sola, Nor. 20/C4
Soledad, Col. 103/H4
Soledad de Graciano, Mex. 101/E4
Soledade, Braz. 108/A4
Soligorsk, Bela. 44/C1
Solihull, Eng, UK 25/E2
Solikamsk, Rus. 43/N4
Solingen, Ger. 28/E6
Sollefteå, Swe. 42/C3
Sollentuna, Swe. 20/F4
Solntsevo, Rus. 43/W9
Solok, Indo. 66/B4
Sololá, Guat. 102/D3
Solomon Islands (ctry.) 68/E6
Solothurn, Swi. 36/D3
Soltau, Ger. 29/G3
Sölvesborg, Swe. 20/E4
Solwezi, Zam. 82/E3
Sōma, Japan 57/G2
Soma, Turk. 44/C5
Somalia (ctry.) 77/Q6
Sombor, Yugo. 40/D3
Sombrerete, Mex. 100/E4
Someren, Neth. 28/C6
Somerset, Ky, US 97/G2
Somerset West, SAfr. 80/L11
Somersworth, NH, US 95/G3
Somoto, Nic. 102/E3
Son La, Viet. 65/C1
Son Tay, Viet. 65/D1
Sønderborg, Den. 26/E1
Sondrio, It. 37/F5
Songea, Tanz. 82/G3
Songkhla, Thai. 65/C5
Songling, China 55/J2
Sŏngnam, SKor. 58/G7
Songt'an, SKor. 58/D4
Sonneberg, Ger. 33/J1
Sonobe, Japan 56/D3
Sonsonate, ESal. 102/D3
Sonthofen, Ger. 37/G2
Sopot, Pol. 27/K1
Sopron, Hun. 40/C2
Sør-Varanger, Nor. 42/F1
Sora, It. 38/C2
Sorel, Qu, Can. 94/F2
Sorgues, Fr. 32/F5
Sorgun, Turk. 44/E5
Soria, Sp. 34/D2
Sorø, Den. 26/F1
Soroca, Mol. 41/J1
Sorocaba, Braz. 108/C2
Sorochinsk, Rus. 45/K1
Sorong, Indo. 67/H4
Soroti, Ugan. 77/M7
Sorrento, It. 38/D2
Sortavala, Rus. 42/F3
Sŏsan, SKor. 58/D4
Soshanguve, SAfr. 80/Q12
Sosnogorsk, Rus. 43/M3
Sosnovka, Rus. 43/L4
Sosnowiec, Pol. 27/K3
Souk Ahras, Alg. 76/G1
Sousa, Braz. 107/L5
South (isl.), NZ 71/R11
South (cape), NZ 71/Q12
South Africa (ctry.) 82/D6
South America (cont.) 105/*
South Augusta, Ga, US 97/H3
South Australia, Austl. 73/B1
South Bend, In, US 94/C3
South Benfleet, Eng, UK 25/G3
South Burlington, Vt, US 94/F2
South Carolina (state), US 97/H3
South China (sea), Asia 48/L8
South Dakota (state), US 91/H4
South Holland, Il, US 99/Q16
South Korea (ctry.) 58/D4
South Lake Tahoe, Ca, US 92/C3
South Milwaukee, Wi, US 99/Q14
South Oxhey, Eng, UK 25/F3
South San Francisco, Ca, US 99/K11
South Saskatchewan (riv.), Sk, Can. 86/E3
South Shields, Eng, UK 23/G2
South Sioux City, Ne, US 93/H2
South Ubian, Phil. 67/F2
Southampton, Eng, UK 25/E5
Southaven, Ms, US 93/K4
Southend-on-Sea, Eng, UK 25/G3
Southern Pines, NC, US 97/J3
Southfield, Mi, US 99/F7
Southgate, Mi, US 99/F7
Southland, Tx, US 101/E1
Southport, Eng, UK 23/E4
Sovetsk, Rus. 27/L1
Sovetskaya Gavan', Rus. 55/N2
Soweto, SAfr. 80/P13
Spain (ctry.) 34/C2
Spalding, Eng, UK 23/H6
Spanaway, Wa, US 99/C3
Spanish Town, Jam. 103/G2
Sparks, Nv, US 92/C3
Sparta, Wi, US 91/L5
Spartanburg, SC, US 97/H3
Spassk-Dal'niy, Rus. 55/L3
Spencer, Ia, US 93/J2
Spennymoor, Eng, UK 23/G2
Speyer, Ger. 33/H2
Spijkenisse, Neth. 28/B5
Spišská Nová Ves, Slvk. 27/L4
Spitsbergen (isl.), Sval. 46/B2
Spittal an der Drau, Aus. 40/A2
Split, Cro. 40/C4
Spokane, Wa, US 90/D4
Spoleto, It. 38/C1
Spring, Tx, US 93/J5
Springdale, Ar, US 93/J3
Springe, Ger. 29/G4
Springfield, Or, US 90/C4
Springfield, Vt, US 95/F3
Springfield, Ma, US 95/F3
Springfield, Mo, US 93/J3
Springfield, Oh, US 97/H2
Springfield, Tn, US 97/G2
Springfield (cap.), Il, US 94/B4
Springs, SAfr. 80/Q13
Sprockhövel, Ger. 29/E6
Squaw Harbor, Ak, US 85/F4
Squinzano, It. 40/D5
Srebrenica, Bosn. 40/D3
Srednogorie, Bul. 41/G4
Śrem, Pol. 27/J2
Sremska Mitrovica, Yugo. 40/D3
Sretensk, Rus. 55/H1
Sri Dungargarh, India 53/K3
Sri Gangānagar, India 53/K3
Sri Jayawardanapura (Kotte), SrL. 62/C6
Sri Lanka (ctry.) 62/D6
Srikākulam, India 62/D4
Srīnagar, India 53/K2
Srīvardhan, India 62/B4
Środa Wielkopolska, Pol. 27/J2
Stabroek, Belg. 28/B6
Stade, Ger. 29/G1
Stadskanaal, Neth. 28/D3
Stadthagen, Ger. 29/G4
Stadtlohn, Ger. 28/D5
Staffanstorp, Swe. 27/G1
Stafford, Eng, UK 23/F6
Staines, Eng, UK 25/F4
Stakhanov, Ukr. 44/F2
Stalowa Wola, Pol. 27/M3
Stalybridge, Eng, UK 23/F5
Stamford, Ct, US 94/F3
Stamford, Eng, UK 25/F1
Standerton, SAfr. 80/Q13
Stanford-le-Hope, Eng, UK 25/G3
Stange, Nor. 20/D3
Stanger, SAfr. 81/E3
Stanley, Eng, UK 23/G2
Stanley (falls), D.R. Congo 77/L8
Stanley (cap.), Falk. 109/E7
Stans, Swi. 37/E4
Stara Pazova, Yugo. 40/E3
Stara Zagora, Bul. 41/G4
Starachowice, Pol. 27/L3
Staraya Russa, Rus. 42/F4
Stargard Szczeciński, Pol. 27/H2
Starkville, Ms, US 97/F3
Starodub, Rus. 44/E1
Starogard Gdański, Pol. 27/K2
Staryy Oskol', Rus. 44/F2
Staszów, Pol. 27/L3
State College, Pa, US 94/E3
Statesboro, Ga, US 97/H3
Statesville, NC, US 97/H3
Staunton, Va, US 97/J2
Stavanger, Nor. 20/C4
Staveley, Eng, UK 23/G5
Stavropol', Rus. 45/G3
Stavropol' Kray, Rus. 46/E5
Steenwijk, Neth. 28/D3
Stein, Neth. 31/E2
Steinhagen, Ger. 29/F4
Steinkjer, Nor. 20/D2
Stekene, Belg. 28/B6
Stellenbosch, SAfr. 80/L10
Stendal, Ger. 26/F2
Stenungsund, Swe. 20/D4
Stephenville, Tx, US 93/H4
Sterling, Co, US 93/G2
Sterling Heights, Mi, US 99/F6
Sterlitamak, Rus. 45/K1
Sterzing (Vipiteno), It. 37/H4
Steubenville, Oh, US 94/D3
Stevenage, Eng, UK 25/F3
Steyr, Aus. 40/B1
Stilfontein, SAfr. 80/P13
Stillwater, Ok, US 93/H3
Štip, FYROM 40/F5
Stjørdal, Nor. 20/D3
Stockholm (cap.), Swe. 42/C4
Stockport, Eng, UK 23/F5
Stockton, Ca, US 99/M11
Stockton-on-Tees, Eng, UK 23/G2
Stoke-on-Trent, Eng, UK 23/F6
Stolac, Bosn. 40/C4
Stolberg, Ger. 31/F2
Stoney Creek, On, Can. 95/T9
Stourbridge, Eng, UK 24/D2
Stourport-on-Severn, Eng, UK 24/D2
Strakonice, Czh. 33/K2
Stralsund, Ger. 26/G1
Strand, SAfr. 80/L11
Strängnäs, Swe. 42/C4
Stratford, On, Can. 94/D3
Stratford-upon-Avon, Eng, UK 25/E2
Straubing, Ger. 33/K2
Strausberg, Ger. 27/G2
Streamwood, Il, US 99/P15
Streator, Il, US 93/K2
Stretford, Eng, UK 23/F5
Strømmen, Nor. 20/D4
Strömsund, Swe. 20/E3
Stroud, Eng, UK 24/D3
Struga, FYROM 40/E5
Strumica, FYROM 41/F5
Strzegom, Pol. 27/J3
Strzelce Opolskie, Pol. 44/A2
Stuart, Fl, US 97/H5
Stupino, Rus. 44/F1
Sturgis, Mi, US 94/C3
Stuttgart, Ger. 33/H2
Subang, Indo. 66/C5
Subotica, Yugo. 40/D2
Suceava, Rom. 41/H2
Sucre (cap.), Bol. 106/E7
Sudan (ctry.) 77/L5
Sudbury, On, Can. 94/D2
Sudbury, Eng, UK 25/G2
Sueca, Sp. 35/E3
Suez (gulf), Egypt 50/C4
Suez (canal), Egypt 77/M1
Suffolk, Va, US 97/J2
Sugar Land, Tx, US 96/E4
Suhāj, Egypt 50/B5
Suhl, Ger. 33/J1
Suifenhe, China 55/L3
Suihua, China 55/K2
Suining, China 60/E2
Suisun City, Ca, US 99/K10
Suizhou, China 61/G2
Sūjāngarh, India 62/B2
Sukabumi, Indo. 66/C5
Sukagawa, Japan 57/G2
Sukhinichi, Rus. 44/E1
Sukhothai, Thai. 65/B2
Sukkur, Pak. 62/A2
Sukumo, Japan 56/C4
Sulawesi (Celebes) (isl.), Indo. 67/E4
Sulechów, Pol. 27/H2
Sulejówek, Pol. 27/L2
Sullana, Peru 106/B4
Sulmona, It. 40/A4
Sulphur, La, US 93/J5
Sulphur Springs, Tx, US 93/J4
Sultānpur, India 62/D2
Suluova, Turk. 44/E4
Sulzbach, Ger. 31/G5
Sulzbach-Rosenberg, Ger. 33/J2
Sumatra (isl.), Indo. 66/B4
Sumbawa Besar, Indo. 67/E5
Sumbawanga, Tanz. 82/F2
Sumenep, Indo. 66/D5
Summerside, PE, Can. 95/J2
Summerville, SC, US 97/H3
Sumoto, Japan 56/D3
Šumperk, Czh. 33/M2
Sumqayıt, Azer. 45/J4
Sumter, SC, US 97/H3
Sumy, Ukr. 44/E2
Sun City, Az, US 92/D4
Sunbury, Pa, US 94/E3
Sunbury, Austl. 73/F5
Sunbury-on-Thames, Eng, UK 25/F4
Sunch'ŏn, SKor. 58/D5
Sundargarh, India 62/D3
Sundarnagar, India 53/L2
Sunderland, Eng, UK 23/G2
Sundern, Ger. 29/F6
Sundsvall, Swe. 42/C3
Sungai Petani, Malay. 66/B2
Sungaipenuh, Indo. 66/B4
Sungurlu, Turk. 44/E4
Sunningdale, Eng, UK 25/F4
Sunnyvale, Ca, US 99/K12
Sunset Beach, Hi, US 88/V12
Sunyani, Gha. 79/E5
Superior, Wi, US 91/K4
Superior (lake), Can.,US 94/C2
Suphan Buri, Thai. 65/C3
Sūq ash Shuyūkh, Iraq 51/F4
Suqian, China 59/D4
Şūr, Leb. 49/D3
Surabaya, Indo. 66/D5
Surakarta, Indo. 66/D5
Surallah, Phil. 67/F2
Surat, India 62/B3
Surat Thani, Thai. 65/B4
Suratgarh, India 62/B2
Surdulica, Yugo. 40/F4
Surendranagar, India 62/B3
Surgut, Rus. 46/H3
Sūri, India 62/E3
Surigao, Phil. 67/G2
Surin, Thai. 65/C3
Suriname (ctry.), Sur. 107/G3
Surrey, BC, Can. 90/C3
Surt, Libya 76/J1
Sürüç, Turk. 50/D2
Sūsah, Tun. 38/B5
Susaki, Japan 56/C4
Suşehri, Turk. 44/F4
Susono, Japan 57/F3
Susurluk, Turk. 50/B2
Sutton Coldfield, Eng, UK 25/E1
Sutton in Ashfield, Eng, UK 23/G5
Suva (cap.), Fiji 69/Y18
Suwa, Japan 57/F2
Suwałki, Pol. 27/M1
Şuwaylih, Jor. 49/D3
Suwŏn, SKor. 58/G7
Suzhou, China 59/D4
Suzhou, China 59/L8
Suzu, Japan 57/E2
Suzuka, Japan 56/E3
Svalbard (isls.), Nor. 46/C2
Svedala, Swe. 27/G1
Svendborg, Den. 26/F1
Sverdlovsk (Yekaterinburg), Rus. 43/P4
Sverdlovsk Oblast, Rus. 46/G4
Svetlogorsk, Bela. 44/D1
Svetlograd, Rus. 45/G3
Svetlyy, Rus. 45/M2
Svetozarevo, Yugo. 40/E4
Svilajnac, Yugo. 40/E3
Svilengrad, Bul. 41/H5
Svishtov, Bul. 41/G4
Svitavy, Czh. 33/M2
Svobodnyy, Rus. 55/K1
Swadlincote, Eng, UK 23/G6
Swakopmund, Namb. 82/B5
Swansea, Wal, UK 24/C3
Swarzędz, Pol. 27/J2
Swaziland (ctry.) 81/E2
Sweden (ctry.) 20/E3
Sweetwater, Tx, US 93/G4
Świdnica, Pol. 27/J3
Świdnik, Pol. 27/M3
Świdwin, Pol. 27/H2
Świebodzice, Pol. 27/J3
Świebozin, Pol. 27/H2
Świecie, Pol. 27/K2
Swift Current, Sk, Can. 90/G3
Swindon, Eng, UK 25/E3
Świnoujście, Pol. 27/H2
Swinton, Eng, UK 23/G5
Switzerland (ctry.) 36/D4
Swords, Ire. 22/B5
Sydney, NS, Can. 95/J2
Sydney, Austl. 72/H8
Syeverodonets'k, Ukr. 44/F2
Syke, Ger. 29/F3
Syktyvkar, Rus. 43/L3
Sylacauga, Al, US 97/G3
Sylhet, Bang. 60/A3
Sylvania, Oh, US 94/D3
Syria (ctry.) 50/D3
Syriam, Myan. 63/G4
Syzran', Rus. 45/J1
Szamotuły, Pol. 27/J2
Szarvas, Hun. 40/E2
Százhalombatta, Hun. 40/D2
Szczecinek, Pol. 27/J2
Szczytno, Pol. 27/L2
Szeged, Hun. 40/E2
Székesfehérvár, Hun. 40/D2
Szekszárd, Hun. 40/D2
Szentendre, Hun. 27/K5
Szentes, Hun. 40/E2
Szolnok, Hun. 40/E2
Szombathely, Hun. 40/C2

T

T'aipei (cap.), Tai. 61/J3
T'bilisi (cap.), Geo. 45/H4
Ta Khmau, Camb. 65/D4
Tabernes de Valldigna, Sp. 35/E3
Tábor, Czh. 33/L2
Tabora, Tanz. 82/F2
Tabrīz, Iran 51/F2
Tabuk, Phil. 61/J5
Tabūk, SAr. 50/D4
Ţaburbah, Tun. 38/A4
Tacámbaro de Codallos, Mex. 101/E5
Tacheng, China 46/J5
Tachikawa, Japan 57/F3
Tacloban, Phil. 68/B3
Tacna, Peru 106/D7
Tacoma, Wa, US 99/B3
Tacoronte, Canl. 35/X16
Tacuarembó, Uru. 109/E3
Tādepallegūdem, India 62/D4
Tadley, Eng, UK 25/E4
Tadmur, Syria 50/D3
Tadotsu, Japan 56/C3
Tādpatri, India 62/C5
T'aebaek, SKor. 58/E4
Taech'ŏn, SKor. 58/D4
Taegu, SKor. 56/A3
Taejŏn, SKor. 58/D4
Tafí Viejo, Arg. 109/C2
Taganrog, Rus. 44/F3
Tagawa, Japan 56/B4
Tagbilaran, Phil. 67/F2
Taguasco, Cuba 103/G1
Tagudin, Phil. 61/J5
Tagum, Phil. 67/G2
Tagus (riv.), Port.,Sp. 34/B3
Tahiti (isl.), FrPol. 67/F5
Tahlequah, Ok, US 93/J4
Tahoe (lake), Ca, US 88/C4
Tahoua, Niger 79/G3
Tai'an, China 59/D3
T'aichung, Tai. 61/J3
T'ainan, Tai. 61/J4
Taiping, Malay. 66/B3
Taisha, Japan 56/C3
T'aitung, Tai. 61/J4
Taiwan (ctry.) 61/J3
Taiyuan, China 59/C3
Taizhou, China 59/D4
Ta'izz, Yem. 52/D6
Tajikistan (ctry.) 46/H6
Tajima, Japan 57/F2
Tajimi, Japan 57/E3
Tajrīsh, Iran 51/G3
Tak, Thai. 65/B2
Takahagi, Japan 57/G2
Takahashi, Japan 56/C3
Takahata, Japan 57/G1
Takamatsu, Japan 56/D3
Takanabe, Japan 56/B4
Takaoka, Japan 57/E2
Takapuna, NZ 71/R10
Takasaki, Japan 57/F2
Takatsuki, Japan 56/D3
Takayama, Japan 57/E2
Takefu, Japan 56/E3
Takehara, Japan 56/C3
Taketa, Japan 56/B4
Takikawa, Japan 55/N3
Takoradi, Gha. 79/E5
Tala, Mex. 100/E4
Talā, Egypt 49/B4
Talara, Peru 106/B4
Talas, Turk. 50/C2
Talavera de la Reina, Sp. 34/C3
Talawakele, SrL. 62/D6
Talca, Chile 109/B4
Talcahuano, Chile 109/B4
Tālcher, India 62/E3
Taldyqorghan, Kaz. 46/H5
Talence, Fr. 32/C4
Talgar, Kaz. 46/H5
Talkhā, Egypt 49/B4
Tall 'Afar, Iraq 50/E2
Talladega, Al, US 97/G3
Tallahassee (cap.), Fl, US 97/G4
Tallinn (cap.), Est. 42/E4
Taloda, India 62/B3
Tāloqān, Afg. 53/J1
Talwāra, India 53/L2
Tam Ky, Viet. 65/E3
Tamale, Gha. 79/E4
Taman, Indo. 66/D5
Tamanrasset, Alg. 76/G3
Tamaqua, Pa, US 94/F3
Tamazula de Gordiano, Mex. 100/E5
Tamazunchale, Mex. 102/B1
Tambacounda, Sen. 78/B3
Tambov, Rus. 45/G1
Tāmiyah, Egypt 49/B5
Tammisaari (Ekenäs), Fin. 42/D4
Tampa, Fl, US 97/H5
Tampere, Fin. 42/D3
Tampico, Mex. 102/B1
Tamra, Isr. 49/G6
Tamworth, Austl. 73/D1
Tamworth, Eng, UK 25/E1
Tamyang, SKor. 58/D5
Tan An, Viet. 65/D4
Tan-Tan, Mor. 76/C2
Tanabe, Japan 56/D4
Tanabi, Braz. 108/B2
Tanagura, Japan 57/G2
Tanambe, Madg. 81/J7
Tandā, India 62/D2
Tānda, India 62/C2
Tandag, Phil. 67/G2

Tandi – Uhers

Tandil, Arg. 109/E4
Tando Ādam, Pak. 62/A2
Tando Allāhyār, Pak. 53/J3
Tando Muhammad Khān, Pak. 62/A2
Tanga, Tanz. 82/G2
Tanganyika (lake), Afr. 82/E2
Tangará da Serra, Braz. 106/G6
Tanger (Tangier), Mor. 34/C5
Tangshan, China 59/J7
Tanjungbalai, Indo. 66/A3
Tanjungkarang-Telukbetung, Indo. 66/C5
Tanjungpandan, Indo. 66/C4
Tanjungpinang, Indo. 66/B3
Tanjungpura, Indo. 66/A3
Tānk, Pak. 53/K2
Ţanţā, Egypt 49/B4
Tantoyuca, Mex. 102/B1
Tanuku, India 62/D4
Tanzania (ctry.) 82/F2
Taolañaro, Madg. 81/H9
Taourirt, Mor. 76/E1
T'aoyüan, Tai. 61/J3
Tapachula, Mex. 102/C3
Tapolca, Hun. 40/C2
Taquara, Braz. 108/B4
Taquari, Braz. 108/B4
Taquaritinga, Braz. 108/B2
Tara, Rus. 46/H4
Ţarābulus, Leb. 49/D2
Tarakan, Indo. 67/E3
Taranto, It. 40/C5
Tarapoto, Peru 106/C5
Tarawa (cap.), Kiri. 68/G4
Tarbes, Fr. 32/D5
Tarboro, NC, US 97/J3
Taree, Austl. 73/E1
Tarhūnah, Libya 76/H1
Tarifa, Sp. 34/C4
Tarija, Bol. 106/F8
Tarin (Torino), It. 33/G4
Tarkwa, Gha. 79/E5
Tarma, Peru 106/C6
Tarnobrzeg, Pol. 27/L3
Tarnów, Pol. 27/L3
Taroudannt, Mor. 76/D1
Tarpon Springs, Fl, US 97/H4
Tarragona, Sp. 35/F2
Tarsus, Turk. 49/D1
Tartagal, Arg. 109/D1
Tartu, Est. 42/E4
Ţarţūs, Syria 49/D2
Tarumizu, Japan 56/B5
Tashkent (cap.), Uzb. 46/G5
Tasikmalaya, Indo. 66/C5
Tasman (sea) 68/E8
Tasmania, Austl. 73/C3
Tata, Hun. 40/D2
Tatabánya, Hun. 27/K5
Tatarsk, Rus. 46/H4
Tatāwīn, Tun. 76/H1
Tateyama, Japan 57/F3
Tatsuno, Japan 57/E3
Tatvan, Turk. 50/E2
Tauá, Braz. 107/K5
Taubaté, Braz. 108/H8
Taufkirchen, Ger. 37/H1
Taungdwingyi, Myan. 60/B4
Taunggyi, Myan. 65/B1
Taunsa, Pak. 53/K2
Taunton, Ma, US 95/G3
Taunton, Eng, UK 24/C4
Taunusstein, Ger. 31/H3
Taupo, NZ 71/S10
Tauragė, Lith. 27/M1
Tauranga, NZ 71/S10
Taverny, Fr. 30/B5
Tavşanlı, Turk. 50/B2
Tawau, Malay. 67/E3
Tawzar, Tun. 76/G1
Taxco, Mex. 101/K8
Tay Ninh, Viet. 65/D4
Taylor, Mi, US 99/F7
Taylorville, Il, US 93/K3
Tayshet, Rus. 47/K4
Taytay, Phil. 67/E1
Taza, Mor. 76/E1
Tchaourou, Ben. 79/F4
Tczew, Pol. 27/K1
Teapa, Mex. 102/C2
Tébessa, Alg. 76/G1
Tebingtinggi, Indo. 66/A3
Tecamachalco, Mex. 101/M8
Tecate, Mex. 92/C4
Tecomán, Mex. 100/E5
Tecpan de Galeana, Mex. 101/E5
Tecuala, Mex. 100/D4
Tecuci, Rom. 41/H3
Tefé, Braz. 106/F4
Tegal, Indo. 66/C5
Tegelen, Neth. 28/D6
Tegucigalpa (cap.), Hon. 102/E3
Tehrān (cap.), Iran 51/G3
Tehuacán, Mex. 101/M8
Tehuantepec (gulf), Mex. 102/C3
Tejen, Trkm. 53/H1
Tejupilco de Hidalgo, Mex. 101/E5
Tekax de Álvaro Obregón, Mex. 102/D1
Tekeli, Kaz. 46/H5
Tekirdağ, Turk. 41/H5
Tekkali, India 62/D4
Tel Aviv-Yafo, Isr. 49/F7
Tela, Hon. 102/E3
T'elavi, Geo. 45/H4
Telde, Canl. 35/X16
Telêmaco Borba, Braz. 108/B3
Telford Dawley, Eng, UK 24/D1
Telgte, Ger. 29/E5
Telica, Nic. 102/E3
Tellicherry, India 62/C5
Telok Anson, Malay. 66/B3
Teloloapan, Mex. 101/K8
Telšiai, Lith. 42/D5
Tema, Gha. 79/E5
Tembilahan, Indo. 66/B4
Tembisa, SAfr. 80/Q13
Temerin, Yugo. 40/D3
Temirtaū, Kaz. 46/H4
Tempe, Az, US 92/E4
Temryuk, Rus. 44/F3
Temse, Belg. 28/B6
Temuco, Chile 109/B4
Tenancingo, Mex. 101/K8
Tendō, Japan 57/G1
Tenggarong, Indo. 67/E4
Tenkodogo, Burk. 79/E4
Tennessee (riv.), US 97/F3
Tennessee (state), US 97/G3
Tenosique de Pino Suárez, Mex. 102/D2
Tenryū, Japan 57/E3
Teófilo Otoni, Braz. 108/D1
Tepalcatepec, Mex. 100/E5
Tepeji del Río de Ocampo, Mex. 101/K7
Tepexpan, Mex. 101/R9
Tepic, Mex. 100/D4
Teplice, Czh. 27/G3
Tepotzotlán, Mex. 101/Q9
Tequila, Mex. 100/E4
Tequisquiapan, Mex. 101/K6
Teramo, It. 40/A4
Teresina, Braz. 107/K5
Teresópolis, Braz. 108/L7
Terlan (Terlano), It. 37/H4
Termas de Río Hondo, Arg. 109/D2
Termini Imerese, It. 38/C4
Termiz, Uzb. 53/J1
Termoli, It. 40/B4
Ternate, Indo. 67/G3
Terneuzen, Neth. 28/A6
Terni, It. 38/C1
Ternopil', Ukr. 44/C2
Terracina, It. 38/C2
Terrassa, Sp. 35/L6
Terrebonne, Qu, Can. 95/N6
Teruel, Sp. 35/E2
Teslić, Bosn. 40/C3
Tessaoua, Niger 79/G3
Tessenie (Teseney), Erit. 52/C5
Tete, Moz. 82/F4
Tétouan, Mor. 34/C5
Tetovo, FYROM 40/E4
Tettnang, Ger. 37/F2
Teverya, Isr. 49/D3
Tewantin-Noosa, Austl. 72/D4
Texarkana, Tx, US 93/J4
Texas (state), US 96/C4
Texas City, Tx, US 93/J5
Texcoco, Mex. 101/R9
Texmelucan, Mex. 101/L7
Teykovo, Rus. 42/J4
Teziutlán, Mex. 101/M7
Tezontepec de Aldama, Mex. 101/K6
Tezpur, India 60/B3
Tezu, India 60/C3
Thai Binh, Viet. 65/D1
Thai Nguyen, Viet. 65/D1
Thailand (ctry.) 65/C3
Thailand (gulf) 65/C4
Thal, Pak. 53/K2
Thalwil, Swi. 37/E3
Thames, NZ 71/S10
Thames (riv.), Eng, UK 25/G3
Thāna, India 62/B4
Thanh Hoa, Viet. 65/D2
Thanjavur, India 62/C5
Tharād, India 62/B3
Thatcham, Eng, UK 25/E4
Thaton, Myan. 65/B2
The Dalles, Or, US 90/C4
The Woodlands, Tx, US 93/J5
Thebes (ruin), Egypt 52/B3
Theodore Roosevelt National Park, US 91/G4
Thessaloníki, Gre. 40/F5
Thetford, Eng, UK 25/G2
Thetford Mines, Qu, Can. 95/G2
Thibodaux, La, US 93/K5
Thiers, Fr. 32/E4
Thiès, Sen. 78/A3
Thika, Kenya 82/G1
Thimphu (cap.), Bhu. 62/E2
Thionville, Fr. 31/F5
Thívai, Gre. 39/H3
Tholen, Neth. 28/B5
Thomaston, Ga, US 97/G3
Thomasville, Ga, US 97/H4
Thomasville, NC, US 97/H3
Thonon-les-Bains, Fr. 36/C5
Thornaby-on-Tees, Eng, UK 23/G2
Thorne, Eng, UK 23/H4
Thornton Cleveleys, Eng, UK 23/E4
Thorold, On, Can. 95/U9
Thoubāl, India 60/B3
Thu Dau Mot, Viet. 65/D4
Thun, Swi. 36/D4
Thunder Bay, On, Can. 91/L3
Tianguá, Braz. 107/K4
Tianjin, China 59/H7
Tianmen, China 61/G2
Tianshui, China 54/F5
Tiaret, Alg. 76/F1
Ticul, Mex. 102/D1
Tidjikdja, Mrta. 78/C2
Tiel, Neth. 28/C5
Tieling, China 58/B1
Tielt, Belg. 30/C2
Tienen, Belg. 31/D2
Tierp, Swe. 42/C3
Tierra Blanca, Mex. 101/N8
Tiffin, Oh, US 94/D3
Tifton, Ga, US 97/H4
Tighina (Bendery), Mol. 41/J2
Tigris (riv.), Iraq 51/F4
Tijuana, Mex. 92/C4
Tīkamgarh, India 62/C3
Tikhoretsk, Rus. 44/G3
Tikhvin, Rus. 42/G4
Tilburg, Neth. 28/C5
Ţīmā, Egypt 50/B5
Timaru, NZ 71/R11
Timashevsk, Rus. 44/F3
Timbaúba, Braz. 107/L5
Timbó, Braz. 108/B3
Timimoun, Alg. 76/F2
Timişoara, Rom. 40/E3
Timmins, On, Can. 94/D1
Timon, Braz. 107/K5
Timor (isl.), Indo. 68/B5
Timóteo, Braz. 108/D1
Timrå, Swe. 42/C3
Tindivanam, India 62/C5
Tindouf, Alg. 76/D2
Tineo, Sp. 34/B1
Tingo María, Peru 106/C5
Tinley Park, Il, US 99/Q16
Tinrhir, Mor. 76/D1
Tiptūr, India 62/C5
Tiranë (cap.), Alb. 40/D5
Tiraspol, Mol. 41/J2
Tirat Karmel, Isr. 49/F6
Tire, Turk. 50/A2
Tîrgovişte, Rom. 41/G3
Tîrgu Jiu, Rom. 41/F3
Tîrgu Mureş, Rom. 41/G2
Tîrgu Neamţ, Rom. 41/H2
Tîrgu Secuiesc, Rom. 41/H2
Tîrnăveni, Rom. 41/G2
Tiruchchirāppalli, India 62/C5
Tiruchendūr, India 62/C6
Tiruchengodu, India 62/C5
Tirunelveli, India 62/C6
Tirupati, India 62/C5
Tiruppattūr, India 62/C5
Tiruppūr, India 62/C5
Tiruvannāmalai, India 62/C5
Titicaca (lake), Peru 106/E7
Titlagarh, India 62/D3
Titov Veles, FYROM 40/E5
Titusville, Fl, US 97/H4
Tivaouane, Sen. 78/A3
Tiverton, Eng, UK 24/C5
Tixtla de Guerrero, Mex. 102/B2
Tizayuca, Mex. 101/L7
Tizimín, Mex. 102/D1
Tiznit, Mor. 76/D2
Tlalnepantla, Mex. 101/Q9
Tlapa de Comonfort, Mex. 102/B2
Tlapacoyan, Mex. 101/M7
Tlaquepaque, Mex. 100/E4
Tlaquiltenango, Mex. 101/K8
Tlaxcala, Mex. 101/L7
Tlemcen, Alg. 76/E1
Toamasina, Madg. 81/J7
Toba, Japan 57/E3
Tobias Barreto, Braz. 107/L6
Tocantins (riv.), Braz. 107/J4
Tochigi, Japan 57/F2
Tochio, Japan 57/F2
Tocopilla, Chile 109/B1
Tocumen, Pan. 103/G4
Toda Bhīm, India 62/C2
Togo (ctry.) 79/F4
Tōkai, Japan 57/E3
Tōkamachi, Japan 57/F2
Tokat, Turk. 44/F4
Tokoroa, NZ 71/S10
Tokorozawa, Japan 57/F3
Tokushima, Japan 56/D3
Tokuyama, Japan 56/B3
Tōkyō (cap.), Japan 57/F3
Tola, Nic. 102/E4
Toledo, Braz. 109/F1
Toledo, Sp. 34/C3
Toliara, Madg. 81/G8
Tolosa, Sp. 34/D1
Tolú, Col. 103/H4
Toluca, Mex. 101/Q10
Tol'yatti, Rus. 45/J1
Tomakomai, Japan 55/N3
Tomar, Port. 34/A3
Tomaszów Lubelski, Pol. 27/M3
Tomaszów Mazowiecki, Pol. 27/L3
Tombouctou, Mali 78/E2
Tomelloso, Sp. 34/D3
Tomsk, Rus. 46/J4
Tonalá, Mex. 102/C2
Tonawanda, NY, US 95/V9
Tonbridge, Eng, UK 25/G4
Tondano, Indo. 67/F3
Tonga (ctry.) 69/H7
Tongaat, SAfr. 81/E3
Tongchuan, China 59/B4
Tongduch'on, SKor. 58/G6
Tongeren, Belg. 31/E2
Tonghae, SKor. 58/E4
Tonghua, China 58/C2
Tongliao, China 59/E2
Tongling, China 61/H2
Tongren, China 61/F3
Tönisvorst, Ger. 28/D6
Tonk, India 62/C2
Tonkin (gulf), Asia 65/D1
Tonoshō, Japan 56/D3
Tønsberg, Nor. 20/D4
Tooele, Ut, US 92/D2
Toowoomba, Austl. 72/C4
Topeka (cap.), Ks, US 93/J3
Topliţa, Rom. 41/G2
Topol'čany, Slvk. 27/K4
Torbalı, Turk. 50/A2
Torbat-e Ḩeydarīyeh, Iran 51/J3
Torghay, Kaz. 46/G4
Torhout, Belg. 30/C1
Torino (Turin), It. 33/G4
Tornio, Fin. 20/H2
Törökszentmiklós, Hun. 40/E2
Toronto (cap.), On, Can. 95/U8
Toropets, Rus. 42/F4
Tororo, Ugan. 77/M7
Torquay, Eng, UK 24/C6
Torrance, Ca, US 92/C4
Torre del Greco, It. 40/B5
Torre-Pacheco, Sp. 35/E4
Torrejón de Ardoz, Sp. 35/N9
Torrelavega, Sp. 34/C1
Torremaggiore, It. 40/B5
Torremolinos, Sp. 34/C4
Torrente, Sp. 35/E3
Torreón, Mex. 96/C5
Tôrres, Braz. 108/B4
Torres Novas, Port. 34/A3
Torres Vedras, Port. 34/A3
Torrevieja, Sp. 35/E4
Tortona, It. 33/H4
Tortosa, Sp. 35/F2
Toruń, Pol. 27/K2
Torzhok, Rus. 42/G4
Tosa, Japan 56/C4
Tosashimizu, Japan 56/C4
Tosno, Rus. 42/F4
Tosu, Japan 56/B4
Tosya, Turk. 44/E4
Totana, Sp. 34/E4
Totness, Sur. 107/G2
Tottori, Japan 56/D3
T'oufen, Tai. 61/J3
Tougan, Burk. 78/E3
Touggourt, Alg. 76/G1
Toul, Fr. 31/E6
Toulon, Fr. 32/F5
Toulouse, Fr. 32/D5
Toungoo, Myan. 65/B2
Tourcoing, Fr. 30/C2
Tourlaville, Fr. 32/C2
Tournai, Belg. 30/C2
Tours, Fr. 32/D3
Towada, Japan 57/G2
Townsville, Austl. 72/B2
Toyama, Japan 57/E2
Toyohashi, Japan 57/E3
Toyokawa, Japan 57/E3
Toyo'oka, Japan 56/D3
Toyoshina, Japan 57/E2
Toyota, Japan 57/E3
Tra Vinh, Viet. 65/D4
Trabzon, Turk. 44/F4
Tracy, Ca, US 99/M11
Tralee, Ire. 21/A10
Tramandaí, Braz. 108/B4
Tramin (Termeno), It. 37/H5
Tranås, Swe. 20/E4
Trang, Thai. 65/B5
Trani, It. 40/C5
Trapani, It. 38/C3
Trappes, Fr. 30/B6
Traralgon, Austl. 73/C3
Traun, Aus. 33/L2
Traunreut, Ger. 40/A2
Traunstein, Ger. 33/K3
Travnik, Bosn. 40/C3
Trbovlje, Slov. 40/B2
Třebíč, Czh. 33/L2
Trebinje, Bosn. 40/D4
Treinta y Tres, Uru. 109/F3
Trelew, Arg. 109/C5
Trelleborg, Swe. 26/G1
Trenčín, Slvk. 27/K4
Trenque Lauquen, Arg. 109/D4
Trento, It. 37/H5
Trenton, On, Can. 94/E2
Trenton (cap.), NJ, US 94/F3
Trenton, Mi, US 99/F7
Tres Arroyos, Arg. 109/D4
Três Corações, Braz. 108/H6
Três Lagoas, Braz. 108/B2
Três Marias, Braz. 108/C1
Três Pontas, Braz. 108/H6
Três Rios, Braz. 108/K7
Tres Valles, Mex. 102/B2
Treviglio, It. 33/H4
Treviso, It. 33/K4
Trichūr, India 62/C5
Trier, Ger. 31/F4
Trieste, It. 40/A3
Triggiano, It. 40/C5
Tríkala, Gre. 39/G3
Trincomalee, SrL. 62/D6
Trindade, Braz. 107/J7
Třinec, Czh. 27/K4
Trinidad, Bol. 106/F6
Trinidad, Uru. 109/E3
Trinidad and Tobago (ctry.), Trin. 104/F5
Triolet, Mrts. 81/T15
Tripoli (cap.), Libya 76/H1
Tripolis, Gre. 39/H4
Tripunittura, India 62/C6
Trivandrum, India 62/C6
Trnava, Slvk. 40/C1
Trois-Rivières, Qu, Can. 95/F2
Troisdorf, Ger. 31/G2
Troitsk, Rus. 43/P5
Trollhättan, Swe. 20/E4
Tromsø, Nor. 20/F1
Trondheim, Nor. 20/D3
Tropic of Capricorn 72/A3
Trowbridge, Eng, UK 24/D4
Troy, NY, US 94/F3
Troy, Oh, US 97/G1
Troy, Al, US 97/G4
Troy, Mi, US 99/F6
Troyan, Bul. 41/G4
Troyes, Fr. 32/F2
Trstenik, Yugo. 40/E4
Trujillo, Ven. 106/D2
Trujillo, Peru 106/C5
Trujillo, Hon. 102/E3
Truro, Eng, UK 24/A6
Truth or Consequences, NM, US 96/B3
Trutnov, Czh. 27/H3
Trzcianka, Pol. 27/J2
Tsabong, Bots. 80/C2
Tsakane, SAfr. 80/Q13
Tsetserleg, Mong. 54/E2
Tsévié, Togo 79/F5
Tshikapa, D.R. Congo 82/D2
Tsiroanomandidy, Madg. 81/H7
Ts'khinvali, Geo. 45/G4
Tsu, Japan 56/E3
Tsubame, Japan 57/F2
Tsubata, Japan 57/E2
Tsuchiura, Japan 57/G2
Tsukumi, Japan 56/B4
Tsuru, Japan 57/F3
Tsuruga, Japan 56/E3
Tsurugi, Japan 56/E2
Tsuyama, Japan 56/D3
Tuamotu (arch.), FrPol. 69/L6
Tuao, Phil. 61/J5
Tuapse, Rus. 44/F3
Tuba, Phil. 61/J5
Tuban, Indo. 66/D5
Tubarão, Braz. 108/B4
Tubbergen, Neth. 28/D4
Tübingen, Ger. 37/F1
Tubize, Belg. 31/D2
Tubou, Fiji 68/H6
Ţubruq (Tobruk), Libya 77/K1
Tucson, Az, US 92/E4
Tucupita, Ven. 106/F2
Tucuruí, Braz. 107/J4
Tudela, Sp. 34/E1
Ţūkh, Egypt 49/B4
Tukums, Lat. 42/D4
Tukwila, Wa, US 99/C3
Tula, Mex. 101/K6
Tula, Rus. 44/F1
Tulancingo, Mex. 101/L6
Tulare, Ca, US 92/C3
Tulcán, Ecu. 106/C3
Tulcea, Rom. 41/J3
Ţūlkarm, WBnk. 49/G7
Tullahoma, Tn, US 97/G3
Tulle, Fr. 32/D4
Tulsa, Ok, US 93/J3
Tultitlán, Mex. 101/Q9
Tuluá, Col. 106/C3
Tulun, Rus. 47/L4
Tumaco, Col. 106/C3
Tumbes, Peru 106/B4
Tumen, China 55/K3
Tumkūr, India 62/C5
Tumwater, Wa, US 99/B4
Tunceli, Turk. 50/D2
Tūnis (cap.), Tun. 38/B4
Tunisia (ctry.) 76/H1
Tunjá, Col. 106/D2
Tunuyán, Arg. 109/C3
Tupã, Braz. 108/B2
Tupaciguara, Braz. 108/B1
Tupelo, Ms, US 97/F3
Tupiza, Bol. 106/E8
Tura, India 62/F2
Turbaco, Col. 103/H4
Turbat, Pak. 53/H3
Turbo, Col. 103/G4
Turčiansky Svätý Martin, Slvk. 27/K4
Turda, Rom. 41/F2
Turek, Pol. 27/K2
Tŭrgovishte, Bul. 41/H4
Turgutlu, Turk. 44/C5
Turhal, Turk. 44/F4
Turkey (ctry.) 50/C2
Türkistan, Kaz. 46/G5
Türkmenbashi (Krasnowodsk), Trkm. 51/H2
Turkmenistan (ctry.) 46/F6
Türkoğlu, Turk. 50/D2
Turks and Caicos (isls.), UK 104/C2
Turlock, Ca, US 92/B3
Turnhout, Belg. 28/B6
Turnu Măgurele, Rom. 41/G4
Turpan, China 54/B3
Tuscaloosa, Al, US 97/G3
Tuskegee, Al, US 97/G3
Tutayev, Rus. 42/H4
Tuticorin, India 62/C6
Tuttlingen, Ger. 37/E2
Tuusula, Fin. 42/E3
Tuvalu (ctry.) 68/G5
Tuxpan, Mex. 100/D4
Tuxpan, Mex. 100/E5
Tuxpan de Rodríguez Cano, Mex. 102/B1
Tuxtla Gutiérrez, Mex. 102/C2
Túy, Sp. 34/A1
Tuy Hoa, Viet. 65/E3
Tuyen Quang, Viet. 65/D1
Tuymazy, Rus. 43/M5
Tuzla, Bosn. 40/D3
Tver', Rus. 42/G4
Tweed Heads, Austl. 73/E1
Twello, Neth. 28/D4
Twin Falls, Id, US 92/D2
Two Rivers, Wi, US 91/M4
Tychy, Pol. 27/K3
Tyldesley, Eng, UK 23/F4
Tyler, Tx, US 93/J4
Tynemouth, Eng, UK 23/G1
Tyrnyauz, Rus. 45/G4
Tyumen', Rus. 43/Q4

U

Ub, Yugo. 40/E3
Ubá, Braz. 108/D2
Übach-Palenberg, Ger. 31/F2
Ubatã, Braz. 107/L6
Ubatuba, Braz. 108/H8
Ube, Japan 56/B4
Úbeda, Sp. 34/D3
Uberaba, Braz. 108/C1
Uberlândia, Braz. 108/B1
Überlingen, Ger. 37/F2
Ubon Ratchathani, Thai. 65/D3
Ubrique, Sp. 34/C4
Ucayali (riv.), Peru 106/D5
Uccle, Belg. 31/D2
Uchaly, Rus. 43/N5
Udagamandalam, India 62/C5
Udaipur, India 62/B3
Uddevalla, Swe. 20/D4
Uden, Neth. 28/C5
Udgīr, India 62/C4
Udhampur, India 53/L2
Udine, It. 40/A2
Udipi, India 62/B5
Udon Thani, Thai. 65/C2
Ueda, Japan 57/F2
Uelzen, Ger. 29/H3
Ueno, Japan 56/E3
Uenohara, Japan 57/F3
Uetersen, Ger. 29/G1
Uetze, Ger. 29/H4
Ufa, Rus. 43/M5
Uganda (ctry.) 77/M7
Uglegorsk, Rus. 55/N2
Uglich, Rus. 42/H4
Uherské Hradiště, Czh. 27/J4

Uíge, Ang. 82/C2
Ŭijŏngbu, SKor. 58/G6
Ŭisŏng, SKor. 56/A2
Uitenhage, SAfr. 80/D4
Uithoorn, Neth. 28/B4
Ujjain, India 62/C3
Ujung Pandang, Indo. 67/E5
Ukhta, Rus. 43/M3
Ukiah, Ca, US 92/B3
Ukmergė, Lith. 42/E5
Ukraine (ctry.) 44/D2
Ulaanbaatar (cap.), Mong. 54/F2
Ulaangom, Mong. 54/C2
Ulan-Ude, Rus. 54/F1
Ulanhot, China 55/J2
Ulchin, SKor. 56/A2
Ulhāsnagar, India 62/B4
Uliastay, Mong. 54/D2
Ulm, Ger. 37/F1
Ulsan, SKor. 56/A3
Ul'yanovka, Rus. 43/T7
Ul'yanovsk, Rus. 45/J1
Umán, Mex. 102/D1
Uman', Ukr. 44/D2
Umarkot, India 62/D4
Umeå, Swe. 42/D3
Umm Durmān, Sudan 52/B5
Umm el Fahm, Isr. 49/G6
Umtata, SAfr. 80/E3
Umuarama, Braz. 109/F1
Unaí, Braz. 107/J7
Unecha, Rus. 44/E1
Ungava (bay), Qu, Can. 87/K3
Ungheni, Mol. 41/H2
União da Vitória, Braz. 108/B3
União dos Palmares, Braz. 107/L5
Union, SC, US 97/H3
Union City, Tn, US 97/F2
Union City, Ca, US 99/K11
Unión de Reyes, Cuba 103/F1
Uniontown, Pa, US 94/E4
United Arab Emirates (ctry.) 52/F4
United Kingdom (ctry.) 18/C3
United States (ctry.) 88/
University Place, Wa, US 99/B3
Unjha, India 62/B3
Unna, Ger. 29/E5
Unnāo, India 62/D2
Unterschleissheim, Ger. 37/H1
Ünye, Turk. 44/F4
Uozu, Japan 57/E2
Upata, Ven. 106/F2
Upington, SAfr. 80/C3
Upleta, India 62/B3
Upper (pen.), Mi, US 89/J2
Upper Hutt, NZ 71/S11
Upplands-Väsby, Swe. 20/F4
Uppsala, Swe. 42/C4
Ural (mts.), Rus. 46/F3
Urawa, Japan 57/F3
Uray, Rus. 46/G3
Urbana, Oh, US 97/H1
Urfa, Turk. 50/D2
Urganch, Uzb. 46/G5
Uriangato, Mex. 101/E4
Urla, Turk. 44/C5
Urmston, Eng, UK 23/F5
Uroševac, Yugo. 40/E4
Uruaçu, Braz. 107/J6
Uruapan, Mex. 100/E5
Uruguaiana, Braz. 109/E2
Uruguay (riv.), SAm. 109/E2
Uruguay (ctry.) 109/E3
Ürümqi, China 54/B3
Uryupinsk, Rus. 45/G2
Urziceni, Rom. 41/H3
Usa, Japan 56/B4
Uşak, Turk. 50/B2
Ushibuka, Japan 56/B4
Ushtobe, Kaz. 46/H5
Ushuaia, Arg. 109/C7
Usibelli, Ak, US 85/J3
Usilampatti, India 62/C6
Uslar, Ger. 29/G5
Usman', Rus. 44/F1
Usol'ye-Sibirskoye, Rus. 54/E1
Uson, Phil. 67/F1
Ussuriysk, Rus. 55/L3
Ust'-Ilimsk, Rus. 47/L4
Ust'-Kut, Rus. 47/L4
Uster, Swi. 37/E3
Ústí nad Labem, Czh. 33/L1
Ustka, Pol. 27/J1
Usuki, Japan 56/B4
Usulután, ESal. 102/D3
Utah (state), US 92/E3
Utraulā, India 62/D2
Utrecht, Neth. 28/C4
Utrera, Sp. 34/C4
Utsunomiya, Japan 57/F2
Utuado, PR 104/E3
Uvalde, Tx, US 93/H5
Uvarovo, Rus. 45/G2
Uwajima, Japan 56/C4
Uxmal (ruin), Mex. 102/D1
Uzbekistan (ctry.) 46/G5
Uzhhorod, Ukr. 27/M4
Užice, Yugo. 40/D4
Uzlovaya, Rus. 44/F1
Uzunköprü, Turk. 41/H5

V

Vaasa (Vasa), Fin. 42/D3
Vác, Hun. 27/K5
Vacaria, Braz. 108/B4
Vacaville, Ca, US 99/L10
Vadodara (Baroda), India 62/B3
Vadsø, Nor. 42/F1
Vaduz (cap.), Lcht. 37/F3
Vaijāpur, India 53/K5
Vakfıkebir, Turk. 44/F4
Val-d'Or, Qu, Can. 94/E1
Valdepeñas, Sp. 34/D3
Valdivia, Chile 109/B4
Valdosta, Ga, US 97/H4
Valença, Braz. 107/L6
Valença, Braz. 108/K7
Valence, Fr. 32/F4
Valencia, Ven. 106/E1
Valencia, Sp. 35/E3
Valenciennes, Fr. 30/C3
Valenza, It. 33/H4
Valera, Ven. 106/D2
Valga, Est. 42/E4
Valinhos, Braz. 108/F7
Valjevo, Yugo. 40/D3
Valkenburg, Neth. 31/E2
Valkenswaard, Neth. 28/C6
Vall de Uxó, Sp. 35/E3
Valladolid, Mex. 102/D1
Valladolid, Sp. 34/C2
Valle de Bravo, Mex. 102/A2
Valle de La Pascua, Ven. 106/E2
Valle de Santiago, Mex. 101/E4
Valle Hermoso, Mex. 101/F3
Valledupar, Col. 103/H4
Vallejo, Ca, US 99/K10
Vallenar, Chile 109/B2
Valletta (cap.), Malta 38/M7
Valley East, On, Can. 94/D2
Valls, Sp. 35/F2
Valmiera, Lat. 42/E4
Vālpārai, India 62/C5
Valparaíso, Chile 109/B3
Valparaiso, In, US 94/C3
Valsād, India 62/B3
Valuyki, Rus. 44/F2
Vammala, Fin. 20/G3
Van, Turk. 51/E2
Van Wert, Oh, US 94/C3
Vanadzor, Arm. 45/H4
Vancouver, Wa, US 90/C4
Vancouver, BC, Can. 90/C3
Vancouver (isl.), BC, Can. 90/B3
Vanderbijlpark, SAfr. 80/P13
Vandœuvre-lès-Nancy, Fr. 31/F6
Vänersborg, Swe. 20/E4
Vangaindrano, Madg. 81/H8
Vanimo, PNG 67/K4
Vanino, Rus. 55/N2
Vannes, Fr. 32/B3
Vantaa, Fin. 42/E3
Vanuatu (ctry.) 68/F6
Varadero, Cuba 103/F1
Varāmīn, Iran 51/G3
Vārānasi, India 62/D2
Varaždin, Cro. 40/C2
Varberg, Swe. 20/E4
Varel, Ger. 29/F2
Varennes, Qu, Can. 95/P6
Vareš, Bosn. 40/D3
Varese, It. 33/H4
Vargem Grande do Sul, Braz. 108/G6
Varginha, Braz. 108/H6
Varkaus, Fin. 42/E3
Varna, Bul. 41/H4
Värnamo, Swe. 20/E4
Várpalota, Hun. 40/D2
Várzea da Palma, Braz. 108/C1
Várzea Grande, Braz. 107/G7
Vaslui, Rom. 41/H2
Vassouras, Braz. 108/K7
Västerås, Swe. 42/C4
Västervik, Swe. 42/C4
Vasto, It. 40/B4
Vasyl'kiv, Ukr. 44/D2
Vaterstetten, Ger. 33/J2
Vatican City (ctry.) 38/C2
Vatican City (cap.), VatC. 38/C2
Vatra Dornei, Rom. 41/G2
Vaudreuil-Dorion, Qu, Can. 95/M7
Vaughan, On, Can. 95/T8
Vaulx-en-Velin, Fr. 36/A6
Vavatenina, Madg. 81/J7
Vavuniya, SrL. 62/D6
Vawkavysk, Bela. 27/N2
Växjö, Swe. 20/E4
Vázea Paulista, Braz. 108/G8
Vechta, Ger. 29/F3
Vecsés, Hun. 27/K5
Veendam, Neth. 28/D2
Veenendaal, Neth. 28/C4
Veghel, Neth. 28/C5
Vejle, Den. 26/E1
Velbert, Ger. 28/E6
Veldhoven, Neth. 28/C6
Vélez-Málaga, Sp. 34/C4
Velika Gorica, Cro. 40/C3
Velika Plana, Yugo. 40/E3
Velikiy Ustyug, Rus. 43/K3
Velikiye Luki, Rus. 42/F4
Veliko Tŭrnovo, Bul. 41/G4
Velletri, It. 38/C2
Vellinge, Swe. 26/G1
Vellmar, Ger. 29/G6
Vellore, India 62/C5
Vel'sk, Rus. 42/J3
Venado Tuerto, Arg. 109/D3
Venâncio Aires, Braz. 108/A4
Venaria, It. 33/G4
Vence, Fr. 33/G5
Vendôme, Fr. 32/D3
Vendrell, Sp. 35/F2
Venezia (Venice), It. 33/K4
Venezuela (ctry.), Ven. 106/E2
Venice, Fl, US 97/H5
Venice (Venezia), It. 33/K4
Vénissieux, Fr. 32/F4
Venkatagiri, India 62/C5
Venlo, Neth. 28/D6
Venray, Neth. 28/C5
Ventspils, Lat. 42/D4
Ventura (San Buenaventura), Ca, US 92/C4
Vera, Arg. 109/D2
Veracruz, Mex. 101/N7
Verāval, India 62/B3
Verbania, It. 37/E6
Vercelli, It. 33/H4
Verde (cape), Sen. 76/B5
Verden, Ger. 29/G3
Verdun, Qu, Can. 95/N7
Verdun, Fr. 31/E5
Vereeniging, SAfr. 80/P13
Vereshchagino, Rus. 43/M4
Verl, Ger. 29/F5
Vermillion, SD, US 93/H2
Vermont (state), US 95/F2
Vernier, Swi. 36/C5
Vernon, BC, Can. 90/D3
Vernon, Tx, US 93/H4
Vernon, Fr. 30/A5
Vernon Hills, Il, US 99/Q15
Vero Beach, Fl, US 97/H5
Véroia, Gre. 40/F5
Verona, It. 33/J4
Verrières-le-Buisson, Fr. 30/B6
Versailles, Fr. 30/B6
Versmold, Ger. 29/F4
Vertientes, Cuba 103/G1
Vertou, Fr. 32/C3
Verviers, Belg. 31/E2
Verwoerdburg, SAfr. 80/Q12
Verzasca (Gerra), Swi. 37/E5
Vesoul, Fr. 36/C2
Vesuvio (Vesuvius) (vol.), It. 38/D2
Veszprém, Hun. 40/C2
Vetlanda, Swe. 20/E4
Vevey, Swi. 36/C5
Vezirköprü, Turk. 44/E4
Viacha, Bol. 106/E7
Viana, Braz. 107/K4
Viana do Castelo, Port. 34/A2
Vianen, Neth. 28/C4
Viareggio, It. 33/J5
Vibo Valentia, It. 38/E3
Viborg, Den. 20/D4
Vic, Sp. 35/G2
Vicenza, It. 33/J4
Vichuga, Rus. 42/J4
Vichy, Fr. 32/E3
Vicksburg, Ms, US 93/K4
Viçosa, Braz. 108/D2
Víctor Rosales, Mex. 100/E4
Victoria, Arg. 109/D3
Victoria, Austl. 73/B2
Victoria, Chile 109/B4
Victoria (cap.), BC, Can. 90/C3
Victoria (isl.), NW,Nun., Can. 86/E1
Victoria (lake), Afr. 77/M8
Victoria, China 61/G4
Victoria (falls), Zim. 82/E4
Victoria de las Tunas, Cuba 103/G1
Victoriaville, Qu, Can. 95/G2
Victorville, Ca, US 92/C4
Vidalia, Ga, US 97/H3
Videira, Braz. 108/B3
Vidin, Bul. 41/F4
Vidisha, India 62/C3
Vidnoye, Rus. 43/W9
Vidor, Tx, US 93/J5
Viedma, Arg. 109/D5
Vienna, WV, US 97/H2
Vienna (cap.), Aus. 40/C2
Vienne, Fr. 32/F4
Vientiane (cap.), Laos 65/C2
Viersen, Ger. 28/D6
Vierzon, Fr. 32/E3
Viet Tri, Viet. 65/D1
Vietnam (ctry.) 65/D2
Vigan, Phil. 61/J5
Vigevano, It. 33/H4
Vigia, Braz. 107/J4
Vigneux-sur-Seine, Fr. 30/B6
Vignola, It. 33/J4
Vigo, Sp. 34/A1
Vihāri, Pak. 53/K2
Vijayawada, India 62/D4
Vila de Sena, Moz. 82/G4
Vila do Conde, Port. 34/A2
Vila Franca de Xira, Port. 35/P10
Vila Nova de Gaia, Port. 34/A2
Vila Real, Port. 34/B2
Vila Velha Argolas, Braz. 108/D2
Viladecans, Sp. 35/K7
Vilafranca del Penedès, Sp. 35/K7
Vilanova i la Geltrù, Sp. 35/K7
Vilhena, Braz. 106/F6
Viljandi, Est. 42/E4
Villa Ángela, Arg. 109/D2
Villa Carlos Paz, Arg. 109/D3
Villa de Costa Rica, Mex. 100/D3
Villa Dolores, Arg. 109/C3
Villa Flores, Mex. 102/C2
Villa Gesell, Arg. 109/E4
Villa María, Arg. 109/D3
Villa Nueva, Guat. 102/D3
Villa Nueva, Nic. 102/E3
Villa Park, Il, US 99/Q16
Villa Regina, Arg. 109/C4
Villa Rosario, Col. 103/H5
Villa Sandino, Nic. 103/E3
Villablino, Sp. 34/B1
Villach, Aus. 40/A2
Villagarcía, Sp. 34/A1
Villaguay, Arg. 109/E3
Villahermosa, Mex. 102/C2
Villajoyosa, Sp. 35/E3
Villalba, Sp. 34/B1
Villanueva, Col. 103/H4
Villanueva de Arosa, Sp. 34/A1
Villanueva de la Serena, Sp. 34/C3
Villarreal de los Infantes, Sp. 35/E3
Villarrica, Par. 109/E2
Villarrica, Chile 109/B4
Villarrobledo, Sp. 34/D3
Villavicencio, Col. 106/D3
Villaviciosa, Sp. 34/C1
Villaviciosa de Odón, Sp. 35/N9
Villazón, Bol. 106/E8
Ville Platte, La, US 93/J5
Villefranche-sur-Saône, Fr. 36/A6
Villejuif, Fr. 30/B6
Villena, Sp. 35/E3
Villeneuve-d'Ascq, Fr. 30/C2
Villeneuve-Saint-Georges, Fr. 30/B6
Villeneuve-sur-Lot, Fr. 32/D4
Villeparisis, Fr. 30/B6
Villers-lès-Nancy, Fr. 31/F6
Villeurbanne, Fr. 36/A6
Villingen-Schwenningen, Ger. 37/E1
Vilnius (cap.), Lith. 27/N1
Vilshofen, Ger. 33/K2
Vilvoorde, Belg. 31/D2
Vimmerby, Swe. 20/E4
Viña del Mar, Chile 109/B3
Vinaroz, Sp. 35/F2
Vincennes, In, US 97/G2
Vineland, NJ, US 94/F4
Vinh, Viet. 65/D2
Vinh Long, Viet. 65/D4
Vinh Yen, Viet. 65/D1
Vinhedo, Braz. 108/G8
Vinica, FYROM 40/F5
Vinkovci, Cro. 40/D3
Vinnytsya, Ukr. 44/D2
Vintar, Phil. 61/J5
Viranşehir, Turk. 50/D2
Virār, India 62/B4
Virgin (isls.), UK,US 104/E3
Virginia, SAfr. 80/D3
Virginia (state), US 97/J2
Virginia Beach, Va, US 97/K2
Virovitica, Cro. 40/C3
Virudunagar, India 62/C6
Viry-Châtillon, Fr. 30/B6
Visākhapatnam, India 62/D4
Visalia, Ca, US 92/C3
Visby, Swe. 42/C4
Visconde do Rio Branco, Braz. 108/D2
Visé, Belg. 31/E2
Višegrad, Bosn. 40/D4
Viseu, Port. 34/B2
Vişeu de Sus, Rom. 41/G2
Visnagar, India 62/B3
Visoko, Bosn. 40/D4
Vista, Ca, US 92/C4
Viterbo, It. 38/C1
Vitória, Braz. 108/D2
Vitoria, Sp. 34/D1
Vitória da Conquista, Braz. 107/K6
Vitória de Santo Antão, Braz. 107/L5
Vitré, Fr. 32/C2
Vitrolles, Fr. 32/F5
Vitry-le-François, Fr. 31/D6
Vitry-sur-Seine, Fr. 30/B6
Vitsyebsk, Bela. 42/F5
Vittoria, It. 38/D4
Vittorio Veneto, It. 33/K4
Viveiro, Sp. 34/B1
Vizianagaram, India 62/D4
Vlaardingen, Neth. 28/B5
Vladikavkaz, Rus. 45/H4
Vladimir, Rus. 42/J4
Vladivostok, Rus. 55/L3
Vlagtwedde, Neth. 29/E2
Vlasenica, Bosn. 40/D3
Vlijmen, Neth. 28/C5
Vlissingen, Neth. 28/A6
Vlotho, Ger. 29/F4
Voerde, Ger. 28/D5
Voghera, It. 33/H4
Vohipeno, Madg. 81/H8
Voiron, Fr. 32/F4
Vöklingen, Ger. 31/F5
Volendam, Neth. 28/C3
Volgodonsk, Rus. 45/G3
Stalingrad (Volgograd), Rus. 45/H2
Volkhov, Rus. 42/G4
Volodymyr-Volyns'kyy, Ukr. 27/N3
Vologda, Rus. 42/H4
Vólos, Gre. 39/H3
Vol'sk, Rus. 45/H1
Volta (riv.), Gha. 76/F6
Volta (lake), Gha. 76/E6
Volta Redonda, Braz. 108/J7
Volzhsk, Rus. 43/L5
Volzhskiy, Rus. 45/H2
Voorburg, Neth. 28/B4
Voorschoten, Neth. 28/B4
Voorst, Neth. 28/D4
Vorkuta, Rus. 43/P2
Voronezh, Rus. 44/F2
Võru, Est. 42/E4
Voskresensk, Rus. 44/F1
Votkinsk, Rus. 43/M4
Votorantim, Braz. 108/C2
Votuporanga, Braz. 108/B2
Voúla, Gre. 39/N9
Voyeykov Ice Shelf, Ant. 83/J
Voznesens'k, Ukr. 41/K2
Vranov nad Teplou, Slvk. 27/L4
Vratsa, Bul. 41/F4
Vrbas, Yugo. 40/D3
Vreden, Ger. 28/D4
Vredenburg-Saldanha, SAfr. 80/K10
Vriezenveen, Neth. 28/D4
Vrindāban, India 62/C2
Vršac, Yugo. 40/E3
Vsetín, Czh. 27/K4
Vsevolozhsk, Rus. 43/T6
Vught, Neth. 28/C5
Vukovar, Cro. 40/D3
Vulcan, Rom. 41/F3
Vung Tau, Viet. 65/D4
Vunisea, Fiji 68/G6
Vyāra, India 62/B3
Vyatskiye Polyany, Rus. 43/L4
Vyazemskiy, Rus. 55/L2
Vyaz'ma, Rus. 42/G5
Vyborg, Rus. 42/F3
Vyksa, Rus. 45/G1
Vynohradiv, Ukr. 27/M4
Vyshniy Volochek, Rus. 42/G4
Vyškov, Czh. 33/M2

W

Wa, Gha. 79/E4
Waalre, Neth. 28/C6
Waalwijk, Neth. 28/C5
Wabash, In, US 94/C3
Waco, Tx, US 93/H5
Wad Medanī, Sudan 52/B6
Waddinxveen, Neth. 28/B4
Wädenswil, Swi. 37/E3
Wadern, Ger. 31/F4
Wadgassen, Ger. 31/F5
Wādī As Sīr, Jor. 49/D4
Wadowice, Pol. 27/K4
Wafangdian, China 58/A3
Wageningen, Neth. 28/C5
Wagga Wagga, Austl. 73/C2
Wągrowiec, Pol. 27/J2
Wāh, Pak. 53/K2
Wahiawa, Hi, US 88/V12
Wai, India 62/B4
Waikiki, Hi, US 88/W13
Wailuku, Hi, US 88/T10
Waipahu, Hi, US 88/V13
Waipio, Hi, US 88/U10
Wajima, Japan 57/E2
Wakayama, Japan 56/D3
Wakefield, Eng, UK 23/G4
Wakema, Myan. 60/B5
Waki, Japan 56/D3
Wakkanai, Japan 55/N2
Wałbrzych, Pol. 27/J3
Walcourt, Belg. 31/D3
Wałcz, Pol. 27/J2
Waldbröl, Ger. 31/G2
Waldkirch, Ger. 36/D1
Waldshut-Tiengen, Ger. 37/E2
Wales, UK 24/B3
Walla Walla, Wa, US 90/D4
Wallasey, Eng, UK 23/E5
Wallenhorst, Ger. 29/F4
Wallis and Futuna (dpcy.), Fr. 68/G6
Wallsend, Eng, UK 23/G2
Walnut Canyon Nat'l Mon., Az, US 92/E4
Walnut Creek, Ca, US 99/K11
Walsall, Eng, UK 24/E1
Walsrode, Ger. 29/G3
Waltham Abbey, Eng, UK 25/G3
Walton-on-Thames, Eng, UK 25/F4
Waltrop, Ger. 29/E5
Wanganui, NZ 71/S10
Wangaratta, Austl. 73/C3
Wangen, Ger. 37/F2
Wanxian, China 61/F2
Wapakoneta, Oh, US 94/C3
Warangal, India 62/C4
Warburg, Ger. 29/G6
Ward Cove, Ak, US 85/M4
Wardha, India 62/C3
Ware, Eng, UK 25/F3
Waregem, Belg. 30/C2
Waren, Ger. 26/G2
Warendorf, Ger. 29/E5
Warin Chamrap, Thai. 65/D3
Warmbad, SAfr. 80/E2
Warminster, Eng, UK 24/D4
Warner Robins, Ga, US 97/H3
Warren, Pa, US 94/E3
Warren, Oh, US 94/D3
Warren, Mi, US 99/F6
Warrensburg, Mo, US 93/J3
Warrenville, Il, US 99/P16
Warri, Nga. 79/G5
Warrington, Fl, US 97/G4
Warrington, Eng, UK 23/F5
Warrnambool, Austl. 73/B3
Warsaw, In, US 94/C3
Warsaw (cap.), Pol. 27/L2
Warstein, Ger. 29/F6
Warwick, RI, US 95/G3
Warwick, Eng, UK 25/E2
Wasco, Ca, US 92/C4
Washington, Pa, US 94/D3
Washington, NC, US 97/J3
Washington, Il, US 93/K2
Washington (cap.), DC, US 94/E4
Washington (state), US 90/C4
Washington, Eng, UK 23/G2
Washington (mt.), NH, US 95/G2
Washington Court House (Washington), Oh, US 97/H2
Waspán, Nic. 103/F3
Wassenaar, Neth. 28/B4
Watampone, Indo. 67/F4
Watari, Japan 57/G1
Waterbury, Ct, US 94/F3
Waterford, Mi, US 99/F6
Waterford, Ire. 21/B10
Waterloo, On, Can. 94/D3
Waterloo, Belg. 31/D2
Watermael-Boitsfort, Belg. 31/D2
Watertown, SD, US 91/J4
Watertown, NY, US 94/F3
Watertown, Wi, US 93/K2
Waterville, Me, US 95/G2
Watford, Eng, UK 25/F3
Wath-upon-Dearne, Eng, UK 23/G4
Watsonville, Ca, US 92/B3
Wattignies, Fr. 30/C2
Wattrelos, Fr. 30/C2
Waukegan, Il, US 99/Q15
Waukesha, Wi, US 99/P13
Wauwatosa, Wi, US 99/P13
Wavre, Belg. 31/D2
Wāw, Sudan 77/L6
Waxahachie, Tx, US 93/H4
Waycross, Ga, US 97/H4
Wayne, Mi, US 99/F7
Waynesboro, Pa, US 94/E4
Waynesboro, Va, US 97/J2
Weatherford, Tx, US 96/D3
Webster City, IA, US 93/J2
Wedel, Ger. 29/G1
Wedemark, Ger. 29/G3
Weert, Neth. 28/C6